YEAR IN REVIEW 2016

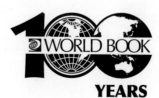

YEARS

World Book, Inc.
www.worldbook.com

ADVISERS

World Book, Inc.
180 North LaSalle Street
Chicago, Illinois 60601
USA
ISBN: 978-0-7166-2764-7

Printed in the United States of America by LSC Communications, Willard, Ohio
1st printing December 2016

STAFF

CONTENTS

IN MEMORIAM

JANUARY 2016

1 **Disasters.** In the Philippines, an island country in the southwest Pacific Ocean, New Year's Eve fireworks cause a blaze that kills one person, injures nearly 400 others, and destroys more than 1,000 homes in Manila, the capital city.

World community. In China, a new "two-child" policy replaces the "one-child" policy introduced in the late 1970's to slow China's massive population growth.

2 **World community.** In the western U.S. state of Oregon, an armed militia occupies the Malheur National Wildlife Refuge's headquarters, which were empty because of the holidays. The occupation is part of an ongoing dispute over the use of western federal lands. The militia is led by Ammon Bundy, son of Nevada rancher Cliven Bundy. In 2014, Cliven was at the center of an armed stand-off between his supporters and agents of the Bureau of Land Management that concerned decades worth of unpaid cattle grazing fees.

3 **World community.** Middle Eastern nations Saudi Arabia and Iran break off diplomatic relations after Saudi Arabia executes a Shī`ite Muslim cleric.

Protests in Iran lead to rioting at the Saudi embassy in Tehran.

4 Government. The parliament of the Marshall Islands, a nation in the North Pacific Ocean, elects former Chief Secretary Casten Nemra as the new president.

5 Disasters. In the northern Chinese region of Ningxia, a bus fire kills 17 passengers and injures 32 others.

Law. U.S. President Barack Obama announces he will push through tougher rules on background checks for gun purchases by

On Jan. 5, 2016, U.S. Army Brigadier General Diana Holland, at left, became the first woman Commandant of Cadets at the U.S. Military Academy at West Point, New York. Holland's command is the latest milestone for U.S. women who can now serve in all military combat roles.

executive order, bypassing the need for legislation by Congress.

6 **World community.** East Asian nation North Korea meets with worldwide condemnation and skepticism after claiming to have successfully tested a hydrogen nuclear bomb.

Sports. Baseball writers elect outfielder Ken Griffey, Jr., and catcher Mike Piazza as the newest members of the National Baseball Hall of Fame.

Arts. The epic space opera *Star Wars: The Force Awakens* surpasses the 2009 film *Avatar* as the highest grossing film in U.S. cinema history.

7 **Terrorism.** In northern Africa, in the coastal Libyan city of Zliten, an Islamic State bomb kills 65 people and injures 200 others at a military training center.

Economy. For the second time in a week, China halts trading on the Shanghai Composite Index to stop tumbling stock prices. The volatility in China's economy has a ripple effect, dropping global stock market values.

8 **World community.** In the northwestern Mexican state of Sinaloa, marines capture notorious drug kingpin Joaquín "El Chapo" Guzmán after a gun battle in the town of Los Mochis.

10 **Arts.** At the annual Golden Globe Awards in Beverly Hills, California, the sci-fi thriller *The Martian* wins best picture, oddly in the comedy or musical category. *The Revenant* wins the drama award and Alejandro G. Iñárritu wins best director for the film. In television, "Mr. Robot" wins best drama and "Mozart in the Jungle" wins best comedy.

Disasters. In southern Mexico, a bus plunges off a bridge into a deep gorge, killing 20 people and injuring 25 others near the city of Cordoba.

11 **Terrorism.** In Iraq, in the Middle East, Islamic State terrorist attacks kill 51 people in Baghdad and in the nearby cities of Baquba and Muqdadiyah in Diyala province.

Sports. In the College Football Playoff National Championship, two Southern universities face off, and the University of Alabama Crimson Tide defeats the Clemson University Tigers of South Carolina 45-40 at the University of Phoenix Stadium in Arizona.

Sports. In soccer, U.S. Women's National Team star Carli Lloyd is named the 2015 FIFA Women's World Player of the Year. U.S. coach Jill Ellis is named FIFA's World Coach of the Year for Women's Football. Argentine star Lionel Messi wins FIFA's Men's World Player of the Year award for the fifth time.

12 **World community.** Rick Snyder, the governor of Michigan, a state in the U.S. Great Lakes region, orders the National Guard to distribute drinking water in the city of Flint, where lead-tainted water has caused a public-health emergency since 2015. An emergency manager appointed by Snyder, in conjunction with the town council, made the fateful decision to switch Flint's water source in 2014 from the Detroit to the Flint River. The corrosive water in the river, however, caused lead to leach into the city's water pipes. The problem was not admitted to or addressed until the autumn of 2015. According to the U.S. Centers for Disease Control and Prevention (CDC), there is no level considered safe when it comes to lead levels in water.

Sports. The National Football League (NFL) approves the return of the St. Louis Rams from the Midwest to the western U.S. city of Los Angeles, California, the team's home from 1946 to 1995.

Government. In the U.S. capital of Washington, D.C., President Barack Obama lists his accomplishments in office and sets a positive tone during his final State of the Union address to Congress.

Terrorism. In Istanbul, Turkey, an Islamic State terrorist bomb kills 10 people and injures 15 others in the Sultanahmet tourist district.

13 **World community.** Three lottery tickets match the numbers drawn for a record $1.6-billion U.S. Powerball lottery.

Terrorism. In south Asia, in the Pakistani city of Quetta, a terrorist bomb kills 15 people—most of them police—outside a polio immunization center.

14 **Government.** In Central America, new Guatemalan President Jimmy Morales is inaugurated at the Miguel Ángel Asturias Cultural Center in Guatemala City.

Disasters. Off the coast of Oahu, Hawaii, in the North Pacific Ocean, two U.S. Marine helicopters collide, killing all 12 crew members aboard the aircraft.

15 **Terrorism.** In Somalia, in east Africa, al-Shabab Islamic terrorists attack an African Union military base in the town of El-Ade, killing 50 people and injuring more than 100.

Terrorism. In the west African nation of Burkina Faso, al-Qa`ida in the Islamic Maghreb (AQIM) terrorists kill 29 people and injure more than 30 others in a hotel and café attack in Ouagadougou, the capital city.

Economy. U.S. retail giant Wal-Mart announces it will close 154 stores in the United States, affecting some 10,000 jobs. The retailer is also closing 115 stores in Latin America.

Living world. U.S. President Barack Obama halts coal mining leases from being issued on federal lands as part of new executive actions to fight climate change.

16 **World community.** The Middle Eastern nation of Iran complies with the opening require-ments of the nuclear arms deal agreed to in 2015, allowing for the lifting of economic sanctions.

Terrorism. In eastern Syria, Islamic State terrorists slaughter 135 people in the city of Deir ez-Zor and take more than 400 others hostage.

Government. Voters in Taiwan, an island in the South China Sea,

elect Democratic Progressive Party candidate Tsai Ing-wen to become that nation's first female president.

17 **Terrorism.** In Afghanistan, in southwestern Asia, a Taliban suicide bomber kills 13 people and injures 14 in the city of Jalalabad.

19 **Health.** The CDC issues a travel alert for people—especially pregnant women or women of child-bearing age who might become pregnant—to avoid travel to Puerto Rico and 13 countries in Latin America out of fear of birth defects associated with the mosquito-borne Zika virus.

20 **Terrorism.** In northern Pakistan, a Taliban attack at Bacha Khan University in the town of Charsadda kills 30 people.

Living world. The U.S. National Aeronautics and Space Administra-tion (NASA) and the National Oceanic and Atmospheric Admin-istration (NOAA) release tempera-ture data showing that 2015 was by far the hottest year on record.

Economy. More than 40 world leaders and 1,500 business leaders open the annual meeting of the World Economic Forum in Davos, Switzerland.

24 Government. Former law professor, newspaper editor, and member of European Parliament Marcelo Rebelo de Sousa wins the presidential election in the western European nation of Portugal.

Sports. Japanese sumo wrestler Kotoshōgiku Kazuhiro wins the annual New Year Grand Sumo Tournament, becoming the first native Japanese wrestler to claim sumo's top division since 2006.

25 Terrorism. In the northern part of the country of Cameroon on Africa's west coast, Boko Haram suicide bombers kill 32 people and injure 65 others in the central market of the village of Bodo.

World community. A Texas grand jury indicts two anti-abortion activists for creating fake videos falsely claiming that Planned Parenthood sold fetal tissue recovered from abortions.

World community. Iranian President Hassan Rouhani visits Italian Prime Minister Matteo Renzi in Rome, becoming the first Iranian leader to visit Europe since 1999. Rouhani will also visit Pope Francis at the Vatican and French President François Hollande in Paris.

26 World community. In Oregon, one right-wing militant is killed and eight others are arrested in a scuffle with FBI agents near the wildlife refuge occupied by the militants in early January.

27 Terrorism. In Nigeria, a western African nation on the Gulf of Guinea, a Boko Haram attack kills 13 people and injures 30 others at a market in the town of Chibok.

28 Government. Hilda Heine becomes the first woman president of the Marshall Islands. Heine succeeded President Casten Nemra, who was ousted in a vote of no-confidence in the nation's parliament after little more than a week in office.

30 Sports. Germany's Angelique Kerber defeats U.S. tennis star Serena Williams at the Australian Open in Melbourne. It is Kerber's first grand slam title.

31 Terrorism. In Nigeria, Boko Haram terrorists kill 86 people and injure hundreds of others in an attack on Dalori Village near Maiduguri.

Sports. Serbian tennis star Novak Djokovic defeats Scotland's Andy Murray for his record sixth Australian Open title.

Urban areas glow beneath Winter Storm Jonas as it hits the Mid-Atlantic coast of the United States on Jan. 22, 2016, in this photo taken by NASA astronaut Scott Kelly. The storm dumped more than two feet (60 centimeters) of snow on the District of Columbia and parts of the states of Maryland, New Jersey, Pennsylvania, and New York. Kelly took the photo during his 340-day stay aboard the International Space Station. See **Out of this World**, p. 362.

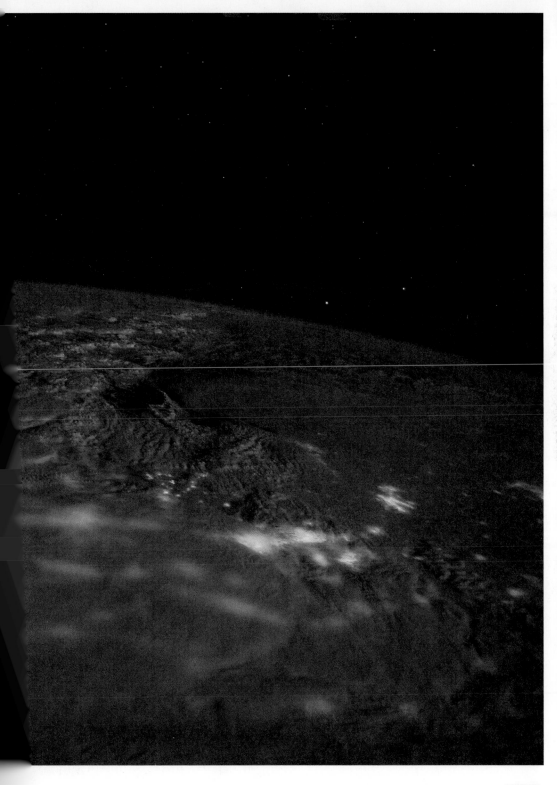

FEBRUARY 2016

1 **Terrorism.** In Afghanistan, a Taliban suicide bomber kills 20 people at a police headquarters in Kabul, the capital city.

World community. The World Health Organization declares the Zika virus a global public health emergency. The mosquito-borne virus has spread "explosively" in 2016, affecting some 4 million people in Brazil and nearby South American countries.

Government. Kicking off the 2016 U.S. presidential election nomination season, Texas Senator Ted Cruz wins the Republican vote in the Iowa caucuses, while former Secretary of State Hillary Clinton edges out Vermont Senator Bernie Sanders on the Democratic side.

2 **Living world.** Criminal charges are filed against Southern California Gas for failing to report a natural gas rupture at the utility's Aliso Canyon storage facility in the Porter Ranch area near Los Angeles. The ongoing leak was first discovered in October 2015, and has forced evacuations in nearby areas.

4 **World community.** Representatives of 12 Pacific rim nations, including the United States, Canada, Japan, and Australia, sign the Trans-Pacific Partnership in Auckland, New Zealand. Member nations now have 2 years to ratify or reject the landmark trade deal.

5 **World community.** A United Nations panel rules that WikiLeaks founder Julian Assange has been "unlawfully detained" in the Ecuadorian embassy in London for the past three years. The ruling states that, as a political refugee, Assange should be allowed asylum in Ecuador. The United Kingdom ignores the ruling and Assange remains in London.

Disasters. In the northwestern Indian state of Gujarat, 37 passengers die when a bus plunges off a bridge into the Purna River.

Disasters. In northern Iraq, a hotel fire kills 13 guest Filipino workers in the Kurdish city of Erbil.

Living world. On the south Japanese island of Kyushu, the Sakurajima volcano erupts, spewing lava down its slopes toward the city of Kagoshima.

6 **Disasters.** In Taiwan, an earthquake topples buildings in the southern city of Tainan, killing 117 people and injuring hundreds.

Disasters. At a college in Tamil Nadu, India, a suspected meteorite kills one person and injures three others. If confirmed, it will be the first fatal meteorite strike in recorded history.

Sports. The Pro Football Hall of Fame announces its 2016 induction class: former players Brett Favre, Kevin Greene, Marvin Harrison, Orlando Pace, Ken Stabler, and Dick Stanfel; coach Tony Dungy; and owner Edward DeBartolo, Jr.

7 **Sports.** At Levi's Stadium in Santa Clara, California, the Denver Broncos defeat the Carolina Panthers 24-10 to win Super Bowl XL, the championship game of the National Football League (NFL).

9 **Disasters.** In the southeastern German state of Bavaria, commuter trains collide killing 11 people and injuring 85 others.

Terrorism. In the northeastern part of the African nation of Nigeria, Boko Haram Islamic terrorists kill 60 people and injure 80 others in a bombing at a refugee camp in Dikma.

Living world. The U.S. Supreme Court puts a hold on the Obama administration's Clean Power Plan meant to reduce climate change. The decision puts off new pollution rules until an appeals court hears challenges from Republican-led U.S. states and fuel industry groups.

Government. In the first U.S. presidential primary in New Hampshire, voters choose New York businessman Donald Trump as the leading Republican candidate, while Vermont Senator Bernie Sanders wins on the Democratic side.

10 **World community.** In northern Mexico, 49 inmates die in a gang fight at Topo Chico prison in Monterrey.

11 **World community.** In Oregon, the last members of a radical armed militia surrender at the Malheur National Wildlife

Sands to Snow National Monument

Mojave Trails National Monument

Refuge headquarters. The group had occupied the empty building since early January over a dispute about federal land rights.

Government. The parliament of the southwest Pacific Island nation of Vanuatu elects Charlot Salwai as the nation's new prime minister.

Science. Scientists from the Laser Interferometer Gravitational-Wave Observatory in Louisiana announce the detection of gravitational waves, tiny ripples in the fabric of space-time predicted by Albert Einstein's general theory of relativity.

Living world. The Southern California Gas Company finally plugs the massive natural gas leak in the Porter Ranch area near Los

On Feb. 12, 2016, U.S. President Barack Obama announced the creation of three new national monuments in California: Mojave Trails, Sand to Snow, and Castle Mountains. The monuments will protect some 1.8 million acres (nearly 7,300 square kilometers) of desert wilderness.

Castle Mountains National Monument

Angeles. The leak drove thousands of residents from the area, and remains to be permanently sealed and inspected.

12 **World community.** Pope Francis stops in Havana, Cuba, for a historic meeting with the head of the Russian Orthodox Church en route to Mexico City, where he begins a week-long visit to Mexico.

13 **Living world.** In Oklahoma, a 5.1-magnitude earthquake strikes northwest of Oklahoma City, the latest seismic activity in areas destabilized by fracking (hydraulic fracturing, the process of injecting water, sand, and chemicals underground at high pressures to extract oil and gas).

Government. In the north-central African nation of Chad, Albert

Pahimi Padacké is appointed the nation's new prime minister.

14 **Government.** In Haiti, Senator Jocelerme Privert takes over as acting president until a popular election can be held later in the year.

Arts. At the British Academy Film Awards in London, *The Revenant* wins five awards, including best film and best actor for the film's lead, Leonardo DiCaprio.

Sports. At the National Basketball Association (NBA) All-Star Game in Toronto, Ontario, the Western Conference All-Stars defeat the Eastern Conference All-Stars 196-173.

15 **Arts.** At the annual Grammy Awards in Los Angeles, U.S. singer Taylor Swift's "1989" wins album of the year. U.S. singer Meghan Trainor wins the best new artist award.

16 **Arts.** At the annual Westminster Dog Show in New York City, California Journey, a German shorthaired pointer, wins the coveted Best in Show award.

World community. The United States and Cuba agree to restore commercial air traffic between the two nations for the first time in 50 years.

17 **Terrorism.** In the Turkish capital of Ankara, Kurdish separatists bomb buses carrying military personnel, killing 28 people and injuring more than 60 others.

18 **Disasters.** In central Ghana in western Africa, a bus and truck collide head-on a highway near the town of Kintampo, killing 71 people.

19 **Terrorism.** U.S. warplanes strike an Islamic State terrorist camp in western Libya, killing 41 militants.

Terrorism. In northern Cameroon in western Africa, Boko Haram terrorists bomb a market in the town of Meme, killing 40 people and injuring more than 100 others.

Law. The U.S. Department of Justice files a motion to compel Apple Inc. to comply with a court order to help the FBI hack a phone used by an attacker in the 2015 San Bernardino mass shooting.

Government. In the Central African Republic, former Prime Minister Faustin-Archange Touadéra is elected the nation's new president.

20 **Disasters.** Cyclone Winston slams into the South Pacific island nation of Fiji, killing 43 people and causing widespread damage.

Crime. In Kalamazoo, Michigan, in the U.S. Great Lakes region, an Uber driver shoots and kills 6 people before being arrested by police.

Government. In Uganda, President Yoweri Museveni wins reelection. He has been in office since 1986.

Government. Hillary Clinton wins the Nevada Democratic presidential caucus while Donald Trump wins the Republican primary in South Carolina.

21 **Terrorism.** In the Syrian Civil War, Islamic State terrorist bombings kill 146 people in the cities of Homs and Damascus.

Sports. In Florida, U.S. auto racer Denny Hamlin wins the 2016 Daytona 500 by 0.011 seconds, the smallest margin of victory in the history of the race.

22 **Terrorism.** In Afghanistan's Parwan Province, a Taliban bomb kills 14 people and injures 11 others at a health clinic.

World community. The United States and Russia conclude a cease-fire agreement between Syria's government and rebel groups that will go into effect February 27. The cease-fire excludes campaigns against terrorist groups also involved in the fighting.

Living world. In northwestern Peru, a ruptured oil pipeline spills some 3,000 barrels of crude oil into the Chiriaco and Morona rivers.

23 **Government.** Donald Trump wins the Nevada Republican presidential caucus.

24 **Disasters.** A Tara Air flight crashes in the mountains of western Nepal, killing all 23 people on board.

World community. In eastern Syria, a United Nations aircraft airdrops 23 tons (21 metric tons) of humanitarian aid in a government-held part of Deir ez-Zor, a city besieged by Islamic State militants.

25 **Terrorism.** In Iraq, Islamic State bombs kill 15 people at a Shī`ite mosque in Baghdad.

Crime. In Hesston, Kansas, a gunman kills 3 people and injures 14 others at a factory before being killed by police.

Disasters. In Vorkuta, Russia, a methane gas leak causes coal mine explosions that kill 36 miners.

On Feb. 25, 2016, surfer John Florence rides 60-foot (18-meter) waves to win the rare Quicksilver Eddie Aikau Big Wave Invitational at Waimea Bay, Hawaii. The surf contest only occurs when wave sizes consistently exceed 30 feet (9 meters).

26 **Terrorism.** On the southern Philippine island of Mindanao, government troops kill 42 members of the Moro Islamic Liberation Front, an Islamist rebel group. Three soldiers die in the fighting.

Crime. In a mass prison break at Buimo jail in the Papua New Guinea city of Lae, 11 inmates are killed, 17 are wounded and recaptured, and more than 50 escape.

Government. In Kosovo, members of parliament elect former Prime Minister Hashim Thaçi as the nation's new president.

Sports. Swiss-Italian soccer administrator Gianni Infantino is elected president of FIFA, soccer's world governing body.

27 **Terrorism.** In eastern Afghanistan's Kunar Province, a Taliban terrorist bomber kills 26 people and injures nearly 50 others at a government compound in Asadabad.

World community. In Syria, violations mar a cease-fire between government and rebel troops. Fighting with terrorist groups continues.

Government. Hillary Clinton wins the Democratic U.S. presidential primary election in South Carolina.

28 **Terrorism.** In Iraq, Islamic State terrorist bombers kill 70 people and injure more than 100 others at a market in Sadr City.

Terrorism. In Somalia, al-Shabab terrorist bombers kill 40 people and injure 30 others in the town of Baidoa.

Crime. In the Indian city of Thane, a man murders 14 members of his own family before killing himself.

Arts. At Hollywood's annual award ceremony for the Academy of Motion Picture Arts and Sciences, *Spotlight* wins the best picture Oscar. *The Revenant* director Alejandro G. Iñárritu wins the award for best director. Brie Larson wins best actress for her role in *Room*, and Leonardo DiCaprio takes best actor as the lead in *The Revenant*.

Sports. Manchester City FC (football club) defeats Liverpool FC to win the Football League Cup, an annual tournament open to all professional soccer clubs in England.

29 **Terrorism.** In Iraq, an Islamic State bomber kills 40 people at a funeral in Muqdadiyah, a town northeast of Baghdad.

World community. In France, police clash with migrants and refugees as they clear parts of the "jungle," a makeshift camp near the coastal city of Calais.

MARCH 2016

1 **Disasters.** In northwestern Oman on the Arabian peninsula, a bus collides head-on with a truck, killing 18 people and injuring 16 others near the Nahdah oasis.

Government. On so-called "Super Tuesday," U.S. presidential caucuses and primary elections are held in 12 states and the territory of American Samoa. On the Democratic side, Hillary Clinton wins 7 states and American Samoa, while Bernie Sanders wins 4 states. Donald Trump wins 7 Republican contests, Ted Cruz tops the voting in 3 states, and Marco Rubio wins 1 state.

Science. U.S. astronaut Scott Kelly and Russian cosmonaut Mikhail Kornienko return to Earth after a record 340 days in space aboard the International Space Station.

2 **Disasters.** In Indonesia, a powerful 7.9-magnitude earthquake strikes off the island of Sumatra, spurring a temporary tsunami alert.

Terrorism. In the Afghanistan city of Jalalabad, 15 people die in an Islamic terrorist attack and gun battle near the Indian Consulate.

3 **Disasters.** In Guyana's capital city of Georgetown, 16 people die in a prison riot and fire sparked by the confiscation of prisoners' mobile phones.

Disasters. In Zimbabwe, 31 people are killed in a collision between two buses on a highway near the central city of Kwekwe.

Science. Using the Hubble Space Telescope, U.S. astronomers discover GN-z11, a galaxy 13.4 billion light years from Earth. It is the remotest galaxy yet found.

4 **Terrorism.** In Yemen, Islamic terrorist gunmen storm a charity retirement home, killing 16 people, including 4 Catholic nuns.

Disasters. In the South American nation of Venezuela, 30 gold miners disappear in Bolívar state. Officials fear the miners fell victim to a criminal gang wanting control of the gold mine.

World community. Former Brazilian President Luiz Inácio

Lula da Silva is briefly detained for questioning in São Paulo amid a corruption probe centered on state-owned oil giant Petrobras.

5 **Terrorism.** In Somalia in eastern Africa, a U.S. drone strike kills at least 150 al-Shabab militants at Raso Camp, a terrorist training facility north of Mogadishu, the capital.

Government. In U.S. presidential primaries and caucuses, Democrat Bernie Sanders wins Kansas, Maine, and Nebraska, while Hillary Clinton wins Louisiana. Republican Ted Cruz wins Kansas and Maine, Donald Trump takes Kentucky and Louisiana, and Marco Rubio wins in Puerto Rico.

6 **Terrorism.** In the Iraqi city of Hillah, south of Baghdad, an Islamic State terrorist bomber kills 60 people and injures 70 others at a busy security checkpoint.

Disasters. In China's Jilin province, a gas leak kills 12 coal miners near the city of Baishan.

7 **Terrorism.** In Tunisia, 50 people die in fighting between government troops and Islamic militants near the Libyan border.

Terrorism. In Pakistan, a Taliban bomber kills 13 people and injures 36 others outside a court in the town of Shabqadar.

Sports. Russian tennis star Maria Sharapova is suspended from tennis after testing positive for a banned substance in January.

Sports. National Football League (NFL) quarterback Peyton Manning announces his retirement from football. Manning was a 5-time NFL Most Valuable Player and won 2 Super Bowls over his 18-year career with the Indianapolis Colts and Denver Broncos.

8 **Disasters.** In the popular Lekki district of Lagos, Nigeria, a building under construction collapses, killing 30 people.

Government. In U.S. presidential caucuses and primaries, Democrats Bernie Sanders and Hillary Clinton win the states of Michigan and Mississippi respectively, while Republican Donald Trump wins three states and Ted Cruz wins one.

9 **World community.** Brazilian prosecutors charge former President Luiz Inácio Lula da Silva with money laundering as part of an ongoing investigation into the state oil company Petrobras.

Living world. Researchers in the Iguaquen Merchan moorlands of Colombia report the discovery of a new species of frog, *Pristimantis macrummendozai*, with distinctive yellow eyebrows.

10 **Disasters.** Heavy rains in Louisiana cause flooding that kills 3 people and displaces more than 1,000 others.

Law. A U.S. federal jury orders the Texas-based Cabot Oil & Gas Corporation to pay more than $4.2 million in damages caused by fracking operations that contaminated ground water in northeastern Pennsylvania.

11 **Disasters.** In Brazil's southern state of São Paulo, heavy rains cause flooding and mudslides that kill 21 people.

12 **Government.** In U.S. presidential caucuses and primaries, Hillary Clinton wins the Democratic caucus in the commonwealth of the Northern Marianas Islands. Republican voters in Washington, D.C., choose Marco Rubio, while Ted Cruz wins the state of Wyoming.

Terrorism. Turkish airstrikes kill 67 Kurdish separatist militants at a camp in northern Iraq.

13 **Terrorism.** In Turkey, a Kurdish separatist bomb kills 37 people and injures 127 others in central Ankara.

Terrorism. In Côte d'Ivoire, al-Qa`ida in the Islamic Maghreb (AQIM) terrorists kill 18 people at two beach hotels in the town of Grand-Bassam.

Government. In Germany, voters advance right wing anti-immigrant candidates in regional elections, weakening the government of Chancellor Angela Merkel.

14 **Terrorism.** In Iraq, Islamic State terrorists kill 47 Iraqi soldiers at a military barracks near the Anbar provincial capital of Ramadi.

World community. In Syria, warring sides resume peace talks that had been postponed several times. On the same day, Russia announces a reduction in military forces in Syria.

World community. In Brazil, more than 1 million anti-government protesters march nationwide, calling for the resignation of President Dilma

A fishing boat near the Indonesian island of Ternate passes beneath the beginning of a total solar eclipse on March 9, 2016. The rare astronomical phenomenon could be partially seen in other parts of Asia, Australia, and many Pacific Islands.

Roussef amid ongoing corruption scandals and economic recession.

15 **Disasters.** An Ecuadorian Air Force transport aircraft crashes in the eastern province of Pastaza, killing all 22 people on board.

Government. Myanmar's Union Assembly elects Htin Kyaw, a long-time ally of democracy activist and Nobel laureate Aung San Suu Kyi, as the nation's new president. On March 30, Kyaw will become Myanmar's first civilian leader since 1962.

Government. In U.S. presidential primaries, Democrat Hillary Clinton sweeps Florida, Illinois, Missouri, Ohio, and North Carolina. Republican Donald Trump wins four states while John Kasich takes his home state of Ohio. Republican Marco Rubio drops out of the race.

World community. Pope Francis announces that nun Mother Teresa, who won the 1979 Nobel Peace Prize, will be canonized in September 2016.

16 **Terrorism.** In northeastern Nigeria, Boko Haram bombers kill 22 people and injure 18 others at a mosque near the city of Maiduguri.

Terrorism. In Pakistan, a Taliban bomb explodes on a bus carrying government employees, killing 15 people and injuring more than 50 others.

Government. U.S. President Barack Obama nominates appellate judge Merrick Garland to fill the vacancy on the Supreme Court left by the February death of Antonin Scalia.

17 **Disasters.** In Saudi Arabia, a bus carrying Palestinian pilgrims overturns, killing 16 people.

World community. In Egypt's Valley of the Kings, radar scans reveal hidden chambers adjoining the tomb of King Tutankhamun, raising hopes of finding the lost tomb of Queen Nefertiti.

18 **Terrorism.** In Brussels, Belgium, police capture Salah Abdeslam, alleged to be a main organizer and participant in the Paris terrorist attack of late 2015.

19 **Disasters.** Flydubai Flight 981, en route from Dubai, crashes during landing in the Russian city of Rostov-on-Don, killing all 62 people on board.

Terrorism. In Egypt's Sinai Peninsula, Islamic State terrorists kill 13 police officers at a security checkpoint in the city of Arish.

20   **Disasters.** A bus carrying European Union Erasmus exchange students crashes near Freginals, Spain, killing 13 people and injuring 34 others.

Disasters. On the Indonesian island of Sulawesi, a military helicopter crashes shortly after takeoff, killing 13 passengers.

Government. Businessman Patrice Talon is elected the next president of the small West African nation of Benin.

World community. U.S. President Barack Obama begins a three-day visit to Havana, Cuba, becoming the first sitting U.S. president to visit the Caribbean island country since 1928.

Economics. U.S.-based paint giant Sherwin-Williams agrees to acquire rival Valspar for $9.3 billion.

21   **World community.** In Havana, President Obama meets with Cuban President Raúl Castro to discuss trade and political reform.

Economics. U.S. hotel giant Marriott International purchases Starwood Hotels and Resorts Worldwide for $13.6 billion.

22   **Terrorism.** In Brussels, Belgium, Islamic State terrorist bombings kill 35 people and injure more than 250 at Zaventem airport and in the Maelbeek metro station.

Government. Mahamadou Issoufou wins a second term as president of the west African nation of Niger.

Government. In U.S. presidential primaries and caucuses, Democrat Bernie Sanders wins Idaho and Utah, while Hillary Clinton takes Arizona. Republican voters chose Donald Trump in Arizona and Ted Cruz in Utah.

23   **Terrorism.** In southern Yemen, U.S. air strikes kill some 50 militants at an al-Qaʾida terrorist training camp.

24   **Terrorism.** Syrian Army troops enter the ancient city of Palmyra, which had been under Islamic State control since May 2015 in Syria's civil war.

World community. In the Hague, Netherlands, the United Nations International Criminal Court sentences former Bosnian Serb leader Radovan Karadžić to 40 years in prison for war crimes during the Bosnian War.

In Cuba, the Rolling Stones' Mick Jagger performs during a free outdoor concert before some 200,000 fans at Havana's Ciudad Deportiva complex on March 25, 2016.

Government. In the west-central African Republic of the Congo, President Denis Sassou Nguesso wins reelection, extending his leadership for another seven years. Except for five years in the 1990's, Nguesso has been in power since 1979.

World community. Dazzling colored powders and splashed water highlight the start of India's two-day *Holi*, an ancient Hindu festival celebrating the arrival of spring.

25 **Terrorism.** In Yemen, Islamic State bombs kill 26 people at security checkpoints in Aden.

Disasters. In central France, a mini-bus carrying Portuguese

dwindling circulation forces a switch to an online-only format.

27 **Terrorism.** In the eastern Pakistan city of Lahore, an Islamic terrorist bombing kills 75 people and injures hundreds of others at a city park filled with people gathered to mark Easter Sunday.

Disasters. In southern Algeria, a military helicopter crash kills 12 soldiers and injures 2 others.

World community. In Dublin, Ireland, thousands attend ceremonies and a parade honoring the 100th anniversary of the 1916 Easter Rising rebellion against British rule.

29 **World community.** The U.S. State Department orders families of diplomats and military personnel to leave posts in southern Turkey due to increased terror threats.

citizens home for Easter collides head-on with a heavy truck, killing all 12 of the bus passengers.

26 **Government.** In Democratic U.S. presidential primaries, Bernie Sanders wins Alaska, Hawaii, and Washington.

World community. London newspaper *The Independent* publishes its last print edition as

30 **Government.** In Naypyidaw, Myanmar, Htin Kyaw is sworn in as the southeast Asian country's first civilian president since 1962.

31 **Disasters.** In Kolkata, India, an overpass under construction collapses, killing 27 people and injuring 80 others.

APRIL 2016

2 **Government.** In the capital city of Hanoi, the Vietnamese parliament elects government security minister Tran Đai Quang—the only candidate—as the Southeast Asian country's new president.

3 **Disasters.** In the northwestern Pakistan province of Khyber Pakhtunkhwa, heavy rains cause flooding that kills 63 people and displaces hundreds of others.

World community. Clashes between Azerbaijani and Armenian forces kill 46 soldiers in the disputed Nagorno-Karabakh region.

World community. In Brussels, Belgium, Zaventem International Airport reopens for the first time since the March 22 Islamic State terrorist attacks that killed 35 people and injured 250 others there and at the Maelbeek metro station.

World community. Millions of confidential documents known as the Panama Papers reveal secret offshore bank accounts used by wealthy world leaders, celebrities, and others for various purposes, including money laundering and to avoid paying taxes in their home countries. Among the people attached to these accounts are the leaders of Argentina, China, Iceland, Pakistan, Russia, Saudi Arabia, Ukraine, the United Arab Emirates, and the United Kingdom.

4 **Terrorism.** In Iraq, a series of Islamic State terrorist bombings and attacks kill 62 people and injure more than 80 others.

Economics. Alaska Airlines buys fellow U.S. airline Virgin America for $4 billion. The deal makes Alaska Air the fifth-largest airline in the United States (by number of passengers).

Sports. At NRG Stadium in Houston, Texas, the Villanova University Wildcats defeat the University of North Carolina Tar Heels 77-74 to win the NCAA Men's Division I Basketball Tournament. Villanova senior guard Ryan Arcidiacono is named the tournament's Most Outstanding Player.

5 **Government.** In Wisconsin, presidential primary voters back Democrat Bernie Sanders and Republican Ted Cruz.

Government. Republican Mississippi Governor Phil Bryant signs into law

"The Religious Liberty Accommodations Act" allowing the use of religion to discriminate against LGBT people at work, at schools, and in their communities. Republican North Carolina Governor Pat McCrory approved a similar state law the month before.

Sports. The University of Connecticut (UConn) Huskies women's basketball team defeats the Syracuse University Orange 82-51 to win their fourth straight NCAA Women's Division I Basketball Tournament. UConn senior forward Breanna Stewart is named Most Outstanding Player.

6 **Government.** In the wake of his attachment to the Panama Papers scandal, Icelandic Prime Minister Sigmundur Davíð Gunnlaugsson resigns from office and is replaced by Agriculture Minister Sigurður Ingi Jóhannsson.

7 **Government.** Vietnam's National Assembly approves Deputy Prime Minister Nguyen Xuân Phúc as the country's new prime minister.

Government. Kosovo's former Prime Minister Hashim Thaçi takes office as the southeastern European nation's new president. Thaçi won the presidential election in February.

8 **Terrorism.** In Syria, Islamic State terrorists murder 175 cement factory workers kidnapped the day before in the town of Dumayr.

Government. Voters in the small northeastern African nation of Djibouti elect President Ismaïl Omar Guelleh to a fourth term.

9 **Terrorism.** On the south Philippine island of Basilan, fighting between government soldiers and Abu Sayyaf Islamic militants kills 23 people and injures more than 70 others.

Disasters. In southeastern Peru, a bus plunges into a river, killing 23 people and injuring 32 others.

10 **Disasters.** In the south Indian coastal town of Paravur, fireworks cause an explosion and fire at the Puttingal Hindu Temple, killing 113 people and injuring more than 350 others.

Sports. Golfer Danny Willett becomes the second Briton to win the Masters Tournament at the Augusta National Golf Club in Georgia.

11 **Terrorism.** In eastern Afghanistan, a Taliban terrorist bomb kills 12 police recruits traveling on a bus near Jalalabad.

World community. In Yemen, a truce allows badly needed aid to reach people trapped by that nation's year-old civil war.

World community. U.S. Secretary of State John Kerry visits the Hiroshima Peace Memorial Museum in Japan. Kerry is the first U.S. secretary of state to visit the memorial, which honors the victims of the atomic bomb dropped on Hiroshima in August 1945.

Economy. U.S. investment banking giant Goldman Sachs agrees to pay a $5 billion settlement for misleading mortgage bond investors during the financial crisis that began in 2007.

13 **Sports.** In the final game of the National Basketball Association (NBA) regular season, the Golden State Warriors win an NBA record 73rd game against just 9 losses. The Warriors broke the 72-10 all-time season record set by the 1995-1996 Chicago Bulls. In Los Angeles, Lakers star Kobe Bryant scores 60 points in the final game of his 20-year NBA career.

14 **Disasters.** In Japan, a 6.2-magnitude earthquake near Kumamoto city knocks down houses and destroys roads, killing 9 people and injuring more than 1,000 others.

Government. The Ukrainian parliament appoints Volodymyr Groysman as the nation's new prime minister, replacing Arseny Yatseniuk, who resigned.

Sports. In the Women's National Basketball Association (WNBA) draft in Connecticut, the Seattle Storm choose University of Connecticut (UConn) superstar

On April 13, 2016, a Buddhist nun leads young novice nuns to receive food during the Songkran Thai New Year's festival in Bangkok, Thailand.

forward Breanna Stewart as the top pick overall. Stewart's UConn teammates Moriah Jefferson and Morgan Tuck are chosen second and third. This marks the first time in a basketball draft that a single school produced the top three selections.

16 **Terrorism.** In northern Afghanistan, 40 Taliban militants and 4 Afghan soldiers are killed in heavy fighting near the city of Kunduz.

World community. On the South Sudan-Ethiopia border in central Africa, 208 people are killed and 125 children kidnapped in clashes between rival ethnic groups.

Disasters. In Ecuador, a 7.8-magnitude earthquake kills over 650 people and injures some 2,500 others near the northern city of Muisne.

Disasters. In the Mediterranean Sea, an overloaded migrant boat sinks near the island of Lampedusa, killing an estimated 500 people.

Disasters. A second, stronger earthquake (7.1-magnitude) hits near Kumamoto city, Japan, killing 40 people.

17 **Disasters.** In India, a bus carrying members of the Bharati Gananatya opera troupe crashes into a gorge in Odisha state, killing 25 people and injuring 11 others.

18 **Disasters.** In Houston, Texas, record rainfalls cause flooding that kills 5 people and displaces more than 1,200 others.

Arts. The annual Pulitzer Prizes for journalism, literature, and music are awarded at Columbia University in New York City. The Associated Press wins the public service award for documenting the use of slave labor in Southeast Asia. The novel *The Sympathizer* by Viet Thanh Nguyen wins the fiction prize. Lin-Manuel Miranda's musical *Hamilton* wins the drama award and Henry Threadgill's jazz album *In for a Penny, In for a*

Pound, takes the award for music.

Sports. In the annual Boston Marathon in Massachusetts, Lemi Berhanu Hayle of Ethiopia wins the men's race, and fellow Ethiopian Atsede Baysa wins the women's race.

19 **Terrorism.** In the Afghan capital of Kabul, a Taliban terrorist bomb kills 71 people and injures more than 350 others at a government security building.

Government. In the New York state presidential primaries, Democrat Hillary Clinton defeats rival Bernie Sanders and Donald Trump wins on the Republican side.

20 **World community.** The U.S. Treasury Department announces that a likeness of anti-slavery crusader Harriet Tubman will replace that of President Andrew Jackson on the front of the $20 bill.

Economics. Japanese automaker Mitsubishi admits faking fuel economy tests in 625,000 vehicles to meet low emissions requirements in Japan. On the same day, German automaker Volkswagen offers to buy back or repair 600,000 U.S. vehicles tainted by similar emissions testing cheating uncovered last year.

21 **Disasters.** In Mexico, an explosion at a petrochemical plant in Coatzacoalcos, Veracruz, kills 28 people and injures 136 others.

Government. In the north-central African nation of Chad, President Idriss Deby is reelected to a fifth term in office against little opposition.

Sports. Chicago Cubs pitcher Jake Arrieta throws Major League Baseball's first no-hitter of the 2016 season. Arrieta struck out 6 and walked 4 in the Cubs' 16-0 win over the Cincinnati Reds.

22 **Disasters.** In northern India, a landslide kills 15 people in the mountainous Tawang District of Arunachal Pradesh state.

World community. In Ohio, eight people—all family members—are found murdered in rural Pike County east of Cincinnati.

Living world. In South America, a coral reef system more than 600 miles (1000 kilometers) long is discovered in the murky waters at the mouth of the Amazon River.

23 **Government.** In the west-African Republic of the Congo, President Denis Sassou Nguesso names former opposition leader Clément Mouamba as prime minister.

Arts. In the United Kingdom, events mark the 400th anniversary of the death of British dramatist William Shakespeare. In Spain, similar events mark the 400th anniversary of the death of Spanish author Miguel de Cervantes.

24 **Government.** In Serbia, voters keep Prime Minister Aleksandar Vučić's Serbian Progressive Party (SNS) in power, countering a far-right threat that would have derailed the nation's efforts to join the European Union.

Sports. In California, the original "Laws of Base Ball," a handwritten document from 1857, sells at auction for over $3.2 million. The laws set such standards as the lengths between bases as well as the number of innings per game and players per team.

25 **Disasters.** In Pakistan's Punjab province, candies tainted with pesticides kill 23 people and sicken dozens of others.

Terrorism. In Syria, an Islamic State bomb kills 15 people and injures 50 others at an army checkpoint in al Diyabiyah, near Damascus.

Sports. A U.S. appeals court reinstates New England Patriots quarterback Tom Brady's 4-game "deflategate" suspension overturned last year.

26 **World community.** In Cape Verde, off the west-African coast, a soldier kills 11 people at the Monte Tchota military barracks.

Government. In South Sudan, Riek Machar returns to his post as vice president after leading a rebellion against the government and President Salva Kiir for more than two years.

Government. Republican Donald Trump sweeps the U.S. presidential primaries in Connecticut, Delaware, Maryland, Pennsylvania, and Rhode Island. Democrat Bernie Sanders wins Rhode Island, while Hillary Clinton wins the remaining four states.

27 **Law.** Republican Dennis Hastert, who served as Speaker of the U.S. House of Representatives from 1999 to 2007, is sentenced to 15 months in prison for making payments to hide sexual misconduct from past decades.

28 **World community.** At a refugee camp in the Libyan town of Bani Walid, 12 people are killed in a dispute between Egyptian and Libyan human traffickers.

World community. Colombia becomes the fourth Latin American country (after Argentina, Brazil, and Uruguay) to legalize same-sex marriage.

Government. Equatorial Guinea President Teodoro Obiang wins reelection against no opposition. Obiang took control of the small western Africa nation in 1979.

Sports. In the 2016 National Football League (NFL) draft in Chicago, the Los Angeles Rams select University of California

In Aleppo, Syria, a man carries a child through the debris left by government airstrikes on April 28, 2016. The airstrikes hit a Médecins Sans Frontières (Doctors Without Borders) hospital, killing 27 people, including doctors, patients, and children. The same day, more than 30 other people died in other air strikes on the city.

quarterback Jared Goff as the top overall pick. The Philadelphia Eagles choose North Dakota State quarterback Carson Wentz with the second pick.

29 **Disasters.** In Kenya, a residential building collapses in Nairobi, killing 93 people.

Disasters. In the Somali capital of Mogadishu, a mosque under renovation collapses, killing 15 people and injuring 40 others.

Disasters. Off the west coast of Norway, a helicopter crashes into the sea between Bergen and the island of Turøy, killing all 13 people on board.

30 **Terrorism.** In Iraq, an Islamic State terrorist bomb kills 23 Shī`ite pilgrims and injures 50 others in south-eastern Baghdad.

MAY 2016

1 **Terrorism.** In Iraq's Al Muthanna Province, Islamic State terrorist bombs kill 32 people and injure 75 others in the city of Samawa.

2 **Terrorism.** In Baghdad, Iraq, Islamic State bombs kill 14 Shī`ite pilgrims commemorating the death anniversary of a celebrated imam.

Economy. The U.S. commonwealth of Puerto Rico is unable to make nearly $370 million in bond payments after failing to solve its catastrophic debt crisis.

Economy. Australian entrepreneur Craig Wright identifies himself as "Satoshi Nakamoto," the mysterious creator of the Bitcoin electronic currency.

World community. In Cuba, the U.S. cruise ship *Adonia* docks in Havana Harbor, reestablishing commercial tourist travel between the nations for the first time since 1978.

Sports. In English soccer, the Football Writers' Association names Leicester City Football Club striker Jamie Vardy as 2016 Footballer of the Year. Later that day, Leicester wins its first Premier League title.

3 **Government.** King Felipe VI of Spain dissolves the Spanish parliament, forcing a new election after politicians chosen in a December 2015 vote fail to agree on the country's next prime minister.

Government. Democrat Bernie Sanders wins the Indiana state presidential primary, while Donald Trump wins on the Republican side. Trump rival Ted Cruz withdraws from the race, as does the far-trailing John Kasich.

Law. Brazilian prosecutors file a $43.5 billion civil lawsuit against mining companies Vale SA and BHP Billiton for the collapse of a mine dam last year that killed 19 people and caused severe damage and pollution.

4 **Disasters.** In northeastern India, a bus falls from a bridge near the city of Raipur, killing 13 people and injuring 53 others.

5 **Disasters.** In Bolivia's eastern Santa Cruz province, a bus plunges into a ravine, killing 12 people and injuring 30 others.

Government. In London, England, voters elect Labour Party candidate

A wildfire rips through the forest along Highway 63 in Alberta, Canada, on May 7, 2016. Days earlier, more than 60,000 people evacuated the nearby oil town of Fort McMurray to escape the fire. Wildfires in the area were not contained until early June.

Sadiq Khan as the city's new and first-ever Muslim mayor.

7 **Sports.** American thoroughbred race horse Nyquist wins the 142nd running of the Kentucky Derby at Louisville's Churchill Downs race track.

Sports. Mexican middleweight boxer Canelo Álvarez knocks out the United Kingdom's Amir Khan to win the WBC middleweight title at T-Mobile Arena in Las Vegas.

8 **Disasters.** In Afghanistan's Ghazni province, two buses and a fuel tanker truck collide, causing a fiery explosion that kills 73 people and injures 50 others.

Disasters. In China's southeastern Fujian province, heavy rains trigger a landslide at a hydroelectric dam under construction, killing 41 people.

Sports. Russian whistleblowers reveal that at least four of Russia's gold medal winners at the 2014 Winter Olympics were using performance-enhancing drugs.

9 **Disasters.** In northern Rwanda, torrential rains cause flooding and landslides that kill 49 people.

Government. Filipino voters elect populist Davao City Mayor Rodrigo Duterte to be the next president of the Philippines.

Government. Austrian Chancellor Werner Faymann resigns after far-right advances in national elections. Deputy Chancellor Reinhold Mitterlehner takes over as chancellor.

Law. North Carolina Republican Governor Pat McCrory sues the U.S. Justice Department instead of repealing an anti-LBGT law passed in the state that the federal government considers a violation of civil rights.

Science. Earth observers watch Mercury as it makes a rare transit of the sun. Mercury was last aligned and visible between Earth and the sun in 2006.

10 **Government.** Democrat Bernie Sanders wins the West Virginia presidential primary. Donald Trump, the only Republican candidate still in the race, is that party's presumptive nominee.

Science. NASA confirms that 1,284 objects discovered by its Kepler telescope are *exoplanets*, planets that orbit stars other than the sun.

11 **Terrorism.** In Iraq, Islamic State terrorist bombs kill 103 people and injure more than 160 others in Shī`ite neighborhoods of Baghdad.

Science. A fragment of the world's oldest ground-edge axe—some 46,000 to 49,000 years old— is found at Carpenter's Gap, a prehistoric site in Windjana Gorge National Park in Western Australia.

12 **Government.** The Brazilian Senate votes to begin impeachment proceedings against President Dilma Rousseff and suspends her from office during the process. Vice President Michel Temer assumes presidential powers and duties.

13 **Terrorism.** In Iraq, Islamic State terrorist gunmen kill 14 people and injure 25 others at a cafe in the predominately Shī`ite town of Balad.

Government. To counter anti-LGBT legislation in Republican-controlled U.S. states, the federal government advises all public schools to allow transgender students to use bathrooms that match their gender identity rather than their gender at birth.

14 **Arts.** In Stockholm, Sweden, Ukrainian pop artist Jamala wins the 2016 Eurovision Song Contest for her song, "1944."

15 **Terrorism.** In Iraq, an Islamic State attack on a natural gas plant and other targets in and near Baghdad kills 29 people and injures dozens of others.

Terrorism. In Yemen, an Islamic State terrorist bombing kills 25 people and injures 17 others in the southern city of Mukalla.

Disasters. In southern India, a truck collides with an overcrowded motorized rickshaw in Hyderabad, killing 16 people and injuring 3 others.

Government. In the Caribbean nation of the Dominican Republic,
voters reelect President Danilo Medina to a second term in office.

Sports. In Florida, Australian golfer Jason Day wins the Players Championship with a 4-day total of 15 under par, 4 strokes ahead of U.S. golfer Kevin Chappell.

16 **World community.** In Colombia's Urabá Antioquia subregion, police seize some 9 tons (8 metric tons) of cocaine in an operation targeting the area's Clan Úsuga gang. It is one of the largest seizures of drugs in Colombian history.

Arts. South Korean author Han Kang's novel, *The Vegetarian,* wins the Man Booker International Prize for best work in English translation, an award shared with the British translator, Deborah Smith.

17 **Terrorism.** In Iraq, Islamic State terrorist attacks kill 77 people and injure more than 140 others in Shī`ite neighborhoods of Baghdad.

Government. Democratic primary voters choose Bernie Sanders in Oregon and Hillary Clinton in Kentucky.

18 **Disasters.** In Sri Lanka's central hills, heavy rains cause landslides that bury three villages, killing 150 people.

19 **Disasters.** EgyptAir Flight 804 crashes into the Mediterranean Sea en route from Paris to Cairo, killing all 66 people on board.

Disasters. In southern Ethiopia, the death toll from flash floods and landslides surpasses 100 people. Rare heavy rains caused by El Niño have displaced some 20,000 others in the northeastern African region.

Law. San Francisco Police Chief Greg Suhr resigns after city police shoot and kill an unarmed black woman in a stolen car.

Science. In Utah, scientists discover a new species of horned dinosaur, *Machairoceratops cronusi*, thought to have lived about 77 million years ago.

World community. At Christie's auction house in Geneva, Switzerland, the "Oppenheimer Blue" diamond sells for 56.8 million Swiss francs ($57.6 million), the most ever paid for a gem.

20 **Living world.** In the northern India desert state of Rajasthan, the temperature hits 123.8 °F (51 °C) in the city of Phalodi, the nation's hottest-ever recorded temperature.

Government. Tsai Ing-wen is sworn in as the first female president of the South China Sea nation of Taiwan.

Government. Oklahoma's Republican-dominated state legislature passes a bill making it a felony for doctors to perform abortions, which are legal in the United States. The state governor vetoes the bill. The same legislature then asks the U.S. Congress to impeach President Barack Obama for recommending that public schools allow transgender students to use bathrooms that match their gender identity.

21 **Disasters.** In the Democratic Republic of the Congo, a bus carrying passengers from nearby Zambia crashes and catches fire, killing 37 people and injuring 22 others.

Terrorism. In Afghanistan, a U.S. drone strike kills Taliban terrorist leader Akhtar Mansour near the town of Ahmad Wa along the Pakistan border.

Sports. American thoroughbred race horse Exaggerator wins the Preakness Stakes at Pimlico Race Course in Baltimore, Maryland.

Sports. Manchester United FC (football club) defeats London's Crystal Palace FC to win the Football Association (FA) Cup, England's oldest and most prestigious professional tournament. It is United's 12th FA Cup title.

22 **Government.** Austrian voters narrowly elect Green Party-backed independent candidate Alexander Van der Bellen as the nation's new president over a far-right candidate.

Arts. At the Cannes Film Festival in southern France, British director Ken Loach's *I, Daniel Blake* wins the Palme d'Or as the festival's best picture.

23 **Disasters.** In northern Myanmar, heavy rains cause a landslide at a jade mine, killing 53 people.

Disasters. In Thailand's northern Chiang Rai Province, an overnight fire in an elementary school dormitory kills 18 young girls.

Terrorism. In Syria, Islamic State terrorist attacks kill 148 people in government-controlled areas of Latakia province.

Terrorism. In Yemen, an Islamic State suicide bomber kills 45 army recruits and injures 60 others near a military base in Aden's Khormaksar district.

World community. U.S. President Barack Obama arrives in Hanoi for a three-day visit to Vietnam, where he announces the lifting of a long-standing embargo on arms sales to the Southeast Asian country.

Government. Cabinet Minister Binali Yıldırım is named prime minister of Turkey, replacing Ahmet Davutoğlu, who resigned.

25 **Terrorism.** In Afghanistan, a Taliban terrorist bomb kills 10 people and injures 4 others on a bus traveling west of Kabul.

World community. U.S. President Barack Obama arrives in Shima, Japan, where he meets with Japanese Prime Minister Shinzo Abe.

Law. Eleven Republican-controlled U.S. states sue the federal government over the Obama administration's directive to public schools to let transgender students use the bathrooms and locker rooms that match their gender identity.

26 **Disasters.** An overloaded migrant boat capsizes in the Mediterranean Sea off the Libyan coast, killing 30 people.

World community. In Japan, world leaders meet in Shima for the two-day Group of Seven (G7) summit focusing on the global economy and international security.

World community. American Airlines says that airport screening delays caused more than 70,000 people and 40,000 checked bags to miss flights so far this year. A shortage of security staff has caused increasingly long lines at airports in the past weeks.

World community. In Washington, D.C., 13-year-old Jairam Hathwar of New York and 11-year-old Nihar Janga of Texas are named co-champions of the 2016 Scripps National Spelling Bee. It is the third straight year the bee has finished in a tie.

World community. In India, a 15-pound (6.8-kilogram) baby girl—the heaviest child ever born in the country—is delivered by Caesarean section at a hospital in the southern state of Karnataka.

Government. Republican Donald Trump officially reaches the 1,238 delegates needed to secure his party's nomination for president.

Sports. Baylor University in Waco, Texas, removes Kenneth Starr as president and fires head football coach Art Briles after a report found administrators mishandled sexual abuse cases involving football players.

28 **Living world.** In Cincinnati, Ohio, zookeepers are forced to shoot and kill Harambe, a 17-year-old male gorilla, to protect a child who had fallen into the gorilla's enclosure.

Sports. At the Stadio Giuseppe Meazza in Milan, Italy, Spanish soccer powerhouse Real Madrid defeats crosstown rival Atlético Madrid on penalty shots to win the Champions League, Europe's elite annual professional club tournament.

29 **Disasters.** In Ukraine, a fire at an unlicensed elderly care facility kills 17 people and injures several others in Litki, a village near Kiev.

Sports. In high-powered auto racing, rookie U.S. driver Alexander Rossi wins the 100th running of the Indianapolis 500.

30 **Terrorism.** In Iraq, government forces battle Islamic State terrorists in the city of Fallujah. In nearby Baghdad, Islamic State bombings kill 24 people.

Living world. In Thailand, a police raid discovers 40 dead tiger cubs in a freezer at the Buddhist "Tiger Temple," a tourist site known for its many tigers. More than 100 living tigers are removed from the temple, which is closed amid suspicions of wildlife trafficking and animal abuse.

31 **Terrorism.** In northern Afghanistan, Taliban terrorists attack buses en route from Kabul to the Takhar and Kunduz provinces, killing 16 people.

On May 27, 2016, U.S. President Barack Obama, *right*, and Japanese Prime Minister Shinzo Abe shake hands after laying wreaths at the Hiroshima Peace Memorial Park in Japan. Obama is the first sitting U.S. president to visit the site of the dropping of the first atomic bomb in warfare in 1945.

Disasters. In the central Indian city of Pulgaon, a fire at a military ammunition depot kills 17 people and injures 19 others.

Disasters. In Texas, the death toll from days of heavy rains and flooding reaches 6 people.

World community. At Christie's Hong Kong Magnificent Jewels sale, the 5.03-carat "Aurora Green" diamond sells for $16.8 million, the most ever paid for a green diamond.

JUNE 2016

1 **Terrorism.** In Somalia, an Al-Shabab terrorist attack kills 16 people outside a hotel in Mogadishu.

World community. In the Swiss Alps, the Gotthard Base Tunnel opens after 17 years of construction. The railway tunnel is the world's longest and deepest.

4 **Sports.** At the Stade Roland Garros near the Bois de Boulogne park in Paris, France, Garbine Muguruza of Spain upsets U.S. tennis star Serena Williams to win the women's tournament at the French Open.

5 **Government.** In Peru, voters elect former business executive Pedro Pablo Kuczynski to be the nation's next president.

Sports. Serbian tennis star Novak Djokovic defeats Andy Murray of the United Kingdom to win the men's tournament at the French Open. The win completed Djokovic's non-calendar year Grand Slam, winning all four major tournaments consecutively.

6 **Disasters.** In Turkey's Osmaniye province, a bus crashes and plunges into a canal, killing 14 people and injuring 26 others.

Terrorism. In Kazakhstan, 19 people die in an Islamic terrorist attack on a military post.

Government. Recent U.S. primary and caucus results give Hillary Clinton the required 2,383 delegates needed to secure the Democratic nomination for president.

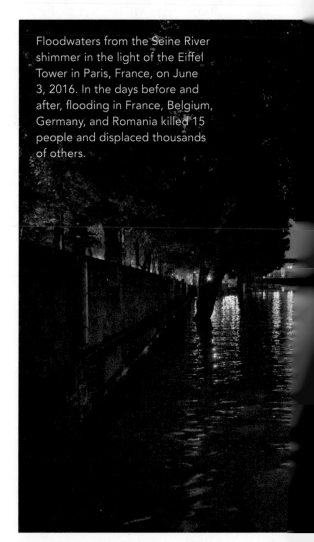

Floodwaters from the Seine River shimmer in the light of the Eiffel Tower in Paris, France, on June 3, 2016. In the days before and after, flooding in France, Belgium, Germany, and Romania killed 15 people and displaced thousands of others.

7 **Terrorism.** In Turkey, Kurdish militants bomb a police bus in Istanbul's main tourist district, killing 11 people and injuring 36 others.

8 **Terrorism.** In Israel, Palestinian gunmen kill 4 people and injure 18 others in the popular Sarona Market area of Tel Aviv.

World community. In Papua New Guinea, dozens of people are injured in police clashes with students calling for the resignation of Prime Minister Peter O'Neill.

Sports. The International Tennis Federation formally suspends Russian star Maria Sharapova for two years for failing a drug test.

9 **Terrorism.** In the central Somalian town of Halgan, 170 people are killed—the majority of them terrorists—in an al-Shabab attack on an African Union military

base garrisoned mostly by Ethiopian soldiers.

Terrorism. In Iraq, Islamic State terrorist bombs kill 28 people and injure dozens of others at a market and army checkpoint in Baghdad.

Disasters. In Brazil's São Paulo state, a bus plunges into a ravine, killing 18 people and injuring 28 others.

Government. U.S. President Barack Obama endorses the presumptive Democratic presidential nominee, Hillary Clinton.

10 **World community.** In Louisville, Kentucky, tens of thousands of people line the funeral procession of late boxer and cultural icon Muhammad Ali, who died on June 3.

11 **Sports.** American thoroughbred race horse Creator wins the 148th running of the Belmont States at New York's Belmont Park.

12 **Terrorism.** In Orlando, Florida, a gunman claiming allegiance to the Islamic State kills 49 people and injures 53 others at a gay nightclub before being killed by police.

Arts. At the Tony Awards at New York City's Beacon Theater, *The Humans* wins best play, and *Hamilton* takes home the award for best musical.

Sports. The Pittsburgh Penguins defeat the San Jose Sharks 3-1 to win the National Hockey League's Stanley Cup Final. The Penguins win the final 4 games to 2, earning their fourth championship in club history.

Sports. Canadian golfer Brooke Henderson wins the 2016 KPMG Women's PGA Championship at Sahalee Country Club in Sammamish, Washington.

13 **Economy.** U.S. software giant Microsoft agrees to buy professional networking site LinkedIn for $26.2 billion.

14 **World community.** In Paris, France, police clash with large crowds of people demonstrating against labor law reforms while strikes halt transport in many other parts of the country.

15 **Disasters.** A deep-sea search vessel finds the main wreckage of EgyptAir flight MS804—which disappeared on May 19—off the Mediterranean coast of Egypt.

World community. Despite Chinese objections, U.S. President Barack Obama meets with the exiled Tibetan spiritual leader, the Dalai Lama, in Washington, D.C.

Sports. Florida Marlins outfielder Ichiro Suzuki sets an unofficial record with his 4,257th career hit—1,278 of which came in Japan and 2,979 in Major League Baseball (MLB). Ichiro surpassed Pete Rose, who holds the official MLB-only record with 4,256 hits.

16 **Disasters.** In the northern Niger desert, the dead bodies of 34 refugees en route to Algeria are found after being abandoned by human traffickers.

Terrorism. In Birstall, England, British Labour Party Member of Parliament Jo Cox is murdered by a local man shouting "Britain First," the name of a right-wing ultraconservative British political party.

World community. After five years of construction, China opens the $5.5-billion Shanghai Disney Resort.

17 **Terrorism.** In northern Nigeria, Boko Haram terrorists murder 18 women at a funeral in the Adamawa State village of Kuda.

Disasters. In southern California, the Sherpa wildfire in Santa Barbara County triples in size to nearly 6,000 acres (2,430 hectares).

18 **Disasters.** In southern China, heavy rains cause severe flooding that kills 25 people and displaces more than 30,000 others.

19 **Disasters.** On the Indonesian island of Java, landslides and flooding kill 24 people and leave many more missing.

Disasters. In the northwestern Russian republic of Karelia, a sudden storm kills 14 people boating on Lake Syamozero.

Government. Voters in Rome, Italy, elect lawyer Virginia Raggi of the populist anticorruption *MoVimento 5 Stelle* (Five Star Movement) as the city's first woman mayor.

Sports. In Oakland, California, the Cleveland Cavaliers defeat the Golden State Warriors 93-89 to win the National Basketball Association championship. The Cavaliers win the finals 4 games to 3, earning their first title.

Sports. American golfer Dustin Johnson wins the U.S. Open Championship at the Oakmont Country Club in Plum, Pennsylvania.

20 **Terrorism.** In Afghanistan, Taliban terrorist bombs kill 22 people in separate attacks in Kabul.

21 **Disasters.** In southern California, wildfires spread in the San Gabriel Mountains near Los Angeles and in the desert scrub southeast of San Diego.

Law. The International Criminal Court sentences former Democratic Republic of the Congo (DRC) vice president Jean-Pierre Bemba to 18 years in prison for war crimes and crimes against humanity committed during conflicts in the DRC and the neighboring Central African Republic in the early 2000's.

22 **Terrorism.** In Karachi, Pakistan, Taliban assassins kill popular Qawwali (Sufi devotional music) singer Amjad Sabri.

World community. In Syria, Russian air strikes targeting Islamic State terrorist positions in Raqqa kill 32 civilians and injure 150 others.

Government. U.S. President Barack Obama signs a bill into law that places stronger regulations on chemicals in such consumer products as automobiles, cleansers, clothing, detergents, and paint thinners.

Government. About 40 Democrats in the U.S. House of Representatives stage a sit-in overnight to protest the Republican-controlled Senate's refusal to approve gun control bills offered earlier in the week.

Sports. In the National Hockey League (NHL) Awards, Chicago Blackhawks forward Patrick Kane wins the Hart Trophy as the league's most valuable player and the Ted Lindsay Award as the most outstanding player as voted by other players. Fellow Blackhawk Artemi Panarin wins the Calder Trophy as the NHL's best rookie. The Vezina Trophy for outstanding goaltender goes to the Washington Capitals' Braden Holtby. Drew Doughty of the Los Angeles Kings wins the Norris Trophy as the league's best defenseman.

23 **Disasters.** In China, severe thunderstorms, hailstorms, and tornadoes kill 98 people and injure hundreds more in the eastern province of Jiangsu.

Disasters. In India, two days of lightning strikes kill 93 farm workers and injure dozens of others during severe monsoon storms in the states of Bihar, Jharkhand, Madhya Pradesh, and Uttar Pradesh.

Government. Voters in the United Kingdom choose to leave the European Union in the contentious "Brexit" referendum, sending shock waves throughout the world and the world's economic markets.

World community. The Colombian government and rebel Revolutionary Armed Forces of Colombia (FARC) guerrillas sign a cease-fire agreement to end decades of conflict.

On June 23, 2016, the solar-powered aircraft *Solar Impulse 2* prepares to land at San Pablo airport in Seville, Spain, after completing a three-day flight across the Atlantic Ocean. The plane completed its record-setting flight around the world on July 26. See **Science and Technology**, p. 347.

Law. The U.S. Supreme Court deadlocks 4-4 on a conservative challenge against President Barack Obama's executive order that would have protected up to five million immigrants from deportation. The tie allows an appeals court ruling blocking the order to stand.

Sports. In the National Basketball Association draft in New York City, the Philadelphia 76ers select Louisiana State University forward Ben Simmons as the overall number one pick. The Los Angeles Lakers choose Duke University forward Brandon Ingram with the second pick.

24 **Disasters.** In West Virginia, the death toll from flash floods reaches 26 people, most of them in hard-hit Greenbrier County.

World community. Global economic markets and currencies drop sharply and British Prime Minister David

Cameron announces he will resign in the coming months in reaction to the United Kingdom's decision to leave the European Union.

Sports. In the National Hockey League draft in Buffalo, New York, the Toronto Maple Leafs select American center Auston Matthews as the overall number one pick. The Winnipeg Jets choose forward Patrik Laine of Finland with the second pick.

25 **Terrorism.** In Somalia, an al-Shabab terrorist attack on Mogadishu's Hotel Nasa Hablod kills 15 people and injures 25 others.

Disasters. In Kenya, 9 people drown—all members of the same music group—in a boating accident while en route to Ndeda Island on Lake Victoria.

Disasters. In southern California, wildfires continue to rage in several areas. Near Bakersfield in Kern County, fires kill 2 people and destroy more than 150 homes.

Government. In Iceland, voters elect independent historian Guðni Jóhannesson to become the nation's next president.

26 **Disasters.** In China's central Hunan Province, a tour bus crashes and catches fire, killing 35 people.

World community. The new $5.25-billion Panama Canal expansion opens, allowing larger ships to pass through the waterway and doubling its capacity.

Sports. In men's soccer, Chile wins the Copa América Centenario tournament by defeating Argentina on penalties after finishing play tied 0-0. After the match, Argentine star Lionel Messi announces his retirement from international soccer.

27 **Terrorism.** In the southern Yemeni port city of Mukalla, Islamic State terrorist bombings at government offices kill 38 people and injure 24 others.

Disasters. In the mountainous central Colombian province of Caldas, bad weather causes a military helicopter crash that kills 17 people.

Law. In a 5-3 decision, the U.S. Supreme Court strikes down a contentious Texas abortion law that imposed strict regulations on abortion facilities. The court then blocks similar laws in Mississippi and Wisconsin.

28 **Terrorism.** In Turkey, Islamic State terrorists kill 43 people and injure more than 230 others at Istanbul Atatürk Airport.

Economy. Volkswagen and the U.S. Justice Department agree on a $14.7 billion fine for the German automaker's emissions-cheating program.

Science. British geologists working with a helium exploration company discover a 54-billion-cubic-foot (1.5-billion-cubic-meter) field of helium in Tanzania's portion of the Great Rift Valley in southeastern Africa.

29 **Government.** In Mongolia, the main opposition Mongolian People's Party wins a landslide victory in parliamentary elections.

World community. Colombian, Italian, and U.S. drug agents seize 12 tons (11 metric tons) of cocaine and arrest 33 people from a Mafia ring operating deep in the Colombian jungle.

Economy. Swedish furniture company IKEA recalls nearly 36 million chests and dressers in the United States and Canada after the deaths of six children were blamed on the furniture's instability.

Economy. Japanese automaker Toyota recalls 3.37 million vehicles because of defects in airbags and emissions control units.

30 **Terrorism.** In Afghanistan, a Taliban terrorist bomb kills 30 police recruits and injures 50 others near Kabul, the capital.

Terrorism. In Somalia, an al-Shabab terrorist bomb kills all 18 people aboard a bus in the town of Lafole, near Mogadishu.

Terrorism. In northern Cameroon, Boko Haram terrorists bomb a video club and mosque, killing 15 people and injuring 50 others.

Government. In the Philippines, Rodrigo Duterte is sworn in as the southwestern Pacific nation's new president.

Law. A U.S. federal judge blocks a Mississippi law discriminating against LGBT people in the state. The same day, the U.S. military ends a ban on transgender people openly serving in the armed services.

Economy. President Obama signs a law creating a federal oversight board with authority to negotiate the restructuring of Puerto Rico's crushing $70 billion debt.

Sports. The Coastal Carolina Chanticleers defeat the Arizona Wildcats 4-3 to win the NCAA College World Series. The Chanticleers win the series 2 games to 1 to claim their first baseball national title.

JULY 2016

1   **Terrorism.** In Bangladesh, Islamic State terrorists kill 22 people in an attack on a restaurant in the upscale Gulshan neighborhood in the capital city of Dhaka. Six terrorists also die in the attack.

World community. Thousands of people, including members of the British royal family, mark the 100th anniversary of the beginning of World War I's 1916 Battle of the Somme at the Thiepval Memorial and other places on the former Somme battlefield in France.

Government. Austria's constitutional court overturns results from May's presidential election because of irregularities, forcing a repeat election scheduled for October.

3   **Terrorism.** In Iraq, Islamic State terrorist bombs kill over 300 people and injure hundreds of others in the Shī`ite majority Karrada district of Baghdad. ·

Disasters. In Pakistan, flash floods kill 31 people in the northwestern province of Khyber Pakhtunkhwa.

4   **Disasters.** In China, torrential rains cause floods that kill 180 people along the Yangtze River in central and southern China.

Science. NASA's space probe Juno enters into orbit around Jupiter, beginning a two-year mission to study the giant planet.

5   **Terrorism.** In Saudi Arabia, Islamic State suicide bombers hit Islamic holy sites in Jeddah, Medina, and Qatif, killing four people and injuring five others.

6   **Terrorism.** In Yemen, an Islamic State suicide bomber kills 26 people at a military base in the port city of Aden.

World community. U.S. President Barack Obama announces that 8,400 U.S. troops will remain in Afghanistan into 2017, eclipsing an earlier estimate of 5,500.

World community. In the United Kingdom, a seven-year inquiry into British involvement in the Iraq War finds that the 2003 invasion of Iraq was based on flawed intelligence and that there was no immediate threat from Iraqi leader Saddam Hussein.

Law. A Spanish court sentences both soccer star Lionel Messi and his father to 21 months probation for tax fraud. The two are also fined $3.8 million.

Law. Former South African runner Oscar Pistorius is sentenced to six years in prison for the 2013 murder of his girlfriend, Reeva Steenkamp.

7 **Terrorism.** In Iraq, Islamic State terrorists kill 35 people and injure 60 others in an attack on a sacred Shī`ite mausoleum north of Baghdad.

Crime. In Texas, a sniper kills five police officers and injures nine other people during a Black Lives Matter rally in Dallas. Police kill the gunman, who was motivated by police killings of African Americans.

World community. In Pamplona, Spain, rockets and the *encierro*, or running of the bulls, begin the annual, week-long Fiesta de San Fermín.

Economy. French food company Danone purchases Colorado's WhiteWave Foods for $10 billion.

8 **Disasters.** On the Indonesian island of Java, 12 people are killed in a traffic pileup.

Living world. Typhoon Nepartak hits the island nation of Taiwan, disrupting transportation and electric power. Three die in the storm and tens of thousands are displaced. The storm later kills six people on the mainland in China.

9 **World community.** In the Indian-controlled part of Kashmir, 30 people are killed and hundreds of others injured in clashes between protesters and Indian soldiers. The protests followed the death of Burhan Wani, a leader of a rebel group that wants to end Indian rule in the area.

World community. In South Sudan, violence between recently warring groups kills some 300 people in Juba, the capital.

Sports. American tennis star Serena Williams defeats Angelique Kerber of Germany to claim her sixth All-England Championships women's title at Wimbledon, near London. Williams had previously won in 2003, 2009, 2010, 2012, and 2015.

Sports. In Spain, matador Victor Barrio is killed by a bull at the Plaza de Las Ventas bullring in Teruel in eastern Aragon. Barrio is the first bullfighter killed in the ring since 1985.

Protestor Ieshia Evans is detained by law enforcement officers during a Black Lives Matter rally in Baton Rouge, Louisiana, on July 9, 2016. The rally followed the police killing of an unarmed African American man in Baton Rouge on July 5.

10 **World community.** Amid severe basic goods shortages in Venezuela, tens of thousands of people take advantage of a brief border opening to buy food and other supplies in neighboring Colombia.

Government. After a week of counting votes in Australia, Prime Minister Malcolm Turnbull's governing coalition of the Liberal and National parties narrowly retains power.

Government. In Japan, Prime Minister Shinzo Abe's Liberal Democratic Party retains power in national elections.

Sports. British tennis star Andy Murray defeats Canada's Milos Raonic to win his second Wimbledon men's title. Murray previously won in 2012.

Sports. Portugal's national men's soccer team defeats France 1-0 to win the UEFA European Championship at the Stade de France near Paris. It is Portugal's first European title.

11 Disasters. In India, monsoon rains cause floods that kill 22 people and displace 100,000 others.

Terrorism. In Somalia, an al-Shabab terrorist assault on an army base near Mogadishu kills 22 people.

12 Disasters. In Italy, a train collision kills 27 people and injures dozens of others near the city of Andria.

Terrorism. In Iraq, an Islamic State terrorist bomb kills 12 people and injures many others at an outdoor market in Rashidiyah, near Baghdad.

World community. The Permanent Court of Arbitration in The Hague rules in favor of the Philippines in territorial arguments with China about the Spratly Islands and nearby areas of the South China Sea.

Economy. Following up on recalls in North America, Swedish furniture company IKEA recalls 1.7 million chests and dressers in China over instability concerns.

Sports. The American League defeats the National League 4-2 at the Major League Baseball All-Star Game at PETCO Park in San Diego, California.

13 Terrorism. In Iraq, an Islamic State terrorist bomb kills 8 people and injures 23 others at a police checkpoint north of Baghdad.

Government. David Cameron resigns as prime minister of the United Kingdom and is replaced by new Conservative Party leader Theresa May.

14 Terrorism. In Nice, France, an Islamic terrorist drives a truck into a large crowd celebrating Bastille Day, killing 85 people and injuring dozens of others.

15 World community. In Turkey, a faction of the Turkish military tries and fails to overthrow the government of President Recep Tayyip Erdoğan. The violent takeover attempt kills over 200 people and injures 1,400 others. Thousands of people suspected of supporting the attempted coup are arrested or suspended from their jobs.

Government. Donald Trump, the presumptive Republican presidential nominee, selects Indiana Governor Mike Pence as his vice presidential running mate.

17 **Crime.** In Louisiana, a gunman motivated by police killings of African Americans kills three Baton Rouge police officers and wounds three others.

Government. In São Tomé and Príncipe in the Gulf of Guinea, voters elect former Prime Minister Evaristo Carvalho as the African two-island nation's new president.

Sports. Swedish golfer Henrik Stenson wins the 2016 Open Championship (commonly known as the British Open) at the Royal Troon Golf Club in South Ayrshire, Scotland. It is Stenson's first major tournament victory.

18 **Economy.** Japanese telecom giant SoftBank agrees to buy the British technology company ARM for $32 billion.

Sports. The World Anti-Doping Agency finds that the Russian government concealed the widespread use of performance-enhancing drugs by Russian athletes at the 2014 Winter Olympic Games.

19 **Terrorism.** In Syria, U.S.-led coalition air strikes targeting Islamic State terrorists in the northern city of Manbij accidentally kill 56 civilians.

Terrorism. In central Mali, Islamic militants attack a military base near Nampala, killing 17 soldiers and injuring 35 others.

Disasters. In Taiwan, a tour bus crashes into a guardrail and catches fire near Taipei, the capital, killing 26 people.

Government. At the Republican National Convention in Cleveland, Ohio, delegates formally nominate Donald Trump as the Republican candidate for president of the United States.

21 **Disasters.** In northern China, torrential rains and flash floods kill 44 people and displace thousands.

Arts. Longtime Fox News Channel chief Roger Ailes resigns amid numerous sexual harassment allegations.

Sports. The Kansas City Royals Major League Baseball team visits the White House in Washington, D.C., where President Obama congratulates them on last year's World Series championship.

Sports. The International Olympic Committee bans Russian track and field athletes from competing in the 2016 Summer Olympic Games because of doping scandals from previous Olympics.

Sports. The National Basketball Association removes its 2017 All-Star

Game from Charlotte, North Carolina, because of the state's anti-LGBT "bathroom law."

22 **Disasters.** An Indian Air Force transport plane with 29 people on board disappears over the Bay of Bengal near the Andaman and Nicobar Islands.

Crime. In Germany, a gunman obsessed with mass killings kills nine people and injures several others at the Olympia-Einkaufszentrum shopping center in Munich. The gunman then shoots and kills himself.

Government. Presumptive Democratic Party presidential nominee Hillary Clinton selects Virginia Senator Tim Kaine as her vice presidential running mate.

23 **World community.** In Key West, Florida, 65-year old Dave Hemingway wins the "Papa" (Ernest) Hemingway Look-Alike Contest. It is the first time that a man named Hemingway (no relation to the famous author) has won the contest, which has been held at Sloppy Joe's Bar—a favorite Hemingway haunt—every year since 1981.

Disasters. In China's northern Hebei province, floods kill 154 people and displace 300,000 others.

Terrorism. In Afghanistan, Islamic State terrorist bombs kill 80 people and injure 260 others in a Shī`ite community in Kabul, the capital.

Disasters. In Madagascar, a three-story thatch house in the district of Ikalamavony catches fire during a party, killing 38 people.

24 **Terrorism.** In Baghdad, Iraq, an Islamic State terrorist bomb kills 21 people and injures 35 others in the Shī`ite district of Kadhimiyah.

Disasters. In central California, the Santa Clarita wildfire kills one person, destroys numerous homes, and doubles in size to more than 51 square miles (132 square kilometers).

Government. Nepal's Prime Minister Khadga Prasad Oli resigns after the defection of allies from his coalition government.

Sports. British cyclist Chris Froome wins the Tour de France men's bicycle race for the third time in the last four years.

Sports. In Cooperstown, New York, outfielder Ken Griffey, Jr., and catcher Mike Piazza are inducted into the National Baseball Hall of Fame.

25 **Terrorism.** In Iraq, an Islamic State terrorist bomb kills 21 people and wounds 32 others near Khalis, a town northeast of Baghdad.

Government. South Sudanese President Salva Kiir replaces Vice President Riek Machar with his personal ally, General Taban Deng.

Economy. U.S. telecom giant Verizon purchases Internet company Yahoo for $4.8 billion.

26 **Crime.** In Japan, a man armed with a knife kills 19 people and injures 25 others at a care center for the disabled in Sagamihara, a city west of Tokyo. Police arrest the attacker, a former employee of the center.

Terrorism. In Somalia, an al-Shabab terrorist attack kills 13 people at an African Union military base near the main airport in Mogadishu.

Terrorism. In Bangladesh, police kill 9 people suspected of ties to a recent terrorist attack in Dhaka, the capital, that killed 22 people.

Government. At the Democratic National Convention in Philadelphia, delegates nominate Hillary Clinton as the first woman major party candidate for president of the United States.

World community. The solar-powered airplane *Solar Impulse 2* lands in Abu Dhabi, United Arab Emirates, completing a record-setting fuel-free circumnavigation of Earth.

27 **Terrorism.** In Syria, Islamic State terrorist bombings kill 44 people in the Kurdish city of al-Qamishli on the Turkish border.

Law. After failing to convict the first three police officers charged in the 2015 death of Freddie Gray, prosecutors in Baltimore, Maryland, drop charges against the remaining three.

28 **Disasters.** In Nepal, monsoon rains cause floods and landslides that kill 64 people in Rupandehi District.

Government. Former Peruvian Prime Minister Pedro Pablo Kuczynski is sworn in as the nation's new president.

29 **Law.** A U.S. federal appeals court strikes down a North Carolina voter identification law, calling it a deliberate effort to suppress African American voter turnout.

30 **World community.** In Turkey, fighting between Turkish soldiers and Kurdish militants kills 35 people in far southeastern Hakkâri Province.

Disaster. In Texas, a hot-air balloon fire and crash kills 16 people near the central city of Lockhart.

Disasters. In Maryland, heavy rains cause flash floods that kill two people and displace thousands in the Baltimore suburb of Ellicott City.

Government. Tunisian lawmakers vote to dismiss Prime Minister Habib Essid from office during a no-confidence ballot in parliament.

Sports. U.S. skydiver Luke Aikins sets a world record by jumping from a height of 25,000 feet (7,620 meters) without a parachute or wing suit. Aikins lands safely in a giant net.

31 **Sports.** U.S. golfer Jimmy Walker wins the PGA Championship at Baltusrol Golf Club in Springfield Township, New Jersey. It is his first major tournament victory.

Sports. Thailand's Ariya Jutanugarn wins the Women's British Open at the Woburn Golf and Country Club in Milton Keynes, England.

Japanese Minister of Defense Yuriko Koike campaigns in Tokyo the day before she is elected the first woman governor of Tokyo prefecture on July 31, 2016.

AUGUST 2016

1   **Terrorism.** The United States launches airstrikes on Islamic State terrorists in the Libyan city of Sirte following a request for help from the Libyan government.

Economy. U.S. telecom giant Verizon agrees to buy GPS vehicle tracking company Fleetmatics for $2.4 billion.

2   **Terrorism.** In Libya, an Islamic State terrorist bomb kills 22 people and injures 20 others in the volatile Guwarsha district of the eastern city of Benghāzī.

Health. In Siberia, an anthrax outbreak—possibly related to the thawing of tundra caused by climate change—kills one person, sickens others, and kills thousands of reindeer.

World community. In the Philippines, the death toll from President Rodrigo Duterte's program of extrajudicial killings of drug dealers and users surpasses 700 since he took office on June 30.

3   **Disasters.** In central California, thousands of firefighters continue to battle wildfires that have scorched some 44,000 acres (17,800 hectares) and killed 6 people.

Government. In Nepal, former Communist rebel leader Pushpa Kamal Dahal becomes prime minister for the second time. In Tunisia, agricultural science specialist and junior minister Youssef Chahed is named the nation's new prime minister.

Science. The U.S. Federal Aviation Administration approves the first contract for a private company, Moon Express, to land a robotic craft on the moon.

4   **Terrorism.** In Iraq, Islamic State terrorists capture some 3,000 fleeing villagers near Kirkuk and execute 12 of them.

5   **Terrorism.** In India's northeastern Assam state, Islamic terrorists kill 13 people and injure dozens of others in Kokrajhar.

6   **Disasters.** In northern France, a fire kills 13 people and injures several others attending a birthday party in Rouen.

On Aug. 5, 2016, the Olympic flame burns during the opening ceremonies of the Summer Olympic Games in Rio de Janeiro, Brazil. The same day, the International Olympic Committee banned 116 Russian athletes from participating in the games for using performance-enhancing drugs.

7 **Disasters.** In eastern Mexico, mudslides triggered by Hurricane Earl kill 48 people in Puebla and Veracruz states. In Macedonia's capital, Skopje, heavy rains cause floods that kill 21 people and leave several others missing.

Government. In Thailand, voters approve a new constitution backed by the ruling military junta. The military took control of the Southeast Asian country in 2014.

Sports. Miami Marlins outfielder Ichiro Suzuki triples for his 3,000th career hit in Major League Baseball. The same day, the International Paralympic Committee bans Russian athletes from participating in the Rio Paralympics for using performance-enhancing drugs.

8 **Terrorism.** In Pakistan, Islamic terrorists attack a government hospital in Quetta, killing 77 people and injuring more than 100 others.

World community. In Ethiopia, days of clashes between protesters and security forces kill 90 people. Protestors are demanding social and political reforms in the impoverished northeastern African nation.

9 **World community.** After months of tension stemming from conflicting aims in Syria, Russia and Turkey reconcile and normalize ties. In Yemen, Saudi warplanes resume airstrikes on Sanaa, the capital, killing 14 people. Peace talks had quieted Yemen's civil war, but the talks ended in failure on August 6.

10 **Disasters.** In Iraq, a fire in Baghdad's Yarmouk maternity hospital kills 12 premature babies. In the Washington, D.C., suburb of Silver Spring, Maryland, an explosion and fire in an apartment building kills 7 people and injures more than 30 others.

Government. Brazilian senators vote 59 to 21 to begin impeachment proceedings against President Dilma Rousseff, who has been suspended since May over alleged budget improprieties.

Law. A U.S. Justice Department study finds that Baltimore, Maryland, police violated the rights of black residents with disproportionate traffic stops, searches, and arrests.

11 **Disasters.** In central China's Hubei province, an explosion and fire at a power plant kill 21 people and injure several others.

Government. In Zambia, voters elect President Edgar Lungu to a full 5-year term in office. Lungu took over in early 2015 after the death of President Michael Sata.

Living world. Scientists find a 400-year-old Greenland shark, making the animal by far the longest-living vertebrate on Earth.

Sports. U.S. swimmer Michael Phelps wins gold in the 200-meter individual medley for the fourth consecutive Olympic Games.

12 **Terrorism.** Two days of terrorist bombings at tourist sites in Thailand kill 4 people and injure several others.

World community. The United States declares a public health emergency in Puerto Rico in response to the commonwealth's Zika virus outbreak. The same day, the United Nations Security Council approves the deployment of 4,000 troops to South Sudan after recent fighting threatened to reignite the east African nation's civil war.

13 **Crime.** In Milwaukee, Wisconsin, riots erupt after police shoot an armed African American man. Several cars and businesses are severely damaged.

World community. In Cuba, former President Fidel Castro attends celebrations in Havana marking his 90th birthday.

14 **Disasters.** In Pakistani-ruled Azad Kashmir, a bus carrying a wedding party crashes into a ravine, killing 25 people and injuring several others.

Sports. Jamaican Usain Bolt becomes the first sprinter to win gold medals in the men's 100-meter race in three consecutive Olympic Games.

15 **Disasters.** In Louisiana, days of heavy rains and flooding kill 13 people, displace thousands of others, and damage some 60,000 homes.

World community. In Syria's civil war, hundreds of people are killed in days of fighting in Aleppo and terrorist attacks in other areas. In war-torn Yemen, Saudi airstrikes accidentally hit a Médecins Sans Frontières (Doctors Without Borders) hospital, killing 11 people and injuring 19 others in north-western Hajjah province.

16 **Disasters.** California Governor Jerry Brown declares a state of emergency in San Bernardino County in response to the Blue Cut

On Aug. 16, 2016, a stifling summer heat wave in China's Sichuan Province drives thousands of people (and their swim rings) into a crowded pool in the resort city of Suining.

wildfire, which has torched some 36,000 acres (14,500 hectares) and displaced 82,000 people.

Arts. The $1.4-billion Westfield World Trade Center, a large, airy mall covering roughly 10 city blocks, opens in New York City as part of the World Trade Center Ground Zero redevelopment.

17 **Science.** HAV 304 Airlander 10, an airship made by Hybrid Air Vehicles, flies for the first time at

19 **Government.** The U.S. Defense Department reveals that the U.S. Army made $6.5 trillion worth of improper accounting adjustments to balance books in 2015.

20 **Terrorism.** In Turkey, an Islamic State terrorist bomb kills 54 people and injures dozens of others at a Kurdish wedding celebration in the southeastern city of Gaziantep.

21 **Terrorism.** In Somalia's Puntland region, al-Shabab terrorists kill 20 people at a local government headquarters in the town of Galkayo.

Sports. In Rio de Janeiro, Brazil, the Olympic Games draw to a close. The United States wins the most gold medals, followed by the United Kingdom and China.

22 **Disasters.** In central and eastern India, heavy rains cause flooding that kills 40 people and displaces hundreds of thousands of others.

Cardington Airfield in Bedfordshire, England. At 302 feet (92 meters) long, it is the world's longest aircraft.

18 **Terrorism.** In southeastern Turkey, Kurdish terrorist bombs targeting police and the military kill 12 people and injure more than 200 others.

World community. In the Philippines, the death toll from President Duterte's program of extrajudicial killings of drug dealers and users surpasses 1,900 since he took office on June 30.

Economics. U.S. pharmaceutical company Pfizer agrees to buy fellow drug company Medivation for $14 billion.

23 **Living world.** A Filipino fisherman turns in a 75-pound (34-kilogram) natural pearl retrieved from a giant clam near the island of Palawan. The gem far exceeds the world's previous largest clam pearl, which weighed 14 pounds (6.4 kilograms).

24 **Disasters.** In mountainous central Italy, a 6.2-magnitude earthquake kills 296 people and leaves thousands of others homeless in the regions of Latium (Lazio), Marches (Marche), and Umbria. In Myanmar, a 6.8-magnitude earthquake kills 4 people and damages ancient temples in the city of Bagan.

Terrorism. Turkish ground forces enter Syria to combat Islamic State terrorists operating near the border. Kurdish militants, who have waged a lengthy guerrilla campaign against the Turkish military, also operate in the area.

Terrorism. At the American University of Afghanistan in Kabul, an Islamic State terrorist attack kills 12 people and injures 44 others.

World community. In Colombia, the government and rebel FARC forces sign the latest in a string of peace treaties meant to end the South American country's long-running insurrection.

Science. European astronomers name Proxima Centauri b as the closest planet beyond our solar system that could possibly have liquid water and support life.

26 **Terrorism.** In Turkey, a Kurdish militant bomb kills 11 police officers and injures 78 others at a checkpoint in the southeastern town of Cizre. In Somalia, an al-Shabab terrorist attack kills 10 people at a beach restaurant in Mogadishu, the capital.

Living world. U.S. President Barack Obama expands Hawaii's Papahānaumokuākea Marine National Monument, making it the world's largest national protected area. The area holds special meaning for native Hawaiians.

27 **Disasters.** In Russia, a warehouse fire kills 17 Kyrgyz migrant workers in Moscow.

Terrorism. In Iraq, an Islamic State terrorist bomb kills 18 people at a wedding in the southern Shī`ite city of Karbala.

Government. In Gabon, President Ali Bongo Ondimba claims victory over his main challenger, former Foreign Minister Jean Ping, in the small west African nation's presidential election. The close vote results in violence and riots in the streets of Libreville, the capital.

28 **Sports.** In South Williamsport, Pennsylvania, an all-star baseball team from Endwell, New York, wins the Little League World Series by defeating a team from Seoul, South Korea, 2-1.

29 **Terrorism.** In Yemen, an Islamic State terrorist bombing kills 70 people in the southern port city of Aden.

World community. In the Philippines, fighting between government troops and Abu Sayyaf Muslim rebels kills 12 people on the southern island of Mindanao.

Science. A team of scientists completes an isolated year-long Mars simulation in Hawaii in preparation for a future visit to the Red Planet.

Living world. In southwestern Mexico, the Volcán de Colima, known as the "Fire Volcano," erupts, spewing columns of smoke and ash into the atmosphere.

30 **Terrorism.** In Somalia, an al-Shabab terrorist bomb kills 22 people and injures many others near the presidential palace in Mogadishu.

Economics. The European Union orders U.S. tech firm Apple Inc. to pay 13 billion euros ($14.5 billion) in back taxes plus interest for illegally running profits through Ireland to avoid paying taxes.

31 **Disasters.** Typhoon Lionrock makes landfall in Japan, causing flooding that kills 11 people on the main island of Honshu.

Government. Brazil's senate impeaches President Dilma Rousseff, formally dismissing her from office. Interim President Michel Temer is sworn in as the new president of Brazil.

World community. JetBlue Airways Flight 387 from Fort Lauderdale, Florida, lands in Santa Clara, Cuba, marking the first commercial passenger air travel between the United States and Cuba since 1961.

SEPTEMBER 2016

1 **World community.** In Venezuela, hundreds of thousands of protestors fill the streets of Caracas, the capital, calling for the removal of President Nicolas Maduro.

2 **Terrorism.** In Pakistan, Taliban terrorist bombs kill 13 people and injure 40 others in northwestern Khyber-Pakhtunkhwa province. On the southern Philippine island of Mindanao, an explosion at a market kills 15 people and injures 60 others in Davao City.

Living world. Hurricane Hermine hits the northern Gulf Coast of Florida with heavy rains and high winds before weakening to a tropical storm.

3 **Living world.** In northern Oklahoma, a 5.6-magnitude earthquake—one of the strongest in the state's history—causes minor damage near the town of Pawnee.

4 **Disasters.** In Afghanistan, a bus crashes into a fuel tanker, killing 35 people and injuring 25 others in southern Zabul province.

5 **Terrorism.** Islamic State terrorist attacks in Syria kill 48 people and injure many others. In Afghanistan, Taliban terrorists kill 35 people

and injure more than 100 others in an attack near the Afghan Ministry of Defense in Kabul, the capital.

Disasters. At Kaliti Prison near Addis Ababa, Ethiopia, 23 inmates are killed in a fire and stampede during an attempted jailbreak.

World community. In the Philippines, the death toll from President Rodrigo Duterte's program of extrajudicial killings of drug dealers and users surpasses more than 2,400 since he took office on June 30.

Sports. U.S. tennis star Serena Williams wins her 308th career Grand Slam match, surpassing the all-time record held by Swiss star Roger Federer.

6 **Disasters.** The death toll from Typhoon Lionrock reaches 120 as dozens die in flooding in North Korea.

Living world. In Mexico, Hurricane Newton's heavy rains and winds cause flooding and mudslides in western Guerrero state before hitting the Baja California resort of Cabo San Lucas. In Spain, wildfires destroy numerous buildings and displace some 1,400 people in the southeastern province of Alicante.

Law. Fox News agrees to pay $20 million to settle sexual harassment lawsuits against the network's former chief Roger Ailes.

Economy. Canadian energy company Enbridge agrees to buy Spectra Energy of Texas for $28 billion.

7 **Sports.** In Rio de Janeiro, Brazil, opening ceremonies mark the official start of the 2016 Paralympic Games for athletes with physical or mental disabilities.

8 **Government.** In Armenia, civil unrest and a poor economy force the

In Cholpon-Ata, Kyrgyzstan, riders compete in the Nomad Games, a competition dedicated to the ethnic sports of Central Asia, on Sept. 8, 2016.

resignation of Prime Minister Hovik Abrahamyan. In Uzbekistan, the parliament appoints Prime Minister Shavkat Mirziyoyev to temporarily replace the late Islam Karimov as president.

Living world. Studies by scientists at the World Conservation Society reveal that the world's wilderness has been reduced by 1.27 million square miles (3.3 million square kilometers)—some 10 percent—since 1993.

9 **World community.** In North Korea, a nuclear weapons test causes a 5.3-magnitude seismic event, violates numerous United Nations Security Council resolutions, and brings international condemnation. Near the French Alps mountain town of Chamonix, helicopter and mountaineer teams rescue 110 people trapped in gondola cable cars as high as 12,500 feet (3,800 meters) above the slopes of Mount Blanc. In the United States, despite ongoing protests, a federal judge allows construction to begin on the controversial Dakota Access Pipeline in North Dakota.

Economy. U.S. automaker General Motors recalls more than 4 million vehicles due to a software defect that can prevent airbags from deploying during a crash.

10 **Disasters.** In Bangladesh, a boiler explosion and fire kills 31

people and injures 70 others at a factory in the city of Tongi. In northern Tanzania, a 5.7-magnitude earthquake kills 13 people and injures 200 others in and around the town of Bukoba.

Sports. In the women's final at the US Open Tennis Championships in New York City, Angelique Kerber of Germany defeats Czech star Karolína Plíšková to win her second grand slam tournament.

11 **World community.** Solemn ceremonies mark the 15th anniversary of the September 11 terrorist attacks in the United States.

Sports. Swiss tennis star Stan Wawrinka defeats Serbian Novak Djokovic to win the US Open men's championship. It is Wawrinka's third grand slam title. In Madrid, Spain, Colombian racer Nairo Quintana wins the Vuelta a España men's bicycle race.

Arts. Miss Arkansas Savvy Shields wins the Miss America pageant in Atlantic City, New Jersey.

12 **Disasters.** In Shelby County, Alabama, the Colonial Pipeline spills an estimated 350,000 gallons of gasoline, poisoning area waters and forcing a partial shutdown of the pipeline. The spill and shutdown cause gas shortages in much of the southeastern United States.

World community. In the Syrian Civil War, an upsurge in violence slackens after Russia and the United States negotiate a temporary cease-fire between government and rebel forces.

Living world. The Piton de la Fournaise volcano erupts on the remote Indian Ocean island of Réunion, an overseas department and region of France.

13 **Government.** Energy executive Karen Karapetyan becomes the new prime minister of Armenia.

Sports. The National Collegiate Athletic Association removes several championship sporting events—including two rounds of the men's March Madness basketball tournament—from North Carolina because of the state's anti-LGBT "bathroom law."

14 **World community.** In Washington D.C., the United States signs a 10-year, $38-billion aid package providing Israel with military assistance. The same day, Myanmar's unofficial head of government Aung San Suu Kyi arrives for her first state visit with President Barack Obama. In Brazil, prosecutors file corruption charges against former president Luiz Inacio Lula da Silva.

Economics. German chemical company Bayer purchases U.S. agrochemical company Monsanto for $66 billion.

Living world. Heavy rains and wind from Typhoon Meranti disrupt transport and electric power on the island of Taiwan.

Government. In Washington, D.C., Carla Hayden is sworn in as the new librarian of Congress. She is the first woman and first African American to hold the post.

15 **Living world.** President Barack Obama establishes the Northeast Canyons and Seamounts marine national monument off the northeast Atlantic coast of the United States.

16 **Terrorism.** In Pakistan, Islamic terrorists bomb a mosque in the northern district of Mohmand Agency, killing 36 people and injuring 34 others.

Disasters. Typhoon Meranti hits coastal China, killing 30 people and displacing thousands of others.

17 **Terrorism.** In northeastern Syria, a U.S.-coalition airstrike meant to hit Islamic State terrorists accidentally kills 62 Syrian soldiers. In New York City, a terrorist bomb detonates in the Chelsea neighborhood of Manhattan, injuring 29 people. Another bomb detonates in New Jersey with no injuries. In St. Cloud, Minnesota, an Islamic terrorist injures 9 people with a knife before being killed by police.

World community. In Munich, Germany, ceremonies mark the beginning of the annual Oktoberfest, a month-long celebration of German beer, food, and culture.

18 **Disasters.** In Thailand, an overcrowded tourist boat capsizes in the Chao Phraya River, killing 26 people.

Terrorism. In Indian-administered Kashmir, Islamic militants attack an Indian military base, leaving 17 soldiers and 4 militants dead.

Government. In Russia, parliamentary elections maintain the majority for President Vladimir Putin's United Russia party. In Germany, elections go against the ruling coalition of Chancellor Angela Merkel.

Arts. At the Emmy Awards in Los Angeles, "Game of Thrones" wins best drama series, "Veep" wins best comedy, and "The People v. O.J. Simpson: American Crime Story" wins best limited series (miniseries).

19 **Terrorism.** In New Jersey, police capture the person suspected of carrying out the weekend bombings in that state and in New York City.

World community. In Syria, a shaky, week-long truce concludes as a Russian airstrike on a United Nations aid convoy kills 20 people and destroys trucks loaded with supplies for stranded refugees. Full-scale

fighting resumes with further airstrikes and violence largely centered on the battered city of Aleppo. In the Democratic Republic of the Congo, 44 people die in clashes between police and protestors calling for the resignation of President Joseph Kabila.

Living world. In Costa Rica, the Volcán Turrialba erupts, spewing ash and smoke into the atmosphere and grounding flights in the region.

20 **World community.** The European Union (EU) formally accepts Bosnia-Herzegovina's application for membership. If approved, the Balkan nation could join the EU as soon as next year.

21 **Disasters.** An overcrowded migrant boat capsizes in the

On Sept. 21, 2016, police form a human barrier to clear rioters from the streets of Charlotte, North Carolina. Protests erupted in the southeastern city following the police shooting of an African American man mistaken for a wanted criminal. The protests turned violent and escalated into riots that injured numerous civilians and police officers. Governor Pat McCrory declared a state of emergency and summoned the National Guard, and the situation quickly calmed.

Mediterranean Sea off the coast of Egypt, killing nearly 400 people.

World community. In Venezuela, bus drivers protesting the administration of President Nicolas Maduro strike and block the streets with buses, paralyzing traffic in Caracas, the capital.

22 **World community.** U.S. Internet company Yahoo announces that 500 million of its accounts were hacked in 2014, the biggest known cyber breach to date.

23 **Crime.** A gunman kills five people at the Cascade Mall in Burlington, Washington. Police capture the shooter the next day.

24 **Sports.** In Manchester, England, Venezuelan boxer Jorge Linares defeats reigning champion Anthony Crolla of the United Kingdom to claim the World Boxing Association lightweight title.

25 **Terrorism.** In northeastern Nigeria, fighting between Boko Haram terrorists and government troops kills 8 soldiers and 25 terrorists.

Sports. At the East Lake Golf Club in Atlanta, Georgia, Northern Irish golfer Rory McIlroy wins the Tour Championship and the PGA Tour season title.

26 **Terrorism.** In Turkey, Kurdish militant attacks kill 10 Turkish soldiers in southeastern Mardin and Sirnak provinces.

World community. In Cartagena, Colombia, FARC rebels sign a peace accord with the Colombian government. Voters will have the opportunity to approve or reject the accord in early October.

Government. U.S. presidential candidates Hillary Clinton and Donald Trump square off in their first debate at Hofstra University in Hempstead, New York.

27 **Terrorism.** In Iraq, Islamic State terrorist bombs kill 17 people and injure 55 others in Baghdad, the capital.

Disasters. In Nepal's central Dhading district, a bus skids off a mountain road and crashes, killing 19 people.

Government. In Gabon, President Ali Bongo is sworn in for a second 7-year term despite unrest in the capital, Libreville, and allegations of electoral fraud.

Health. The World Health Organization announces that measles has been eliminated in the Americas, the first time the virus has been eradicated in an entire region.

28 **Disasters.** Typhoon Megi causes landslides that kill 32 people in eastern China's Zhejiang Province a day after the storm killed 4 people and injured hundreds on Taiwan.

World community. International investigators find that a Russian-made Buk missile brought down a Malaysian airliner in eastern Ukraine in July 2014, contradicting Russia's claim that Ukrainian rebels shot down the civilian plane.

Economy. Low oil prices force the Organization of the Petroleum Exporting Countries (OPEC) to reduce output from 33.24 million barrels per day to 32.5 million, the group's first oil production cut since 2008.

Government. The U.S. Congress overrides President Barack Obama's veto of the Justice Against Sponsors of Terrorism Act. The act allows victims of terrorist attacks in the United States to sue any foreign government that "aids and abets" terrorism.

Living world. In Australia, severe thunderstorms cause widespread blackouts, knocking out electric power throughout the state of South Australia.

29 **Disasters.** In Hoboken, New Jersey, a commuter train derails and crashes into a station during morning rush hour, killing 1 person and injuring more than 100 others.

30 **Crime.** In southern China's Yunnan Province, police capture a man who killed his parents and 17 others in a village near Kunming.

Law. Alabama Supreme Court Chief Justice Roy Moore is suspended for violating judicial ethics. Moore refused to accept and prevented others from enforcing the 2015 legalization of gay marriage.

Science. The European Space Agency's Rosetta space probe ends its 12-year mission studying comet 67P/Churyumov–Gerasimenko with a controlled crash landing on the comet's surface.

OCTOBER 2016

1 **Sports.** At the Melbourne Cricket Ground in Australia, 100,000 fans watch the Western Bulldogs defeat the Sydney Swans for their first Australian Football League title since 1954.

2 **Disasters.** In Ethiopia's central Oromia Region, police clashes with protestors and a panicked stampede kill 52 people in the town of Bishoftu.

World community. In Colombia, voters narrowly reject a referendum that would have concluded a peace agreement between FARC rebels and the government.

Sports. On the final day of the Major League Baseball regular season, Los Angeles Dodgers sportscaster Vin Scully calls the final game of his 67-year career as the voice of the Dodgers. At the Hazeltine National Golf Club in Chaska, Minnesota, the United States defeats the European team to win the Ryder Cup for the first time since 2008. In Australia, at ANZ Stadium in Sydney, the Cronulla Sharks defeat the Melbourne Storm to win their first National Rugby League title.

3 **Terrorism.** In Iraq, Islamic State terrorist bombs kill 11 people and injure more than 40 others participating in Shī`ite processions in Baghdad.

Government. The Estonian parliament elects European Union accountant Kersti Kaljulaid to become the Baltic nation's first woman president.

Economy. U.S. outdoor sports retailer Bass Pro Shops purchases rival Cabela's for $5.5 billion.

Science. Japan's Yoshinori Ohsumi wins the Nobel Prize in medicine for his discovery of how cells break down and recycle their content.

4 **Government.** U.S. Democratic and Republican vice-presidential candidates Tim Kaine and Mike Pence debate at Longwood University in Farmville, Virginia.

Science. British scientists Duncan Haldane, J. Michael Kosterlitz, and David J. Thouless share the 2016 Nobel Prize in physics for their research on unusual forms of matter.

5 **World community.** The United Nations Security Council nominates former Portuguese Prime Minister António Guterres to be the world body's next secretary-general.

Science. European scientists Jean-Pierre Sauvage, Sir Fraser Stoddart, and Ben Feringa share the 2016 Nobel Prize in chemistry for their research on nanotechnology (molecular machines). In Van Horn, Texas, U.S. aerospace firm Blue Origin successfully tests its New Shepard reusable launch system.

6 **Disasters.** The death toll in Haiti from Hurricane Matthew surpasses 800 as the storm rolls over the Bahamas and churns toward the southeast coast of the United States.

Terrorism. In the west African nation of Niger, Islamic militants kill 22 soldiers guarding a camp for refugees from neighboring Mali.

7 **World community.** Colombian President Juan Manuel Santos is awarded the Nobel Peace Prize for negotiating a peace deal with FARC rebels that ended 52 years of conflict. Santos earned the prize despite a Colombian referendum that rejected the deal.

8 **Disasters.** Hurricane Matthew ravages the southeast Atlantic coast of the United States, causing flooding and accidents that kill 24 people in North Carolina. In Haiti, where the storm struck days earlier, the death toll passes 1,000.

World community. In Yemen's civil war, Saudi air strikes accidentally kill 140 people and injure hundreds of others attending a funeral reception in the capital, Sanaa.

9 **Terrorism.** In Turkey's southeast Hakkâri Province, a Kurdish militant bomb kills 17 people and injures 27 others at a military camp in Şemdinli district.

Government. U.S. Democratic and Republican presidential candidates Hillary Clinton and Donald Trump debate for a second time at Washington University in St. Louis, Missouri.

Sports. In the annual Chicago Marathon, Abel Kirui of Kenya wins the men's race, and fellow Kenyan Florence Kiplagat wins her second straight women's race.

10 **Terrorism.** In Afghanistan's southern Helmand province, a Taliban terrorist bomb kills 14

People await the arrival of aid in Anse d'Hainault, Haiti, on Oct. 14, 2016, the week after Hurricane Matthew ravaged the area. United States military personnel delivered drinking water, food, medicine, and other badly needed relief supplies to the remote town at the tip of Haiti's Tiburon Peninsula, where the devastation was made worse by outbreaks of cholera.

people and injures 15 others in the provincial capital, Lashkar Gah.

World community. In South Sudan, a rebel ambush kills 21 people and injures 20 others in Central Equatoria State, threatening to reignite the nation's recent civil war.

Economics. British economist Oliver Hart and Bengt Holmström of Finland share the Nobel Prize in economics for their research in corporate contract theory.

11 **Terrorism.** In Afghanistan, an Islamic State terrorist attack kills 18 people as they gather to celebrate the mainly Shī`ite Ashura festival in Kabul. Near the city of Lashkar Gah, a large Taliban attack kills 100 Afghan police and soldiers.

Disasters. In China, a residential building collapses in the eastern city of Wenzhou, killing 22 people.

12 **Terrorism.** In Afghanistan, an Islamic State terrorist bomb kills

14 Shī`ite worshipers and injures 36 others at a mosque in the Balkh Province capital of Mazar-i-Sharif.

Economy. John Stumpf resigns as chief executive and chairman of U.S. bank giant Wells Fargo following a scandal over illegal sales practices.

Sports. Toronto Maple Leafs rookie Auston Matthews sets an all-time record by scoring four goals in his first National Hockey League game.

13 **Terrorism.** In the Central African Republic, Islamic Seleka militants kill 30 people and injure 57 others during an attack on a refugee camp in the northern village of Kaga-Bandoro.

World community. Under pressure to reform its political system and restore democracy, the Indian Ocean island nation of the Maldives quits the Commonwealth of Nations. In New York City, the United Nations General Assembly approves the nomination of Antonio Guterres as the world body's ninth secretary-general. Guterres will take office on Jan. 1, 2017. In the Syrian Civil War, Russian and Syrian air strikes pound the beleaguered, rebel-held city of Aleppo, killing hundreds of people. In Yemen's civil war, a U.S. Navy warship retaliates against failed Houthi rebel missile attacks by destroying radar stations along Yemen's southwestern coast.

Government. In Thailand, military chief and Privy Council President Prem Tinsulanonda is named regent pro tempore until the succession of Crown Prince Maha Vajiralongkorn to replace King Bhumibol Adulyadej, who died earlier that day.

Arts. U.S. music icon Bob Dylan is awarded the Nobel Prize in literature.

14 **Terrorism.** In Iraq, Islamic State terrorists execute 58 people suspected of trying to help Iraqi government troops capture the Islamic State-held city of Mosul. In Egypt, fighting at a checkpoint in northern Sinai kills 15 Islamic State terrorists and 12 security personnel.

World community. In Somalia, clashes between rival regional groups kill 11 people and displace thousands of others.

15 **Terrorism.** In Iraq, an Islamic State terrorist attack kills 55 people at a Shī`ite gathering in Baghdad. In Egypt, government air strikes kill more than 100 Islamic State terrorists at a camp in northern Sinai.

Disasters. In India, a panic among pilgrims causes a stampede that kills 24 people and injures 20 others at a sacred Hindu site in the ancient city of Varanasi.

16 **Disasters.** In central Vietnam, flooding caused by Typhoon Sarika kills 31 people and displaces many thousands of others. The day before, the storm killed two people and displaced more than 150,000 in the Philippines.

17 **Disasters.** In Pakistan, buses collide in the town of Khanpur in Rahimyar Khan district, killing 30 people and injuring 70 others. In the east Indian state of Odisha, a fire in a hospital kills 20 people and injures over 100 others in the capital city of Bhubaneswar.

Terrorism. In Iraq, Kurdish and Iraqi government forces (with support from the U.S.-led coalition) launch an offensive on the Islamic State-held city of Mosul.

Crime. In Brazil's northern Roraima state, a prison riot and fighting between rival gangs kill 25 inmates.

18 **World community.** In the Democratic Republic of the Congo, clashes between rival ethnic groups kill 20 people in the southeastern province of Tanganyika.

19 **Government.** U.S. presidential candidates Hillary Clinton and Donald Trump meet for a final debate at the University of Nevada, Las Vegas. In Croatia, the parliament names Croatian Democratic Union leader Andrej Plenković as the nation's next prime minister.

Science. The European Space Agency's Schiaparelli lander is lost as it descends to land on Mars.

Sports. In Major League Baseball, the Cleveland Indians win the American League Championship Series, advancing to their first World Series appearance since 1997.

20 **Disasters.** Typhoon Haima hits the Philippines, causing flooding and landslides that kill seven people and knock out electric power on the northern island of Luzon.

Sports. In the deciding game five of the Women's National Basketball Association Finals, the Los Angeles Sparks defeat the Minnesota Lynx 77-76 to win their first league title since 2002.

21 **Disasters.** In central Cameroon, a passenger train derails near the village of Eséka, killing 75 people and injuring hundreds of others. In Russia's northern Yamal Peninsula, a military helicopter crash kills 19 people and injures 3 others. In northeastern Kansas, a chemical spill at the MGP Ingredients plant injures 34 people and forces the evacuation of thousands of people from the town of Atchison.

Terrorism. In Iraq, Islamic State terrorists kill 19 people in attacks on government buildings, police stations, and a power station in the city of Kirkuk.

22 **Terrorism.** In the embattled city of Mosul, Iraq, Islamic State terrorists execute nearly 300 people after using them as human shields in fighting against Kurdish and Iraqi troops.

Crime. In Arcahaie, Haiti, 174 inmates escape from a prison after killing a guard and stealing weapons.

Sports. In Major League Baseball, the Chicago Cubs win the National League Championship Series, advancing to their first World Series appearance since 1945.

23 **Disasters.** In southern California, a collision between a tour bus and a truck kills 13 people and injures 31 others near Palm Springs.

25 **Terrorism.** In Pakistan, Islamist militants kill 60 people and injure 117 others in an attack on a police academy in the western city of Quetta. In Afghanistan, Islamic State terrorists kill 30 people after abducting them from a village in the remote province of Ghor. In northeastern Kenya, al-Shabab terrorists kill 12 people in an attack on Christians in the town of Mandera.

Disasters. In the north-central Chinese province of Shaanxi, illegally stored explosives detonate in a house in the town of Xinmin, killing 14 people and injuring 147 others.

Arts. U.S. writer Paul Beatty becomes the first American to win the Man Booker Prize, the United Kingdom's highest literary award.

29 **Sports.** In Japanese baseball, the Hokkaido Nippon-Ham Fighters defeat the Hiroshima Toyo Carp 10-4 to win the best-of-7 Japan Series 4 games to 2.

On Oct. 24, 2016, authorities begin clearing refugees and migrants from the so-called Calais Jungle, a sprawling and troubled temporary camp in northwestern France. Some 6,300 people were removed from the camp and taken to other parts of France.

IN MEMORIAM

NOTABLE DEATHS IN 2016*

Albee, Edward (1928-September 16), U.S. playwright. Albee's plays earned multiple Tony Awards and Pulitzer Prizes. His most famous works included *The Zoo Story, The Sandbox, Who's Afraid of Virginia Woolf?,* and *A Delicate Balance.*

Ali, Muhammad (1942-June 3), U.S. boxer and activist. **See page 192.**

Aylwin Azócar, Patricio (1918-April 19), former Chilean president. Aylwin led Chile from 1990 to 1994, helping restore democracy to the nation after a brutal 17-year military dictatorship.

Babenco, Héctor (1946-July 13), Argentine-Brazilian film director, producer, and screenwriter. Babaenco's directing career included the acclaimed films *Kiss of the Spider Woman, Ironweed,* and *At Play in the Fields of the Lord.*

Bagaza, Jean-Baptiste (1946-May 4), former president of Burundi. Bagaza led the small central African country from 1976 to 1987 before losing power in a military coup.

Bhumibol Adulyadej (1927-October 13), king of Thailand. Bhumibol, who was crowned in 1946, was the ninth sovereign in the Chakri dynasty, which was founded in 1782.

Bley, Paul (1932-January 3), Canadian jazz pianist. Bley's career included numerous albums, world tours, and collaborations with such jazz greats as Ornette Coleman, Charles Mingus, and Sonny Rollins.

Boutros-Ghali, Boutros (1922-February 16), Egyptian diplomat and politician. Boutros-Ghali was a law professor and Egyptian foreign minister before serving as Secretary-General of the United Nations from 1992 through 1996.

Bowie, David (David Jones) (1947-January 10), British pop music star and artist, actor, and producer. **See page 267.**

Cáceres, Berta (1971-March 3), Honduran human rights activist and environmentalist. **See page 399.**

Carr, Charmian (1942-September 17), U.S. actress and singer. Carr's most famous role was Liesl, the eldest Von Trapp daughter in the film version of *The Sound of Music.*

Ciampi, Carlo Azeglio (1920-September 16), Italian banker and politician. Ciampi served as Italy's prime minister from 1993 to 1994 and as president from 1999 to 2006.

*January through October 2016

Edward Albee

Cimino, Michael (1939-July 2), U.S. film director, producer, and screenwriter. Cimino's many films included the 1978 Best Picture and Best Director winner, *The Deer Hunter*.

Collins, Bud (Arthur Worth Collins, Jr.) (1929-March 4), award-winning U.S. sports journalist and broadcaster. Collins was most famous for his decades of tennis coverage.

Conroy, Pat (1945-March 4), U.S. author. Conroy's many works included the novels *The Great Santini, The Lords of Discipline,* and *The Prince of Tides*.

Cruyff, Johan (1947-March 24), former Dutch soccer star and coach. Cruyff was a three-time European Footballer of the Year in the 1970's. He later enjoyed a successful coaching career.

DeHaven, Gloria (1925-July 30), U.S. actress and singer. DeHaven began her film career as a child and later appeared in numerous musicals alongside such stars as Fred Astaire, Charlie Chaplin, Tony Curtis, Gene Kelly, and Frank Sinatra.

De Jong, Piet (1915-July 27), Dutch naval officer and politician. De Jong, a decorated World War II veteran, served as prime minister of the Netherlands from 1967 to 1971.

Duke, Patty (1946-March 29), U.S. actress. Duke's career included roles in such films as *The Miracle Worker* and *The Valley of the Dolls*. She also starred in the television comedy "The Patty Duke Show."

Dyson, Tony (1947-March 4), British robotics expert. Dyson created robotic models for toy companies and a number of movies, but he was

José Fernández

most famous for building working models of R2-D2 for the *Star Wars* cinema franchise.

Eco, Umberto (1932-February 19), Italian author, critic, philosopher, and scholar. **See page 258.**

Elliott, Bob (1923-February 2), U.S. actor and comedian. Elliott co-starred in the long-running television comedy "Bob and Ray."

Emerson, Keith (1944-March 10), British musician. Emerson co-founded the progressive rock supergroup Emerson, Lake & Palmer in 1970.

Fernández, José (1992-September 25), Cuban-American professional baseball player. Fernández pitched for the Miami Marlins from 2013 until his accidental death in 2016.

Fo, Dario (1926-October 13), Italian playwright and actor. Fo, who won the 1997 Nobel Prize in literature, was best known for his political plays *Accidental Death of an Anarchist* and *Can't Pay, Won't Pay*.

Ford, Rob (1969-March 22), Canadian politician. Ford was a longtime Toronto city councilman before serving as the city's mayor from 2010 to 2014.

Frey, Glenn (1948-January 18), U.S. musician and founding member of the rock band the Eagles. Frey and the Eagles enjoyed immense success in the 1970's. Frey later enjoyed solo success before rejoining the Eagles later in his career.

Gabriel, Juan (Alberto Aguilera Valadez) (1950-August 28), Mexican singer and songwriter. Gabriel, nicknamed *El Divo de Juárez,* was a hugely popular figure in Latin American music. His most popular hit songs include *Amor Eterno* (Eternal Love) and *Hasta Que Te Conoci* (Until I Met You).

Garagiola, Joe (1926-March 23), former U.S. professional baseball player and broadcaster. **See page 177.**

Gaynes, George (George Jongejans) (1917-February 15), U.S. actor. Among many other roles, Gaynes starred in the *Police Academy* film franchise and the 1980's television comedy "Punky Brewster."

Hadid, Zaha (1950-March 31), Iraqi-British architect. **See page 254.**

Haggard, Merle (1937-April 6), U.S. country music singer and songwriter. **See page 266.**

Hamilton, Guy (1922-April 20), British film director. Hamilton's directing career included the classic James Bond films *Diamonds Are Forever, Goldfinger, Live and Let Die,* and *The Man with the Golden Gun.*

Hanson, Curtis (1945-September 20), U.S. film director and screenwriter. Hanson's hit films included *The Hand That Rocks the Cradle, L.A. Confidential,* and *8 Mile*

Havelange, João (1916-August 16), Brazilian athlete and sports executive. Havelange represented Brazil at the 1936 and 1952 Olympic Games. He later served as president of FIFA, soccer's world governing body, from 1974 to 1998. He also served on the International Olympic Committee from 1963 to 2011.

Herr, Michael (1940-June 23), U.S. author. Herr's work as a correspondent covering the Vietnam War led to his book *Dispatches,* a critically acclaimed account of the U.S. combat soldier's experience in the war. Herr later wrote parts of the Vietnam War films *Apocalypse Now* and *Full Metal Jacket.*

Howard, Ken (1944-March 23), U.S. actor and former Screen Actors Guild president. Howard, who played in numerous television, film, and stage productions, was best known for his starring role in the TV drama "The White Shadow."

Howe, Gordie (1928-June 10), Canadian hockey legend. **See page 215.**

Huddleston, David (1930-August 2), U.S. actor. Huddleston was a character actor in numerous television shows and films over his long career, including *Blazing Saddles, Santa Claus: The Movie,* and *The Big Lebowski.*

Irvin, Monte (Monford) (1919-January 11), former U.S. professional baseball player. Irvin starred as an outfielder in the Negro leagues before joining the New York Giants of Major League Baseball in 1949. Irvin was elected to the National Baseball Hall of Fame in 1973.

Kantner, Paul (1941-January 28), U.S. musician and founding member of the psychedelic rock band Jefferson Airplane. Kantner and Jefferson Airplane were a central musical element of the counterculture era of the late 1960's. Kantner later led the spin-off group Jefferson Starship.

Karimov, Islam (1938-September 2), Uzbek politician. Karimov was the first president of independent Uzbekistan, serving unopposed from 1991 until his death.

Kelly, Frank (Francis O'Kelly) (1938-February 28), Irish actor and writer. Kelly's roles included Father Jack Hackett on the popular 1990's television comedy, "Father Ted."

Kennedy, George (1925-February 28), U.S. actor. Kennedy's long career included major roles in the popular films *Cool Hand Luke, The Dirty Dozen,* and *Airport,* as well as in the television drama, "Dallas."

Kiarostami, Abbas (1940-July 4), Iranian film director, screenwriter, and producer. Kiarostami's many films included the 1997 Palme d'Or-winning *Taste of Cherry,* the *Koker* trilogy, and *Close-Up.*

Kinsella, W.P. (William Patrick) (1935-September 16), Canadian novelist. Kinsella's most famous work, *Shoeless Joe,* was the basis for the hit baseball movie *Field of Dreams.*

Kives, Philip (1929-April 27), Canadian entrepreneur and advertising pitchman. Kives founded the "As-Seen-On-TV" marketing company, K-tel, known for its innovative hard-sell commercials.

Kwouk, Burt (1930-May 24), British-Chinese actor. Kwouk was best known for his comedic portrayal of Cato, the often-dangerous manservant of Inspector Clouseau in the *Pink Panther* film franchise.

LeBeau, Madeleine (1923-May 1), French actress. LeBeau was the last surviving credited cast member from the 1942 classic film, *Casablanca.*

Lee, Harper (1926-February 19), U.S. author. **See page 257.**

Marisol (Marisol Escobar) (1930-April 30), French-born American sculptor. Marisol's boxy sculptural personages—often enhanced with photographs—gained her fame in the pop art world of 1960's New York City.

Marshall, Garry (1934-July 19), U.S. film director, producer, and writer. Marshall created the popular 1970's television comedies "Happy Days," "Laverne and Shirley," and "Mork & Mindy," and directed the movie hits *Beaches* and *Pretty Woman.*

Garry Marshall

Joseph Medicine Crow

Martin, Sir George (1926-March 8), British record producer. Martin produced each of the Beatles' original albums as well as numerous albums for other artists over his career.

McLaughlin, John (1927-August 16), U.S. television personality and political commentator. McLaughlin created and hosted the PBS commentary program "The McLaughlin Group" from 1982 until his death.

McPherson, James Alan (1943-July 27), U.S. short story writer and essayist. McPherson, a MacArthur Fellow and member of the American Academy of Arts and Sciences, was the first African American to win the Pulitzer Prize for his 1978 fiction collection, *Elbow Room*.

Medicine Crow, Joseph (1913-April 3), Native American author and historian. Medicine Crow, the historian and last war chief of Montana's Crow Nation, was best known for his works on the 1876 Battle of Little Bighorn.

Moman, Lincoln "Chips" (1937-June 13), U.S. music producer and songwriter. Moman co-wrote songs and produced albums for such legendary performers as Aretha Franklin, Merle Haggard, and Elvis Presley.

Mondavi, Peter (1914-February 20), U.S. winemaker and entrepreneur. Mondavi had run Napa Valley's Charles Krug Winery, the oldest

Shimon Peres

Doris Roberts

winery in California, since 1959.

O'Brian, Hugh (Hugh Charles Krampe) (1925–September 5), U.S. actor. O'Brian was best known for starring in the 1950's TV western "The Life and Legend of Wyatt Earp."

Palmer, Arnold (1929-September 25), U.S. champion golfer. **See page 211.**

Pappas, Milt (Miltiades Papastergios) (1939-April 19), former U.S. professional baseball player. Pappas, an All-Star pitcher, won 209 games and threw 43 shutouts over his 17-year Major League Baseball career.

Paul, Billy (Paul Williams) (1934-April 24), U.S. soul singer. Paul's recording career included the 1972 number-one hit, "Me and Mrs. Jones."

Peres, Shimon (1923-September 28), served as president of Israel from 2007 to 2014. He also served as prime minister from 1984 to 1986 and from 1995 to 1996. Peres shared the 1994 Nobel Peace Prize for his efforts to establish peace in the Middle East.

Prince (Prince Rogers Nelson) (1958-April 21), U.S. rock musician and singer. **See page 268.**

Rabinowitz, Harry (1916-June 22), South African-British composer and conductor. Rabinowitz conducted scores for such films as *Chariots of Fire* and *The English Patient*.

Reagan, Nancy Davis (Anne Frances Robbins) (1921-March 6), former

U.S. First Lady. **See page 303.**

Reid, Clarence "Blowfly" (1939-January 17), U.S. musician, songwriter, and producer. Blowfly experimented in various forms of often-humorous music beginning in the 1960's and is considered the "Godfather" of the hip-hop genre.

Rickman, Alan (1946-January 14), British actor. **See page 263.**

Rivette, Jacques (1928-January 29), French film director and critic. Rivette started as editor of the magazine *Cahiers du Cinéma* in the 1950's. Part of the French New Wave movement of the 1950's and 1960's, his best known films include *Paris Belongs to Us, The Nun,* and *Va savoir* (Who Knows?).

Roberts, Doris (1925-April 17), U.S. actress. Roberts, whose long career began in the 1950's, was best known for her later motherly role in the television comedy "Everybody Loves Raymond."

Ryan, Buddy (James David) (1934-June 28), former National Football League defensive coordinator and head coach. Ryan gained fame leading the defense of the Chicago Bears in the 1980's. He later served as head coach of the Philadelphia Eagles and Arizona Cardinals.

Safer, Morley (1931-May 19), U.S.-Canadian journalist. **See page 277.**

Saunders, John (1955-August 10), U.S.-Canadian sportscaster. Saunders joined the ESPN sports network in 1986, working as a studio host and play-by-play broadcaster.

Scalia, Antonin (1936-February 13), U.S. Supreme Court justice. **See page 300.**

Scheel, Walter (1919-August 24), German politician. Scheel, a veteran of World War II, was briefly chancellor of West Germany before serving as president from 1974 to 1979.

Shaffer, Peter (1926-June 6), British playwright and screenwriter. Shaffer's plays *Equus* and *Amadeus* each won Tony Awards for Best Play. His film adaptations for both plays were nominated for Academy Awards. *Amadeus* won the 1985 Oscar for Best Adapted Screenplay.

Shandling, Garry (1949-March 24), U.S. actor, comedian, and writer. Shandling enjoyed a successful stand-up comedy career before creating the popular TV comedies "It's Garry Shandling's Show" and "The Larry Sanders Show."

Slice, Kimbo (Kevin Ferguson) (1974-June 6), U.S. mixed martial artist. Slice gained fame as an underground street fighter before joining the popular Ultimate Fighting Championship, a mixed martial arts promotion company.

Sinatra, Frank, Jr. (1944-March 16), U.S. singer, actor, and entertainer. Sinatra, son of American music icon Frank Sinatra, enjoyed a successful singing career and appeared in numerous television programs.

Stigwood, Robert (1934-January 4), Australian music producer and manager. Stigwood's career began in the 1960's in England, where he managed Cream and the Bee Gees. He later produced the hit films *Grease* and *Saturday Night Fever*.

Summitt, Pat (1952-June 28), legendary University of Tennessee women's basketball coach. **See page 191.**

Thielemans, Jean Baptistse "Toots" (1922-August 22), Belgian jazz musician. Thielemans played guitar and harmonica with such jazz legends as Charlie Parker, Miles Davis, and Max Roach. He also played on scores for such films as *Midnight Cowboy, Jean de Florette,* and *The Getaway,* as well as the closing credits of the children's television program "Sesame Street."

Thurmond, Nate (1941-July 16), former U.S. professional basketball player. **See page 185.**

Tomlinson, Ray (1941-March 5), U.S. computer scientist. In 1971, Tomlinson created the first email program on the ARPANET system, a precursor to the Internet. He also first used the @ sign to differentiate between email users.

Van Gelder, Rudy (1924-August 25), U.S. recording engineer. Van Gelder specialized in jazz and recorded such legends as John Coltrane, Miles Davis, and Thelonius Monk.

Vigoda, Abe (1921-January 26), U.S. actor. Vigoda's long career included famous roles in the 1972 film *The Godfather* and the 1970's television comedy "Barney Miller."

Voinovich, George (1936-June 12), U.S. politician. Voinovich served as mayor of Cleveland in the 1980's. He later served as Ohio's governor and in the U.S. Senate.

Wajda, Andrzej (1926-October 9), Oscar-winning Polish film director. Wajda was best known for his 1950's war trilogy *A Generation, Kanał,* and *Ashes and Diamonds.*

Washington, Dwayne "Pearl" (1964-April 20), former U.S. professional basketball player. Washington starred for Syracuse University and played three seasons in the National Basketball Association.

White, Maurice (1941-February 4), U.S. singer, musician, and songwriter. White co-founded the R & B group Earth, Wind & Fire in 1969. White was the lead singer for the band, which was inducted into the Rock 'n' Roll Hall of Fame in 2000.

Wiesel, Elie (Eliezer) (1928-July 2), Romanian-American Holocaust activist and author. **See page 259.**

Wilder, Gene (Jerome Silberman) (1933-August 29), U.S. actor and screenwriter. **See page 264.**

Worsley, Henry (1960-January 24), British explorer. Worsley died of an infection during his solo attempt to cross Antarctica "unassisted and unsupported."

Yelchin, Anton (1989-June 19), Russian-American actor. Yelchin was best known for his portrayals of Mr. Chekov in the most recent *Star Trek* movie series.

Young, Alan (1919-May 19), English-Canadian-American actor. Young, best known for starring in the television comedy "Mister Ed," also hosted "The Alan Young Show."

Zewail, Ahmed (1946-August 2), Egyptian-American scientist and California Institute of Technology professor. Zewail won the 1999 Nobel Prize for chemistry for his experiments showing how molecules change during chemical reactions.

Zsigmond, Vilmos (1930-January 1), Hungarian-U.S. cinematographer. Zsigmond worked on many acclaimed films over his long career. He won the 1977 Oscar for

Buckwheat Zydeco

Best Cinematography for the sci-fi classic *Close Encounters of the Third Kind.*

Zydeco, Buckwheat (Stanley Dural, Jr.) (1947-September 24), U.S. accordionist and zydeco musician. Zydeco took his name from the music genre he made famous. Zydeco and his band made numerous television appearances and played celebrated world tours.

THROUGH THE YEARS

Events from history that reached a milestone anniversary in 2016.

200 YEARS AGO
ARGENTINE INDEPENDENCE, 1816

Representatives signed Argentina's declaration of independence at the Congress of Tucumán on July 9, 1816.

On July 9, 2016, Argentines celebrated the 200th anniversary of the signing of their nation's declaration of independence. The 1816 signing took place during a turbulent period in Argentina's history—a period, in fact, before the nation was called Argentina. It was then known as the United Provinces of the Río de la Plata, and it covered only the nation's current northern half above Patagonia. The declaration of independence also came six years after the formation of a government independent of Spain on May 25, 1810, in Buenos Aires. The area had been part of a Spanish colony since the late 1500's.

After establishing self-rule in 1810, it took awhile to unite Buenos Aires with the various Argentine provinces. Eventually, representatives met at the Congress of Tucumán, and on July 9, 1816, declared their nation's independence. The new nation had a rough go of it, suffering through a civil war and decades of dictatorship before the constitution of 1853 established a republic, which was renamed Argentina in 1860. The nation grew to include Patagonia in 1881.

200 YEARS AGO
INDIANA'S BICENTENNIAL, 1816

A commemorative stamp celebrating Indiana's 200th birthday features a sunset over cornfields near Milford in northern Indiana's Kosciusko County.

Indiana's bicentenary took place on Dec. 11, 2016. Looking back 200 years to 1816, when Indiana became the 19th state in the Union, many people may be surprised that statehood did not come easily. Aside from convincing the U.S. Congress to accept Indiana as a state, there were some Hoosiers themselves that needed convincing. Many people were perfectly happy living in the Indiana *territory* and wanted nothing to do with the trappings of statehood. Some feared the higher taxes that came with statehood, as well as an increase in laws and regulations. Chief among the "just say no to statehood" faction was William Henry Harrison himself, the recent champion of Tippecanoe and *appointed* (not elected) governor of the Indiana territory. Harrison stood to lose considerable, almost dictatorial powers if the territory became a state. Statehood would also mean the abolition of slavery in Indiana, a practice many conservative landowners wanted to preserve.

A majority of Hoosiers, however, favored statehood and its democratic benefits, as well as its increased protection. Indiana was on the western frontier in the early 1800's, and violence often overruled territorial statutes and ordinances. Hostility between Native Americans and settlers continued, too, as ever more of Indiana's fertile soils were claimed for farming. The introduction of federal laws—as well as federal troops—would do much to calm Indiana's frontier turbulence. Hoosiers also wanted the hospitals, schools, transportation, and other far-reaching benefits of statehood. Additionally, Indiana settlers wanted to *elect* a governor with limited power. Last, but perhaps most important, most Hoosiers wanted slavery to be outlawed.

The Indiana Territorial Assembly listened to the Hoosier majority and petitioned for statehood in late 1815. Congress approved the petition the next year, and President James Madison signed it into law.

100 YEARS AGO
BATTLE OF VERDUN, 1916

Feb. 21, 2016, marked the 100th anniversary of the beginning of the Battle of Verdun in France during World War I (1914-1918). The battle was fought between German and French troops around Verdun, an ancient fortress city on the Meuse River. The brutal battle lasted more than nine months (until late December 1916) and ended in a slim and costly French victory. Together with the Battle of the Somme, which began a few months later, Verdun was one of the bloodiest examples of trench warfare in history. Verdun is a city of great historic and strategic value to France. The Germans knew the French would defend it at all cost.

The Battle of Verdun began on February 21 with a massive German attack on French positions around Verdun. For months, French defenses held the city against overwhelming force. However, a number of key positions—including forts Douaumont and Vaux—fell to the German attack. As the battle dragged into summer, both sides suffered major casualties. In July, after the start of the Allied offensive on the Somme River, the Germans reduced their efforts at Verdun. In the autumn, repeated French attacks regained the lost forts. By battle's end in December, the lines were almost exactly where they had been in February.

General Henri Pétain led the French at Verdun, and troops rallied to the cry: *On ne passe pas! (They shall not pass!)* It was a French "victory," but the battle came to symbolize the slaughter of modern war. More than 2 million soldiers fought in the battle, and more than 700,000 of them were killed, wounded, or went missing. Verdun and the surrounding area were almost completely destroyed.

100 YEARS AGO
DUBLIN'S EASTER RISING, 1916

Dubliners gather amidst the ruins of Lower Sackville Street (now O'Connell Street) after the Easter Rising in 1916.

On Easter weekend (March 25-28) 2016, events in Dublin, Ireland, marked the 100th anniversary of the Easter Rising, a 1916 rebellion in which Irish rebels fought against British rule. The rebellion began on Easter Monday that year and lasted less than a week. The events of that week had lasting effects, however, leading to further rebellion, civil war, and, eventually, independence for Ireland's 26 southern counties.

On April 24, 1916, roughly 1,000 Irish rebels took control of several Dublin locations, including the General Post Office, where poet Patrick Pearse read the Proclamation of the Irish Republic.

British troops responded quickly, and battles erupted on the city's streets. The Irish held out for several days, but they were outgunned and outnumbered. They surrendered on April 29, ending the Easter Rising. Nearly 500 people died in the fighting. Sixteen of the rebel leaders, including Pearse, were executed.

After the Easter Rising, the Irish fought the British in a war of independence from 1919 to 1921. The 26 counties of southern Ireland then became a *dominion* (self-governing country) of the British Commonwealth. Ireland eventually broke all political ties with the United Kingdom, becoming the Republic of Ireland in 1949.

THROUGH THE YEARS

Poppies and the names of war dead line the Roll of Honour at the Australian War Memorial in Canberra, Australia.

100 YEARS AGO
ANZAC DAY, 1916

April 25, 2016, was the 100th anniversary of the first Anzac Day, a patriotic holiday honoring current and former members of the armed forces of Australia and New Zealand. *ANZAC* stands for the *Australian and New Zealand Army Corps*, the name of the combined overseas force that fought in World War I (1914-1918). Anzac Day marks the anniversary of the Allied invasion of Turkey's Gallipoli Peninsula on April 25, 1915. The costly invasion and campaign at Gallipoli first "bloodied" the Anzacs. Services in Australia and New Zealand marked the first Anzac Day in 1916 to remember the fallen of Gallipoli.

By the 1920's, Anzac Day had become a legal holiday and expanded to include all 46,000 Australians and 18,000 New Zealanders killed in World War I. After World War II (1939-1945), the holiday expanded again to honor Australians and New Zealanders killed in all wars, as well as veterans and those still serving in the armed forces of the two nations.

Anzac Day services are now held throughout Australia and New Zealand, as well as at Gallipoli's "Anzac Cove." In Sydney, the dawn service begins each year at 4:30 a.m. at the Cenotaph in Martin Place, where many young men enlisted to fight in World War I. War memorial *cenotaphs* (empty tombs) honor dead soldiers whose bodies lie elsewhere. The solemn service includes a reading of the "Ode of Remembrance," part of the poem "For the Fallen" written by British poet Laurence Binyon soon after the outbreak of war in 1914. The ode contains the memorable lines, "They shall grow not old, as we that are left grow old... We will remember them."

National ceremonies begin a few hours later in Canberra and Wellington, the capital cities of Australia and New Zealand.

100 YEARS AGO
BATTLE OF THE SOMME, 1916

A soldier begins Somme commemorations during a night vigil amongst British graves at Thiepval, France, on June 30, 2016.

July 1, 2016, was the 100th anniversary of the beginning of the 1916 Battle of the Somme during World War I (1914-1918). To mark the solemn occasion, thousands of people, including members of the British royal family, gathered at the Thiepval Memorial to the Missing and other poignant places on the former Somme battlefield in northern France. At Thiepval—a village central to the battle that was completely destroyed in the war—a two-minute silence was followed by a reading by Prince Charles and the hymn "Abide With Me." Then the Archbishop of Canterbury, the Most Reverend Justin Welby, said a prayer: "On this day we remember all those caught up by the battle on the Somme; those who faced the terrible waste and devastation, those who fought against all the odds, who endured the clinging mud and squalor of the trenches."

The Somme campaign took place from July 1 to November 18, 1916, and consisted of a series of largely unsuccessful offenses by British and French troops against part of Germany's western battlefront. The Battle of the Somme was one of the bloodiest examples of trench warfare in history. Experts believe that more than 1 million soldiers died—including 20,000 British on the battle's first day— for the exchange of about 7 miles (11 kilometers) of muddy, war-ravaged Somme territory.

THROUGH THE YEARS

100 YEARS AGO
NATIONAL PARK SERVICE , 1916

Conservationist John Muir was instrumental in the creation of Yosemite National Park, *seen here*, in California.

Aug. 25, 2016, was the 100th anniversary of the creation of the National Park Service (NPS). The NPS is a bureau of the United States Department of the Interior. It manages the approximately 400 areas of the National Park System. The NPS preserves many natural landscapes and historic and archaeological sites and structures. To mark the NPS centenary, special events took place across the country, and all national parks had free admission from August 25 to 28. The events included a solar-powered vehicle race through nine parks in seven Midwestern states; classical music performances and naturalization ceremonies in several parks; and a special Girl Scout and Boy Scout chat from Lewis and Clark National Historical Park with an astronaut aboard the International Space Station. The bureau's 100th birthday was also celebrated at several major and minor league baseball parks.

Conservationist John Muir and President Theodore Roosevelt did much to create the parks and the protected lands that led to the formation of the NPS in 1916. Stephen T. Mather, the first NPS director, actively promoted and expanded the bureau and its protected lands. From 1916 to 1929, Mather increased the number of national parks from 16 to 25; the number of national monuments from 21 to 32; and doubled the total system area from nearly 5 million acres (2 million hectares) to about 10 million acres (4 million hectares). Today, the National Park System includes more than 84 million acres (34 million hectares).

The U.S. Mint commemorated the NPS centenary by issuing three limited edition coins: a five-dollar gold coin, a silver dollar, and a half-dollar coin. The coins feature images of parks, the NPS arrowhead logo, depictions of the exploration of nature, and portrayals of the multicultural heritage of the United States. The U.S. Postal Service celebrated the NPS centennial with 16 new Forever stamps featuring national parks.

The NPS logo symbolizes history and archaeology (arrowhead); vegetation and wildlife (a Sequoia tree and bison); and scenery and recreation (mountains and water).

Trunk Bay Overlook, Virgin Islands National Park

Historic Henry House and cannons at Virginia's Manassas National Battlefield Park

The World Book Encyclopedia began the celebration of the 100th anniversary of its first edition in 2016. The first set, published in 1917, contained eight volumes complete with illustrations—an innovation for the time. Chicago's Hanson-Roach-Fowler Company produced that first set, which was the project of University of Wisconsin professor M. V. O'Shea. *The World Book*, "organized knowledge

1917 Publisher J. H. Hanson produces the first edition of *The World Book Encyclopedia.*

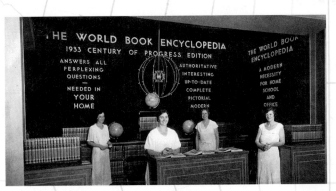

1933 World Book is a key part of Chicago's Century of Progress Exposition, a world's fair marking the city's centennial.

in story and picture," was an instant hit, and, by 1929, had been expanded and completely revised to keep pace with world events. World Book managed to expand further during the tough years of the Great Depression, and the first international edition reached readers in 1937.

In 1945, Chicago publishing magnate and department store heir Marshall Field III purchased World Book. The encyclopedia was then heavily revised and expanded to cover the tragic years of World War II. In 1959, World Book

1959 World Book creates the first Braille encyclopedia.

1961 A World Book expedition led by famed mountaineer Sir Edmund Hillary searches for the legendary Yeti and studies the people and climate of the Himalaya mountain ranges of southern Asia.

produced a Braille edition—a mammoth undertaking that included 145 volumes and 38,000 pages. A large type edition for the visually impaired soon followed.

World Book continued to expand in the 1960's and 1970's and entered the "modern era" with software titles on floppy disks in the late 1980's and its first digital encyclopedia on CD-ROM in 1990. *World Book Online* went live in 1998. It expanded during the 2000's to its current total of 21 different digital products. World Book also offers over 2,000 eBooks while continuing to publish a revised edition of the print encyclopedia each and every year. The commemorative 2017 centennial edition of *The World Book Encylopedia* counts more than 14,000 pages in its 22 accurate and informative volumes.

1990 *The World Book Encyclopedia* goes electronic with a CD-ROM edition.

2016 World Book celebrates 100 years of serving readers everywhere who strive to learn and to know.

80 YEARS AGO
JESSIE OWENS'S FIRST GOLD MEDAL, 1936

On Aug. 3, 1936—80 years ago—African American track and field star Jesse Owens won the gold medal in the men's 100-meter dash at the Summer Olympic Games in Berlin, Germany. It was the first of four gold medals that Owens would win over the next week—a remarkable performance by a remarkable athlete. Owens's accomplishment transcended the sports world, however, and took on a much greater importance. The Nazis controlled Germany in 1936, and German Chancellor Adolf Hitler hoped the Olympics would help prove—athletically, anyway—his theory of *Aryan* racial superiority. Aryan was a term the Nazis used for Germans and certain other white peoples of northern Europe. Owens (and his American teammates) disappointed Hitler, but he won the admiration of the crowds watching in Berlin. Owens's Olympic performance made him one of the most famous athletes in sports history.

In the 100-meter dash, Owens edged out his African American teammate Ralph Metcalf by 1/10th of a second to win gold. German runner Erich Borchmeyer finished fifth. The next day, August 4, Owens set an

Jesse Owens competes in the broad jump at the 1936 Summer Olympics.

Olympic record in the broad jump (now called the long jump), winning gold over German jumper Luz Long. On August 5, Owens set a world record in the 200-meter dash, nosing out another African American teammate, Mack Robinson (older brother of baseball legend Jackie Robinson). Four days later, Owens and Metcalfe joined American teammates Foy Draper and Frank Wykoff in the 400-meter relay, setting a world record and winning gold over the second-place Italian team and third-place Germans.

On June 16, 2016, South Africans marked the 40th anniversary of the bloody Soweto Uprising of 1976. The uprising began as a protest against education programs under South Africa's policy of racial segregation known as *apartheid*. Apartheid lasted from the late 1940's to the early 1990's. The Soweto uprising and its aftermath motivated black Africans to become more organized in their struggle for freedom. It also forced the South African government to make gradual reforms that slowly led to the end of apartheid.

In 1975, protests started in African schools after the government decreed that Afrikaans had to be used equally with English as languages of instruction in secondary schools. Although Afrikaans—the language of the ruling white minority—was at best a third language for most black Africans, the education problems under apartheid were much broader. Black students had separate schools and universities, and the facilities were old, ill funded, overcrowded, and often led by inadequately trained teachers. The protests, then, were the result of years of frustration and discrimination.

On June 16, 1976, thousands of schoolchildren marched through Soweto (now part of Johannesburg). Police opened fire on the children, prompting disturbances in many parts of South Africa during the next few months. Several clashes erupted between black Africans and the police, and at least 575 people, almost all of them young black Africans, were killed.

Police confront kneeling Soweto youths on June 16, 1976, the first day of protests in what became known as the Soweto Uprising.

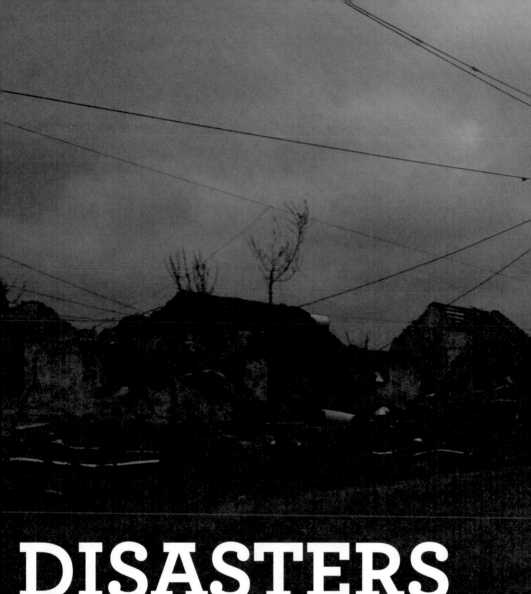

DISASTERS

Rescue workers search for survivors in the eastern Chinese village of Beichen after tornadoes ripped through the area on June 23, 2016. The destruction in China was just one part of a wild 24-hour weather spectrum that hit opposite ends of Earth with fires, flooding, lightning storms, and tornadoes.

FLYDUBAI **FLIGHT 981**
CRASHES IN RUSSIA

Early on the morning of March 19, 2016, Flydubai Flight 981 crashed during landing in the Russian city of Rostov-on-Don, killing all 62 passengers and crew on board. Rostov sits on the Don River about 590 miles (950 kilometers) south of Moscow. Flydubai is a government-owned airline based at Dubai International Airport in the United Arab Emirates (U.A.E.). Flight 981, a Boeing 737-800 aircraft, took off from Dubai on March 18 at 10:10 p.m. local time—about 35 minutes behind schedule. The flight arrived at Rostov-on-Don roughly four hours later, but heavy rain and *wind shear* (a dangerous change in wind speed and direction) forced the pilots to abort their first landing attempt. The flight crew—an experienced team of a Cypriot captain and Spanish first officer—took Flight 981 into a holding pattern as other arriving flights also attempted but aborted landings in the bad weather.

The crew of Flight 981 tried a second landing at roughly 3:30 a.m. local time, but conditions again forced them to abort. As the 737 banked and began to ascend, however, the plane—at an elevation just below 3,000 feet (900 meters)—suddenly pitched into a steep dive and slammed into the runway in a fiery explosion.

Russia's Interstate Aviation Committee led the investigation into the crash of Flight 981, aided by aviation authorities from the U.A.E. as well as from France and the United States (where the engines and aircraft were built). An initial report said the crash was most likely the result of pilot error. Some experts believed the error was caused by a form of disorientation known as *somatogravic illusion*. Such an illusion occurs during high accelerations or decelerations when a pilot has no clear visual reference. Flight 981—flying in the dark and in heavy weather—climbed into a cloud just before nosing down and out of control. Crashes blamed on somatogravic illusion are fairly common, and several have occurred in recent years.

The crash of Flight 981 was the first for Flydubai since it began operating in 2009. The possibility of terrorism—as is so often suspected these days—was ruled out due to the crash circumstances and the lack of any trace of explosives at the crash site.

FIERY BLASTS **SCORCH HINDU TEMPLE** IN INDIA

In the dark morning hours of April 10, 2016, explosions and fire severely damaged parts of the Puttingal Hindu Temple complex in the Indian town of Paravur, killing 113 people and injuring more than 350 others. Paravur is located in Kerala, a coastal state in India's southwestern tip. The inferno and its debris also damaged more than 100 homes near the temple, which was packed with thousands of oracles, pilgrims, and other devotees for the annual *Meena Bharani* festival—a boisterous 10-day celebration of the Hindu goddess Bhadrakali. The fire erupted during a spectacular fireworks display, an event for which the festival and the 100-year-old Puttingal temple are famous.

Apparently, a stray aerial rocket struck the ground and exploded, shooting sparks into a stockpile of other fireworks, which ignited, rocking the temple with deafening blasts. The series of explosions collapsed a large building—causing most of the casualties—and set fire to others. The explosions also knocked out the temple's electric power, causing further panic among the crowds already fleeing the rapidly spreading fire.

Emergency crews descended on the temple, extinguishing the fire and working with survivors to help those who could be helped. That afternoon, Indian Prime Minister Narendra Modi visited the temple, describing the scene as "heart-rending and shocking beyond words." Modi also visited some of the injured at a hospital in nearby Thiruvananthaupuram.

Temple pyrotechnics are banned in Paravur's Kollam district, with exceptions sometimes given for religious festivals. Puttingal officials were denied a temporary permit for this year's Meena Bharani, however, due to safety concerns and complaints from people who live in the area. The temple went ahead with the fireworks display regardless, relenting to pressure from the large crowds. Several temple officals were arrested for reckless endangerment, while the fireworks contractor—who would have faced murder charges—was among the dead.

Ring of Fire Earthquakes Shake Japan and Ecuador

In April 2016, deadly earthquakes struck Ecuador and Japan—
and, although they both took place on the infamous *Ring of Fire*,
they were not connected. The Ring of Fire is a turbulent zone of
frequent seismic and volcanic activity along the islands and
continents rimming the Pacific Ocean. In Japan, an earthquake
measuring 6.2 on the Richter scale struck the south island of
Kyushu on April 14, killing 9 people. Two days later, 40 people
died when a 7.0-magnitude quake hit Kyushu again. At the same
time—on April 16—a much stronger 7.8-magnitude earthquake
killed more than 650 people some 9,000 miles (14,500
kilometers) away in Ecuador.

Large earthquakes often lead to more quakes—but only in the
same region, along or near the same *fault* (a break in Earth's

◄ A hard-hatted woman stands in shock before a toppled house in Mashiki, Japan, after earthquakes hit the town and other areas of the south island of Kyushu on April 14 and April 16, 2016.

Most of the world's earthquakes occur in the notoriously unstable *Ring of Fire* circling the Pacific Ocean.

crust). Thus, distant Ring of Fire events are not connected, regardless of their suspicious timing. Further, the April 2016 earthquakes were of different types. In Japan, they were of the *strike-slip* variety—a horizontal scrubbing along a fault line. The Ecuadorian quake was a *megathrust* event caused by tectonic plate activity at a subduction zone, where one plate (in this case, the Nazca) slips diagonally beneath another (the South American Plate).

A car smashed and buried by earthquake debris waits for its driver in the coastal city of Manta, Ecuador, on April 17, 2016. The day before, a powerful earthquake toppled buildings and damaged nearly 300 schools in the small South American country.

EARTHQUAKE *SHOCKS* CENTRAL ITALY

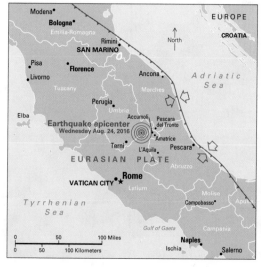

On Aug. 24, 2016, a 6.2-magnitude earthquake shook the mountains of central Italy. The earthquake struck in the early morning, toppling homes and buildings in the region of Latium (often called Lazio) and causing damage in nearby Marches (or Marche) and Umbria as well. The earthquake killed 296 people, injured hundreds of others, and left thousands of people homeless. The mountain towns hit by the quake are popular with tourists, and many of the dead were travelers staying in hotels and hostels. A week after the disaster, Italian President Sergio Mattarella and Prime Minister Matteo Renzi attended mass funerals held amongst piles of collapsed masonry, destroyed vehicles, and dust-covered possessions.

The earthquake struck at 3:36 a.m. local time and centered near the mountain village of Amatrice, about 85 miles (140 kilometers) northeast of Rome, the Italian capital. The quake reduced much of the town to ruins, including several historic buildings dating from the 1400's. Most of the earthquake victims—232 of them—were in Amatrice, but scores died in such nearby villages as Accumoli, Arquata del Tronto, and Pescara del Tronto. The earthquake woke startled residents in Rome and was felt as far away as Bologna to the north and Naples to the south. In the first 12 hours

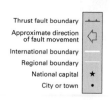

This map shows the location of the earthquake that devastated Amatrice and other mountain towns in central Italy on Aug. 24, 2016.

Survivors and rescue workers begin searching the ruins of Amatrice, Italy, after an earthquake struck on Aug. 24, 2016.

after the initial quake, the region trembled through some 150 aftershocks, the strongest of which measured 5.5 on the Richter scale. Survivors stumbled amidst the destruction, helping those who could be reached, and huddled in vehicles and tents as rescue workers arrived on the scene. Helicopters carried rescue workers to the area's more isolated villages to retrieve survivors trapped by landslides and rubble.

Amatrice has a population of about 2,000 people, but that number swells many times during the summer tourist season. Last year, Amatrice was voted one of Italy's most beautiful historic towns, and the town's popular spa-ghetti festival was scheduled for the weekend after the quake. Amatrice's heartbroken mayor, Sergio Pirozzi, surveyed the destruction, saying, "The town is no more."

The August 24 earthquake was the worst in Italy since 2009, when 308 people died in a powerful quake just south of Amatrice in the region of Abruzzo. That earthquake destroyed parts of the medieval city of L'Aquila. Italy sits on a major fault line, making it one of the most seismically active areas of Europe.

A THURSDAY IN JUNE

BY JAKE BUMGARDNER

Thursday, June 23, 2016, was a wild weather day for the ages. In the space of just 24 hours, extreme storms of wind, fire, electricity, and water struck at opposite ends of Earth. Winds came in the form of deadly tornadoes in eastern China's Jiangsu Province, where 98 people were killed. Heavy rains and painful hailstorms hampered rescue efforts in the region, as flooding killed still more people in nearby areas. The Erskine Wildfire in southern California tripled in size on June 23, scorching large swaths of Kern County, killing two people, and destroying hundreds of buildings. In northern India, lightning strikes killed 93 farm workers and injured dozens more as they tried to work during torrential monsoon rains. And in West Virginia, torrential rains caused flash floods on June 23, washing out roads and bridges and killing 23 people.

In recent years, the frequency and severity of storms have increased on all continents—a likely product of climate change, according to scientists—and 2016 saw more than its share of fierce seasonal storms. But no single day could match the weather fury of that Thursday in June.

Firefighters from Cal Fire's Sonoma-Lake-Napa Unit contemplate the wildfire roaring through California's Kelso Valley east of Bakersfield early on June 24, 2016.

▲

Residents gather amongst the ruins of Lixin village in eastern China's Jiangsu Province on June 24, 2016. The day before, a powerful tornado ravaged Lixin and other Jiangsu villages, killing 98 people and injuring more than 800 others.

In India, lightning strikes on June 22 and 23, 2016, killed 93 people and injured many others during monsoon storms in the states of Bihar, Jharkhand, Madhya Pradesh, and Uttar Pradesh. The dangerous electrical storms also passed over India's capital city of New Dehli, *seen here*, in Haryana. ▶

An officer of the West Virginia Department of Natural Resources searches flooded homes and surveys the damage in Rainelle, West Virginia, on June 25, 2016, two days after heavy rains pummeled the state. Eight counties were included in a federal disaster area. Of those, Greenbrier (home of Rainelle), Kanawha, and Nicholas counties were the hardest hit.
▼

WORLD COMMUNITY

A giant rainbow flag—a symbol of gay pride—billows along the LGBT Pride March route in New York City on June 26, 2016. The annual event runs down Manhattan's Fifth Avenue and ends near the historic Stonewall Inn in Greenwich Village. This year's parade, themed "Equality Needs You," was the largest in its 47-year history, with 32,000 marchers and nearly 3 million people lining the parade route.

see page 126 for

A CLOSER
LOOK

OREGON STAND-OFF

On Jan. 2, 2016, two brothers from Nevada—Ammon and Ryan Bundy—led a group of armed militants in the take-over and occupation of the Malheur National Wildlife Refuge in Harney County, Oregon. The Bundys are sons of Cliven Bundy, a Nevada rancher who refuses to pay the U.S. Bureau of Land Management (BLM) rents he owes for grazing his cattle on government-owned land. This refusal is part of a larger movement in the western United States, where some people feel the U.S. government should not be allowed to own land. The Malheur take-over was an antigovernment protest in support of two Oregon ranchers jailed for lighting fires on federal lands.

During the resulting stand-off between the Federal Bureau of Investigation (FBI) and the occupiers, the FBI wanted to avoid conflict with the armed militants. The occupiers were free to enter and leave the refuge until January 26. On that day, Ammon and Ryan Bundy and several supporters were driving from the refuge to a small town for a community meeting. The militants attempted to ram an FBI roadblock, and the driver was killed by police. The Bundys and three others were arrested. The remaining militants surrendered on February 11, ending the occupation.

A federal grand jury indicted 26 militants for conspiring against the government. Most made plea deals to avoid trial and lighten their prison sentences. The Bundy brothers and five others went on trial in September, but they were acquitted of the most serious charges.

The Bundy family's problems with the government dated back to 2014, when BLM agents arrived to seize Bundy-owned cattle in lieu of $1 million owed in unpaid grazing fees. Armed protesters refused to let the BLM take action, and the BLM backed off, choosing to avoid violent confrontation and pursue the matter in court.

PRESIDENT OBAMA IN CUBA

On March 20, 2016, U.S. President Barack Obama arrived in Havana, Cuba, for a three-day visit. Obama's arrival made him the first sitting U.S. president to visit Cuba since Calvin Coolidge in 1928. Obama's historic trip was the latest step in the accelerating *rapprochement* (renewal of friendly relations) between Cuba and the United States. The president began his visit with a tour of Old Havana and a meeting with Cardinal Jaime Ortega, who was a key participant in the negotiations between the nations.

On March 21, Obama laid a wreath at the memorial to Cuban national hero José Julián Martí in the Plaza de la Revolución. A military honor guard then welcomed Obama to the Revolution Palace, where he met with Cuban President Raúl Castro. The two

U.S. President Barack Obama meets with Cuban President Raúl Castro at the Revolution Palace on March 21, 2016, in Havana, Cuba.

leaders discussed trade and political reforms aimed at lifting longstanding U.S. sanctions against the Communist island country. Obama pressed Castro to provide greater Internet access for Cubans, while the Cuban delegation repeated the goal of reclaiming Cuba's Guantánamo Bay Naval Base, which has been under formal U.S. control since 1903.

On March 22, 2016, Obama addressed the Cuban people on television before joining Castro for an exhibition game between the Tampa Bay Rays of Major League Baseball (MLB) and the Cuban National Team at Havana's Estadio Latinoamericano.

CANADA'S **FIERY** MAY

On May 1, 2016, authorities in the Canadian province of Alberta declared a local state of emergency as wildfires broke out during a period of record-high temperatures and low humidity. By May 2, around 7,500 acres (3,000 hectares) of forested area were burning. On May 3, as flames threatened Fort McMurray, the city's entire population—more than 60,000 people—was forced to evacuate. The fires then reached Fort McMurray, destroying parts of the city. Nearby areas—including the Anzac, Gregoire Lake Estates, and Fort McMurray First Nation communities—were evacuated as the fire spread south.

Canadian authorities scrambled to fight the fires, which found much fuel in the Athabasca tar sands region. The heavily forested area is home to recovery plants (similar to refineries) for oil extracted from the sands. The recovery plants are filled with flammable oil and chemicals. The fire temporarily stopped oil production in much of Canada's energy region as the fires spread out of control, covering some 390,000 acres (156,000 hectares) by May 7. Areas of safe haven that had accepted earlier evacuees were themselves then forced to evacuate.

By May 21, the fires had expanded into Saskatchewan province and reached a peak coverage area of over 1¼ million acres (500,000 hectares)—an area larger than Prince Edward Island. By then, members of the Canadian Armed Forces had joined firefighters from several provinces in the effort to contain the fires. Millions of dollars, too, came in to aid and house the tens of thousands of people displaced by the fires. By early June, the region's 17 fires had been largely contained, with just 1 still listed as "out of control."

Residents then began returning to the often-charred remains of their homes and businesses in Alberta and Saskatchewan. Thousands of structures burned to the ground. Many buildings untouched by flames were uninhabitable, contaminated by toxic ash from the fires. Estimated losses from the fires reached $7 billion but, remarkably, the fires directly caused no deaths.

ORLANDO TERROR

On June 12, 2016, at the Pulse nightclub in Orlando, Florida, a gunman entered carrying an assault rifle and a handgun and started shooting. The gunman shot several people before retreating deeper into the club and taking hostages. Orlando police, paramedics, and firefighters were quickly on the scene, but, unsure of what they were dealing with, they awaited the arrival of heavily armed Special Weapons and Tactics (SWAT) officers. About 5:00 a.m., SWAT officers broke through a wall of the nightclub. In a brief gunfight, the gunman was killed and one officer was wounded. Thirty hostages were freed, wounded bar patrons were treated and evacu-

Mourners attend a candlelight vigil in downtown Orlando, Florida, on June 13, 2016, the day after an attack on a gay nightclub killed 49 people.

ated, and a suspected explosive device was destroyed. Forty-nine people died in the attack—plus the shooter—and 53 others were injured, making it the deadliest mass shooting in United States history. Some 350 patrons were in Pulse for a Latin music event at the time of the attack.

The gunman, a U.S. Muslim born to Afghan parents in New York City, targeted the nightclub because it caters predominantly to the lesbian, gay, bisexual, and transgender (LGBT) community.

LGBT / USA

BY SHAWN BRENNAN

On May 31, 2016, United States President Barack Obama, as he had done in every year of his administration, proclaimed June to be LGBT Pride Month. President Bill Clinton proclaimed the first Gay and Lesbian Pride Month in June 2000, his last summer in office, but the proclamations disappeared during the George W. Bush administration. Obama revived the June celebration, however, and no other U.S. president has done more to further the cause of LGBT equality.

In his 2016 Pride Month proclamation, Obama urged Americans to eliminate prejudice and celebrate diversity. Recalling the landmark 2015 Supreme Court decision guaranteeing marriage equality in all 50 states, Obama said, "for every partnership that was not previously recognized under the law and for every American who was denied their basic civil rights, this monumental ruling instilled newfound hope, affirming the belief that we are all more free when we are treated as equals."

The 2015 decision was celebrated across the country and the world as supporters waved U.S. and rainbow LGBT pride flags outside the Supreme Court. The White House was illuminated in rainbow colors to commemorate the historic ruling.

However, the gay marriage ruling had its opponents. A number of states proposed anti-LGBT legislation—some cloaked in religious objections, some blatantly discriminatory—in the year after the ruling. According to the Human Rights Campaign (HRC), the largest LGBT civil rights advocacy group and

Messages carried by LGBT Pride participants in 2016 reflected the dark turn of anti-LGBT legislation in some states and a mass shooting in Florida targeting the LGBT community.

#WEARENOTTHIS

Don't Tread On Me

THIS ISN'T
ABOUT
BATHROOMS

REPEAL HATE BILL 2!
#WE ARE NOT THIS

People gather on May 16, 2016, across the street from the North Carolina State Legislative Building in Raleigh to protest House Bill 2 (HB2), which became known as the *bathroom law*.

political lobbying organization in the United States, 36 states drafted some 200 anti-LGBT bills in 2016.

In March, Republican North Carolina Governor Pat McCrory signed the controversial Public Facilities Privacy and Security Act (commonly known as House Bill 2 or HB2) into law. HB2 banned North Carolina cities from passing their own *anti*-discrimination ordinances, forcing them to accept state-level discriminatory anti-LGBT legislation. HB2 also barred transgender people from using bathrooms that match their gender identity.

HB2—quickly dubbed the *bathroom law*—outraged many people as well as a number of influential corporations. PayPal canceled plans to create 400 jobs and invest $3.6 million in North Carolina, while Apple, Facebook, Google Ventures, and Bank of America—the state's largest corporation—put a hold on new investments there. The National Basketball Association removed its 2017 All-Star Game from Charlotte; the National Collegiate Athletic Association removed future tournament basketball games from the state; rock stars Bruce Springsteen and Ringo Starr canceled concerts; and Cyndi Lauper turned her Raleigh concert into a rally to repeal HB2. Even the North Carolina attorney general's office snubbed the law, refusing to enforce it and calling it unconstitutional.

In other states, anti-LGBT legislation gave businesses the right to deny services to LGBT people and allowed judges to refuse to marry same-sex couples. A number of these bills were state versions of the 1993 Religious Freedom Restoration Act (RFRA). The intent of the act was to protect religious practices from government interference. So-called "religious freedom" bills were proposed in 17 states. Mississippi Governor Phil Bryant approved one such law in April 2016. Mississippi's law specifically stated that marriage is between "one man and one woman" and that "male" or "female" refers to an individual's "immutable biological sex." The law also protected doctors who refuse to provide fertility treatment or to perform gender reassignment surgery and employers who make sex-specific grooming rules or limit "access to restrooms, spas, baths, showers, dressing rooms [or] locker rooms."

On July 1, however, U.S. District Court Judge Carlton W. Reeves blocked the Mississippi law just before it went into effect. Reeves said it created "a vehicle for state-sanctioned discrimination on the basis of sexual orientation and gender identity." Reeves further compared Governor Bryant's remarks on a state's "right to self-governance" to former Mississippi Governor Ross Barnett's 1962 opposition to the integration of the University of Mississippi.

Despite some recent local setbacks, the American LGBT community has made many important strides under the Obama administration. In 2009, Obama became the first president to appoint openly LGBT candidates to U.S. Senate-confirmed positions. That same year, he signed into law the Matthew Shepard and James Byrd, Jr., Hate Crimes Prevention Act, which strengthens federal protections against crimes based on gender identity or sexual orientation. Obama also renewed the Ryan White CARE Act, which provides life-saving medical services and support to Americans living with HIV/AIDS. He also ended a 22-year ban on HIV-positive people traveling to the United States.

In 2010, President Obama signed a presidential memorandum directing hospitals receiving Medicare and Medicaid funds to give LGBT patients "the compassion and security they deserve in their time of need," including the ability to choose someone other than an immediate family member to visit them and make medical decisions. The Department of Health and Human Services then launched the National Resource Center on LGBT Aging, the country's first resource center aimed at improving services offered to older LGBT adults. In addition, President Obama, Vice President Joe Biden, and other officials recorded "It Gets Better" video messages to address suicides among LGBT youth that occurred after bullying or harrassment.

In 2011, the government ended the "Don't Ask, Don't Tell" policy barring openly homosexual soldiers from serving in the armed forces. President Obama also directed the Department of Justice (DOJ) to cease its legal defense of the Defense of Marriage Act (DOMA), a 1996 law that defined marriage as a union between a man and a woman. The law excluded same-sex marriage from legal recognition by the federal government. The Supreme Court later declared DOMA unconstitutional.

In 2012, new regulations in the Department of Housing and Urban Development (HUD) ensured that housing programs were open to all eligible persons, regardless of sexual orientation or gender identity. In 2013, HUD released the first-ever national study of discrimination against members of the LGBT community in the rental and sale of housing. Beginning in 2014, under the Patient Protection

On July 21, 2014, in the East Room of the White House in Washington, D.C., President Obama signs an executive order protecting federal LGBT employees from workplace discrimination.

and Affordable Care Act (commonly known as "Obamacare"), insurers were prohibited from denying coverage based on a consumer's sexual orientation or gender identity. Also in 2014, an Obama executive order prohibited discrimination against federal employees and contractors on the basis of sexual orientation or gender identity. In 2015, the Family Medical Leave Act was extended to cover all legally married same-sex couples and the DOJ amended its equal opportunity program to protect service members against discrimination because of sexual orientation.

On June 24, 2016, President Obama capped eight years of promoting LGBT rights by designating New York City's landmark gay bar the Stonewall Inn as part of the Stonewall National Monument—the first National Park Service monument to honor the LGBT equality movement. The monument also includes Christopher Park, a historic community park at the intersection of Christopher Street, West 4th Street, and Grove Street across from the Stonewall Inn in Greenwich Village. The monument area was the site of demonstrations for gay rights in late June and early July 1969. The demonstrations followed a raid at the inn as police sought to enforce a law prohibiting the sale of alcoholic beverages to homosexuals. The demonstrations evolved into a series of riots that lasted, on and off, for several days. The anniversary of the Stonewall uprising is commemorated every summer as part of gay pride celebrations in the United States.

"Stonewall will be our first national monument to tell the story of the struggle for LGBT rights," President Obama said. "I believe our national parks should reflect the full story of our country, the richness and diversity and uniquely American spirit that has always defined us. That we are stronger together. That out of many, we are one."

Earlier that month, on June 12, 2016, the Stonewall was also the site of a gathering of LGBT people and their supporters who came to mourn the deaths of 49 people killed by a gunman at a gay nightclub in Orlando, Florida—the deadliest mass shooting up to that time in U.S. history. The White House, in its announcement about the Stonewall monument, referred to the Orlando shooting, stating, "As seen two weeks ago in Orlando, Florida, LGBT Americans continue to face acts of violence, discrimination, and hate. LGBT people of color are especially at risk. The administration is committed to continuing the fight for dignity, acceptance and equal rights for all Americans—no matter who they are or who they love."

Finally, on June 30, the last day of LGBT Pride Month, the Pentagon announced the end of a ban on transgender people openly serving in the U.S. military.

In his final LGBT Pride Month proclamation, President Obama remarked on the great progress made toward the equal treatment of LGBT Americans. But, he added, "there remains much work to do to extend the promise of our country to every American. But because of the acts of courage of the millions who came out and spoke out to demand justice and of those who quietly toiled and pushed for progress, our nation has made great strides in recognizing what these brave individuals long knew to be true in their hearts—that love is love and that no person should be judged by anything but the content of their character."

On June 13, 2016, New York's Stonewall Inn became a gathering site for momentos and messages of caring and grief after the mass shooting at a gay club in Orlando, Florida.

PANAMA CANAL
EXPANSION

On June 26, 2016, thousands of people lined the Panama Canal's new Cocolí Locks as the colossal Chinese container ship *Cosco Shipping Panama* made the inaugural voyage through the canal's new $5.25-billion expansion. The expansion, 10 years in the making and 2 years overdue, doubles the waterway's previous shipping capacity. The new longer, wider, and deeper lock complexes allow the passage of most *post-Panamax* ships—gargantuan tankers and container and cruise ships that were once too large to fit through the canal (such ships are now described as *neo*-Panamax).

With the expansion, the Panama Canal can now accommodate about 98 percent of all ships afloat. (The largest supertankers and aircraft carriers are still too big.) For neo-Panamax ships, the expansion significantly shortens the trip from China to the east

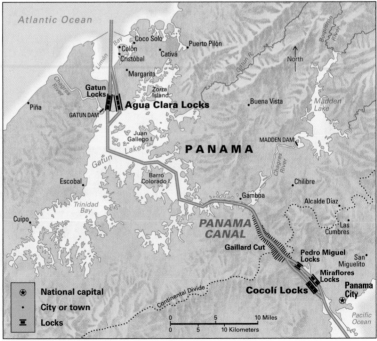

The Panama Canal's newly expanded locks are at each end of the waterway.

Tugboats nuzzle the container ship *Cosco Shipping Panama* as it prepares to enter the Panama Canal's new Cocolí Locks on June 26, 2016.

coast of the United States—the canal's most important commercial route. The expansion's new lock chambers measure 1,400 feet (427 meters) long, 180 feet (55 meters) wide, and 60 feet (18.3 meters) deep. The older locks—still very much in use—measure 1,000 feet (304 meters) long, 110 feet (33.5 meters) wide, and 42 feet (12.8 meters) deep.

Construction on the expansion began in 2007 with the aim of opening on the canal's 100th birthday in 2014. Various setbacks—including construction disputes, design flaws, funding and water shortages, leaky concrete, and work stoppages—delayed the expansion's opening until June 2016. But Panamanian officials and citizens alike celebrated the better-late-than-never achievement, welcoming the increase in revenue and prestige brought by the expansion. The Panama Canal cuts across the Isthmus of Panama and links the Atlantic Ocean and the Pacific Ocean. It ranks as one of the greatest engineering achievements in the world.

BRAZIL'S CHALLENGING YEAR

Brazil had a challenging year in 2016, but the South American nation persevered and, by autumn, things were reasonably calm. January entered on the heels of a decision by Congress to begin impeachment proceedings against President Dilma Rousseff. The main reasons for impeachment were alleged budget improprieties, but Rousseff insisted (to the bitter end, as it turned out) the allegations were baseless and that her impeachment was pure political spite.

In February, the World Health Organization declared a global public health emergency following an outbreak of the Zika virus centered on Brazil. The virus struck Brazil in 2015, and it was soon connected to microcephaly birth defects in newborn babies (see **Season of Zika**, p. 372). Pregnant women were advised not to travel to Brazil, creating second thoughts for those planning to attend the 2016 Summer Olympic Games in Rio de Janeiro (see **Games from Ipanema**, p. 226).

In March, millions of people protested as an ongoing corruption scandal further troubled Rousseff and her dwindling government allies. The state-run oil company, Petrobras, had been caught bribing officials, as had Brazil's largest construction company. Rousseff tried to protect her predecessor and ally, Luiz Inácio Lula da Silva, but he was hit with money laundering charges and will go on trial in 2017. In May 2016, Congress suspended Rousseff from office as impeachment proceedings formally began, and Vice President Michel Temer took control.

In June and July, officials scrambled to complete Olympic preparations. Maintenance and infrastructure work lagged behind, and many athlete dormitories and arenas and venues remained unfinished or in states of disrepair. As for Zika, mosquito areas had been sprayed, the weather had turned (to winter), and, the government insisted, if people took simple precautions—such as wearing long sleeves and insect repellent—then there was little to fear.

As it turned out, the government was right. The August Olympics went rather well. Minor complaints abounded, but the biggest fears (such as Zika, work strikes, and terrorism) went unrealized.

Late in August, Rousseff was officially kicked out and Temer officially took over. Brazil's economic difficulties (a recession has persisted since 2014) continued, however, as did further political problems, but Brazil's challenging year of 2016 could have turned out much worse.

EASTER BOMBING IN PAKISTAN

On Easter Sunday, March 27, 2016, in the eastern Pakistan city of Lahore, an Islamic terrorist bombing killed 75 people and injured hundreds of others. Most of the victims were women and children. Lahore, near the border between India and Pakistan, is the capital of the province of Punjab.

The bomb detonated in Gulshan-e-Iqbal Park (Garden of Iqbal—named for Pakistani poet Muhammad Iqbal), a large public space featuring walking paths, playgrounds, and carnival rides for children. The park was filled with families celebrating the Easter holiday. The bomb exploded near the park's playground swings.

Jamaat-ul-Ahrar, a faction of the Pakistani Taliban, claimed responsibility for the suicide bombing. The attack specifically targeted Christians, but most of the victims were Muslims.

On the same day, thousands turned out in Islamabad, Pakistan's capital, to protest the execution of a police officer convicted of assassinating the governor of the province, Salman Taseer, in 2011. Taseer had spoken against Pakistan's strict blasphemy laws, which sometimes lead to vigilante violence and extremism in the south Asian nation.

Pakistani mourners embrace the coffin of a victim of the terrorist bombing in Lahore on March 27, 2016. The Easter Sunday attack targeted Pakistan's minority Christian community.

OBAMA IN HIROSHIMA:
DEATH FELL FROM THE SKY

On May 27, 2016, Barack Obama became the first sitting United States president to visit Hiroshima, Japan, site of the world's first atomic bombing in 1945. Accompanied by Japanese Prime Minister Shinzo Abe, the president visited the haunting Hiroshima Peace Memorial Museum before laying a wreath at the Memorial Cenotaph at the center of the Peace Memorial Park. The park—situated near the bombing's *hypocenter* (area immediately below the atomic explosion)—was once the site of the city's bustling commercial district. The saddle-shaped cenotaph bears the names of people killed in the attack.

President Obama then addressed a large, somber, and silent crowd: "Seventy-one years ago, on a bright cloudless morning, death fell from the sky and the world was changed," he began. "A flash of light and a wall of fire destroyed a city, and demonstrated that mankind possessed the means to destroy itself." He later added: "We come to mourn the dead, including over 100,000 Japanese men, women and children, thousands of Koreans, and a dozen Americans held prisoner. Their souls speak to us." The president did not apologize for the bombing, which was done by the United States near the end of World War II. He painted the Japanese as neither victims nor aggressors, but merely called for an end to senseless wars. He also reiterated the need to rid the world of nuclear weapons.

Following his speech, President Obama met with survivors of the bombing. He embraced a visibly moved Shigeaki Mori, a 79-year-old survivor who helped create a memorial to the 12 American prisoners of war killed in the bombing.

On Aug. 6, 1945, a U.S. Army plane, the *Enola Gay*, dropped an atomic bomb on Hiroshima. The explosion and aftermath killed an estimated 140,000 people. Three days later, on August 9, another atomic bomb was dropped on Nagasaki. These were the first and last times that nuclear weapons were used in warfare. The United States dropped the bombs to convince Japan to surrender—and it worked. World War II unofficially ended a few days later with Japan's agreement on August 14 to stop fighting. The official surrender came on September 2.

MOTHER TERESA BECOMES A SAINT

The Roman Catholic nun Mother Teresa was *canonized* (formally declared) a saint on Sept. 4, 2016, one day before the 19th anniversary of her death in 1997. Tens of thousands of faithful attended the canonization service led by Pope Francis outside St. Peter's Basilica in Vatican City. Francis praised the Nobel Peace Prize-winning Teresa, saying she embodied the ideal of a "poor church for the poor." Sometimes referred to as the *saint of the gutters,* Teresa founded a religious order in Calcutta (now Kolkata), India, called the Missionaries of Charity. The order provides food and services for the needy.

Mother Teresa's original name was Agnes Gonxha Bojaxhiu. She was born on Aug. 27, 1910, in what is now Skopje, Macedonia. In 1928, she joined a religious order, which sent her to India.

Mother Teresa cradles an armless baby girl at her order's orphanage in Calcutta, India, in 1978. A champion among the poor, Mother Teresa received the Nobel Peace Prize on Oct. 17, 1979.

She took the name *Teresa* after joining the order. A few years later, she began teaching in Calcutta. In 1948, the Catholic Church granted her permission to leave her convent and work among the city's poor people. She founded the Missionaries of Charity in 1950. Teresa died on Sept. 5, 1997.

In 2003, Pope John Paul II *beatified* Mother Teresa. Beatification is an important step toward declaring an individual a saint in the Roman Catholic Church. A saint is a holy person who exemplifies a virtue or virtues of his or her religion. The word comes from the Latin word *sanctus,* meaning *a holy one.*

AFGHANISTAN SMOLDERS

As it has for much of its troubled history, Aghanistan continued to smolder in 2016. Islamic militants, government troops, and international security forces came in frequent violent contact during the year, resulting in numerous small battles and hit-and-run attacks. After years on the decline, Taliban forces reemerged in strength in 2015 and continued to cause trouble in 2016. Al-Qa`ida too has gained strength, and terrorists loyal to the Islamic State group have also entered the fray. The increase in Islamic militant attacks can be linked to the steep reduction in foreign troops and security forces after the official end of the Afghanistan War in December 2014. Since that time, a new conflict has emerged (or merely continued) in Afghanistan, a conflict that pits Taliban militants against government workers and troops—and terrorists against civilians. In less than two years, this "new" conflict has taken the lives of more than 20,000 people.

The Taliban and other antigovernment groups control large parts of Aghanistan (from 15 to 20 percent by most estimates). And of the provincial capitals still in government hands, about half are under constant threat of Islamic militant attack. Govern-

Afghan soldiers guard a highway checkpoint on the outskirts of Kabul, Afghanistan, on July 19, 2016. Since the end of the Afghanistan War in December 2014—and a steep reduction in U.S. troops—violence has once again gripped the long-troubled nation.

ment attempts to quiet the chaos have been largely ineffectual, often stymied from within by fractious power grabs by rival politicians and government-allied militias.

In 2016, U.S. military forces—which were supposed to be on their way home—reengaged Afghanistan's Islamic militants, stepping up air attacks and commando raids. Operations against the Islamic State were

particularly successful, but the political situation in Afghanistan has limited what U.S. forces can do against the still somewhat-widely-supported Taliban. The main American role has been to supply Afghan troops with intelligence, air support (including drone strikes), and weapons and equipment. The nation's instability, however, has forced an increase (from 5,000 to 8,500) in the number of U.S. troops that will remain in Afghanistan into 2017—along with hundreds of troops from other supporting nations.

Meanwhile, the Afghan people continue to pay the price. In 2016, Taliban and other Islamic extremist attacks killed hundreds of civilians in Kabul, the capital, and in the surrounding provinces of Ghazni, Helmand, Kandahar, Kunduz, and Urōzgān.

AUSTRALIAN RULING COALITION CLAIMS VICTORY

Australian Prime Minister Malcolm Turnbull speaks at the government offices in Sydney on July 10, 2016. Turnbull's conservative coalition government was reelected for a second three-year term. Australia's coat of arms is seen at right.

On July 10, 2016, Australian Prime Minister Malcolm Turnbull declared victory in the country's recent parliamentary election. Turnbull, who leads a governing coalition of Australia's Liberal and National parties, made the announcement after opposition leader Bill Shorten, who heads the Labor Party, conceded defeat. More than a week after the July 2 poll, the vote count showed Turnbull's coalition winning exactly enough seats—76—to secure a majority in the House of Representatives.

Turnbull became prime minister in September 2015 after successfully challenging Prime Minister Tony Abbott for the leadership of the Liberal Party. Using a provision of Australia's Constitution, he enacted a *double dissolution* in early 2016—both houses of the federal Parliament were dissolved and fresh elections were called. Turnbull had hoped for an increase in power, but the election gamble had the opposite effect. The coalition's majority fell from 90 to 76, while Labor increased its presence in the House from 55 to 69 seats.

REMEMBERING THE BATTLE OF LONG TAN

Australian Vietnam War veterans were frustrated when the Vietnamese government canceled a memorial event the day before it was to occur on Aug. 18, 2016. The day marks Australia's annual Vietnam Veterans Day, but this year the day also marked the 50th anniversary of the Battle of Long Tan, Australia's first major fight in the Vietnam War. In that battle, a small group of soldiers from Australia and New Zealand defeated a larger Vietnamese force. The war is a sensitive subject for the Vietnamese government. More than 1,000 Australians had already traveled to Vietnam for the ceremony.

Australia's involvement in the Vietnam War began in 1962, when the country sent Army advisers to South Vietnam in support of its allies from the United States. Australian soldiers first arrived in Vietnam in 1966. That year, the Australians began to set up a base at Nui Dat, near the village of Long Tan about 70 miles (110 kilometers) east of Saigon (now Ho Chi Minh City).

On August 17, the Viet Cong (Communist-led South Vietnamese guerrillas) fired artillery at Nui Dat. The next day, a group of Australian soldiers searched for the Viet Cong at a rubber plantation near Long Tan. The group, led by Major Harry Smith, consisted of 105 Australians and 3 New Zealanders. They soon encountered a group of some 2,000 Viet Cong troops.

In a monsoon rain, Smith's force fought the Viet Cong. American and Australian forces supported Smith's company with artillery fired from the base at Nui Dat. After about three hours of fighting, and after Smith's group had fought off several waves of Viet Cong attacks, Australian reinforcements arrived. Nightfall and the arrival of the reinforcements ended the battle.

Eighteen Australian soldiers died in the battle, and several more were injured. The Australians buried 245 Viet Cong dead after the battle, though captured documents indicated that hundreds more had been killed.

A memorial called the Long Tan Cross marks the site of the battle. In 2016, a group of Australian veterans—including 83-year-old Harry Smith, who led the Australians at Long Tan 50 years ago—had scheduled a low-key service there before a "friendship dinner" with Vietnamese veterans and a memorial concert. The Vietnamese government, however, decided to allow only small groups to access the battle site for a limited amount of time, and the dinner and concert were canceled.

TERRORISTS BOMB BRUSSELS

On March 22, 2016, terrorist bombs struck the Belgian capital of Brussels, killing 32 people—plus 3 terrorists—and injuring more than 300 others. Two explosions occurred at Brussels Airport in the suburb of Zaventem. About an hour later, a third explosion hit a train in the Maelbeek *metro* (subway) station in Brussels's city center. The three explosions killed 28 people outright, and 4 more died later of wounds. The Islamic State terrorist group (also called ISIS, ISIL, or DAESH) claimed responsibility for the bombings, which comprised the deadliest acts of terrorism in Belgium's history.

Closed-circuit television footage showed the airport attackers— three of them—entering Brussels Airport and pushing luggage believed to have contained the bombs. Two of the terrorists detonated their explosives, killing themselves, but the third bomb did not go off, and the surviving suspect escaped in the chaos following the bombs' detonations. Police found and destroyed the third bomb, and later captured the third would-be bomber. A taxi driver recognized the attackers in the video footage, and, realizing he had transported them, led police to the address where he had picked them up. When police raided the address, they found a nail bomb, explosive chemicals, and an Islamic State flag. In the Malbeeck subway attack, one bomber killed himself while another terrorist escaped, only to be arrested in the coming weeks. Several people believed to have helped the bombers were also later arrested.

The attacks forced authorities to temporarily shut down all public transport in Brussels, but the airport and most city trains were up and running again by early April. Three official days of mourning were declared, and Belgian Prime Minister Charles Michel stated, "To those who have chosen to be barbarous enemies of freedom, democracy and fundamental values ... we remain united as one."

Brussels is the unofficial capital of the European Union (EU), and so a strike at Brussels is, in some ways, a strike at the heart of Europe. In addition, Belgium has a large immigrant population that has not been well integrated into the fabric of the small nation, so religious extremism has been a problem in certain areas.

QUEEN ELIZABETH II TURNS 90

On April 21, 2016, people wish happy birthday to Queen Elizabeth II as she walks the streets of Windsor, England, the home of Windsor Castle near London. It was the queen's 90th birthday.

April 21, 2016, was the 90th birthday of Britain's Queen Elizabeth II. She is the oldest monarch in British history. The next oldest monarchs were Elizabeth's great-great grandmother, Victoria (1819-1901), and ancestor George III (1738-1820), who both reached 81. Elizabeth II is also the British monarch with the longest reign. She surpassed Victoria, who ruled for more than 63 years, in 2015.

In addition to the actual day of her birth, Queen Elizabeth II has a second, official birthday during the summer. In 2016, it was held on June 11. The tradition of an official birthday for the monarch began with George II (1683-1760). He was born in November, but it was often too cold in London, the British capital, for his birthday ceremony. The celebration—and his birthday—moved to the warmer months of summer. Since George II, all British monarchs have had the option of celebrating a summertime "official" birthday in addition to their actual day of birth.

Birthday celebrations for Queen Elizabeth II took place throughout the United Kingdom.

SADIQ KHAN: LONDON'S FIRST MUSLIM MAYOR

On May 5, 2016, in London, England, voters elected the Labour Party's Sadiq Khan as the city's new mayor. Khan, a London native, is a Muslim of Pakistani descent. His election win made him London's first Muslim mayor and just the second Muslim mayor (after Rotterdam's Ahmed Aboutaleb) of a major European city. Khan's win reflected the choice of Londoners to focus on issues and a candidate's policies and abilities rather than a candidate's race, religion, or ethnic identity. Billionaire Conservative Party candidate Zac Goldsmith—who lost with just 35 percent of the vote—tried to use Khan's religion against him, hoping his Islamic faith would turn voters away. Goldsmith also tried to link Khan—and the liberal Labour Party in general—to Islamist extremists. The tactics fell flat, however, and Khan's electoral support—strong from the start—never faltered, carrying him to a comfortable victory.

Sadiq Khan was born in London on Oct. 8, 1970, the son of Pakistani immigrants. His father was a bus driver and his mother a seamstress. Khan joined the Labour Party while still in high school. He practiced as a human rights lawyer before entering Parliament in 2005 as representative for Greater London's Tooting constituency (where he grew up) in the House of Commons. He held different ministry positions before concentrating on his run for London mayor in 2015.

GOTTHARD BASE TUNNEL

On June 1, 2016, authorities in Switzerland announced the completion and official opening of the Gotthard Base Tunnel. After 17 years of construction, the 35-mile (57-kilometer) railroad tunnel is now the world's longest, surpassing Japan's 33.5-mile (53.9-kilometer) Seikan rail tunnel.

The Gotthard Base Tunnel, which opens to commercial traffic in December, is also the world's deepest, running up to 1.4 miles (2.3 kilometers) underground. European heads of state inaugurated the tunnel, and a lucky few hundred people were chosen by lottery to be the first to travel the tunnel's flat route beneath the Swiss Alps. A few days later, public festivities took place at each end of the new tunnel—Erstfeld in the north and Bodio in the south—as well as at connecting train stations and other places.

The first blast on the $12-billion Gotthard Base Tunnel's main shaft took place in 1999. Engineers then drilled, dug, and blasted through 73 different types of rock—and removed more than 31 million tons (28 million tonnes) of it—which was used in the concrete to build the tunnel. The long, difficult task claimed the lives of nine workers who are commemorated in a memorial marker at Erstfeld.

Swiss authorities anticipate that about 260 freight trains and 65 passenger trains—running up to 150 miles (250 kilometers) per hour—will pass through the tunnel each day. The tunnel will cut nearly an hour off the 3 hour and 40 minute trip from Zurich to Milan, Italy—a very busy route. The tunnel will also remove thousands of road-clogging and polluting trucks from Switzerland's highways.

This photo shows the view from the driver's cabin during a train test run through Switzerland's Gotthard Base Tunnel on March 10, 2016. The world's longest rail tunnel officially opened on June 1 and began carrying commercial traffic in December.

BASTILLE DAY TERROR IN FRANCE

On July 14, 2016, an Islamic terrorist drove a truck into a large crowd in Nice, France, killing 86 people and injuring more than 200 others. The brutal attack took place on the resort city's famed Promenade des Anglais seafront as it was packed with people celebrating Bastille Day, France's great national holiday. A fireworks show was just finishing, around 11 p.m. local time, when the large commercial truck began ramming pedestrians at high speed along the promenade. Terrified people scrambled to get out of the way, but there was little time and little room for escape. The driver continued his rampage for some 1¼ miles (2 kilometers). The battered truck finally came to a halt, and the terrorist began firing a handgun from behind the wheel. Police killed him in a quick shootout.

French President François Hollande, who was elsewhere in the south of France for Bastille Day, rushed back to a national crisis center in Paris. "France is filled with sadness by this new tragedy," Hollande said. "There's no denying the terrorist nature of this attack."

The terrorist driver was identified as a 31-year-old Tunisian-French Nice resident with a history of domestic violence and petty crimes. The Islamic State terror group claimed responsibility for the attack, but evidence suggested the driver acted on his own initiative—a so-called "lone wolf" attack. Police later arrested several people alleged to have aided in the attack's planning and preparation.

Nice is a popular resort city on the French Riviera and a Mediterranean port. It lies at the foot of the Alps near Italy. The Promenade des Anglais (English Walkway)—often called La Prom by locals—stretches along the sea with luxury hotels, shops, and villas on one side and lovely beaches on the other. It is the city's most famous landmark. An estimated 30,000 people were along the walkway at the time of the attack.

People place flowers on the Promenade des Anglais at the scene of a truck attack that killed 86 people at Nice's popular waterfront walkway on Bastille Day, July 14, 2016.

SYRIA'S MISERY OF WAR

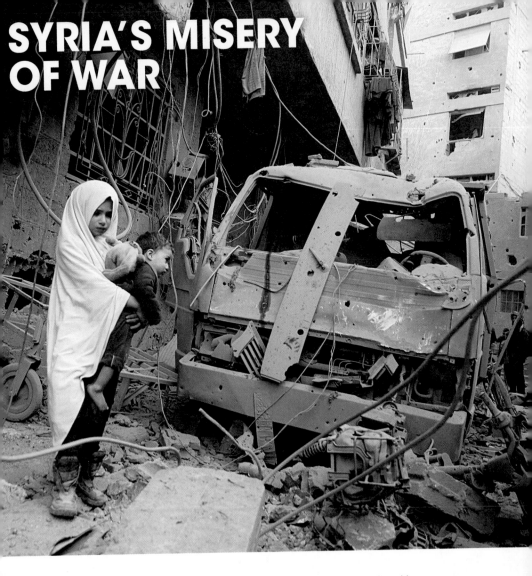

Despite multiple efforts at peace, the Syrian Civil War (which began in 2011) flared with ever greater violence in 2016. The Syrian government, led by President Bashar al-Assad, concentrated its military efforts on the rebel-held city of Aleppo, which has been largely reduced to ruins. The Syrian Army surrounded Aleppo in July, but

On Jan. 10, 2016, a girl and her young brother survey the damage from Russian air strikes on the rebel-held town of Duma, northeast of Damascus, the Syrian capital.

rebel troops quickly forced a southern breach, allowing badly needed supplies to trickle into the city. The ordinary people of Aleppo continued to suffer from famine, air raids, and shelling, and humanitarian aid was largely prevented from reaching them. In August, Syrian government troops and their allied militias again cut off the rebel supply route, and increased air strikes (many flown by Russia, Syria's main ally in the war) put added pressure on Aleppo's surviving population. Russia's involvement in Syria increased rapidly in 2016. Russian warships, troops, and missile defense systems arrived, and their warplanes flew daily sorties against rebel positions, inflicting thousands of casualties among both rebel troops and civilians.

Many aid workers, including doctors, nurses, drivers, and the celebrated "white helmets," were killed and wounded in Syria in 2016. The white helmets—officially known as the Syrian Civil Defense—are civilian volunteers who rush into the often still-burning debris left by air strikes to retrieve anyone who might have survived. Well-publicized rescues, often of children, gained the white helmets attention in 2016, and the group was among the strongest contenders for the Nobel Peace Prize.

Coalition forces, led by the United States, continued to steer away from the fighting between government and rebel forces, centering their efforts instead on destroying the Islamic State terror group (also called ISIS, ISIL, or DAESH). Islamic State terror attacks killed thousands of people in 2016, nearly all of them

civilians, in both Syria and Iraq, but the territory under their control shrank decidedly. U.S. and coalition air strikes hit Islamic State camps, convoys, and infrastructure, while special forces troops conducted pinpoint raids and worked closely on the ground with Kurdish forces in Syria's north as well as with certain rebel groups engaged against Islamic State militants.

Turkey, too, took on a larger role in Syria in 2016, sending troops across the border to nullify nearby Islamic State positions. Turkey's aim, too, included the reduction of Kurdish militants in the same area. Kurdish troops are fighting the Islamic State in northern Syria and Iraq, but they are also involved in a long-running and still-simmering conflict with the Turkish government.

Large anti-Islamic State efforts took place in neighboring Iraq in 2016 as well. Iraqi and Kurdish troops (closely supported by the U.S.-led coalition) made significant gains throughout the year, continuing with a large effort to liberate the northern city of Mosul starting in October. Mosul has been under Islamic State control since June 2014, and it represents the terror group's last stronghold in Iraq. The main military threat posed by the Islamic State may be nearing its end, but their bloody acts of terror continue in Iraq, Syria, and elsewhere.

NIGERIA'S NIGER DELTA AVENGERS

On June 13, 2016, Nigeria's Niger Delta Avengers (NDA) announced they were ready to talk with the west African nation's federal government. The NDA—a militant group that has attacked petroleum and natural gas installations in the Niger River Delta—has strict preconditions, however, before a dialogue can be arranged. The NDA insists that damaged pipelines and facilities remain out of service, and that the selling of crude oil be suspended. The group wants international oil companies at the talks and a commitment from the government to improve conditions in the impoverished and badly polluted delta. The government, desperate to stop the attacks and regain the delta's fossil fuel wealth, has recently called off military efforts against the NDA. The government, however, may be unwilling or unable to comply with the militant group's pretalk conditions.

The NDA grabbed the government's attention earlier in 2016 by launching "Operation Red Economy," systematic attacks meant to cripple the Niger Delta's rich oil and gas industry. NDA sabotage has destroyed or forced the closures of pipelines, terminals, and wells belonging to such oil giants as Chevron, Royal Dutch Shell, and Italy's ENI. Nigeria's oil production has since been reduced to its lowest level in 20 years.

The NDA emerged from the remains of previous militant groups in the Niger Delta that fought for control of the region's oil wealth as well as independence from the Nigerian government. The NDA's crusade, however, has largely centered on the economic well-being of delta citizens and the restoration of land and water contaminated by spills and irresponsible oil and gas exploration. The NDA has thus far avoided open warfare with Nigerian troops and has followed self-imposed rules against kidnapping or killing. The NDA has ominously warned, however, that these rules could change.

The Niger Delta forms the southernmost region of Nigeria, along the Gulf of Guinea. It consists of deposits of clay, mud, and sand at the mouth of the Niger River. Lagoons and mangrove swamps cover much of the region. Large-scale oil and gas extraction in the delta began in the 1950's.

TERROR STRIKES ISTANBUL

On June 28, 2016, a terrorist attack killed 41 people and injured 239 others at Istanbul Atatürk Airport in Turkey. The attack, blamed on Islamic State terrorists, occurred at the international terminal of the airport, which is Turkey's busiest and one of the world's major travel hubs. The attack began as three armed terrorists fired at airport guards and passengers near the terminal entrance. Guards returned fire, and the terrorists then detonated body explosives in succession—one—two—three. The explosions killed and wounded dozens of people in the ground floor arrivals area, the first floor departures area, and the nearby parking area. Security personnel swarmed to help as survivors gaped in shock at the carnage, the scattered luggage, and the shattered glass and gutted walls and ceilings of the terminal. The airport

On June 29, 2016, a young girl attends a prayer service for the 41 victims of an Islamic State terrorist attack on Turkey's Istanbul Atatürk Airport the day before.

shut down and heavily armed security prowled the terminals. Would-be travelers were evacuated to safety, and incoming flights were diverted to other airports. The injured were taken to hospitals, and the dead were slowly identified. Hours later, flights resumed at the airport.

The June 28 airport attack was the most recent in a flurry of terror attacks in Turkey. Some of the blame has fallen on Kurdish separatists, who primarily target Turkish soldiers and police. The Islamic State terror group, based in neighboring Iraq and Syria, has carried out the deadly civilian attacks. Since July 2015, Islamic State attacks have killed some 200 people within Turkey's borders.

AFRICA'S DEEP HELIUM POOL

In late June 2016, British researchers working with the Norwegian mining company Helium One announced the discovery of a vast helium reserve in Tanzania's portion of eastern Africa's Great Rift Valley. Helium is an important gas, but supplies are limited, so the discovery was welcome news. The researchers presented their findings at the Goldschmidt Geochemical Conference in Yokohama, Japan.

Helium is a lightweight gas and chemical element. It is called an *inert* gas or *noble gas*. These terms are used because helium does not combine with other elements.

Helium is the second most common element in the universe, next to hydrogen, but it is rare on Earth. Scientists think that early in the formation of the solar system, Earth and the other three inner planets (Mercury, Venus, and Mars) had atmospheres of hydrogen and helium. But the constant outflow of particles from the sun, called the *solar wind*, blew away most of these elements. Only larger planets orbiting farther from the sun, such as Jupiter and Saturn, were able to hold on to their hydrogen and helium atmospheres.

The research group thinks that volcanic activity at rift sites, such as the Great Rift Valley, provides the heat necessary to release helium from ancient rocks where it had been trapped for billions of years. Geologists hope to find more reserves in similar locations. Until the Rift Valley discovery, most of the major supplies of helium were found among natural gas deposits in the United States, but these reserves are dwindling.

The newly discovered helium pool contains an estimated 54 billion cubic feet (1.5 billion cubic meters) of the gas—and the researchers believe there is much more helium to be found there. Annual global helium consumption is about 8 billion cubic feet (227 million cubic meters), so the African reserve will provide nearly seven years' use of the gas.

Helium has many important uses. The gas fills weather (and other) balloons and shields welded joints from oxygen (strengthening the joint). Liquid helium cools rocket engines and the magnets in magnetic resonance imaging (MRI) devices.

The helium reserve was found here, near the Ngorongoro caldera (extinct volcano crater) in Tanzania's portion of eastern Africa's Great Rift Valley.

TERROR RETURNS TO BAGHDAD

Early on the morning of July 3, 2016, an Islamic State terrorist bomber drove a truck packed with explosives into the crowded Karrada commercial district of Baghdad, Iraq. People filled the streets of the Shī`ite majority neighborhood as they shopped for the upcoming Id al-Fitr holiday marking the end of the holy month of Ramadan. Just after midnight, the truck exploded in a massive blast that killed 292 people and injured hundreds of others. A second terrorist bomber also struck that night in the city's Shī`ite market district of al-Shaab, killing two more people. The July 3 bombings marked the fourth major terrorist attack in Baghdad since the beginning of May 2016.

The second, smaller bombing was typical of the daily existence for many Iraqis as they deal with the constant threat of terrorist violence. The larger bombing, while atypical because of its size and impact, illustrated the ruthlessness of the Islamic State and the most frequent targets of its attacks—other Muslims. The Islamic State is a radical Sunni group, and the vast majority of its victims belong to the Shī`ite division of Islam. The Islamic State is slowly losing Iraqi territory it captured in the past two years, but its reach is obviously still deadly and extensive. The Karrada bombing was the worst in Iraq this year.

Naturally, the Islamic State does not speak for most Sunni Muslims. The Association of Muslim Scholars in Iraq, the nation's highest Sunni religious body, called the Karrada bombing a "bloody crime, regardless of who carried it out or what their motivations were."

The victims of the bombings were more than just numbers. Entire families were among the dead in Karrada—fathers, mothers, and children all destroyed in one moment of tragic terrorist hatred. The dead had names, too, like Adel al-Jaf, a promising young dancer and rapper also known as Adel Euro; Zulfikar Oraibi, the son of former Iraqi soccer star Ghanim Oraibi; and Adnan Abu Altman, who graduated from law school last week and died with his father and brother. Some of the dead—badly mangled in the violence of the explosion—were never identified.

INDEPENDENT COUNTRIES OF THE WORLD

This map shows each continent in a different color. The names of continents and independent nations are printed in capital letters. The table on the following pages gives the most current estimate for each country's area and population. It also has the country's capital and the key to locate the country on the map.

*Populations are current estimates based on the latest figures from official government, United Nations, and other sources.

†Not on map; key shows general location.

‡Claimed by China.

INDEPENDENT COUNTRIES OF THE WORLD

Name	Area in mi²	Area in km²	Population*	Capital	Map key
Afghanistan	251,827	652,230	32,795,000	Kabul	D 13
Albania	11,100	28,748	3,038,000	Tirane	C 11
Algeria	919,595	2,381,741	40,137,000	Algiers	D 10
Andorra†	181	468	81,000	Andorra la Vella	C 10
Angola	481,354	1,246,700	23,525,000	Luanda	F 10
Antigua and Barbuda	171	442	93,000	Saint John's	E 6
Argentina	1,073,519	2,780,400	43,438,000	Buenos Aires	G 6
Armenia	11,484	29,743	3,049,000	Yerevan	D 12
Australia	2,969,907	7,692,024	24,272,000	Canberra	G 16
Austria	32,386	83,879	8,546,000	Vienna	C 10
Azerbaijan	33,436	86,600	9,730,000	Baku	D 12
Bahamas	5,382	13,939	390,000	Nassau	D 6
Bahrain	296	767	1,399,000	Manama	D 12
Bangladesh	56,977	147,570	161,487,000	Dhaka	D 14
Barbados	166	430	289,000	Bridgetown	E 7
Belarus	80,155	207,600	9,432,000	Minsk	C 11
Belgium	11,787	30,528	11,171,000	Brussels	C 10
Belize	8,867	22,966	356,000	Belmopan	E 5
Benin	43,484	112,622	10,862,000	Porto-Novo	E 10
Bhutan	14,824	38,394	775,000	Thimphu	D 14
Bolivia	424,165	1,098,581	11,205,000	La Paz; Sucre	F 6
Bosnia-Herzegovina	19,772	51,209	3,813,000	Sarajevo	C 10
Botswana	224,607	581,730	2,138,000	Gaborone	G 11
Brazil	3,287,613	8,514,877	205,515,000	Brasília	F 7
Brunei	2,226	5,765	435,000	Bandar Seri Begawan	E 15
Bulgaria	42,819	110,900	7,060,000	Sofia	C 11
Burkina Faso	105,877	274,220	18,874,000	Ouagadougou	E 9
Burundi	10,747	27,834	11,170,000	Bujumbura	F 11
Cambodia	69,898	181,035	15,550,000	Phnom Penh	E 15
Cameroon	183,650	475,650	23,979,000	Yaoundé	E 10
Canada	3,855,103	9,984,670	36,224,000	Ottawa	C 4
Cape Verde	1,557	4,033	524,000	Praia	E 8
Central African Republic	240,535	622,984	4,992,000	Bangui	E 10
Chad	495,755	1,284,000	14,006,000	N'Djamena	E 10
Chile	291,930	756,096	18,002,000	Santiago	G 6
China	3,697,002	9,575,191	1,385,400,000	Beijing	D 14
Colombia	440,831	1,141,748	48,992,000	Bogotá	E 6
Comoros	719	1,862	789,000	Moroni	F 12

Name	Area in mi²	Area in km²	Population*	Capital	Map key
Congo, Democratic Republic of the	905,355	2,344,858	75,126,000	Kinshasa	F 11
Congo, Republic of the	132,047	342,000	4,797,000	Brazzaville	F 10
Costa Rica	19,730	51,100	4,890,000	San José	E 5
Côte d'Ivoire (Ivory Coast)	124,504	322,463	22,529,000	Yamoussoukro	E 9
Croatia	21,851	56,594	4,252,000	Zagreb	C 10
Cuba	42,426	109,884	11,223,000	Havana	D 6
Cyprus	3,572	9,251	1,178,000	Nicosia	D 11
Czech Republic	30,451	78,867	10,553,000	Prague	C 10
Denmark	16,639	43,094	5,672,000	Copenhagen	C 10
Djibouti	8,958	23,200	924,000	Djibouti	E 12
Dominica	290	751	74,000	Roseau	E 6
Dominican Republic	18,792	48,670	10,680,000	Santo Domingo	E 6
East Timor	5,774	14,954	1,274,000	Dili	F 16
Ecuador	105,037	272,045	16,331,000	Quito	F 6
Egypt	386,662	1,001,450	88,371,000	Cairo	D 11
El Salvador	8,124	21,041	6,466,000	San Salvador	E 5
Equatorial Guinea	10,831	28,051	822,000	Malabo	E 10
Eritrea	45,406	117,600	6,840,000	Asmara	E 12
Estonia	17,462	45,227	1,308,000	Tallinn	C 11
Ethiopia	426,373	1,104,300	101,485,000	Addis Ababa	E 11
Fiji	7,055	18,272	900,000	Suva	F 1
Finland	130,670	338,435	5,507,000	Helsinki	B 11
France	212,935	551,500	65,163,000	Paris	C 10
Gabon	103,347	267,667	1,771,000	Libreville	F 10
Gambia	4,361	11,295	2,031,000	Banjul	E 9
Georgia	26,911	69,700	4,482,000	Tbilisi	C 12
Germany	137,885	357,121	80,722,000	Berlin	C 10
Ghana	92,098	238,533	27,596,000	Accra	E 9
Greece	50,949	131,957	11,121,000	Athens	D 11
Grenada	133	344	108,000	Saint George's	E 6
Guatemala	42,042	108,889	16,657,000	Guatemala City	E 5
Guinea	94,926	245,857	12,197,000	Conakry	E 9
Guinea-Bissau	13,948	36,125	1,782,000	Bissau	E 9
Guyana	83,000	214,969	759,000	Georgetown	E 7
Haiti	10,714	27,750	10,797,000	Port-au-Prince	E 6
Honduras	43,433	112,492	8,558,000	Tegucigalpa	E 5
Hungary	35,919	93,030	9,892,000	Budapest	C 10
Iceland	39,769	103,000	336,000	Reykjavík	B 9
India	1,222,548	3,166,384	1,299,580,000	New Delhi	D 13
Indonesia	737,815	1,910,931	258,553,000	Jakarta	F 16

Name	Area in mi²	Area in km²	Population*	Capital	Map key
Iran	636,372	1,648,195	79,892,000	Tehran	D 12
Iraq	168,049	435,244	36,361,000	Baghdad	D 12
Ireland	27,133	70,273	4,714,000	Dublin	C 9
Israel	8,522	22,072	8,110,000	Jerusalem	D 11
Italy	116,346	301,336	61,375,000	Rome	C 10
Jamaica	4,244	10,991	2,828,000	Kingston	E 6
Japan	145,932	377,962	126,698,000	Tokyo	D 16
Jordan	34,495	89,342	6,969,000	Amman	D 11
Kazakhstan	1,052,090	2,724,900	17,716,000	Astana	C 13
Kenya	224,961	582,646	45,564,000	Nairobi	E 11
Kiribati	313	811	107,000	Tarawa	F 1
Korea, North	46,540	120,538	24,982,000	Pyongyang	C 16
Korea, South	38,572	99,900	50,673,000	Seoul	D 16
Kosovo	4,212	10,908	1,863,000	Priština	C 11
Kuwait	6,880	17,818	3,544,000	Kuwait	D 12
Kyrgyzstan	77,201	199,949	5,776,000	Bishkek	C 13
Laos	91,429	236,800	7,042,000	Vientiane	E 15
Latvia	24,928	64,562	2,015,000	Riga	C 11
Lebanon	4,036	10,452	4,603,000	Beirut	D 11
Lesotho	11,720	30,355	2,095,000	Maseru	G 11
Liberia	43,000	111,369	4,635,000	Monrovia	E 9
Libya	679,362	1,759,540	6,524,000	Tripoli	D 10
Liechtenstein†	62	160	38,000	Vaduz	C 10
Lithuania	25,212	65,300	2,976,000	Vilnius	C 11
Luxembourg	998	2,586	566,000	Luxembourg	C 10
Macedonia	9,928	25,713	2,111,000	Skopje	C 11
Madagascar	226,756	587,295	24,898,000	Antananarivo	F 12
Malawi	45,747	118,484	17,802,000	Lilongwe	F 11
Malaysia	127,724	330,803	30,976,000	Kuala Lumpur	E 15
Maldives	115	298	365,000	Male	E 13
Mali	478,841	1,240,192	16,872,000	Bamako	E 9
Malta	122	316	426,000	Valletta	D 10
Marshall Islands	70	181	56,000	Majuro	E 18
Mauritania	397,956	1,030,700	3,965,000	Nouakchott	D 9
Mauritius	788	2,040	1,310,000	Port Louis	G 12
Mexico	758,450	1,964,375	122,628,000	Mexico City	D 4
Micronesia, Federated States of	271	702	106,000	Palikir	E 17
Moldova	13,068	33,846	3,477,000	Chisinau	C 11
Monaco†	0.75	1.95	39,000	Monaco	C 10
Mongolia	603,909	1,564,116	2,968,000	Ulaanbaatar	C 15

Name	Area in mi²	Area in km²	Population*	Capital	Map key
Montenegro	5,333	13,812	622,000	Podgorica	C 10
Morocco	172,414	446,550	34,424,000	Rabat	D 9
Mozambique	308,642	799,380	26,355,000	Maputo	F 11
Myanmar	261,228	676,578	54,612,000	Naypyidaw	D 14
Namibia	318,772	825,615	2,435,000	Windhoek	G 10
Nauru	8	21	10,000	–	F 18
Nepal	56,827	147,181	28,637,000	Kathmandu	D 14
Netherlands	16,040	41,543	16,920,000	Amsterdam	C 10
New Zealand	103,362	267,707	4,586,000	Wellington	H 18
Nicaragua	50,337	130,373	6,299,000	Managua	E 5
Niger	489,191	1,267,000	19,212,000	Niamey	E 10
Nigeria	356,669	923,768	186,486,000	Abuja	E 10
Norway	148,718	385,178	5,203,000	Oslo	B 10
Oman	119,499	309,500	3,354,000	Muscat	E 12
Pakistan	341,311	883,992	195,999,000	Islamabad	D 13
Palau	177	459	21,000	Melekeok	E 16
Panama	29,119	75,417	4,018,000	Panama City	E 5
Papua New Guinea	178,704	462,840	7,799,000	Port Moresby	F 17
Paraguay	157,048	406,752	7,048,000	Asunción	G 7
Peru	496,225	1,285,216	31,371,000	Lima	F 6
Philippines	115,831	300,000	103,528,000	Manila	E 16
Poland	120,728	312,685	38,228,000	Warsaw	C 10
Portugal	34,397	89,089	10,103,000	Lisbon	D 9
Qatar	4,473	11,586	2,229,000	Doha	D 12
Romania	92,043	238,391	21,176,000	Bucharest	C 11
Russia	6,601,670	17,098,246	143,085,000	Moscow	C 13
Rwanda	10,169	26,338	12,772,000	Kigali	F 11
Saint Kitts and Nevis	101	261	56,000	Basseterre	E 6
Saint Lucia	238	616	185,000	Castries	E 6
Saint Vincent and the Grenadines	150	389	109,000	Kingstown	E 6
Samoa	1,097	2,840	194,000	Apia	F 1
San Marino†	24	61	33,000	San Marino	C 10
São Tomé and Príncipe	372	964	204,000	São Tomé	E 10
Saudi Arabia	830,000	2,149,690	30,459,000	Riyadh	D 12
Senegal	75,955	196,722	14,718,000	Dakar	E 9
Serbia	29,913	77,474	7,080,000	Belgrade	C 11
Seychelles	176	455	96,000	Victoria	F 12
Sierra Leone	27,699	71,740	6,446,000	Freetown	E 9
Singapore	276	716	5,666,000	Singapore	E 15
Slovakia	18,933	49,036	5,465,000	Bratislava	C 11

INDEPENDENT COUNTRIES OF THE WORLD, CONTINUED

Name	Area in mi²	Area in km²	Population*	Capital	Map key
Slovenia	7,827	20,273	2,078,000	Ljubljana	C 10
Solomon Islands	11,157	28,896	623,000	Honiara	F 18
Somalia	246,201	637,657	11,099,000	Mogadishu	E 12
South Africa	471,359	1,220,813	54,021,000	Cape Town; Pretoria; Bloemfontein	G 11
South Sudan	248,777	644,329	12,714,000	Juba	E 11
Spain	195,341	505,930	47,549,000	Madrid	C 9
Sri Lanka	25,332	65,610	20,985,000	Sri Jayewardenepura Kotte	E 14
Sudan	718,723	1,861,484	40,418,000	Khartoum	E 11
Suriname	63,251	163,820	556,000	Paramaribo	E 7
Swaziland	6,704	17,363	1,339,000	Mbabane	G 11
Sweden	173,860	450,295	9,855,000	Stockholm	B 10
Switzerland	15,940	41,285	8,304,000	Bern	C 10
Syria	71,498	185,180	23,135,000	Damascus	D 11
Taiwan‡	13,902	36,006	23,512,000	Taipei	D 16
Tajikistan	54,810	141,958	8,581,000	Dushanbe	D 13
Tanzania	365,756	947,303	53,851,000	Dodoma	F 11
Thailand	198,117	513,120	68,148,000	Bangkok	E 15
Togo	21,925	56,785	7,356,000	Lomé	E 10
Tonga	288	747	106,000	Nuku'alofa	F 1
Trinidad and Tobago	1,981	5,130	1,352,000	Port-of-Spain	E 6
Tunisia	63,170	163,610	11,330,000	Tunis	D 10
Turkey	302,535	783,562	78,966,000	Ankara	D 11
Turkmenistan	188,456	488,100	5,442,000	Ashgabat	D 12
Tuvalu	10	26	11,000	Funafuti	F 1
Uganda	93,263	241,551	39,253,000	Kampala	E 11
Ukraine	233,032	603,550	44,698,000	Kiev	C 11
United Arab Emirates	32,278	83,600	9,880,000	Abu Dhabi	D 12
United Kingdom	93,628	242,495	64,298,000	London	C 9
United States	3,618,233	9,371,180	323,873,000	Washington, D.C.	C 4
Uruguay	68,037	176,215	3,442,000	Montevideo	G 7
Uzbekistan	172,742	447,400	30,300,000	Tashkent	D 13
Vanuatu	4,707	12,190	282,000	Port-Vila	F 18
Vatican City†	0.17	0.44	1,000	–	C 10
Venezuela	352,145	912,050	31,107,000	Caracas	E 6
Vietnam	127,783	330,957	92,523,000	Hanoi	E 15
Yemen	203,850	527,968	27,274,000	Sanaa	E 12
Zambia	290,585	752,612	15,729,000	Lusaka	F 11
Zimbabwe	150,872	390,757	15,377,000	Harare	G 11

50 LARGEST URBAN CENTERS IN THE WORLD

Rank	Urban center*	Population
1.	Tokyo, Japan	38,065,000
2.	Delhi, India	26,385,000
3.	Shanghai, China	24,376,000
4.	Mumbai, India	21,387,000
5.	São Paulo, Brazil	21,272,000
6.	Mexico City, Mexico	21,169,000
7.	Beijing, China	21,084,000
8.	Osaka, Japan	20,294,000
9.	Cairo, Egypt	19,115,000
10.	New York City, United States	18,633,000
11.	Dhaka, Bangladesh	18,218,000
12.	Karachi, Pakistan	17,103,000
13.	Buenos Aires, Argentina	15,320,000
14.	Kolkata, India	15,032,000
15.	Istanbul, Turkey	14,345,000
16.	Chongqing, China	13,687,000
17.	Lagos, Nigeria	13,671,000
18.	Manila, Philippines	13,138,000
19.	Rio de Janeiro, Brazil	12,986,000
20.	Guangzhou, China	12,950,000
21.	Los Angeles, United States	12,338,000
22.	Moscow, Russia	12,227,000
23.	Kinshasa, Dem. Rep. of Congo	12,045,000
24.	Tianjin, China	11,510,000
25.	Paris, France	10,927,000
26.	Shenzhen, China	10,854,000
27.	Jakarta, Indonesia	10,509,000
28.	London, United Kingdom	10,418,000
29.	Bengaluru, India	10,410,000
30.	Chennai, India	10,144,000
31.	Lima, Peru	10,062,000
32.	Bogotá, Colombia	9,943,000
33.	Seoul, South Korea	9,783,000
34.	Johannesburg, South Africa	9,582,000
35.	Bangkok, Thailand	9,436,000
36.	Nagoya, Japan	9,423,000
37.	Hyderabad, India	9,192,000
38.	Lahore, Pakistan	8,986,000
39.	Chicago, United States	8,770,000
40.	Tehran, Iran	8,525,000
41.	Wuhan, China	7,995,000
42.	Chengdu, China	7,780,000
43.	Nanjing, China	7,575,000
44.	Ahmadabad, India	7,549,000
45.	Dongguan, China	7,493,000
46.	Ho Chi Minh City, Vietnam	7,487,000
47.	Hong Kong, China	7,360,000
48.	Foshan, China	7,107,000
49.	Taipei, Taiwan	7,047,000
50.	Kuala Lumpur, Malaysia	7,025,000

*The United Nations defines an urban center as a city surrounded by a continuous built-up area having a high population density.

Source: 2016 estimates based on data from the United Nations and other official government sources.

2016 CANADIAN POPULATION ESTIMATES

PROVINCE AND TERRITORY POPULATIONS

Alberta	4,272,000
British Columbia	4,729,900
Manitoba	1,306,300
New Brunswick	753,100
Newfoundland and Labrador	526,700
Northwest Territories	44,200
Nova Scotia	943,900
Nunavut	37,700
Ontario	13,902,400
Prince Edward Island	146,700
Quebec	8,313,200
Saskatchewan	1,144,900
Yukon	37,800
Canada	36,158,800

CITY AND METROPOLITAN AREA POPULATIONS

	Metropolitan area	City
Toronto, Ont.	6,213,900	2,734,000
Montreal, Que.	4,099,200	1,679,100
Vancouver, B.C.	2,538,000	630,600
Calgary, Alta.	1,483,300	1,222,000
Edmonton, Alta.	1,404,300	907,300
Ottawa-Gatineau, Ont.-Que.	1,346,900	
Ottawa, Ont.		963,700
Gatineau, Que.		291,800
Quebec, Que.	812,900	544,000
Winnipeg, Man.	805,300	695,800
Hamilton, Ont.	778,500	535,900
Kitchener-Cambridge-Waterloo, Ont.	515,500	
Kitchener, Ont.		235,100
Cambridge, Ont.		133,700
Waterloo, Ont.		100,200
London, Ont.	510,300	380,600
Halifax, N.S.	421,800	408,600
St. Catharines-Niagara, Ont.	409,700	
St. Catharines, Ont.		130,900
Niagara Falls, Ont.		84,000
Oshawa, Ont.	394,100	158,300
Victoria, B.C.	369,200	82,000
Windsor, Ont.	337,500	205,400
Saskatoon, Sask.	312,300	244,700
Regina, Sask.	246,700	208,500
St. John's, Nfld. Lab.	217,000	112,100
Sherbrooke, Que.	216,700	162,500
Barrie, Ont.	205,100	143,600
Kelowna, B.C.	202,300	129,000
Abbotsford-Mission, B.C.	186,100	
Abbotsford, B.C.		143,700
Mission, B.C.		38,400
Kingston, Ont.	171,300	130,000
Greater Sudbury/Grand Sudbury, Ont.	164,400	162,800
Saguenay, Que.	159,900	145,800
Trois-Rivières, Que.	157,100	136,800
Guelph, Ont.	154,800	129,000
Moncton, N.B.	149,800	74,500
Brantford, Ont.	145,000	97,200
Saint John, N.B.	126,400	72,100
Thunder Bay, Ont.	124,500	107,400
Peterborough, Ont.	122,400	82,200

Source: World Book estimates based on data from Statistics Canada.

2016 UNITED STATES POPULATION ESTIMATES

50 LARGEST METROPOLITAN AREAS

Rank	Metropolitan area†	Population*
1.	New York–Newark–Jersey City, NY-NJ-PA	20,277,271
2.	Los Angeles–Long Beach–Anaheim, CA	13,428,584
3.	Chicago–Naperville–Elgin, IL-IN-WI	9,553,867
4.	Dallas–Fort Worth–Arlington, TX	7,248,782
5.	Houston–The Woodlands–Sugar Land, TX	6,827,366
6.	Washington–Arlington–Alexandria, DC-VA-MD-WV	6,165,795
7.	Miami–Fort Lauderdale–West Palm Beach, FL	6,089,773
8.	Philadelphia–Camden–Wilmington, PA-NJ-DE-MD	6,086,728
9.	Atlanta–Sandy Springs–Roswell, GA	5,807,604
10.	Boston–Cambridge–Newton, MA-NH	4,812,918
11.	San Francisco–Oakland–Hayward, CA	4,721,387
12.	Phoenix–Mesa–Scottsdale, AZ	4,664,886
13.	Riverside–San Bernardino–Ontario, CA	4,541,211
14.	Detroit–Warren–Dearborn, MI	4,304,527
15.	Seattle–Tacoma–Bellevue, WA	3,795,902
16.	Minneapolis–St. Paul–Bloomington, MN-WI	3,557,049
17.	San Diego–Carlsbad, CA	3,338,352
18.	Tampa–St. Petersburg–Clearwater, FL	3,027,894
19.	Denver–Aurora–Lakewood, CO	2,873,869
20.	St. Louis, MO-IL	2,816,945
21.	Baltimore–Columbia–Towson, MD	2,809,445
22.	Charlotte–Concord–Gastonia, NC-SC	2,473,149
23.	Orlando–Kissimmee–Sanford, FL	2,447,406
24.	San Antonio–New Braunfels, TX	2,436,586
25.	Portland–Vancouver–Hillsboro, OR-WA	2,427,808
26.	Pittsburgh, PA	2,348,824
27.	Sacramento–Roseville–Arden-Arcade, CA	2,303,195
28.	Cincinnati, OH-KY-IN	2,167,737
29.	Las Vegas–Henderson–Paradise, NV	2,159,830
30.	Kansas City, MO-KS	2,103,871
31.	Austin–Round Rock, TX	2,062,667
32.	Cleveland–Elyria, OH	2,058,792
33.	Columbus, OH	2,047,856
34.	Indianapolis–Carmel–Anderson, IN	2,006,910
35.	San Jose–Sunnyvale–Santa Clara, CA	2,001,481
36.	Nashville-Davidson–Murfreesboro–Franklin, TN	1,867,446
37.	Virginia Beach–Norfolk–Newport News, VA-NC	1,734,071
38.	Providence–Warwick, RI-MA	1,617,105
39.	Milwaukee–Waukesha–West Allis, WI	1,578,024
40.	Jacksonville, FL	1,477,102
41.	Oklahoma City, OK	1,377,688
42.	Memphis, TN-MS-AR	1,345,419
43.	Raleigh, NC	1,304,403
44.	Louisville/Jefferson County, KY-IN	1,286,166
45.	Richmond, VA	1,283,999
46.	New Orleans–Metairie, LA	1,273,762
47.	Hartford–West Hartford–East Hartford, CT	1,209,517
48.	Salt Lake City, UT	1,184,799
49.	Birmingham–Hoover, AL	1,148,981
50.	Buffalo–Cheektowaga–Niagara Falls, NY	1,134,841

50 LARGEST CITIES

Rank	City	Population
1.	New York, NY	8,608,359
2.	Los Angeles, CA	4,007,448
3.	Chicago, IL	2,719,702
4.	Houston, TX	2,337,541
5.	Phoenix, AZ	1,588,647
6.	Philadelphia, PA	1,572,857
7.	San Antonio, TX	1,499,422
8.	San Diego, CA	1,412,601
9.	Dallas, TX	1,320,546
10.	San Jose, CA	1,038,713
11.	Austin, TX	955,706
12.	Jacksonville, FL	880,259
13.	San Francisco, CA	877,212
14.	Columbus, OH	863,263
15.	Indianapolis, IN	858,049
16.	Fort Worth, TX	853,577
17.	Charlotte, NC	844,618
18.	Seattle, WA	700,543
19.	Denver, CO	700,510
20.	Washington, DC	683,968
21.	El Paso, TX	682,843
22.	Boston, MA	675,033
23.	Detroit, MI	670,818
24.	Nashville, TN	664,589
25.	Memphis, TN	654,505
26.	Portland, OR	643,842
27.	Oklahoma City, OK	641,726
28.	Las Vegas, NV	634,217
29.	Baltimore, MD	621,167
30.	Louisville, KY	617,964
31.	Milwaukee, WI	600,197
32.	Albuquerque, NM	560,246
33.	Tucson, AZ	533,414
34.	Fresno, CA	525,267
35.	Sacramento, CA	496,211
36.	Kansas City, MO	479,512
37.	Mesa, AZ	478,471
38.	Long Beach, CA	475,956
39.	Atlanta, GA	471,931
40.	Colorado Springs, CO	464,038
41.	Raleigh, NC	461,236
42.	Virginia Beach, VA	454,572
43.	Miami, FL	451,255
44.	Omaha, NE	445,403
45.	Oakland, CA	425,117
46.	Minneapolis, MN	416,306
47.	Tulsa, OK	405,914
48.	New Orleans, LA	395,116
49.	Arlington, TX	392,389
50.	Wichita, KS	391,246

†The U.S. Census Bureau defines a metropolitan area as a large population nucleus with adjacent communities having a high degree of economic and social integration.

*2015 World Book estimates based on data from the U.S. Census Bureau.

SPORTS

The famous statue *Christ the Redeemer* stands atop Mount Corcovado above Rio de Janeiro, Brazil, site of the 2016 Summer Olympic Games.

see page 226 for
A CLOSER
LOOK

ROOKIE TAKES 100TH INDIANAPOLIS 500

On May 29, 2016, Alexander Rossi, a 24-year old rookie driver from California, pushed his race car to the limit in the waning laps of the 100th running of the Indianapolis 500. As other contenders took late refueling pit stops—including Colombian Carlos Muñoz, who was leading with three laps to go—Rossi took a chance and kept going. His fuel gauge was sitting on *E*—a pins-and-needles moment of fearful exhilaration for any driver—but this was the Indianapolis 500, the premier event of the Indy Racing League (IRL) and one of the world's most famous and prestigious auto races. Rossi, who began the race in the 11th position out of 33, saw his only chance was to literally finish on fumes—and he did. His car conked out as he crossed the finish line 4.5 seconds ahead of Munoz

Alexander Rossi's yellow-and-blue Honda (98) leads the pack during the Indianapolis 500 on May 29, 2016.

to win the race. "I'm out of fuel, guys," Rossi radioed his crew after taking the checkered flag. A topping up of fuel gave his car the boost it needed to make the celebration in the victory lane.

The Indianapolis 500 (or *Indy 500*) takes place on the 2 ½-mile (4.02-kilometer) oval track at the Indianapolis Motor Speedway in Speedway, Indiana. The first driver to complete 200 laps around the track—a distance of 500 miles (805 kilometers)—wins the race. The first Indy 500 took place in 1911, but racing was suspended for two years during World War I (1914-1918) and four more years during World War II (1939-1945).

NEW YORK'S LITTLE LEAGUE CHAMPS

On Aug. 28, 2016, an all-star baseball team from Maine-Endwell, New York, won the Little League World Series by defeating a team from Seoul, South Korea, 2-1. The Little League World Series is a competition played each year in South Williamsport, Pennsylvania, among kids aged 11 to 13. The tournament, first played in 1947, includes 16 Little League teams from the United States and other nations. Little League Baseball is the world's largest organized youth-sports program with nearly 180,000 teams. Endwell's Little League title was the first for a U.S. team since 2011, and the first for a New York team since Staten Island won in 1964.

Pitching and defense dominated the title game at South Williamsport's Howard J. Lamade Stadium. Endwell's Ryan Harlost and Seoul's Junho Jeong mowed down hitters, and both teams made sparkling defensive plays to help keep the game scoreless through three innings. New York's first hits came in the decisive fourth as the team pushed two runs across on three singles and a passed ball. South Korea's Yoomin Lee homered in the fifth, narrowing the score to 2-1. The Seoul Little Leaguers kept the pressure on in the sixth and final frame, putting two runners aboard with two outs. Harlost fanned young Minho Choi to end the game, however, and Endwell hats and gloves flew into the air before a miniature team pile formed near home plate. A raucous and happy home crowd cheered the New York champions, who gathered with the gracious South Koreans for a group jog and wave around the ball field. U.S. President Barack Obama took a few minutes from his busy schedule to place a congratulatory phone call to the champs after the game.

The Seoul all-stars rolled through the international bracket of the tournament, downing a tough Panama team 7-2 to advance to the World Series title game. The undefeated Endwell ball club won the U.S. championship 4-2 over the all-stars of Goodlettsville, Tennessee. The tournament's 32 games drew a total of nearly 500,000 fans.

MAJOR LEAGUE BASEBALL

World Series. The Chicago Cubs ended the most storied championship drought in the history of professional sports on Nov. 2, 2016, winning their first Major League Baseball (MLB) World Series title in 108 years. The Cubs beat the Cleveland Indians 8-7 in a tense and exhausting Game 7 that carried into the 10th inning.

Indians ace Corey Kluber dominated the Cubs in Game 1 of the series, a 6-0 shutout in Cleveland on October 25. The Cubs struck back in Game 2, also in Cleveland, on October 26, winning 5-1 behind 5 1/3 shutout innings by Cubs starter Jake Arrieta. Chicago slugger Kyle Schwarber drove in two runs and reached base three times. Schwarber got his first hits of the year in the series, having battled back from a regular season-ending knee injury on April 7. The series then moved to Chicago for the first World Series games played at the Cubs' home Wrigley Field since 1945. Cleveland won 1-0 on October 28 and 7-2 on October 29, pushing the Cubs to the brink of elimination. The Cubs won 3-2 in Chicago on October 30 and routed the Indians 9-3 in Cleveland on November 1 to force a Game 7.

Leading off Game 7 in Cleveland on November 2, Chicago outfielder Dexter Fowler started the scoring by hitting a home run off Indians ace Corey Kluber. The Cubs built their lead to 6-3 by the 8th inning, when Cleveland tied it with a 3-run rally. The scoring was capped by a dramatic 2-run blast by Indians outfielder Rajai Davis off Cubs flamethrowing reliever Aroldis Chapman. Chapman, Chicago's usual closer, appeared spent, having pitched multiple innings in the previous two games. Following a short rain delay after the 9th

Chicago Cubs players celebrate their Game 7 victory over the Cleveland Indians to win the World Series on Nov. 2, 2016. It was the first World Series title for the Cubs since 1908.

inning, the Cubs scored twice on hits by 2016 World Series Most Valuable Player Ben Zobrist and catcher Miguel Montero. In a tense bottom of the 10th, the Indians pushed a run across and were threatening to score again, but Cubs star third baseman Kris Bryant made a tough play on an infield chopper to record the last out. The Cubs players then erupted into a joyous team pile around the pitcher's mound, celebrating the long-awaited and hard-fought championship.

Cubs catcher David Ross, who was playing his last MLB game before retirement, homered in the 6th inning of Game 7. At age 39, Ross became the oldest player ever to homer in a World Series Game 7.

With the victory, the Cubs became the first team to battle back from a 3-games-to-1 World Series deficit since the Kansas City Royals did so in 1985. The Cubs were the first team to pull off the feat on the road since the 1979 Pittsburgh Pirates won the last two games of the World Series against the Orioles in Baltimore, Maryland. It was the Cubs first championship since defeating the Detroit Tigers in the series in 1908. The Cubs last World Series appearance (which they lost to the Tigers) came in 1945.

For Cleveland, the gut-wrenching near miss in the World Series carried a bitter reminder. The Indians last chance at the title came in 1997, when they also lost Game 7 of the World Series in extra innings, that time to the Florida Marlins.

Playoffs. The Cubs reached the World Series by beating the Los Angeles Dodgers four games to two in the National League Championship Series (NLCS). In the deciding Game 6, the Cubs faced Dodgers ace Clayton Kershaw, who had blanked them in Game 2 of the series. Cubs starter Kyle Hendricks and Aroldis Chapman combined for a shutout, winning 5-0. Series standouts included pitcher Jon Lester, both of whose starts the Cubs won, and infielder Javier Baez. Baez hit .318 with four doubles and 5 RBI's in the series. He also stole two bases and dazzled spectators with his agile defensive play.

The Cubs had reached the NLCS by defeating the San Francisco Giants 3 games to 1 in the NL Division Series. The Dodgers entered the championship series having bested the Washington Nationals 3 games to 2. The NL wild card game offered an epic pitching matchup, pitting ace Madison Bumgarner of the San Francisco Giants against New York Mets' fireballer Noah Syndergaard. Bumgarner pitched a complete game shutout. Syndergaard threw 7 shutout innings, but the Giants finally broke through against Mets reliever Jeurys Familia, winning 3-0 in New York on October 5.

In the American League Championship Series (ALCS), the Indians beat the Toronto Blue Jays 4 games to 1. In the decisive game, played in Toronto on October 19, rookie pitcher Ryan Merritt took the mound for Cleveland. Merritt, in only his second career MLB start, shut out the heavy-hitting Jays for 4 1/3 innings before handing the ball to Cleveland's vaunted bullpen. Indians slugger Mike Napoli hit a run-scoring double in the first. Outfielder Coco Crisp and first baseman Carlos Santana notched solo home runs in the 3-0 Indians victory.

The Indians swept the Boston Red Sox in the AL Division Series. The Blue Jays swept the Texas Rangers in their division series. In the wild card game, the Blue Jays and Baltimore Orioles carried a 2-2 tie into the 11th inning, when Jays slugger Edwin Encarnación blasted a walk-off three-run homer. Toronto won 5-2 at home on October 4.

Regular season. The Cubs finished the regular season with the best record in baseball, taking the NL Central at 103-58. It was the club's best finish since 1910. The Dodgers won their fourth straight NL West title at 91-71. The Nationals, at 95-67, took the NL East for the third time in five years. Washington featured a strong starting rotation anchored by 20-game winner Max Scherzer. The Giants had the best record in the majors at the All-Star break. But they struggled in the second half, limping into a wild card spot at 87-75. The Mets, whose dominant rotation was plagued by injuries, took the other wild card slot, also at 87-75. The Mets had recovered from a dismal slump that saw them hit 2 games under .500 on Aug. 19. The St. Louis Cardinals fell just short of the wild card slot at 86-76, missing the playoffs for the first time in six years.

The Rangers finished with the best record in the American League, taking the West at 95-67. The Indians took the Central Division for the first time since 2007. Though plagued by injuries, the Indians rode ace Corey Kluber, a league-leading stolen base percentage, and a surprisingly effective bullpen to a 94-67 finish. Their season included a 14-game winning streak, starting in mid-June, a record for the franchise and the longest in the AL since 2002. The Boston Red Sox surged into the playoffs with a 93-69 record, rattling off an 11-game win streak in the season's final weeks. The Orioles and Blue Jays slugged their way into the AL wild card slots, both finishing 89-73. The Orioles led the majors in home runs with 253; the Jays were next among postseason contenders at 221. The reigning MLB champion Kansas City Royals failed to make the postseason with an 81-81 record.

FINAL STANDINGS IN MAJOR LEAGUE BASEBALL

AMERICAN LEAGUE

American League champions—
Cleveland Indians
(defeated Toronto Blue Jays, 4 games to 1)

NATIONAL LEAGUE

National League champions—
Chicago Cubs
(defeated Los Angeles Dodgers, 4 games to 2)

World Series champions—
Chicago Cubs
(defeated Cleveland Indians, 4 games to 3)

Eastern Division

	W.	L.	Pct.	G.B.
Boston Red Sox	93	69	.574	—
Baltimore Orioles*	89	73	.549	4
Toronto Blue Jays*	89	73	.549	4
New York Yankees	84	78	.519	9
Tampa Bay Rays	68	94	.420	25

Central Division

	W.	L.	Pct.	G.B.
Cleveland Indians	94	67	.584	—
Detroit Tigers	86	75	.534	8
Kansas City Royals	81	81	.500	13.5
Chicago White Sox	78	84	.481	16.5
Minnesota Twins	59	103	.364	35.5

Western Division

	W.	L.	Pct.	G.B.
Texas Rangers	95	67	.586	—
Seattle Mariners	86	76	.531	9
Houston Astros	84	78	.519	11
Los Angeles Angels	74	88	.457	21
Oakland Athletics	69	93	.426	26

Eastern Division

	W.	L.	Pct.	G.B.
Washington Nationals	95	67	.586	—
New York Mets*	87	75	.537	8
Miami Marlins	79	82	.491	15.5
Philadelphia Phillies	71	91	.438	24
Atlanta Braves	68	93	.422	26.5

Central Division

	W.	L.	Pct.	G.B.
Chicago Cubs	103	58	.640	—
St. Louis Cardinals	86	76	.531	17.5
Pittsburgh Pirates	78	83	.484	25
Milwaukee Brewers	73	89	.451	30.5
Cincinnati Reds	68	94	.420	35.5

Western Division

	W.	L.	Pct.	G.B.
Los Angeles Dodgers	91	71	.562	—
San Francisco Giants*	87	75	.537	4
Colorado Rockies	75	87	.463	16
Arizona Diamondbacks	69	93	.426	22
San Diego Padres	68	94	.420	23

Offensive leaders

Batting average	Jose Altuve, Houston	.338
Home runs	Mark Trumbo, Baltimore	47
Runs batted in	Edwin Encarnacion, Tor.	127
	David Ortiz, Boston	
Runs scored	Mike Trout, Los Angeles	123
Hits	Jose Altuve, Houston	216
Stolen bases	Rajai Davis, Cleveland	43
OPS (On-base plus slugging)	David Ortiz, Boston	1.021

Offensive leaders

Batting average	D. J. LeMahieu, Colorado	.348
Home runs	Nolan Arenado, Colorado	41
	Chris Carter, Milwaukee	
Runs batted in	Nolan Arenado, Colorado	133
Runs scored	Kris Bryant, Chicago	121
Hits	Jean Segura, Arizona	203
Stolen bases	Jonathan Villar, Milwaukee	62
OPS (On-base plus slugging)	Daniel Murphy, Washington	.985
	Joey Votto, Cincinnati	

Leading pitchers

Wins	Rick Porcello, Boston	22
ERA	Aaron Sanchez, Toronto	3.00
Strikeouts	Justin Verlander, Detroit	254
Saves	Zach Britton, Baltimore	47

Leading pitchers

Wins	Max Scherzer, Washington	20
ERA	Kyle Hendricks, Chicago	2.13
Strikeouts	Max Scherzer, Washington	284
Saves	Jeurys Familia, New York	51

*Qualified for wild-card playoff spot.

AL ALL-STARS TOP NL

On July 12, 2016, the powerful All-Star bats of the American League (AL) triumphed over the National League (NL) 4-2 at the Major League Baseball (MLB) All-Star Game at PETCO Park in San Diego, California. The annual "Midsummer Classic" features the best MLB players and determines which league will have home field advantage in that year's World Series.

The NL jumped to a 1-0 lead in the first inning as Chicago Cubs star Kris Bryant homered off the AL starting pitcher and crosstown rival, Chris Sale of the Chicago White Sox. The AL quickly rallied in the second, however, as Kansas City Royals teammates Eric Hosmer and Salvador Perez each hit home runs off NL starter Johnny Cueto of the San Francisco Giants for a 3-1 lead. Hosmer drilled a run-scoring single in the third inning, as well, and the NL added a run in the fourth, but the pitching took over after that and no more All-Stars crossed home plate. The only hold-your-breath moment came in the eighth when the NL loaded the bases with two outs. Houston Astros closer Will Harris fanned St. Louis Cardinals rookie Aledmys Diaz on a 3-2 pitch to end the NL threat. Hosmer, playing in his first Midsummer Classic, was named the All-Star Game Most Valuable Player.

Much fanfare surrounded the final All-Star appearance by Boston Red Sox slugger David Ortiz, who retired at season's end. Ortiz had a superb season, capping a career that began in 1997 with the Minnesota Twins but took off once he reached Boston in 2003. Ortiz finished his career with over 500 home runs and 1,700 runs batted in–stats that win most players a place in the Hall of Fame. Ortiz started the All-Star Game at designated hitter and left for a pinch-runner in the third inning after drawing a walk.

In other All-Star festivities, Miami Marlins slugger Giancarlo Stanton pounded a record 61 home runs to win the Home Run Derby. In the All-Star Futures Game, the World Team downed the United States side 11-3 in a match-up of the best of Minor League Baseball.

The first MLB All-Star Game was played on July 6, 1933, at Comiskey Park on Chicago's south side. That first game, which featured legendary players Lou Gehrig, Jimmie Foxx, Babe Ruth, and other Hall of Famers, was expected to be a one-time event and was thus called the "Game of the Century." The AL beat the NL 4-2 in that game, too.

ICHIRO 3000

On Aug. 7, 2016, Miami Marlins outfielder Ichiro Suzuki collected his 3,000th career hit in Major League Baseball (MLB). Ichiro, as he is widely called, reached the milestone with a sky-high triple off the right field wall in the 7th inning of a game against the Colorado Rockies at Coors Field in Denver. Rockies fans—despite their team's 8-6 deficit at the time—gave Ichiro a standing ovation as the 42-year-old outfielder was mobbed at third base by his Marlins teammates. Ichiro politely doffed his helmet to the Coors Field faithful before resuming the game and scoring the Marlins' 9th run. Ichiro—just the 30th player in

Miami Marlins outfielder Ichiro Suzuki watches his 3,000th career hit soar toward the right field wall during a game against the Colorado Rockies at Denver's Coors Field on Aug. 7, 2016.

MLB history to gather 3,000 hits—is a sure-fire bet to join most of the other "3,000-hit club" members in the National Baseball Hall of Fame, including Paul Molitor, the only other player to triple for his 3,000th hit. The month before, in June 2016, Ichiro's 2,979th MLB hit gave him a combined career hit total of 4,257 (including 1,278 over 9 professional seasons in Japan), one more than Pete Rose's career MLB hit record of 4,256.

TEARS OF JOY IN COOPERSTOWN

On July 24, 2016, Ken Griffey, Jr., and Mike Piazza became the newest members of the National Baseball Hall of Fame in Cooperstown, New York. At a ceremony attended by previous Hall of Fame members and some 50,000 fans, both players paid tribute to supportive parents and—with baseball-sized lumps in their throats—they each broke down in tears. Griffey, a graceful outfielder with a legendary swing, dedicated his inauguration "to my dad, who taught me how to play this game and to my mom, the strongest woman I know." Piazza, one of the game's all-time great catchers, was grateful for the freedom and opportunity to play baseball: "Dad always dreamed of playing in the major leagues. He could not follow that dream because of the realities of life. My father's faith in me, often greater than my own, is the single most important factor of me being inducted into this Hall of Fame." Griffey is the highest draft pick—number 1 overall in 1987—ever to enter the Hall of Fame. Conversely, Piazza was drafted in 1988 in the 62nd round at number 1,390—the lowest draft pick to end up in Cooperstown. The Major League Baseball (MLB) draft was first held in 1965 and is now limited to 40 rounds.

Griffey played 22 seasons in his MLB career, split mainly between the Seattle Mariners and Cincinnati Reds. He hit 630 home runs (sixth all time), drove in 1,836 runs, made 13 All-Star teams, won 10 Gold Gloves in center field, and was the 1997 American League Most Valuable Player. Griffey is the first Mariners player enshrined in Cooperstown. In Hall of Fame voting (cast by members of the Baseball Writers' Association of America), he was named on 437 of 440 ballots. His vote percentage of 99.3 was the highest since Hall of Fame voting began in 1936.

Piazza played 16 years in the big leagues, primarily as a catcher. He spent most of his career with the Los Angeles Dodgers and the New York Mets. Piazza retired with a .308 career batting average and 427 home runs, including an MLB record 396 as a catcher. He was selected to 12 All-Star teams. He is the second Mets player (after Tom Seaver) to enter the Hall of Fame. Piazza received 83 percent of the Hall of Fame vote. No other players reached the minimum of 75 percent.

LAST TIME AROUND THE BASES

Retirements in 2016. Three-time AL MVP and 14-time All-Star Álex Rodríguez played his final game on August 12. Rodríguez's retirement ended a stellar-but-tainted (by performance-enhancing drugs) 22-year career in which he hit 696 home runs with 2,086 RBI's with the Mariners, Rangers, and Yankees. Ten-time All-Star designated hitter David Ortiz called it quits after 20 seasons with the Twins and Red Sox. Ortiz led Boston to World Series titles in 2004, 2007, and 2013. He finished with 2,472 hits, 541 home runs, and 1,768 RBI's. Three-time All-Star first baseman Mark Teixeira ended his 14-year career spent mostly with the Rangers and Yankees. He hit 409 home runs with 1,298 RBI's. Injuries forced the retirement of six-time All-Star first baseman Prince Fielder on July 18, 2016. Fielder hit 319 home runs with 1,028 RBI's over 12 seasons with the Brewers, Tigers, and Rangers.

Deaths in 2016. Third baseman Jim Davenport (1933-February 18); Miami Marlins pitcher José Fernández (1992-September 25); Joe Garagiola (see **p. 179**); outfielder/infielder Jim Hickman (1937-June 25); outfielder Monte Irvin (1919-January 11); infielder Dick McAuliffe (1939-May 13); pitcher Milt Pappas (1939-April 19); outfielder/infielder Tony Phillips (1959-February 17); pitcher Frank Sullivan (1930-January 19); outfielder Walt Williams (1943-January 23).

Legendary sportscaster Vin Scully waves to the crowd during his last home broadcast for the Los Angeles Dodgers on Sept. 24, 2016. The Hall of Famer retired after the 2016 season, his 67th with the team. Scully joined the Dodgers in 1950, when the team was still in Brooklyn, New York.

JOE GARAGIOLA 1926-2016

On March 23, 2016, former baseball player and broadcaster Joe Garagiola died at age 90 in Phoenix, Arizona. Garagiola, a catcher, played nine seasons in Major League Baseball (MLB) before embarking on a lengthy television career that landed him in the broadcasters wing of the National Baseball Hall of Fame. He also received MLB's Buck O'Neil Lifetime Achievement Award "for his lifelong dedication to enriching the game."

Joseph Henry Garagiola was born on Feb. 12, 1926, in St. Louis, Missouri. He grew up in "The Hill," an Italian-American neighborhood, across the street from lifelong friend and fellow MLB catcher Yogi Berra. In 1942, when he was just 16 years old, Garagiola signed a professional baseball contract with his hometown Cardinals. World War II interrupted his career in 1944, but he returned to pro baseball, making his big league debut for St. Louis on May 26, 1946.

Garagiola was a good defensive catcher, but his left-handed bat never found enough fastballs to make him an every-day starter. In 1951, Garagiola was traded to the Pittsburgh Pirates, where he put up the best numbers of his career—but still as a part-time player. Garagiola later played for the Chicago Cubs and briefly for the New York Giants. He retired as a player after the 1954 season.

In 1955, Garagiola began calling Cardinals games on KMOX radio. His broadcasting career took off in 1961, when he began doing nationally televised games on NBC. He remained with NBC for the next 30 years, working ballgames with such legendary partners as Curt Gowdy, Tony Kubek, and Vin Scully. In the late 1990's, Garagiola worked as a part-time commentator for the Arizona Diamondbacks, where his son, Joe Garagiola, Jr., served as general manager. Garagiola called his last game in 2012.

PROFESSIONAL BASKETBALL IN 2016

On June 19, 2016, the Cleveland Cavaliers brought their city its first major professional sports championship in 52 years, outlasting the Golden State Warriors 93-89 to win the National Basketball Association (NBA) Finals. Cleveland's thrilling victory completed the first-ever comeback from a 3-games-to-1 deficit in the best-of-7 NBA championship series. It was the first title for the Cavs, and the first major sports championship in Cleveland since the Browns topped the National Football League in 1964. The win was also sweet revenge for Cleveland against Golden State, who had downed the Cavaliers in the 2015 NBA Finals.

LeBron James, a native of Akron, Ohio, just south of Cleveland, led the way for the Cavaliers, earning the Finals Most Valuable Player (MVP) Award. James and teammates Kyrie Irving, Tristan Thompson, Kevin Love, and J. R. Smith overcame a flashy, often scintillating Warriors team that had passed and swished its way to a best-ever NBA season record of 73-9, surpassing the 72-10 mark set by the 1995-1996 Chicago Bulls. The Warriors built a 3-1 series lead despite the uneven play of two-time league MVP Stephen Curry and his backcourt mate Klay Thompson—standout guards nicknamed the "Splash Brothers" for their uncanny accuracy sinking long-range three-point shots. A year earlier, Warriors do-everything swingman Andre Iguodala contained James and the Cavaliers en route to his own Finals MVP Award. This year, however, no Warrior could match James's will to win as the Cavalier forward amassed a Game 7 "triple-double" with 27 points, 11 rebounds, and 11 assists.

In leading his team to the comeback win—the Cavs trailed 49-42 at halftime—James completed a storybook turnaround for his team, his reputation, and his own place in league history. The Cavaliers drafted "King James" straight out of high school in 2003. He led the team to a Finals appearance in 2007, but the Cavs couldn't get by the more broadly talented San Antonio Spurs.

Many championship-starved Cleveland fans burned their James jerseys in 2010 after he spurned the Cavs to seek titles with the Miami Heat. The Heat played in the next four consecutive Finals, winning titles in 2012 and 2013. Following the 2013-14 season, a sentimental James returned to Cleveland, where he joined young point guard Kyrie Irving and the embattled Kevin Love, a crafty rebounder who, despite a sweet shooting touch, had never led his prior Minnesota teams to a playoff appearance. "I came back for a reason," James said. "I came back to bring a championship to our city."

Cavs General Manager David Griffin fired Coach David Blatt on Jan. 22, 2016, despite the team's conference-best 30-11 record, and promoted Assistant Coach Tyronn Lue. Blatt, who won numerous championships coaching in Europe for 20-plus years, had been hired prior to the 2014 season to lead a rebuilding effort around Irving and top draft pick Andrew Wiggins. Blatt's role changed dramatically once the Cavs re-signed James and traded Wiggins to acquire Love. Though the star-laden team advanced to the 2015 Finals, the coach and the players failed to jell. Taking over at this season's midway point, Coach Lue, a former point guard shedding the "assistant" label, soothed team divisions while leading the team to a 27-14 finish. More importantly, he prepared his team for a long run in the NBA playoffs.

The dynamic Irving—a 2011 first overall draft pick—had something of a national coming-out party in the 2016 Finals' crucial Game 5, when he converted numerous spinning, off-balance baskets, making 17-of-24 shots en route to a 41-point performance. James matched Irving's point total and added 16 rebounds in the game, which proved a turning point in the series. Warriors hero/goat Draymond Green watched Game 5 from outside the arena while serving an automatic one-game suspension for his fourth flagrant foul of the playoffs. Green proved rusty in his return in Game 6, but he brought his team close to a second consecutive title with a 32-point, 15-rebound, 9-assist performance in the deciding Game 7.

As for the Warrior's backcourt duo of Curry and Thompson, the Splash Brothers showed flashes in the series, but overall both struggled against the Cavs dialed-up perimeter defense. Curry, having suffered ankle and knee sprains earlier in the playoffs, looked particularly out of sync, lagging his season averages in points, rebounds, assists, and steals.

Regular season. On April 13, 2016, the NBA regular season finished in dazzling style. In Oakland, California, the Golden State Warriors dismantled the Memphis Grizzlies 125-104. The home win was nothing new for Curry and the Warriors, who ended the year 39-2 at Oracle Arena. The Warriors played well on the road, too, disappointing other teams' fans 34 out of 41 times. Golden State finished 73-9, an all-time season best.

During the 2015-16 regular season, Curry sank a league-record 402 three-pointers, obliterating his year-old mark of 286. He won the

NATIONAL BASKETBALL ASSOCIATION STANDINGS

EASTERN CONFERENCE

Atlantic Division

	W.	L.	Pct.	G.B.
Toronto Raptors*	56	26	.683	—
Boston Celtics*	48	34	.585	8
New York Knicks	32	50	.390	24
Brooklyn Nets	21	61	.256	35
Philadelphia 76ers	10	72	.122	46

Central Division

	W.	L.	Pct.	G.B.
Cleveland Cavaliers*	57	25	.695	—
Indiana Pacers*	45	37	.549	12
Detroit Pistons*	44	38	.537	13
Chicago Bulls	42	40	.512	15
Milwaukee Bucks	33	49	.402	24

Southeast Division

	W.	L.	Pct.	G.B.
Miami Heat*	48	34	.585	—
Atlanta Hawks*	48	34	.585	—
Charlotte Bobcats*	48	34	.585	—
Washington Wizards	41	41	.500	7
Orlando Magic	35	47	.427	13

WESTERN CONFERENCE

Northwest Division

	W.	L.	Pct.	G.B.
Oklahoma City Thunder*	55	27	.671	—
Portland Trail Blazers*	44	38	.537	11
Utah Jazz	40	42	.488	15
Denver Nuggets	33	49	.402	22
Minnesota Timberwolves	29	53	.354	26

Pacific Division

	W.	L.	Pct.	G.B.
Golden State Warriors*	73	9	.890	—
Los Angeles Clippers*	53	29	.646	20
Sacramento Kings	33	49	.402	40
Phoenix Suns	23	59	.280	50
Los Angeles Lakers	17	65	.207	56

Southwest Division

	W.	L.	Pct.	G.B.
San Antonio Spurs*	67	15	.817	—
Dallas Mavericks*	42	40	.512	25
Memphis Grizzlies*	42	40	.512	25
Houston Rockets*	41	41	.500	26
New Orleans Pelicans	30	52	.366	37

NBA champions—Cleveland Cavaliers
(defeated Golden State Warriors, 4 games to 3)
*Made playoffs.

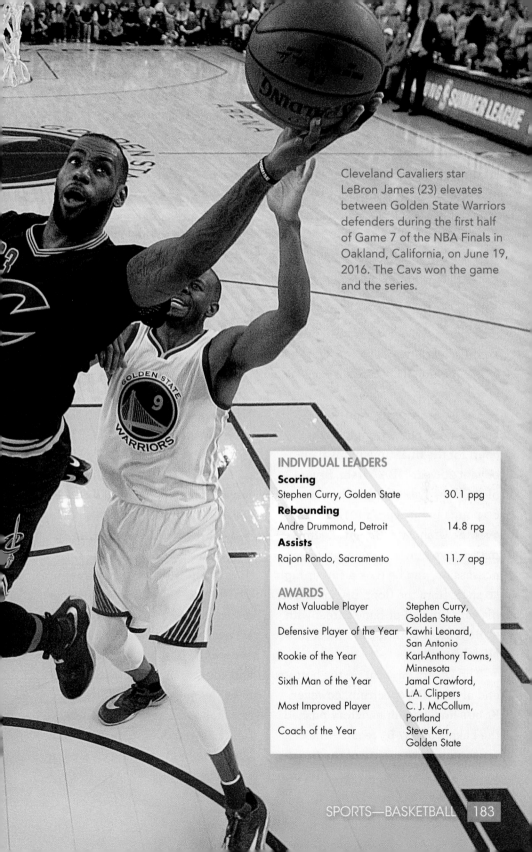

Cleveland Cavaliers star LeBron James (23) elevates between Golden State Warriors defenders during the first half of Game 7 of the NBA Finals in Oakland, California, on June 19, 2016. The Cavs won the game and the series.

INDIVIDUAL LEADERS

Scoring
Stephen Curry, Golden State   30.1 ppg

Rebounding
Andre Drummond, Detroit   14.8 rpg

Assists
Rajon Rondo, Sacramento   11.7 apg

AWARDS

Most Valuable Player	Stephen Curry, Golden State
Defensive Player of the Year	Kawhi Leonard, San Antonio
Rookie of the Year	Karl-Anthony Towns, Minnesota
Sixth Man of the Year	Jamal Crawford, L.A. Clippers
Most Improved Player	C. J. McCollum, Portland
Coach of the Year	Steve Kerr, Golden State

league scoring title with 30.2 points per game. Warriors Coach Steve Kerr missed the first half of the season following complications from back surgery. Assistant Coach Luke Walton filled in ably, guiding the team to a 24-0 start and a 39-4 record before Kerr's return. League scribes and broadcasters unanimously selected Curry for Most Valuable Player. Kawhi Leonard of the San Antonio Spurs finished second, just ahead of LeBron James in third. Top draft pick Karl-Anthony Towns delighted Minnesota Timberwolves fans all season, averaging 18.3 points and 10.5 rebounds per game en route to his unanimous choice for Rookie of the Year.

On April 13 in Los Angeles, Lakers star Kobe Bryant took the court for the final time in his flamboyant 20-year NBA career. Bryant pleased the Laker faithful by scoring 60 points in his team's 101-96 win over the Utah Jazz. Bryant's teammates gave him the ball nearly every possession, and he took a career-high 50 shots from the floor. Bryant ended his sure-fire hall-of-fame career with 33,643 career points, third-most in NBA history.

The Lakers brought up the bottom end of the NBA spectrum, however. Kobe's final headline victory pushed the Lakers to a 17-65 record—their worst season ever, but not the worst in the NBA this year. That distinction fell to the lowly Philadelphia 76ers, who finished 10-72. The 76ers fell one defeat shy of breaking their own record for losses in an 82-game NBA season. The 'Sixers went 9-73 in '73.

WNBA. The Women's National Basketball Association (WNBA) played its 20th season from May through October 2016. In the WNBA Finals, the No. 2 seed Los Angeles Sparks defeated the top seed and defending champion Minnesota Lynx in a thrilling and deciding game five, 77-76. Sparks swing forward Candace Parker was named Finals Most Valuable Player.

All-Star Game leaves Charlotte. On July 21, 2016, the NBA pulled the 2017 All-Star Game from Charlotte, North Carolina, in protest of the state's controversial anti-LGBT "bathroom bill" (see **LGBT / USA**, p. 126). NBA Commissioner Adam Silver had stated in April that the league would pull the popular game—which features the three-point and slam-dunk contests among three days of fan-friendly activities—from Charlotte if North Carolina lawmakers refused to change the law. "While we recognize that the NBA cannot choose the law in every city, state, and country in which we do business," league officials stated in July, "we do not believe we can successfully host our All-Star festivities in Charlotte in the climate created by the current law."

Big men move on. Fifteen-time All-Star Tim Duncan of the San Antonio Spurs announced his retirement in July following a 19-season career that featured five NBA titles and two MVP awards. 2014 MVP Kevin Durant left heavy hearts in Oklahoma City after the Thunder forward opted to sign with the already talented Warriors.

NATE THURMOND 1941-2016

NBA Hall of Famer Nate Thurmond died at age 74 on July 16, 2016, after a short battle with leukemia. Thurmond, a 6'11" center and power forward, played 14 seasons in the NBA, most of them with the San Francisco (later Golden State) Warriors. Thurmond hailed from Akron, Ohio, and played college ball at Bowling Green State University.

During his time with the Warriors (1963 to 1974), Thurmond made seven All-Star teams and was the runner-up MVP for the 1966-1967 season (behind NBA legend and former Warriors teammate, Wilt Chamberlain). The Warriors made it to the NBA Finals that year, losing to Chamberlain's Philadelphia 76ers.

In 1974, Thurmond moved to Chicago, where he recorded the NBA's first *quadruple-double* (double digits in four of five statistical categories in a single game) with 22 points, 14 rebounds, 13 assists, and 12 blocked shots in his Bulls debut against the Atlanta Hawks. He was traded to the Cleveland Cavaliers in 1975 and retired after the 1976-1977 season.

Thurmond averaged 15 points and 15 rebounds per game over his long career, reaching career totals of 14,437 points and 14,464 rebounds. He was inducted into the Basketball Hall of Fame in 1985 and was named one of the 50 Greatest Players in NBA History in 1996.

Thurmond, whose NBA career made him a Bay Area celebrity, ran the popular San Francisco restaurant Big Nate's BBQ from 1990 until 2010.

VILLANOVA WINS NCAA TITLE

On April 4, 2016, a three-point, buzzer-beating jump shot clinched victory for the Villanova University Wildcats over the University of North Carolina Tar Heels in the NCAA Men's Division I Basketball Tournament. In a thrilling game with multiple lead changes, North Carolina led 39-34 at halftime before Villanova roared back to take their largest lead of the game, 67-57, with 5:29 to go. The Tar Heels closed the margin to 3 points with 14 seconds remaining. A wild three-point jumper by North Carolina senior guard Marcus Paige then tied the game at 74-74.

With just 4.7 seconds left, the Wildcats inbounded the ball and scrambled down the court. Villanova star point guard Ryan Arcidiacono dumped the ball to forward Kris Jenkins, who squared up and drained a clean three-pointer as time expired for a 77-74 Villanova title victory. Arcidiacono, a senior, was named the tournament's Most Outstanding Player. It was the second national title for Villanova. The school's first came in 1985.

Villanova entered the tournament as the No. 2 seed in the South region. The Wildcats advanced to the championship game after a record-setting 95-51 pasting of Oklahoma in the semifinal. The Wildcats also knocked out No. 1 seed Kansas in the Elite Eight. North Carolina, the No. 1 seed out of the East, beat Notre Dame in the Elite Eight before blowing out Syracuse in their semifinal to advance to the championship.

This year's March Madness tournament lived up to its nickname, as low-seeded teams picked off the powerhouses at the tops of the brackets in early rounds. All four No. 1 seeds—Kansas, North Carolina, Oregon, and Virginia—cruised into the Elite Eight, but only North Carolina pushed on to the Final Four.

AUSTRALIAN SIMMONS TOPS NBA DRAFT

On June 23, 2016, the Philadelphia 76ers selected Louisiana State University (LSU) forward Ben Simmons as the number one overall pick of the National Basketball Association (NBA) draft in Brooklyn, New York. A 19-year-old out of Australia, Simmons decided to go pro after his first collegiate season, in which he averaged 19.2 points, 11.8 rebounds, and 4.8 assists per game for the LSU Tigers. Simmons earned Freshman of the Year honors in LSU's Southeastern Conference and was named to the National Collegiate Athletic Association (NCAA) Men's Basketball All-American first team.

Simmons was born in the Melbourne suburb of Fitzroy in 1996, the son of Dave Simmons, a former star of Australia's National Basketball League. Ben grew up playing basketball, rugby, and Australian Rules football. In 2013, Simmons moved to Florida, where he graduated from high school in 2015. Simmons is the third Australian to be chosen number one in the NBA draft, after Kyrie Irving (born in Melbourne but raised in New Jersey) in 2011 and Andrew Bogut (born and raised in Melbourne) in 2005. Simmons is the second top pick out of LSU—the first was Hall of Fame center Shaquille O'Neal.

The Los Angeles Lakers, fresh off the worst season in team history, chose Duke University forward Brandon Ingram with the second pick in the draft. With the third pick, the Boston Celtics chose forward Jaylen Brown out of the University of California. The Milwaukee Bucks rounded out the "down under" portion of the first round by choosing 7'1" power forward Thon Maker, a Sudanese-Australian out of Perth who has most recently lived in Canada, as the 10th overall pick.

COLLEGE BASKETBALL TOURNAMENT CHAMPIONS

NCAA	(Men)	Division I	Villanova
		Division II	Augustana (SD)
		Division III	St. Thomas (MN)
	(Women)	Division I	Connecticut
		Division II	Lubbock Christian (TX)
		Division III	Thomas More (KY)
NAIA	(Men)	Division I	Mid-America Christian (OK)
		Division II	Indiana Wesleyan
	(Women)	Division I	MidAmerica Nazarene (KS)
		Division II	Marian (IN)
NIT	(Men)		George Washington
	(Women)		South Dakota

UCONN CAN: CHAMPS AGAIN

On April 5, 2016, the University of Connecticut (UConn) Huskies women's basketball team defeated the Syracuse University Orange 82-51 to win an unprecedented fourth straight NCAA Women's Division I Basketball Tournament. It was the 11th NCAA title for UConn and their coach Geno Auriemma, who now has more titles than legendary UCLA men's coach John Wooden. The women's tournament has been played every year since 1982, and UConn first won it in 1995. This year's title game was played at Bankers Life Fieldhouse in Indianapolis, Indiana.

UConn's 31-point margin of victory looks large, but the game really wasn't even that close. During an apparent breather in the third quarter, UConn let Syracuse rattle off 16 points in a row. UConn was even playing short-handed. Their top 3-point shooter, freshman Katie Lou Samuelson, watched the game from the bench with an injured foot. The cakewalk win was more of the same for UConn, which has done more than dominate women's college basketball. They own it. The win was the 75th in a row for the Huskies. This year, 25 of their 38 wins (with no losses, obviously) were by 40 points or more.

UConn senior center Breanna Stewart scored 24 points, grabbed 10 rebounds, and dished out 6 assists on her way to winning the tournament's Most Outstanding Player award. She won it last year, too, and the year before, and the year before that.

On April 5, 2016, Connecticut Huskies star Breanna Stewart (30) scores inside during her team's victory over the Syracuse Orange in the national championship game at Bankers Life Fieldhouse in Indianapolis, Indiana.

UCONN 1-2-3 IN WNBA DRAFT

On April 14, 2016, the Women's National Basketball Association (WNBA) draft was held—fittingly—in Connecticut (home of the perennial women's NCAA champs). The Seattle Storm surprised no one with the top overall pick: University of Connecticut (UConn) superstar Breanna Stewart. In her four years at UConn, Stewart redefined greatness in women's college basketball. First, she led her team to four consecutive NCAA national titles. Second, she earned the NCAA tournament's Most Outstanding Player award all four of those years. Third, as the top women's player overall, Stewart was named Naismith College Player of the Year the past three years. So no, it was no surprise that "Bre" went number one. The Seattle Storm are no doubt counting their lucky stars to have her.

But then came the next two picks, chosen by the San Antonio Stars and the Connecticut (that state again) Sun: UConn guard Moriah Jefferson and UConn forward Morgan Tuck. Yes, UConn again and again. For the first time, a single school produced the top three basketball picks in the same draft. It is fitting that a team with four straight NCAA championships and a 75-game winning streak should have its top players go 1-2-3 in the draft. No doubt the college basketball world beyond UConn is happy to see them go. But UConn, as always, surely has terrific players waiting to replace them. Now that Stewart, Jefferson, and Tuck will be professionals on different teams at opposite ends of the country, they'll have to get used to playing against each other. Will the camaraderie endure?

The fourth player chosen in the draft was University of Minnesota guard Rachel Banham, and the rest of the first round was dispersed evenly to colleges around the United States. Sorry, UConn, you can't have them all... Twice before in the WNBA draft, players from the same school were selected one and two. In the inaugural 1997 draft, USC's Tina Thompson and Pamela McGee were the top picks. In 2002, the top two selections were Sue Bird and Swin Cash from—where else?—UConn.

PAT SUMMITT 1952-2016

basketball while attending the University of Tennessee at Martin. She graduated in 1974 with a B.S. degree in physical education. She received an M.S. degree in physical education in 1975 from the University of Tennessee in Knoxville.

Summitt was co-captain of the United States women's basketball team that won the silver medal at the 1976 Summer Olympic Games and coached the United States team that won gold at the 1984 Olympics. In 2000, she was inducted into the Naismith Memorial Basketball Hall of Fame and was honored as the Naismith Coach of the 20th Century in women's basketball.

On June 28, 2016, legendary women's basketball coach Pat Summitt died at age 64. Summitt coached the University of Tennessee Lady Vols from 1974 to 2012, leading them to eight National Collegiate Athletic Association (NCAA) championships. She ended her career with more wins (1,098) than any other coach in NCAA Division I history. Summitt stepped down as head coach at Tennessee in 2012 after being diagnosed with early onset dementia, Alzheimer's type.

Patricia Sue Head was born in Henrietta, Tennessee, on June 14, 1952. She married R. B. Summitt, a bank executive, in 1980. She starred in

In March 2005, Summitt won her 880th game as a head coach, breaking the NCAA record held by Dean Smith of the University of North Carolina. In February 2009, Summitt became the first NCAA coach to win 1,000 games. Named the NCAA Coach of the Year seven times, Summitt led the Lady Vols to 16 Southeastern Conference tournament titles and 22 Final Fours. Her University of Tennessee teams won NCAA titles in 1987, 1989, 1991, 1996, 1997, 1998, 2007, and 2008. In 2012, U.S. President Barack Obama presented Summitt with the Presidential Medal of Freedom, one of the country's highest civilian honors.

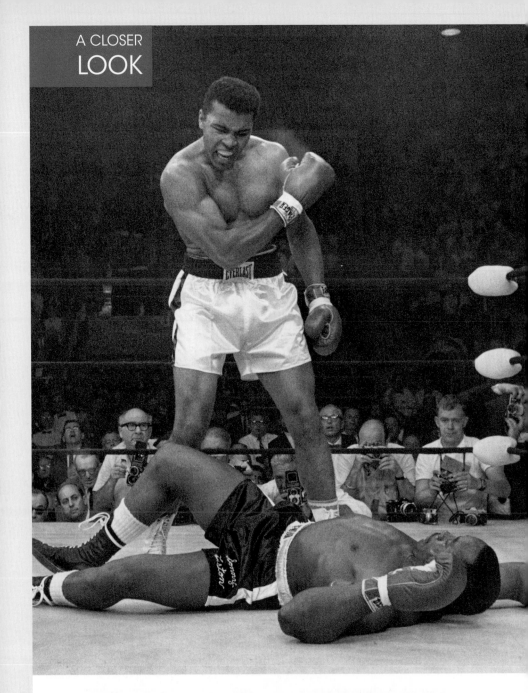

THE GREATEST

BY DAN ZEFF

American boxing legend and cultural icon Muhammad Ali died on June 3, 2016. Tributes flowed in from leaders and celebrities from around the world, praising Ali as a great sportsman, humanitarian, and goodwill ambassador. Millions of people watched the television coverage of his elaborate funeral and memorial service in his hometown of Louisville, Kentucky.

Ali was one of the most colorful and controversial boxing champions in the history of the sport. But Ali was much more than an athlete. He was also a towering cultural figure, standing up for political, religious, and social causes regardless of their popularity. In the 1960's, Ali refused to be drafted into the army during the Vietnam War. He rejected racial integration at the height of the civil rights movement. He joined the Nation of Islam (later converting to traditional Islam) and changed his name from Cassius Clay (what Ali called his "slave" name) to Muhammad Ali. Conservatives considered Ali a serious threat to the establishment at the time, while liberals often saw courage and nobility in his acts of defiance. Ali became an icon of the 20th century itself and was well known throughout the world. After a long fight with Parkinson disease, a progressive disorder of the brain that inhibits movement and speech, Ali died at the age of 74.

Ali was born Cassius Marcellus Clay, Jr., in Louisville in 1942. Growing up in segregated Southern society, he experienced racial prejudice first hand. Ali starting boxing at the age of 12, and by the time he was 18 he had won two national Golden Gloves titles and two Amateur Athletic Union national titles while compiling a record of 100 victories against only 18 losses. After graduating from high school, he won the light heavyweight gold medal at the 1960 Summer Olympic Games in Rome, Italy.

Heavyweight champion Muhammad Ali stands over fallen challenger and former champion Sonny Liston, on May 25, 1965, in Lewiston, Maine. The bout lasted only one minute into the first round. Ali had taken the title from Liston the year before in a six-round fight in Miami Beach, Florida.

Ali turned professional late in 1960, winning his first 19 fights, 15 by knockouts. His boxing skills featured quick, powerful jabs and foot speed, but it was his self-promoting personality that captured the attention of the public and the sports media. He bragged continually about his boxing ability and even his good looks. He composed short poems ridiculing his opponents and sometimes predicting the round in which he would win. Modern boxing had not seen anything like him before. Some people were charmed while others were annoyed at his outsized self-confidence. But everyone had to agree that the young man brought a freshness to boxing, and he definitely could fight.

The turning point in Ali's rise to stardom came on Feb. 25, 1964, in Miami Beach, Florida, when he fought the powerful and intimidating heavyweight champion Sonny Liston. The 22-year-old challenger was a huge underdog in the fight. But Ali taunted Liston before the bout, promising to "float like a butterfly, sting like a bee." Ali boastfully predicted a victory by a knockout, and when Liston failed to answer the bell to begin the seventh round, Ali became the heavyweight champion of the world. Immediately after the fight he shouted, "I am the greatest!" The cocky young man from Louisville was now an international celebrity. Ali knocked out Liston in the first round of their rematch on May 25, 1965, and successfully defended his title eight more times.

At a press conference the morning after the first Liston fight, Ali confirmed rumors that he had converted to Islam. Nation of Islam leader Elijah Muhammad gave him the name of Muhammad Ali, a name he retained until his death.

During the mid-1960's, the Vietnam War was dividing the United States. Ali reported for his induction into the U.S. Army on April 28, 1967, but refused to serve, citing his religious beliefs. Ali was arrested, and the New York State Athletic Commission suspended his boxing license and revoked his heavyweight championship. Ali was convicted of draft evasion and sentenced to a maximum of five years in prison and a $10,000 fine. He remained at liberty while his conviction was appealed.

Ali was widely attacked as a draft dodger, and his popularity declined sharply. Boxing organizations banned him from fighting for three years, but he made numerous antiwar appearances on college campuses, where he was popular with students. By the late 1960's the public was turning against the Vietnam War, and in 1970 the New York State Supreme Court ordered Ali's boxing license restored. In 1971, the U.S. Supreme Court unanimously overturned his conviction. But the suspension cost Ali more than three prime years of his boxing career.

Ending his exile from fighting, Ali returned to the sport in 1970, retaining the World Boxing Council (WBC) title that was withheld from him during his suspension. Ali soon became a partner in one of the great rivalries in boxing history with his three bouts against the powerful Joe Frazier. Ali and Frazier first met in 1971, when both were undefeated. Frazier was the World Boxing Association (WBA) champion, and Ali was the WBC champion. Ali lost the fight in a unanimous decision in a bout called the "Fight of the Century." The defeat was Ali's first as a professional fighter.

Ali defeated Frazier by a decision in a nontitle fight in 1974, setting up a title match against the champion at the time, George Foreman. Foreman had won the title from Frazier in 1973. The 1974 Ali-Foreman fight in Kinshasa, Zaire (now the Democratic Republic of the Congo), was labeled the "Rumble in the Jungle." Ali was the underdog but won out with his "rope-a-dope" strategy. Ali leaned on the ring ropes, absorbing a flurry of punches from Foreman. The younger Foreman eventually tired, and Ali won in an eighth-round knockout. In 1975, Ali met Frazier for the third time and won by a technical knockout after the 14th round. The brutal bout, held in Manila in the Philippines, was known as the "Thrilla in Manila."

Ali continued to defend his title successfully, but he was

> "I AM AN ORDINARY MAN WHO WORKED HARD TO DEVELOP THE TALENT I WAS GIVEN. I BELIEVED IN MYSELF, AND I BELIEVE IN THE GOODNESS OF OTHERS."
>
> ~MUHAMMAD ALI

beginning to show his age. On Feb. 15, 1978, little-known Leon Spinks defeated the Champ in a 15-round split decision. Ali regained the title seven months later, defeating Spinks in a unanimous 15-round decision. In the process, he became the first fighter to win the world heavyweight boxing championship three different times.

In 1979, Ali gave up his title and announced his retirement. In 1980, however, he came out of retirement and fought defending heavyweight champion Larry Holmes, seeking to win the World Boxing Council version of the title. Holmes defeated Ali by a technical knockout. In 1981, Ali lost a unanimous 10-round decision to Trevor Berbick, a former heavyweight champion. After the Berbick fight, the 39-year old Ali retired for good, with a career record of 56 victories (37 by knockout) and 5 losses.

In 1984, Ali was diagnosed with Parkinson disease, a disorder that gradually destroys cells in certain regions of the brain involved in body movements. There has been speculation that Ali's condition was at least partly the result of the many blows to the head he absorbed during his boxing career. In spite of the disease, Ali remained a public figure, traveling internationally on charitable, humanitarian, and goodwill missions. He met with Saddam Hussein, the leader of Iraq, in 1990 to negotiate the release of American hostages. In 2002, Ali traveled to Afghanistan as a United Nations Messenger of Peace.

Ali also became active in philanthropy. He raised money for the Muhammad Ali Parkinson Center in Phoenix, Arizona. He also raised money for such organizations as the Special Olympics (athletic competitions for intellectually challenged individuals) and the Make-A-Wish Foundation, which assists sick and disabled children.

In 1990, Ali was inducted into the International Boxing Hall of Fame. At the 1996 Summer Olympic Games in Atlanta, Georgia, he was the final carrier of the Olympic torch. For the Olympic Games, runners transport the Olympic flame in a torch relay from Greece to the site of the games. In the last leg of the relay, the runner carries the torch into the stadium and lights the Olympic cauldron. To be the torch's final carrier is considered a high honor.

In a White House ceremony in 2005, President George W. Bush presented Ali with the Presidential Medal of Freedom. Also in 2005, the nonprofit Muhammad Ali Center opened in downtown Louisville. The $80-million Center consists of a museum and cultural center built as a tribute to Ali and his beliefs. Ali discussed his boxing career and religious views in his autobiography, *The Greatest: My Own Story* (1975). His memoir *The Soul of a Butterfly: Reflections on Life's Journey*, written with his daughter Hana Yasmeen Ali, was published in 2004.

Ali was married four times and had seven daughters and two sons.

Muhammad Ali kisses an orphaned child at a mission for Liberian refugees in San Pedro, Côte d'Ivoire, on Aug. 20, 1997. Ali came on a goodwill visit to donate food, wheelchairs, and medicine after receiving a letter asking for help from the mission's organizer, Sister M. Sponsa Beltran.

FROOME TAKES THIRD
TOUR DE FRANCE

On July 24, 2016, British cyclist Chris Froome raced to his third Tour de France victory in the last four years. The 31-year-old Froome, who previously won in 2013 and 2015, established a comfortable 4-minute lead over the race's grueling first 20 stages and 2,000 miles (3,200 kilometers). Wearing the leader's distinctive yellow jersey, Froome coasted through the largely ceremonial 21st and final stage, finishing on the famous Avenue des Champs-Élysées in Paris arm-in-arm with other members of his Team Sky. As Froome accepted the winner's trophy, he reflected on the terrorist attack that took place 10 days earlier in Nice, France, as the cyclists competed roughly 175 miles (280 kilometers) away. "This Tour has obviously taken place against the backdrop of terrible events in Nice and we pay tribute to those who have lost their lives," he said. "These events put sport into perspective, but it also shows the value of sport to free society."

Froome, a veteran racer, stayed near the front during the tour's first week before snatching the lead in stage 8 at Bagnères-de-Luchon on the Spanish border. On Bastille Day, July 14 (the day of the Nice attack), Froome crashed ascending Mont Ventoux in Provence, disabling his bicycle. Losing time, he trotted up the course on foot until the arrival of a replacement bike. In the Swiss Alps, Froome pulled away from the pack, padding his lead despite another crash coming down from the mountains on stage 19. Two days later, he completed his second straight Tour de France victory. Only two rest days are included over the course of the three-week endurance event.

French cyclist Romain Bardet finished second in the race, followed closely by Colombia's Nairo Quintana and the United Kingdom's Adam Yates. Aside from the race winner's *maillot jaune* (yellow jersey), the *maillot blanc* (white jersey) signifies the race's best young rider (worn by Yates); the best climber in the tough mountain stages wears the *maillot à pois rouges* (polka dot jersey); and the *maillot vert* (green jersey) marks the overall leader in points (awarded for consistently high stage finishes). This year, the climbing "King of the Mountain" was Rafal Majka of Poland, while Slovakia's Peter Sagan won the green jersey. The Tour de France is one of three major touring races of cycling; the others are the Giro d'Italia and the Vuelta a España.

SUPER BOWL 50

On Feb. 7, 2016, the Denver Broncos overwhelmed the Carolina Panthers 24-10 in a defense-dominated Super Bowl 50 at Levi's Stadium in Santa Clara, California. Denver linebacker Von Miller recorded 2 ½ quarterback sacks and two forced fumbles, including one that was returned for the game's first touchdown. Miller was named the National Football League (NFL) championship game's Most Valuable Player (MVP). It was the third Super Bowl victory for the Broncos in team history and the first since the team won consecutive titles after the 1997 and 1998 regular seasons.

The Carolina Panthers were slightly favored to win the game. Led by their quarterback, NFL 2015 season MVP Cam Newton, Carolina had the NFL's top offense, averaging 31.3 points per game. The Panthers finished the regular season 15-1. But the Broncos, sporting the NFL's top-rated defense, contained Newton for much of the game. He completed only 18 of 41 passes for 265 yards, with one interception and two fumbles lost. The key play occurred with Denver already up 3-0 in the first quarter. On the Panthers' own 15-yard-line, Von Miller charged off the line and sacked Newton, stripping the football and knocking it into the Panthers' end zone, where Broncos defensive end Malik Jackson fell on the ball for a touchdown and a 10-0 Denver lead. It was the first fumble recovery for a touchdown in a Super Bowl in 22 years. Denver running back C. J. Anderson added a touchdown late, and kicker Brandon McManus kicked three field goals in the win.

Denver's Peyton Manning, who at age 39 was the oldest quarterback to start a Super Bowl game, completed 13 of 23 passes for only 141 yards, with one interception and one lost fumble. But the stifling Denver defense did not require any more offense as they thoroughly controlled the game. The victory gave Manning his second NFL championship in four Super Bowl appearances. The victory proved to be the crowning achievement for the Hall of Fame-bound quarterback, as he announced his retirement exactly one month after the Super Bowl.

NFL UPDATE—2016

NFL playoffs. The 2016 National Football League (NFL) playoffs began with the wild card games. The Kansas City Chiefs trounced the Houston Texans 30-0 on January 9 in Houston. Texans quarterback Brian Hoyer threw 4 interceptions and lost a fumble in the blowout loss. The same day, the visiting Pittsburgh Steelers defeated the Cincinnati Bengals 18-16 in a wild and ugly game where referees often struggled to maintain control. On January 10, the Seattle Seahawks barely got past the Minnesota Vikings 10-9 in Minneapolis. In Washington, D.C., the Green Bay Packers pulled away after a close first half, downing the Redskins 35-18.

In the divisional round on January 16, the defending NFL champion New England Patriots defeated Kansas City 27-20 in Foxborough, Massachusetts.

WILD CARD		DIVISIONAL		CHAMPIONSHIP		CHAMPIONSHIP		DIVISIONAL		WILD CARD	
6 Pittsburgh	**18**									**6 Seattle**	**10**
3 Cincinnati	16									**3 Minnesota**	9
		6 Pittsburgh	16					**6 Seattle**	24		
		1 Denver	**23**					**1 Carolina**	**31**		
				2 New England	18	**2 Arizona**	15				
				1 Denver	**20**	**1 Carolina**	**49**				
		5 Kansas City	20					**5 Green Bay**	20		
		2 New England	**27**					**2 Arizona**	**26**		
5 Kansas City	**30**									**5 Green Bay**	**35**
4 Houston	0									**4 Washington**	18

SUPERBOWL

1 Carolina	10
1 Denver	**24**

The Arizona Cardinals needed overtime to beat the Packers 26-20 in Glendale, Arizona. On January 17, the Carolina Panthers survived a late surge by the visiting Seahawks to eke out a 31-24 win and advance to the NFC championship game. Carolina was up 31-0 at the half, but the lead evaporated in the second half as Seattle mounted a furious-but-not-good-enough comeback. In Denver, the Broncos downed the Steelers 23-16 to advance to the AFC Championship.

On Sunday, Feb. 7, 2016, Denver Broncos linebacker Von Miller (58) rushes against Carolina Panthers tackle Mike Remmers (74) during Super Bowl 50 in Santa Clara, California. Miller was named the game's MVP.

On January 24, the Broncos nipped their nemesis New England 20-18 in the AFC Championship game, punching their ticket to Super Bowl 50. Denver quarterback Peyton Manning led the Broncos the entire way. A strong New England drive in the final 2 minutes came up short. That same day, the Carolina Panthers thoroughly controlled the visiting Cardinals in the NFC Championship game in Charlotte. Carolina quarterback Cam Newton put on a show as the offense racked up 476 total yards in a 49-15 win to push the Panthers to their second Super Bowl.

Rams back in L.A. After a day of meetings on Jan. 13, 2016, NFL owners voted to allow the St. Louis Rams to move to Los Angeles, California, ending a 21-year football drought in the country's second largest media market. The Rams will play home games in Los Angeles Memorial Coliseum until the team moves into a new stadium being built in Inglewood, southwest of downtown Los Angeles. The stadium is expected to be ready for the 2019 season. The Rams were originally founded in Cleveland in 1937. The team moved to Los Angeles in 1946 and then to St. Louis in 1995. The Rams have not made the playoffs since 2004.

The NFL vote also gave the San Diego Chargers the option to join the Rams and share the new stadium in Los Angeles. The Chargers play just 120 miles south of Inglewood, and the team owner has been trying to negotiate a new stadium to replace the aging Qualcomm Stadium in San Diego. The Chargers will remain at Qualcomm for the 2016 regular season, but the decision to stay likely depends on the approval of a new stadium initiative in the November elections. If voters approve a new stadium deal, the Chargers will have the option of moving to Los Angeles until the new San Diego stadium is ready. The Oakland Raiders were also in the mix for a move to Los Angeles, as the team owner is also involved in negotiations for a new stadium. However, the Raiders joining the Rams in Los Angeles seems unlikely. Raiders owner Mark Davis's first choice is a move to Las Vegas if he cannot get a new stadium in Oakland.

NFL draft. Representatives from all 32 NFL teams and the top-ranked college prospects from across the country gathered in Chicago on April 28-30, 2016, for the NFL Draft. This was the second year in a row that the draft was held in Chicago. Before that, the event had been held each year at Radio City Music Hall in New York City. NFL Commissioner Roger Goodell indicated that future drafts would be held in a different city each year. The 2017 draft will be in Philadelphia. The event regularly draws big crowds and high TV ratings.

Drama marked the draft from the beginning as teams traded future picks for higher first round choices in order to land coveted players. The newly restored L.A. Rams traded a number of future picks to the Tennessee Titans in return for the number one overall pick. The Rams chose University of California quarterback

Jared Goff. The Philadelphia Eagles had the next pick, which they obtained in a trade with the Cleveland Browns. The Eagles chose North Dakota State quarterback Carson Wentz. This was the second consecutive year that quarterbacks were selected one-two in the draft. In all, seven teams traded for better first round positions.

As usual, most of the first round picks were selected from the top college teams. Eight players were selected from the powerful Southeastern Conference. Five players from The Ohio State University of the Big 10 Conference were among the first 20 players selected in the first round, one player short of the record, six, set by the University of Miami in 2004.

Manning retires. With a win in Super Bowl 50 to cap a brilliant career, Broncos quarterback Peyton Manning announced his retirement in an emotional press conference on March 7, 2016, in Denver. Manning, who was drafted by the Indianapolis Colts in 1998, signed with Denver in 2012. Over 18 seasons, Manning passed for 71,940 yards and 539 regular season touchdowns, finishing with a career quarterback rating of 96.5. A shoo-in for the Pro Football Hall of Fame when he becomes eligible, Manning is one of just 12 NFL quarterbacks to win multiple championships and is the only starting quarterback to win a Super Bowl with two different franchises. His victory in Super Bowl 50

over Carolina gave him 200 career wins, moving him past 2016 Hall of Fame inductee Brett Favre into first place on the all-time list of wins by a quarterback.

Hall of Fame. The 2016 NFL Hall of Fame inductees were enshrined in a ceremony on Aug. 6, 2016 in Canton, Ohio. A total of 108 players from the NFL modern era (since 1970) were eligible for induction. The inductees recognized for their play were linebacker Kevin Greene (Rams, Steelers, 49ers, and Panthers); wide receiver Marvin Harrison (Colts); offensive tackle Orlando Pace (Rams); and quarterback Brett Favre (Packers). Quarterback Ken Stabler (Raiders) and offensive guard Dick Stanfel (Redskins and Lions) were inducted by the NFL Seniors Committee posthumously. Both died in 2015.

Longtime head coach Tony Dungy was also named to the NFL Hall of Fame. Dungy amassed 148 wins over 13 seasons as head coach of the Tampa Bay Buccaneers and Indianapolis Colts. He became the first African American head coach to win a Super Bowl, when the Colts defeated the Chicago Bears in Super Bowl XLI in Miami in 2007. Dungy was named NFL Coach of the year in 1997 and 2005. Eddie DeBartolo Jr., who owned the San Francisco 49ers from 1977 to 2000, was also inducted. During his tenure, the 49ers won 13 division titles and 5 Super Bowls.

2015 NFL FINAL STANDINGS
AMERICAN CONFERENCE

North Division

North Division	W.	L.	T.	Pct.
Cincinnati Bengals*	12	4	0	.750
Pittsburgh Steelers*	10	6	0	.625
Baltimore Ravens	5	11	0	.313
Cleveland Browns	3	13	0	.188

East Division

East Division	W.	L.	T.	Pct.
New England Patriots*	12	4	0	.750
New York Jets	10	6	0	.625
Buffalo Bills	8	8	0	.500
Miami Dolphins	6	10	0	.375

South Division

South Division	W.	L.	T.	Pct.
Houston Texans*	9	7	0	.563
Indianapolis Colts	8	8	0	.500
Jacksonville Jaguars	5	11	0	.313
Tennessee Titans	3	13	0	.188

West Division

West Division	W.	L.	T.	Pct.
Denver Broncos*	12	4	0	.750
Kansas City Chiefs*	11	5	0	.688
Oakland Raiders	7	9	0	.438
San Diego Chargers	4	12	0	.250

*Made playoffs

TEAM STATISTICS

Leading offenses	Points per game	Yards per game
Pittsburgh Steelers	26.4	395.4
New England Patriots	29.1	374.4
San Diego Chargers	20.0	371.8
New York Jets	24.2	370.3
Buffalo Bills	23.7	360.9

Leading defenses	Avg. points against	Yards per game
Denver Broncos	18.5	283.1
Houston Texans	19.6	310.2
New York Jets	19.6	318.6
Kansas City Chiefs	17.9	329.3
Baltimore Ravens	25.1	337.4

INDIVIDUAL STATISTICS

Quarterbacks

Passing yards	Philip Rivers San Diego Chargers	4,792
Touchdowns	Tom Brady New England Patriots	36
QB Rating (min. 224 passes)	Andy Dalton Cincinnati Bengals	106.2

Running backs

Rushing yards	Chris Ivory New York Jets	1,070
Touchdowns	Jeremy Hill Cincinnati Bengals DeAngelo Williams Pittsburgh Steelers	11
Yards per carry (min. 100 rushes)	Le'Veon Bell Pittsburgh Steelers	4.9

Wide receivers

Receiving yards	Antonio Brown Pittsburgh Steelers	1,834
Receptions	Antonio Brown Pittsburgh Steelers	136
Touchdowns	Brandon Marshall New York Jets Allen Robinson Jacksonville Jaguars	14
Yards per catch (min. 30 catches)	Malcom Floyd San Diego Chargers	18.7

Scoring

Touchdowns	Brandon Marshall New York Jets Allen Robinson Jacksonville Jaguars	14

Kickers

Points	Stephen Gostkowski New England Patriots	151
Longest field goal	Jason Myers Jacksonville Jaguars	58 yds

Punters

Yards per punt (min. 40 punts)	Pat McAfee Indianapolis Colts	47.7

Defense

Sacks	J. J. Watt Houston Texans	17.5
Interceptions	Reggie Nelson Cincinnati Bengals Marcus Peters Kansas City Chiefs	8

NATIONAL CONFERENCE

North Division

	W.	L.	T.	Pct.
Minnesota Vikings*	11	5	0	.688
Green Bay Packers*	10	6	0	.625
Detroit Lions	7	9	0	.438
Chicago Bears	6	10	0	.375

East Division

	W.	L.	T.	Pct.
Washington Redskins*	9	7	0	.563
Philadelphia Eagles	7	9	0	.438
New York Giants	6	10	0	.375
Dallas Cowboys	4	12	0	.250

South Division

	W.	L.	T.	Pct.
Carolina Panthers*	15	1	0	.938
Atlanta Falcons	8	8	0	.500
New Orleans Saints	7	9	0	.438
Tampa Bay Buccaneers	6	10	0	.375

West Division

	W.	L.	T.	Pct.
Arizona Cardinals*	13	3	0	.813
Seattle Seahawks*	10	6	0	.625
St. Louis Rams	7	9	0	.438
San Francisco 49ers	5	11	0	.313

*Made playoffs

TEAM STATISTICS

Leading offenses	Points per game	Yards per game
Arizona Cardinals	30.6	408.3
New Orleans Saints	25.5	403.8
Seattle Seahawks	26.4	378.6
Tampa Bay Buccaneers	21.4	375.9
Atlanta Falcons	21.2	374.4

Leading defenses	Avg. points against	Yards per game
Seattle Seahawks	17.3	291.8
Arizona Cardinals	19.6	321.7
Carolina Panthers	19.2	322.9
Tampa Bay Buccaneers	26.1	340.4
Minnesota Vikings	18.9	344.2

INDIVIDUAL STATISTICS

Quarterbacks

Passing yards	Drew Brees New Orleans Saints	4,870
Touchdowns	Eli Manning New York Giants Cam Newton Carolina Panthers Carson Palmer Arizona Cardinals	35
QB Rating (min. 224 passes)	Russell WIlson Seattle Seahawks	110.1

Running backs

Rushing yards	Adrian Peterson Minnesota Vikings	1,485
Touchdowns	Devonta Freeman Atlanta Falcons Adrian Peterson Minnesota Vikings	11
Yards per carry (min. 100 rushes)	Thomas Rawls Seattle Seahawks	5.6

Wide receivers

Receiving yards	Julio Jones Atlanta Falcons	1,871
Receptions	Julio Jones Atlanta Falcons	136
Touchdowns	Doug Baldwin Seattle Seahawks	14
Yards per catch (min. 30 catches)	Torrey Smith San Francisco 49ers	20.1

Scoring

Touchdowns	Doug Baldwin Seattle Seahawks Devonta Freeman Atlanta Falcons	14

Kickers

Points	Graham Cano Carolina Panthers	146
Longest field goal	Greg Zuerlein St. Louis Rams	61 yds

Punters

Yards per punt (min. 40 punts)	Johnny Hekker St. Louis Rams	47.9

Defense

Sacks	Ezekiel Ansah Detroit Lions	14.5
Interceptions	Kurt Coleman Carolina Panthers Trumaine Johnson St. Louis Rams	7

Notable deaths. Lineman Marion Campbell, who played 8 seasons in the NFL and later became a head coach, died on July 13, 2016, at age 87. Campbell played two years for San Francisco before moving to Philadelphia, where he helped the Eagles win the 1960 NFL Championship. He later coached for the Eagles and Atlanta Falcons.

Buddy Ryan, who coached 26 seasons in the NFL and was part of three Super Bowl-appearing coaching staffs, died on June 28, 2016, at age 85. The defensive mastermind who invented the legendary "46" defense, Ryan's career highlight came as defensive coordinator for the 1985 Chicago Bears, who won Super Bowl XX with one of the NFL's all-time great defenses. Ryan later served as head coach of the Eagles and Cardinals. His twin sons, Rex and Rob Ryan, are currently head coach and assistant head coach for the Buffalo Bills.

Former Vikings and Cardinals head coach Dennis Green died on July 21, 2016, at age 67. Green became the second African American head coach in NFL history when he took the helm in Minnesota in 1992. The Vikings had winning records from '92 through 2000, but Green's teams never reached the Super Bowl. Green coached the Cardinals from 2004 through 2006.

Deflategate. The inflated scandal that will not go away continued to make news in 2016. After the 2015 AFC Championship game, the Indianapolis Colts accused the New England Patriots of intentionally deflating footballs used by Patriots quarterback Tom Brady during the game. Such an act would allow Brady to grip the ball better in cold weather, giving him an unfair advantage over Colts quarterback Andrew Luck, whose footballs were filled to regulation capacity. In May 2015, NFL Commissioner Roger Goodell suspended Brady for four games without pay, but the suspension was appealed. On July 13, 2016, the U.S. Second Circuit Court of Appeals upheld the suspension, leaving the Patriots Brady-less for the first four games of the 2016 season.

Free agents. The top off-season free agent moves of 2016 included Broncos defensive lineman Malik Jackson joining the Jacksonville Jaguars and Miami Dolphins defensive end Olivier Vernon moving to the New York Giants. Quarterback Brock Osweiler, who had been groomed to replace the retired Manning in Denver, jumped ship to the Houston Texans. Carolina All-Pro cornerback Josh Norman was enticed north to Washington, D.C., and Bengals receiver Marvin Jones left to play in Detroit.

Sharper sentenced. On Aug. 18, 2016, a federal court sentenced former NFL All-Pro defensive back Darren Sharper to 18 years in prison on rape and drug charges. Sharper played 14 seasons with the Packers, Vikings, and Saints.

TIDE *ROLL* TO A TITLE

On Jan. 11, 2016, the University of Alabama Crimson Tide defeated the Clemson University Tigers 45-40 to win the College Football Playoff National Championship. The title was the fourth in the past seven seasons for Alabama, a 7-year period of excellence matched only once before in NCAA history by Notre Dame in the late 1940's.

The game broke a recent string of one-sided championship games that lacked suspense down the stretch. The lead went back and forth for the first three quarters until Alabama took control with 17 points over a three-minute span in the fourth quarter. The contest was loaded with big moments. Four touchdowns came on plays of more than 50 yards, including a 95-yard kickoff return by Alabama's Kenyan Drake. The two teams combined for 1,012 yards of total offense, plus almost 300 yards more in punt and kickoff returns. Alabama and Clemson scored 40 points between them in the fourth quarter alone.

Each team's offensive star gave a center stage performance. Alabama's Heisman Trophy winner Derrick Henry rushed for 158 yards and three touchdowns, including a 50-yard sprint that opened the scoring 5 minutes and 18 seconds into the game. Clemson's All-American sophomore quarterback Deshaun Watson passed for 405 yards and four touchdowns and added another 73 yards rushing.

For all the excitement provided by both teams offensively, the key play of the evening was a kickoff that went only 15 yards. Alabama had kicked a field goal to tie the score 24-24 with 10 minutes and 34 seconds remaining in the game. Alabama coach Nick Saban then elected to try an on-side kick to retain possession of the ball. The kick was executed perfectly against the surprised Clemson team as an Alabama player caught the kick in midair. Two plays later, quarterback Jake Coker hit tight end O. J. Howard with a 51-yard touchdown pass to give Alabama a lead they would not surrender with 9 minutes and 45 seconds left in the game.

The teams still had time to dazzle and thrill for four more touchdowns and a field goal, however. The last touchdown, by Clemson, reduced Alabama's lead to 45-40 with just 12 seconds left. Clemson tried its own on-side kick, but the ball went out of bounds and Alabama ran out the clock to end one of the most memorable title games in college football history.

COLLEGE FOOTBALL SEASON

NATIONAL CHAMPIONSHIP GAMES

NCAA Div. I	Alabama	45	Clemson	40
NCAA FCS	North Dakota State	37	Jacksonville State	10
NCAA Div. II	NW Missouri State	34	Shepherd	7
NCAA Div. III	Mount Union	49	St. Thomas (MN)	35
NAIA	Marian (IN)	31	Southern Oregon	14

NCAA DIV. I CHAMPIONSHIP SEMIFINAL BOWL GAMES

Bowl	Result			
Cotton	Alabama	38	Michigan State	0
Orange	Clemson	37	Oklahoma	17

BOWL GAMES IN 2015-2016

Bowl	Result			
Alamo	TCU	47	Oregon	41
Armed Forces	California	55	Air Force	36
Arizona	Nevada	28	Colorado State	23
Bahamas	Western Michigan	45	Middle Tennessee	31
Belk	Mississippi State	51	NC State	28
Birmingham	Auburn	31	Memphis	10
Boca Raton	Toledo	32	Temple	17
Cactus	West Virginia	43	Arizona State	42
Camellia	Appalachian State	31	Ohio	29
Celebration	North Carolina A&T	41	Alcorn State	34
Citrus	Michigan	41	Florida	7
Cure	San Jose State	27	Georgia State	16
Fiesta	Ohio State	44	Notre Dame	28
Foster Farms	Nebraska	37	UCLA	29
GoDaddy	Georgia Southern	58	Bowling Green	27
Hawaii	San Diego State	42	Cincinnati	7
Heart of Dallas	Washington	44	Southern Miss	31
Holiday	Wisconsin	23	USC	21
Idaho Potato	Akron	23	Utah State	21
Independence	Virginia Tech	55	Tulsa	52
Las Vegas	Utah	35	BYU	28
Liberty	Arkansas	45	Kansas State	23
Miami Beach	Western Kentucky	45	South Florida	35
Military	Navy	44	Pittsburgh	28
Music City	Louisville	27	Texas A&M	21
New Mexico	Arizona	45	New Mexico	37
New Orleans	Louisiana Tech	47	Arkansas State	28
Outback	Tennessee	45	Northwestern	6
Peach	Houston	38	Florida State	24
Pinstripe	Duke	44	Indiana	41
Poinsettia	Boise State	55	Northern Illinois	7
Quick Lane	Minnesota	21	Central Michigan	14
Rose	Stanford	45	Iowa	16
Russell Athletic	Baylor	49	North Carolina	38
St. Petersburg	Marshall	16	Connecticut	10
Sugar	Ole Miss	48	Oklahoma State	20
Sun	Washington State	20	Miami (FL)	14
Taxslayer	Georgia	24	Penn State	17
Texas	LSU	56	Texas Tech	27

ALL-AMERICAN TEAM (FBS)
(as chosen by the Associated Press)

Offense

Quarterback	Deshaun Watson, Clemson
Running backs	Leonard Fournette, LSU; Derrick Henry, Alabama
Wide receivers	Corey Coleman, Baylor; Josh Doctson, TCU
Tight end	Hunter Henry, Arkansas
Center	Jack Allen, Michigan State
Tackles	Taylor Decker, Ohio State; Spencer Drango, Baylor
Guards	Joshua Garnett, Stanford; Landon Turner, North Carolina
Place-kicker	Ka'imi Fairbairn, UCLA
All-purpose player	Christian McCaffrey, Stanford

Defense

Defensive ends	Shaq Lawson, Clemson; Carl Nassib, Penn State
Defensive tackles	Andrew Billings, Baylor; A'Shawn Robinson, Alabama
Linebackers	Tyler Matakevich, Temple; Reggie Ragland, Alabama; Jaylon Smith, Notre Dame
Cornerbacks	Vernon Hargreaves III, Florida; Desmond King, Iowa
Safeties	Vonn Bell, Ohio State; Jeremy Cash, Duke
Punter	Tom Hackett, Utah

Player awards

Heisman Trophy (best player)
　　　　　Derrick Henry, Alabama
Bednarik Trophy (best defenseman)
　　　　　Tyler Matakevich, Temple

NCAA PREVIEW

Alabama entered the 2016 college football season as the odds-on favorite to repeat as NCAA champions. The NFL took the Crimson Tide's Heisman-winning running back, their quarterback, and most of their defensive line, but prognosticators believed the program's famed "process" of reloading star players would continue.

Deshaun Watson returned to lead second-ranked Clemson, as did quarterback Baker Mayfield of third-ranked Oklahoma. Florida State came in at No. 4 with steady senior quarterback Sean Maguire behind center. Fifth-ranked Ohio State—also NFL-depleted—looked to reload with a bevy of redshirted young talent, including junior quarterback J. T. Barrett, running back Mike Weber, and receivers Noah Brown and Terry McLaurin.

Usual suspects rounded out the preseason top 10: Lousiana State at No. 6, followed by Stanford, Michigan, Notre Dame, and Tennessee.

The Southeastern Conference stocked the preseason top 25 with 6 teams. Five teams from the Pac-12 were in the top 25, and 4 each came from the Atlantic Coast Conference, Big 10, and Big 12, leaving odd spots for just Notre Dame and Houston.

GOLF 2016

On April 8, 2016, British golfer Danny Willett hits from a bunker during the Masters Tournament at the Augusta National Golf Club in Georgia. Willett won the tournament by three strokes over Lee Westwood and defending champion Jordan Spieth.

MAJOR GOLF CHAMPIONSHIPS

This table lists the winners of golf's major tournaments in 2016.

Men's		Women's	
Masters Tournament	Danny Willett	U.S. Women's Open	Brittany Lang
U.S. Open	Dustin Johnson	KPMG Women's PGA	Brooke Henderson
British Open	Henrik Stenson	Women's British Open	Ariya Jutanugarn
U.S. PGA Championship	Jimmy Walker	ANA Inspiration	Lydia Ko
		Evian Championship	In Gee Chun

ARNOLD PALMER 1929-2016

Champion U.S. golfer Arnold Palmer—one of golf's most famous and popular stars—died from complications of heart problems on Sept. 25, 2016. Palmer was 87 years old.

Palmer's most successful period on the links was from 1958 to 1964, when he won seven major titles: two British Opens, one U.S. Open, and four Masters Tournaments (1958, 1960, 1962, and 1964). Palmer's appealing personality and bold playing style helped to greatly increase the popularity of golf. Throughout his career, Palmer attracted a huge crowd of supporters called "Arnie's Army" at tournaments. His charisma also was largely responsible for making golf a popular television sport. Palmer's fellow pros nicknamed him "the King," and he was the first athlete to receive three of the United States' highest civilian honors: the Presidential Medal of Freedom, the Congressional Gold Medal, and the National Sports Award.

Palmer ranks fifth on the all-time PGA Tour victories list with 62 (behind Sam Snead, Tiger Woods, Jack Nicklaus, and Ben Hogan). Palmer, Nicklaus, and South African Gary Player made up the "Big Three" of golf from the late 1950's into the early 1980's. Palmer played his final competitive tournament in 2006 at the age of 77.

Arnold Daniel Palmer was born in Latrobe, Pennsylvania, on Sept. 10, 1929. The son of a golf pro, Palmer began playing golf as a child. He turned professional after winning the United States Amateur tournament in 1954. He won the U.S. Open in 1960 and the British Open in 1961 and 1962. Palmer joined the Senior PGA Tour in 1980. Palmer's autobiography was published as *A Golfer's Life*.

Aside from his playing career, Palmer was also an accomplished pilot and golf course designer. He also popularized an iced tea and lemonade drink, the "Arnold Palmer."

NHL UPDATE—2016

On June 12, 2016, the Pittsburgh Penguins of the National Hockey League (NHL) defeated the San Jose Sharks 3-1 to win the best-of-7 Stanley Cup Final 4 games to 2, capturing their first title in 7 years. The quick, confident Penguins made themselves at home on the ice at the SAP Center in San Jose, California, thoroughly outskating the Sharks to nab the championship series-clinching win. It was the fourth NHL title for the Penguins—often called the *Pens*.

Pittsburgh star forward Sidney Crosby, who won the Conn Smythe Trophy as the playoffs' most valuable player, scored 19 points—6 goals and 13 assists—through the Pens' 24-game playoff run. He had 2 assists in the championship clincher. "It's special," Crosby said about the MVP trophy. "It's the one you play for." The Penguins also received valuable ice time from forwards Phil Kessel and Evgeni Malkin, defenseman Kris Letang, and rookie goaltender Matthew Murray.

Penguins owner and Hockey Hall of Fame inductee Mario Lemieux (himself a two-time Conn Smythe winner while leading the Pens to titles in 1991 and 1992) lifted the Stanley Cup during the postgame celebration. "It's so hard to win it year after year," Lemieux said, referencing the team's playoff failures since their most recent

title in 2009. "Hopefully there's a few more for them."

It was quite a turnaround season for the Pens, who languished near the bottom of the NHL's Eastern Conference before firing coach Mike Johnston and hiring Mike Sullivan in December 2015. Sullivan improved the team's pace of play and empowered Crosby as a leader. Crosby finished the regular season ranked third in points behind Chicago's Patrick Kane and Dallas's Jamie Benn.

Pittsburgh reached the Stanley Cup Final by defeating the New York Rangers and Washington Capitals—who won the President's Trophy for compiling the league's best regular season record—in the playoffs' first two rounds. They then dispatched the Tampa Bay Lightning in a hard-fought, 7-game series for the Eastern Conference title. The nimble Pens then overwhelmed the Western Conference champion Sharks, taking leads in 5 of the 6 games.

The Sharks, playing in their first Stanley Cup Final, looked tired at times against the faster Penguins. Centers Joe Thornton and Logan Couture and goalie Martin Jones were standouts on the losing side. The Sharks reached the Final by defeating the St. Louis Blues for the Western Conference title. The Sharks had earlier outlasted the Los Angeles Kings and the Nashville Predators.

In 2016, no Canadian teams qualified for the NHL playoffs for the first time since 1970.

NHL notes. Seven NHL teams began the 2015-16 season with new coaches. Three teams—including eventual Cup winners Pittsburgh—replaced their coaches after opening the season with disappointing results. Three games were played outdoors in 2016. The Montreal Canadiens defeated the Boston Bruins 5-1 on January 1 in the Bridgestone 2016 NHL Winter Classic at Gillette Stadium in Foxborough, Massachusetts. Two alfresco games were played in the Stadium Series. On February 21, the Minnesota Wild topped the Chicago Blackhawks, 6-1, at the University of Minnesota's TCF Bank Stadium in Minneapolis. On February 27, the Detroit Red Wings came back to beat the Colorado Avalanche, 5-3, at Denver's Coors Field.

Following the conclusion of the 2015-16 season, Blackhawks forward Patrick Kane won the Hart Trophy as the league's most valuable player. Kane, who led the league with 106 points, was the first player born and raised in the United States to win the award. Kane's teammate Artemi Panarin won the Calder Trophy (top rookie). Other winners included the Kings' Anze Kopitar, who received the Lady Byng (sportsmanship) and Frank Selke (top defensive forward) trophies, and Kopitar's teammate Drew Doughty, who won the Norris Trophy (best defenseman). The Capitals' Braden Holtby won the Vezina Trophy (top goaltender).

On June 22, the NHL announced that it had awarded an expansion team to Las Vegas, Nevada, to begin play in the 2017-18 season. In an expansion draft set for 2017, the new franchise will select one player left unprotected from each of the 30 existing teams. In the league's regular annual draft on June 24, 2016, the Toronto Maple Leafs selected Arizona native Auston Matthews, a center who played the year in the Swiss National League A, with the first overall pick. The draft brought a particular distinction to the relatively ice-free city of St. Louis, Missouri, as five players who grew up there were selected in the opening round.

College. The Fighting Hawks of the University of North Dakota overwhelmed Quinnipiac University 5-1 to win the school's eighth National Collegiate Athletic Association (NCAA) Division I hockey championship on April 9, 2016, in Tampa, Florida. On March 20 in Durham, New Hampshire, the University of Minnesota women's ice hockey team upset previously undefeated Boston College 3-1 to repeat as national champions. It was the school's seventh women's hockey title.

NATIONAL HOCKEY LEAGUE STANDINGS

WESTERN CONFERENCE

Central Division

	W	L	OT†	Pts
Dallas Stars*	50	23	9	109
St. Louis Blues*	49	24	9	107
Chicago Blackhawks*	47	26	9	103
Nashville Predators*	41	27	14	96
Minnesota Wild*	38	33	11	87
Colorado Avalanche	39	39	4	82
Winnipeg Jets	35	39	8	78

Pacific Division

	W	L	OT†	Pts
Anaheim Ducks*	46	25	11	103
Los Angeles Kings*	48	28	6	102
San Jose Sharks*	46	30	6	98
Arizona Coyotes	35	39	8	78
Calgary Flames	35	40	7	77
Vancouver Canucks	31	38	13	75
Edmonton Oilers	31	43	8	70

EASTERN CONFERENCE

Atlantic Division

	W	L	OT†	Pts
Florida Panthers*	47	26	9	103
Tampa Bay Lightning*	46	31	5	97
Detroit Red Wings*	41	30	11	93
Boston Bruins	42	31	9	93
Ottawa Senators	38	35	9	85
Montreal Canadiens	38	38	6	82
Buffalo Sabres	35	36	11	81
Toronto Maple Leafs	29	42	11	69

Metropolitan Division

	W	L	OT†	Pts
Washington Capitals*	56	18	8	120
Pittsburgh Penguins*	48	26	8	104
New York Rangers*	46	27	9	101
New York Islanders*	45	27	10	100
Philadelphia Flyers*	41	27	14	96
Carolina Hurricanes	35	31	16	86
New Jersey Devils	38	36	8	84
Columbus Blue Jackets	34	40	8	76

*Made playoffs

†Overtime/shoot-out losses

STANLEY CUP CHAMPIONS—Pittsburgh Penguins (defeated San Jose Sharks, 4 games to 2)

LEADING SCORERS

	G	A	Pts
Patrick Kane, Chicago	46	60	106
Jamie Benn, Dallas	41	48	89
Sidney Crosby, Pittsburgh	36	49	85
Joe Thornton, San Jose	19	63	82
Erik Karlsson, Ottawa	16	66	82

G = Goals, A = Assists, Pts = Points

LEADING GOALIES

	GP	GA	GAA
Ben Bishop, Tampa Bay	61	123	2.06
John Gibson, Anaheim	40	79	2.07
Brian Elliott, St. Louis	42	78	2.07
Cory Schneider, New Jersey	58	122	2.15
Braden Holtby, Washington	66	141	2.20

GP = Games played, GA = Goals against,
GAA = Goals against average

AWARDS

Art Ross Trophy (most points scored)	Patrick Kane, Chicago
Bill Masterton Trophy (perseverance, sportsmanship, dedication to hockey)	Jaromir Jagr, Florida
Calder Memorial Trophy (best rookie)	Artemi Panarin, Chicago
Conn Smythe Trophy (Most Valuable Player in Stanley Cup)	Sidney Crosby, Pittsburgh
Frank J. Selke Trophy (best defensive forward)	Anze Kopitar, Los Angeles
Hart Trophy (Most Valuable Player)	Patrick Kane, Chicago
Jack Adams Award (coach of the year)	Barry Trotz, Washington
James Norris Trophy (best defenseman)	Drew Doughty, Los Angeles
King Clancy Memorial Trophy (leadership)	Henrik Sedin, Vancouver
Lady Byng Memorial Trophy (sportsmanship)	Anze Kopitar, Los Angeles
Maurice Richard Trophy (most goals scored)	Alex Ovechkin, Washington
Ted Lindsay Award (best player as voted by NHL players)	Patrick Kane, Chicago
Vezina Trophy (best goalkeeper)	Braden Holtby, Washington
William Jennings Trophy (goalkeeper[s] for team with fewest goals against)	Frederik Andersen and John Gibson, Anaheim

On June 12, 2016, Pittsburgh Penguins center Nick Bonino (13) and San Jose Sharks left wing Matt Nieto (83) fight to control the puck during the deciding Game 6 of the NHL Stanley Cup Final at the SAP Center in San Jose, California. Pittsburgh won the game and the series.

NHL: THE FOURTH PERIOD

Hockey Hall of Fame. On Nov. 14, 2016, center Eric Lindros headlined the newest class inducted into the Hockey Hall of Fame in Toronto, Ontario. Lindros, in his seventh year of eligibility, was joined by right wing Sergei Makarov, goaltender Rogie Vachon, and longtime coach and executive Pat Quinn.

Lindros, one of the most highly regarded junior hockey players in history, made his much-awaited debut for the Philadephia Flyers in 1992. He earned the Hart Trophy as the NHL MVP in 1995 and led Philadelphia to a Stanley Cup Final in 1997. Lindros was traded to the New York Rangers in 2001 and later played injury-short-ened seasons for the Maple Leafs and Stars before retiring in 2007. A six-time All-Star, Lindros scored 372 goals and had 493 career assists.

Sergei Makarov starred in the former Soviet Union—scoring a goal in the famous "Miracle on Ice" loss to the United States in 1980—before being allowed to join the Flames in 1989 as a 31-year-old "rookie." He played four seasons in Calgary before taking on diminished roles with the Sharks and Stars. Over seven NHL seasons and 424 games, Makarov scored 134 goals and had 250 assists.

Rogie Vachon joined the Montreal Canadiens in 1966 and shared the Vezina Trophy with teammate Gump Worsley as the NHL's top goalies of 1968. Vachon and the Canadiens won the Stanley Cup that season and again in 1969 and 1971. Vachon then joined the Kings, where he made three All-Star teams and set several team goaltending records. Vachon later played for the Red Wings and Bruins before retiring in 1982 to serve as an NHL coach and executive.

Pat Quinn (1943-2014) played nine seasons in the NHL before joining the Flyers as an assistant coach in 1977. From 1979 to 2010, he served in executive roles for the Flyers, Kings, Vancouver Canucks, Maple Leafs, and Edmonton Oilers. He won the Jack Adams Award in 1980 and 1992 as the NHL's coach of the year. In 2002, he led Team Canada to a gold medal at the Winter Olympic Games. At the time of his death in November 2014, Quinn was chairman of the Hockey Hall of Fame.

Rogers Place. The Edmonton Oilers left 42-year-old Rexall Place in favor of the stylish new Rogers Place to start the 2016-2017 NHL season. Rogers Place arena holds 18,641 hockey fans (slightly more people for concerts and other events) with plenty of room for all five of the team's Stanley Cup banners and the freshly refurbished 27-year-old bronze statue of Oilers great Wayne Gretzky.

GORDIE HOWE 1928-2016

Gordie Howe, one of the greatest players in hockey history, died on June 10, 2016, at the age of 88. Howe—nicknamed "Mr. Hockey"—played most of his professional career as a right wing for the Detroit Red Wings of the National Hockey League (NHL). Howe was one of the most complete and respected—and physically feared—players in hockey history.

Howe played on four Stanley Cup champion teams in Detroit. He won six Hart Trophies as the NHL's Most Valuable Player and six Art Ross Trophies as the league's leading scorer. He retired holding NHL records for career goals (801), assists (1,049), and points (1,850). Those records were later broken by Wayne Gretzy. Howe still holds the record for games played in the NHL (1,767). He was elected to the Hockey Hall of Fame in 1972.

During his long career, Howe earned a reputation as one of the roughest players in the NHL. His son Mark—himself a Hockey Hall of Fame inductee—said his father was "the toughest, meanest guy I've ever seen on a pair of skates." Howe's physical play forced opposing players to make room for him on the ice—a factor in Howe's prolific scoring and lack of serious injury over his long career.

Gordon Howe was born on March 31, 1928, in Floral, Saskatchewan. He joined the Red Wings in 1946 at the age of 18. Two years after he retired in 1971, Howe joined the Houston Aeros of the new World Hockey Association (WHA) to play with his sons Mark and Marty. He then moved to the WHA's New England Whalers for the 1977-1978 and 1978-1979 seasons. He remained with the Whalers for one more season after the team joined the NHL as the Hartford Whalers. Howe appeared in a single game in 1997 for the Detroit Vipers of the International Hockey League when he was almost 70, his record sixth decade on the ice.

NYQUIST WINS 2016 KENTUCKY DERBY

The table below lists the winners of the major international horse races run in 2016.

MAJOR HORSE RACES OF 2016

Race	Winner
THOROUGHBRED RACING	
American Triple Crown	
Kentucky Derby	Nyquist
Preakness Stakes	Exaggerator
Belmont Stakes	Creator
United Kingdom Triple Crown	
Two Thousand Guineas	Galileo Gold
Epsom Derby	Harzand
St. Leger Stakes	Harbour Law
Other major races	
Irish Derby (Ireland)	Harzand
King George VI and Queen Elizabeth Diamond Stakes (United Kingdom)	Highland Reel
Prix de l'Arc de Triomphe (France)	Found
HARNESS RACING	
Trotting Triple Crown	
Hambletonian	Marion Marauder
Kentucky Futurity	Marion Marauder
Yonkers Trot	Marion Marauder
Pacing Triple Crown	
Cane Pace	Control The Moment
Little Brown Jug	Betting Line
Messenger Stakes	Racing Hill

Jockey Mario Gutierrez rides Nyquist to victory during the 142nd running of the Kentucky Derby horse race at Churchill Downs on May 7, 2016, in Louisville, Kentucky.

LEICESTER CITY'S
SHOCKING SUCCESS

On May 2, 2016, London soccer clubs Tottenham Hotspur and Chelsea FC (football club) battled to a 2-2 tie—a common result in the Barclays Premier League. The result of that tie, however, was extraordinarily *uncommon*. Tottenham's failure to overcome Chelsea crowned an unlikely Premier League champion: Leicester City FC, commonly known as the Foxes. After *132 years* of coming up short (the team was founded in 1884), Leicester (pronounced Lester) had finally won its first top-flight league title.

The Premier League has 20 teams. Each year, the worst three teams are *relegated* (sent down) to a lower soccer league. In return, the top three lower-league teams are promoted. In 2015, a late-season spurt pushed Leicester City from a 20th- to a 14th-place finish, just a few points above the teams doomed to demotion. The Foxes saved their Premier League status, but the future looked dim, so they set to work. They fired their head coach in favor of the unassuming 64-year-old Claudio Ranieri, who last coached in the Premier League in 2004. Leicester raised their payroll to £57 million ($82 million), which sounds like a lot, but top teams Arsenal, Chelsea, and the Manchesters (United and City) all hover around £200

million ($292 million) with individual players earning as much as the Foxes take home altogether. These efforts made Leicester 5,000-1 favorites (if one can say such a thing) to win the 2015-2016 Premier League.

Leicester City came through, however, and built momentum after the season began in August 2015. Midfielder Riyad Mahrez and striker Jamie Vardy quickly showed the form that would earn them each player of the year awards (as chosen by the footballers' union and football writers respectively). The East Midlands club consistently beat their "big-city betters," culminating in a dominating 3-1 win over Manchester City FC in February 2016. The team finished the season with 81 points (23 wins, 12 draws, and just 3 losses), 10 points ahead of second-place Arsenal.

For sports fans beyond England, the scope of Leicester's achievement may not be clear. To put it in perspective, it's like the Cubs winning baseball's World Series—the *Iowa* Cubs of the Triple-A Pacific Coast League. Superlatives thrown around included *shocking, immortal, biggest thing ever,* and *greatest sport story of all time.* Generations of Foxes' fans shed tears and no doubt mumbled something like, *I never thought I'd see the day.*

PORTUGAL TAKES EURO 16

On July 10, 2016, Portugal's national men's soccer team upset home favorite France 1-0 to win the 2016 UEFA European Championship at the Stade de France near Paris. *UEFA* stands for the *Union of European Football Associations*. It was Portugal's first European title and first major tournament win of any kind. It wasn't Portuguese superstar Cristiano Ronaldo, however, who pushed the red-clad *Seleção* (Selection) to victory. Ronaldo, a three-time *Ballon d'Or*

(Golden Ball) award winner as the world's most outstanding player, left the pitch early after suffering a knee injury. Portuguese heroics were then left to sure-handed goalkeeper Rui Patrício and—in the match's 109th minute—late substitute forward Éder.

In the match's 8th minute, Ronaldo collided with French midfielder Dimitri Payet. Ronaldo went to the turf, clutching his knee, but he remained in the game. A few minutes later, the hobbling Ronaldo went down again, receiving treatment on the sideline before returning to action. Finally, just 25 minutes into the match, the superstar forward could take no more. Grimacing and hugely disappointed, Ronaldo left the pitch on a stretcher. At the time, Ronaldo's injury seemed to spell doom for the Portuguese. The *Seleção* have a poor track record in international tournaments, and it looked like the grit that got them through the month-long Euro 16 would not be enough to win it as well.

France dominated the first half, but several scoring opportunities turned up nothing—thanks largely to Patrício, who made several outstanding saves and repeatedly snatched the ball amidst pockets of French attackers and Portuguese defenders. After a lackluster second half, time expired with the score still 0-0—the first time a Euro championship final had remained scoreless through 90 minutes.

Extra time, too, began uneventfully, and the match seemed destined to end in a penalty shootout. But then, shortly after a Portuguese miss off the crossbar, Éder, who had

Portugal's Cristiano Ronaldo lifts the Euro 2016 trophy as his teammates celebrate their 1-0 championship win over France on July 10, 2016.

entered the match in the 79th minute, snaked a goal past French keeper Hugo Lloris to put the Portuguese up 1-0—a lead they would not relinquish.

Portugal's victory ended a run of 10 straight losses to France, which lost a major tournament on home soil for the first time since 1960. Ronaldo, who had languished and then cheered and then celebrated on the sideline, was the first to raise the Henri Delaunay Cup for Portugal in the *Seleção's* finest moment to date.

MAJOR LEAGUE SOCCER

The 2016 Major League Soccer (MLS) regular season ended with a dramatic Decision Day on October 23. A final game loss knocked last year's MLS champion, the Portland Timbers, out of the Audi 2016 MLS Cup Playoffs. (2015's runner-up, Columbus Crew SC, suffered a rough season and slipped well below the playoff mark in the Eastern Conference.) With a win, the Colorado Rapids had a chance to tie first-place FC Dallas in the Western Conference, but they fell short by drawing against the lowly Houston Dynamo. FC Dallas, who also drew on Decision Day, won the Supporters' Shield as the MLS team with the best regular season record (17-8-9). Four teams—the Philadelphia Union, Real Salt Lake, the Seattle Sounders, and Sporting Kansas City—slid into playoff spots on the season's last day.

New York's two teams—the Red Bulls and NYCFC—enjoyed outstanding seasons and finished 1-2 in the Eastern Conference. The other playoff teams in the east were Toronto FC, D.C. United, the Montreal Impact, and Philadelphia. In the west, the LA Galaxy finished third ahead of the Decision Day latecomers.

Red Bulls forward Bradley Wright-Phillips led MLS in scoring with 24 goals, edging out his cross-town rival, David Villa of NYCFC, who scored 23 goals during the year. Red Bulls midfielder Sacha Kljestan led the league in assists with 19. Not surprisingly, the Red Bulls and NYCFC finished 1-2 in team scoring for the year.

In July, the MLS All-Stars lost to English soccer powerhouse Arsenal FC, 2-1. In September, Dallas defeated the New England Revolution in the final of the 2016 Lamar Hunt U.S. Open Cup. In October, Atlanta United FC and Minnesota United FC—two new MLS teams that will begin play in 2017—made selections in an expansion draft held ahead of the MLS SuperDraft in January 2017.

On July 20, 2016, FC Dallas forward Fabian Castillo (11) heads in the winning goal late in the Lamar Hunt US Open Cup Quarterfinal match against the Houston Dynamo at BBVA Compass Stadium in Houston, Texas.

SHARAPOVA'S MELDONIUM MIX-UP

In June 2016, the International Tennis Federation (ITF) suspended Russian star Maria Sharapova from competition for two years for using the banned drug *meldonium*. Sharapova, a five-time grand slam champion, tested positive for the drug during the Australian Open in January 2016, just weeks after the drug was officially banned by the World Anti-Doping Agency (WADA). Meldonium is used to treat heart disease and diabetes, but the drug, which increases blood flow, has also been used to enhance athletic performance. Sharapova, who has taken the drug for 10 years, said she had used it for legitimate medical reasons—a magnesium deficiency and a family history of diabetes. Sharapova also claimed not to have known about meldonium's ban, which went into effect on January 1. She appealed her suspension to the Court of Arbitration for Sport (CAS) in Lausanne, Switzerland. In October, the CAS reduced the suspension to 15 months, saying Sharapova's level of fault did not merit the full 2-year suspension. The reduction in the suspension (which dates from her positive drug test in January 2016) allows Sharapova to return to competition in time for the 2017 French Open in May. Sharapova, who turned 29 in April 2016, has played professional tennis since she was 14. She has reached the ranking of number-one women's player in the world several times.

Meldonium, also known as mildronate, is manufactured in Latvia and only distributed in Baltic countries and Russia. It is not approved by the United States Food and Drug Administration and is not authorized for use in the rest of Europe. Drug tests of Russian athletes in 2015 found that 17 percent of them had taken meldonium (globally, just 2 percent of athletes tested positive for the drug). Some gray area followed the drug's ban in 2016, as it was unclear exactly how long the drug remained in a person's system. This did not affect Sharapova's case, however, as she never denied taking the drug. More than 60 athletes, including Olympic medalists and world champions, tested positive for meldonium in the early months of 2016.

TENNIS IN 2016

At the Stade Roland Garros in Paris, France, Novak Djokovic of Serbia serves during the men's final of the French Open on June 5, 2016. Djokovic defeated British tennis star Andy Murray for his 12th career grand slam victory.

MAJOR TENNIS TITLES

This table lists the winners of the 2016 grand slam tennis tournaments.

Australian Open

Men's singles	Novak Djokovic, Serbia
Women's singles	Angelique Kerber, Germany

French Open

Men's singles	Novak Djokovic, Serbia
Women's singles	Garbiñe Muguruza, Spain

Wimbledon

Men's singles	Andy Murray, United Kingdom
Women's singles	Serena Williams, United States

US Open

Men's singles	Stan Wawrinka, Switzerland
Women's singles	Angelique Kerber, Germany

THE GAMES FROM IPANEMA (RIO 2016)

BY JAKE BUMGARDNER

Despite fears of crime, political unrest, pollution, terrorism, and the Zika virus, the 2016 Summer Olympic Games in Rio de Janeiro, Brazil, were largely problem-free and will be remembered—as they should be—for the often awe-inspiring and thrilling athletic performances. The opening ceremonies took place on Friday, August 5, celebrating Brazilian history and culture through bossa nova and hip hop and elaborately choreographed dance numbers. More than 11,000 athletes from 206 nations (plus a refugee team and an "independent" team) entered Rio's famous Maracanã Stadium that Friday night. (If you're counting, there are 196 independent countries in the world, but some dependencies, such as Bermuda and Puerto Rico, have their own teams.) There was no shortage of pomp and circumstance, and above it all were the many shots of Christ the Redeemer, the famous statue lording over Mount Corcovado above the beautiful city and Guanabara Bay. The myriad athletic competitions—which actually began two days before—then took place, seemingly round-the-clock, in more

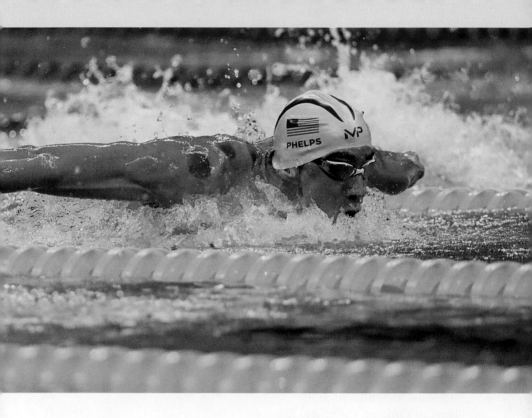

than 30 locations around Rio for the next 16 days.

United States athletes dominated the competition, winning 46 gold medals and 121 medals overall. The United Kingdom and China finished with 27 and 26 golds respectively, and 133 total medals between them. Russian athletes—despite having their ranks thinned significantly by doping scandals—pulled in the fourth-most medals, followed by Germany, France, and Japan. Olympic stars included such familiar faces as Jamaica's Usain Bolt (who won gold in the 100-meter dash for a third straight Olympics) and U.S. swimmer Michael Phelps (who upped his Olympic-record gold medal tally to 23). New Olympic legacies were created, too, particularly by U.S. swimmer Katie Ledecky and U.S. gymnast Simone Biles. Brazil's men's soccer team restored its dignity by winning gold at Rio, while the heavily favored U.S. women's soccer team flopped out in the quarterfinals. Team USA raked in the nation's 1,000th gold medal in its Summer Olympics history,

U.S. swimmer Michael Phelps competes in the men's 200-meter butterfly at Olympic Aquatics Stadium in Rio de Janeiro on Aug. 8, 2016. Phelps, who won gold in the event, bears "cupping" marks on his shoulders from a suction therapy used to help muscles recover quickly from stress.

while Fiji, Kosovo, Puerto Rico, Singapore, Tajikistan, and Vietnam each won their first.

The games saw some problems, however, like the murky green waters of the Maria Lenk Aquatic Center—called "the swamp" by some Olympic divers. The emerald green waters, tinted by an accidental mixture of hydrogen peroxide with chlorine, "posed no health risks," but the water had to be drained and replaced—all 1 million gallons of it—for clear-water acts such as synchronized swimming and water polo. Crime too was an issue after a few athletes were mugged in the night streets of Rio, but the biggest "crime" was a false mugging claim made by partying U.S. swimmers prior to leaving for home. There were maintenance problems in some athletic dorms, wave-demolished platforms, nonhuman spectators in some Olympic venues, and a host of other small complaints, but the biggest fears went unrealized, leaving Vinicius, the offical Rio 2016 mascot, a happy "mix of all the animals found in Brazil."

MEDAL WINNING NATIONS

Nation	GOLD	SILVER	BRONZE	Total
United States	46	37	38	121
China	26	18	26	70
United Kingdom	27	23	17	67
Russia	19	18	19	56
Germany	17	10	15	42
France	10	18	14	42
Japan	12	8	21	41
Australia	8	11	10	29
Italy	8	12	8	28
Canada	4	3	15	22

ARCHERY

Men's Individual
GOLD   Ku Bon-chan, South Korea
SILVER   Jean-Charles Valladont, France
BRONZE   Brady Ellison, United States

Men's Team
GOLD   South Korea
SILVER   United States
BRONZE   Australia

Women's Individual
GOLD   Chang Hye-jin, South Korea
SILVER   Lisa Unruh, Germany
BRONZE   Ki Bo-bae, South Korea

Women's Team
GOLD   South Korea
SILVER   Russia
BRONZE   Taiwan

BADMINTON

Men's Singles
GOLD   Chen Long, China
SILVER   Lee Chong Wei, Malaysia
BRONZE   Viktor Axelsen, Denmark

Men's Doubles
GOLD   Fu Haifeng and Zhang Nan, China
SILVER   Goh V Shem and Tan Wee Kiong, Malaysia
BRONZE   Marcus Ellis and Chris Langridge, United Kingdom

Women's Singles
GOLD   Carolina Marin, Spain
SILVER   Pusarla V. Sindhu, India
BRONZE   Nozomi Okuhara, Japan

Women's Doubles
GOLD   Misaki Matsutomo and Ayaka Takahashi, Japan
SILVER   Kamilla Rytter Juhl and Christinna Pedersen, Denmark
BRONZE   Jung Kyung-eun and Shin Seung-chan, South Korea

Mixed Doubles
GOLD   Tontowi Ahmad and Liliyana Natsir, Indonesia
SILVER   Chan Peng Soon and Goh Liu Ying, Malaysia
BRONZE   Zhang Nan and Zhao Yunlei, China

BASKETBALL

Men

GOLD	United States
SILVER	Serbia
BRONZE	Spain

Women

GOLD	United States
SILVER	Spain
BRONZE	Serbia

U.S. teammates Kyle Lowry (7) and Carmelo Anthony fight for a rebound with Serbia's Stefan Markovic at Carioca Arena in Rio de Janeiro on Aug. 21, 2016. U.S. teams won gold in both men's and women's basketball.

A CLOSER LOOK

Named after Brazilian poet and musician Vinícius de Moraes, "Vinicius" was the offical mascot of the Rio games.

BEACH VOLLEYBALL

Men
GOLD   Alison Conte Cerutti and Bruno Schmidt, Brazil
SILVER   Daniele Lupo and Paolo Nicolai, Italy
BRONZE   Alexander Brouwer and Robert Meeuwsen, Netherlands

Women
GOLD   Laura Ludwig and Kira Walkenhorst, Germany
SILVER   Ágatha Bednarczuk and Bárbara Seixas, Brazil
BRONZE   April Ross and Kerri Walsh Jennings, United States

BOXING

Men's Light Flyweight 49 kg (108 lb)
GOLD   Hasanboy Dusmatov, Uzbekistan
SILVER   Yurberjen Herney Martinez, Colombia
BRONZE   Joahnys Argilagos, Cuba, and Nico Hernández, United States

Men's Flyweight 52 kg (114 lb)
GOLD   Shakhobidin Zoirov, Uzbekistan
SILVER   Misha Aloyan, Russia
BRONZE   Yoel Finol, Venezuela, and Hu Jianguan, China

Men's Bantamweight 56 kg (123 lb)
GOLD   Robeisy Ramirez Carrazana, Cuba
SILVER   Shakur Stevenson, United States
BRONZE   Murodjon Akhmadaliev, Uzbekistan and Vladimir Nikitin, Russia

Men's Lightweight 60 kg (132 lb)
GOLD   Robson Conceicão, Brazil
SILVER   Sofiane Oumiha, France
BRONZE   Dorjnyambuu Otgondalai, Mongolia, and Lázaro Álvarez, Cuba

Men's Light Welterweight 64 kg (141 lb)
GOLD   Fazliddin Gaibnazarov, Uzbekistan
SILVER   Lorenzo Sotomayor Collazo, Azerbaijan
BRONZE   Vitaly Dunaytsev, Russia, and Artem Harutyunyan, Germany

Men's Welterweight 69 kg (152 lb)
GOLD   Daniyar Yeleussinov, Kazakhstan
SILVER   Shakhram Giyasov, Uzbekistan
BRONZE   Souleymane Cissokho, France, and Mohammed Rabii, Morocco

Men's Middleweight 75 kg (165 lb)
GOLD   Arlen López, Cuba
SILVER   Bektemir Melikuziev, Uzbekistan
BRONZE   Misael Rodriguez, Mexico, and Kamran Shakhsuvarly, Azerbaijan

Men's Light Heavyweight 81 kg (178 lb)
GOLD   Julio César La Cruz, Cuba
SILVER   Adilbek Niyazymbetov, Kazakhstan
BRONZE   Mathieu Bauderlique, France, Joshua Buatsi, United Kingdom

Men's Heavyweight 91 kg (200 lb)
GOLD   Evgeny Tishchenko, Russia
SILVER   Vassiliy Levit, Kazakhstan
BRONZE   Erislandy Sávon, Cuba, and Rustam Tulaganov, Uzbekistan

Men's Super-Heavyweight over 91 kg (over 200 lb)
GOLD   Tony Yoka, France
SILVER   Joe Joyce, United Kingdom
BRONZE   Ivan Dychko, Kazakhstan, and Filip Hrgovic, Croatia

Women's Flyweight 51 kg (112 lb)
GOLD   Nicola Adams, United Kingdom
SILVER   Sarah Ourahmoune, France
BRONZE   Ren Cancan, China, and Ingrid Valencia, Colombia

Women's Lightweight 60 kg (132 lb)
GOLD   Estelle Mossely, France
SILVER   Yin Junhua, China
BRONZE   Anastasiia Beliakova, Russia, and Mira Potkonen, Finland

Women's Middleweight 75 kg (165 lb)
GOLD   Claressa Shields, United States
SILVER   Nouchka Fontijn, Netherlands
BRONZE   Li Qian, China, and Dariga Shakimova, Kazakhstan

CANOEING AND KAYAKING

MEN'S KAYAK

Kayak Slalom Singles
GOLD   Joseph Clarke, United Kingdom
SILVER   Peter Kauzer, Slovenia
BRONZE   Jiří Prskavec, Czech Republic

Kayak Single 200m
GOLD   Liam Heath, United Kingdom
SILVER   Maxime Beaumont, France
BRONZE   Saúl Craviotto, Spain and Ronald Rauhe, Germany

Kayak Double 200m
GOLD   Saúl Craviotto and Cristian Toro, Spain
SILVER   Liam Heath and Jon Schofield, United Kingdom
BRONZE   Aurimas Lankas and Edvinas Ramanauskas, Lithuania

Kayak Single 1,000m
GOLD   Marcus Walz, Spain
SILVER   Josef Dostál, Czech Republic
BRONZE   Roman Anoshkin, Russia

Kayak Double 1,000m
GOLD   Marcus Gross and Max Rendschmidt, Germany
SILVER   Marko Tomicevic and Milenko Zoric, Serbia
BRONZE   Lachlan Tame and Ken Wallace, Australia

Kayak Four 1,000m
GOLD   Germany
SILVER   Slovakia
BRONZE   Czech Republic

MEN'S CANOE

Canoe Slalom Singles
GOLD   Denis Gargaud Chanut, France
SILVER   Matej Benus, Slovakia
BRONZE   Takuya Haneda, Japan

Canoe Slalom Doubles
GOLD   Ladislav Skantár and Peter Skantár, Slovakia
SILVER   David Florence and Richard Hounslow, United Kingdom
BRONZE   Gauthier Klauss and Matthieu Péché, France

Canoe Single 200m
GOLD   Yuriy Cheban, Ukraine
SILVER   Valentin Demyanenko, Azerbaijan
BRONZE   Isaquias Queiroz dos Santos, Brazil

Canoe Single 1,000m
GOLD   Sebastian Brendel, Germany
SILVER   Isaquias Queiroz dos Santos, Brazil
BRONZE   Serghei Tarnovschi, Moldova

Canoe Double 1,000m
GOLD   Sebastian Brendel and Jan Vandrey, Germany
SILVER   Erlon Silva and Isaquias Queiroz dos Santos, Brazil
BRONZE   Dmytro Ianchuk and Taras Mishchuk, Ukraine

WOMEN'S

Kayak Slalom Singles
GOLD   Maialen Chourraut, Spain
SILVER   Luuka Jones, New Zealand
BRONZE   Jessica Fox, Australia

Kayak Single 200m
GOLD   Lisa Carrington, New Zealand
SILVER   Marta Walczykiewicz, Poland
BRONZE   Inna Osipenko-Rodomska, Azerbaijan

Kayak Single 500m
GOLD   Danuta Kozák, Hungary
SILVER   Emma Jørgensen, Denmark
BRONZE   Lisa Carrington, New Zealand

Kayak Double 500m
GOLD   Danuta Kozák and Gabriella Szabó, Hungary
SILVER   Tina Dietze and Franziska Weber, Germany
BRONZE   Beata Mikolajczyk and Karolina Naja, Poland

Kayak Four 500m
GOLD   Hungary
SILVER   Germany
BRONZE   Belarus

CYCLING

MEN
TRACK

Men's Sprint
GOLD   Jason Kenny, United Kingdom
SILVER   Callum Skinner, United Kingdom
BRONZE   Denis Dmitriev, Russia

Men's Team Sprint
GOLD   United Kingdom†
SILVER   New Zealand
BRONZE   France

Men's Keirin
GOLD   Jason Kenny, United Kingdom
SILVER   Matthijs Buchli, Netherlands
BRONZE   Azizulhasni Awang, Malaysia

Men's Team Pursuit
GOLD   United Kingdom
SILVER   Australia
BRONZE   Denmark

Men's Omnium
GOLD   Elia Viviani, Italy
SILVER   Mark Cavendish, United Kingdom
BRONZE   Lasse Norman Hansen, Denmark

BMX
Men's BMX
GOLD   Connor Fields, United States
SILVER   Jelle van Gorkom, Netherlands
BRONZE   Carlos Ramirez, Colombia

MOUNTAIN BIKE
Men's Cross-country
GOLD   Nino Schurter, Switzerland
SILVER   Jaroslav Kulhavy, Czech Republic
BRONZE   Carlos Coloma Nicolas, Spain

† Olympic record

CYCLING, continued

ROAD
Men's Road Race
GOLD   Greg van Avermaet, Belgium
SILVER Jakob Fuglsang, Denmark
BRONZE Rafal Majka, Poland

Men's Individual Time Trial
GOLD   Fabian Cancellara, Switzerland
SILVER Tom Dumoulin, Netherlands
BRONZE Christopher Froome, United Kingdom

WOMEN
TRACK
Women's Sprint
GOLD   Kristina Vogel, Germany
SILVER Becky James, United Kingdom
BRONZE Katy Marchant, United Kingdom

Women's Team Sprint
GOLD   Gong Jinjie and Zhong Tianshi, China
SILVER Daria Shmeleva and Anastasia
        Voynova, Russia
BRONZE Kristina Vogel and Miriam Welte,
        Germany

Women's Keirin
GOLD   Elis Ligtlee, Netherlands
SILVER Rebecca James, United Kingdom
BRONZE Anna Meares, Australia

Women's Team Pursuit
GOLD   United Kingdom*
SILVER United States
BRONZE Canada

Women's Omnium
GOLD   Laura Trott, United Kingdom
SILVER Sarah Hammer, United States
BRONZE Jolien D'Hoore, Belgium

BMX
Women's BMX
GOLD   Mariana Pajón, Colombia
SILVER Alise Post, United States
BRONZE Stefany Hernandez, Venezuela

MOUNTAIN BIKE
Women's Cross-country
GOLD   Jenny Rissveds, Sweden
SILVER Maja Wloszczowska, Poland
BRONZE Catharine Pendrel, Canada

ROAD
Women's Road Race
GOLD   Anna van der Breggen, Netherlands
SILVER Emma Johansson, Sweden
BRONZE Elisa Longo Borghini, Italy

Women's Individual Time Trial
GOLD   Kristin Armstrong, United States
SILVER Olga Zabelinskaya, Russia
BRONZE Anna van der Breggen, Netherlands

DIVING

Men's 3m Springboard
GOLD   Cao Yuan, China
SILVER Jack Laugher, United Kingdom
BRONZE Patrick Hausding, Germany

Men's 10m Platform
GOLD   Chen Aisen, China
SILVER Germán Sánchez, Mexico
BRONZE David Boudia, United States

Men's Synchronized 3m Springboard
GOLD   Jack Laugher and Chris Mears,
        United Kingdom
SILVER Sam Dorman and Mike Hixon,
        United States
BRONZE Cao Yuan and Qin Kai, China

Men's Synchronized 10m Platform
GOLD   Chen Aisen and Lin Yue, China
SILVER David Boudia and Steele Johnson,
        United States
BRONZE Thomas Daley and Daniel
        Goodfellow, United Kingdom

Women's 3m Springboard
GOLD   Shi Tingmao, China
SILVER He Zi, China
BRONZE Tania Cagnotto, Italy

Women's 10m Platform
GOLD   Ren Qian, China
SILVER Si Yajie, China
BRONZE Meaghan Benfeito, Canada

Women's Synchronized 3m Springboard
GOLD   Shi Tingmao and Wu Minxia,
        China
SILVER Tania Cagnotto and Francesca
        Dallapé, Italy
BRONZE Maddison Keeney and Anabelle
        Smith, Australia

Women's Synchronized 10m Platform
GOLD   Chen Ruolin and Liu Huixia, China
SILVER Cheong Jun Hoong and Pandelela
        Rinong Pamg, Malaysia
BRONZE Meaghan Benfeito and Roseline
        Filion, Canada

* World record

EQUESTRIAN

INDIVIDUAL EVENTS

Individual Dressage
GOLD Charlotte Dujardin, United Kingdom
SILVER Isabell Werth, Germany
BRONZE Kristina Bröring-Sprehe, Germany

Individual Jumping
GOLD Nick Skelton, United Kingdom
SILVER Peder Fredricson, Sweden
BRONZE Eric Lamaze, Canada

Individual Eventing
GOLD Michael Jung, Germany
SILVER Astier Nicolas, France
BRONZE Phillip Dutton, United States

TEAM EVENTS

Team Dressage
GOLD Germany
SILVER United Kingdom
BRONZE United States

Team Jumping
GOLD France
SILVER United States
BRONZE Germany

Team Eventing
GOLD France
SILVER Germany
BRONZE Australia

FENCING

INDIVIDUAL

Men's Foil
GOLD Daniele Garozzo, Italy
SILVER Alexander Massialas, United States
BRONZE Timur Safin, Russia

Men's Épée
GOLD Park Sang-young, South Korea
SILVER Géza Imre, Hungary
BRONZE Gauthier Grumier, France

Men's Sabre
GOLD Áron Szilágyi, Hungary
SILVER Daryl Homer, United States
BRONZE Kim Jung-hwan, South Korea

Women's Foil
GOLD Inna Deriglazova, Russia
SILVER Elisa Di Francisca, Italy
BRONZE Ines Boubakri, Turkey

Women's Épée
GOLD Emese Szász, Hungary
SILVER Rossella Fiamingo, Italy
BRONZE Sun Yiwen, China

Women's Sabre
GOLD Yana Egorian, Russia
SILVER Sofya Velikaya, Russia
BRONZE Olga Kharlan, Ukraine

TEAM

Men's Team Épée
GOLD France
SILVER Italy
BRONZE Hungary

Men's Team Foil
GOLD Russia
SILVER France
BRONZE United States

Women's Team Épée
GOLD Romania
SILVER China
BRONZE Russia

Women's Team Sabre
GOLD Russia
SILVER Ukraine
BRONZE United States

FIELD HOCKEY

Men
GOLD Argentina
SILVER Belgium
BRONZE Germany

Women
GOLD United Kingdom
SILVER Netherlands
BRONZE Germany

GOLF

Men
GOLD Justin Rose, United Kingdom
SILVER Henrik Stenson, Sweden
BRONZE Matt Kuchar, United States

Women
GOLD Inbee Park, South Korea
SILVER Lydia Ko, New Zealand
BRONZE Shanshan Feng, China

GYMNASTICS

MEN

Men's Team All-Around

GOLD	Japan
SILVER	Russia
BRONZE	China

Men's Individual All-Around

GOLD	Kohei Uchimura, Japan
SILVER	Oleg Verniaiev, Ukraine
BRONZE	Max Whitlock, United Kingdom

Men's Floor Exercise

GOLD	Max Whitlock, United Kingdom
SILVER	Diego Hypólito, Brazil
BRONZE	Arthur Mariano, Brazil

Men's Pommel Horse

GOLD	Max Whitlock, United Kingdom
SILVER	Louis Smith, United Kingdom
BRONZE	Alexander Naddour, United States

Men's Rings

GOLD	Eleftherios Petrounias, Greece
SILVER	Arthur Zanetti, Brazil
BRONZE	Denis Ablyazin, Russia

Men's Vault

GOLD	Ri Se-gwang, North Korea
SILVER	Denis Ablyazin, Russia
BRONZE	Kenzo Shirai, Japan

Men's Parallel Bars

GOLD	Oleg Verniaiev, Ukraine
SILVER	Danell Leyva, United States
BRONZE	David Belyavskiy, Russia

Men's Horizontal Bars

GOLD	Fabian Hambüchen, Germany
SILVER	Danell Leyva, United States
BRONZE	Nile Wilson, United Kingdom

Men's Trampoline

GOLD	Uladzislau Hancharou, Belarus
SILVER	Dong Dong, China
BRONZE	Gao Lei, China

WOMEN

Women's Team All-Around

GOLD	United States
SILVER	Russia
BRONZE	China

Women's Individual All-Around

GOLD	Simone Biles, United States
SILVER	Aly Raisman, United States
BRONZE	Aliya Mustafina, Russia

Women's Vault

GOLD	Simone Biles, United States
SILVER	Maria Paseka, Russia
BRONZE	Giulia Steingruber, Switzerland

Women's Uneven Bars

GOLD	Aliya Mustafina, Russia
SILVER	Madison Kocian, United States
BRONZE	Sophie Scheder, Germany

Women's Beam

GOLD	Sanne Wevers, Netherlands
SILVER	Laurie Hernandez, United States
BRONZE	Simone Biles, United States

Women's Floor Exercise

GOLD	Simone Biles, United States
SILVER	Aly Raisman, United States
BRONZE	Amy Tinkler, United Kingdom

Women's Trampoline

GOLD	Rosannagh MacLennan, Canada
SILVER	Bryony Page, United Kingdom
BRONZE	Li Dan, China

U.S. gymnast Simone Biles competes on the beam during the women's team all-around on Aug. 9, 2016. The U.S. women's team took gold in the competition.

A CLOSER
LOOK

Australia's Chloe Esposito rides during the show jumping event of the women's modern pentathlon in Rio de Janeiro on Aug. 19, 2016. Esposito took gold in the competition.

MODERN PENTATHLON

Men

GOLD	Aleksander Lesun, Russia[†]
SILVER	Pavlo Tymoshchenko, Ukraine
BRONZE	Ismael Hernandez Uscanga, Mexico

Women

GOLD	Chloe Esposito, Australia[†]
SILVER	Elodie Clouvel, France
BRONZE	Oktawia Nowacka, Poland

[†] Olympic record

RHYTHMIC GYMNASTICS

Individual All-Around

GOLD	Margarita Mamun, Russia
SILVER	Yana Kudryavtseva, Russia
BRONZE	Ganna Rizatdinova, Ukraine

Team All-Around

GOLD	Russia
SILVER	Spain
BRONZE	Bulgaria

JUDO

Men

Men's Extra Lightweight 60 kg (132 lb)

GOLD	Beslan Mudranov, Russia
SILVER	Yeldos Smetov, Kazakhstan
BRONZE	Naohisa Takato, Japan, and Diyorbek Urozboev, Uzbekistan

Men's Half-lightweight 66 kg (145 lb)

GOLD	Fabio Basile, Italy
SILVER	An Baul, South Korea
BRONZE	Masashi Ebinuma, and Rishod Sobirov, Uzbekistan

Men's Lightweight 73 kg (161 lb)

GOLD	Shohei Ono, Japan
SILVER	Rustam Orujov, Azerbaijan
BRONZE	Lasha Shavdatuashvili, Georgia, and Dirk Van Tichelt, Belgium

Men's Half-middleweight 81 kg (179 lb)

GOLD	Khasan Khalmurzaev, Russia
SILVER	Travis Stevens, United States
BRONZE	Takanori Nagase, Japan, and Sergiu Toma, United Arab Emirates

Men's Middleweight 90 kg (198 lb)

GOLD	Mashu Baker, Japan
SILVER	Varlam, Liparteliani, Georgia
BRONZE	Gwak Dong-han, South Korea, and Cheng Xunzhao, China

Men's Half-heavyweight 100 kg (220 lb)

GOLD	Lukás Krpálek, Czech Republic
SILVER	Elmar Gasimov, Azerbaijan
BRONZE	Ryunosuke Haga, Japan, and Cyrille Maret, France

Men's Heavyweight over 100 kg (220 lb)

GOLD	Teddy Riner, France
SILVER	Hisayoshi Harasawa, Japan
BRONZE	Or Sasson, Israel, and Rafael Silva, Brazil

Women

Women's Extra Lightweight 48 kg (106 lb)
GOLD   Paula Pareto, Argentina
SILVER   Bo Kyeong Jeong, South Korea
BRONZE   Otgontsetseg Galbadrakh, Kazakhstan, and Ami Kondo, Japan

Women's Half-lightweight 52 kg (114 lb)
GOLD   Majlinda Kelmendi, Kosovo
SILVER   Odette Giuffrida, Italy
BRONZE   Misato Nakamura, Japan, and Natalia Kuziutina, Russia

Women's Lightweight 57 kg (125 lb)
GOLD   Rafaela Silva, Brazil
SILVER   Dorjsürengiin Sumiya, Mongolia
BRONZE   Kaori Matsumoto, Japan, and Telma Monteiro, Portugal

Women's Half-middleweight 63 kg (139 lb)
GOLD   Tina Trstenjak, Slovenia
SILVER   Clarisse Agbegnenou, France
BRONZE   Yarden Gerbi, Israel, and Anicka van Emden, Netherlands

Women's Middleweight 70 kg (154 lb)
GOLD   Haruka Tachimoto, Japan
SILVER   Yuri Alvear, Colombia
BRONZE   Sally Conway, United Kingdom, and Laura Vargas Koch, Germany

Women's Half-heavyweight 78 kg (172 lb)
GOLD   Kayla Harrison, United States
SILVER   Audrey Tcheuméo, France
BRONZE   Mayra Aguiar, Brazil, and Anamari Velensek, Slovenia

Women's Heavyweight over 78 kg (over 172 lb)
GOLD   Émilie Andéol, France
SILVER   Idalys Ortiz, Cuba
BRONZE   Yu Song, China, and Kanae Yamabe, Japan

ROWING

MEN

Men's Single Sculls
GOLD   Mahé Drysdale, New Zealand
SILVER   Damir Martin, Croatia
BRONZE   Ondrej Synek, Czech Republic

Men's Double Sculls
GOLD   Martin Sinkovic and Valent Sinkovic, Croatia
SILVER   Mindaugas Griskonis and Saulius Ritter, Lithuania
BRONZE   Kjetil Borch and Olaf Tufte, Norway

Men's Lightweight Double Sculls
GOLD   Jeremie Azou and Pierre Houin, France
SILVER   Gary O'Donovan and Paul O'Donovan, Ireland
BRONZE   Kristoffer Brun and Are Strandli, Norway

Men's Quadruple Sculls
GOLD   Germany
SILVER   Australia
BRONZE   Estonia

Men's Pair
GOLD   Hamish Bond and Eric Murray, New Zealand
SILVER   Lawrence Brittain and Shaun Keeling, South Africa
BRONZE   Giovanni Abagnale and Marco Di Costanzo, Italy

Men's Four
GOLD   United Kingdom
SILVER   Australia
BRONZE   Italy

Men's Lightweight Four
GOLD   Switzerland
SILVER   Denmark
BRONZE   France

Men's Eight
GOLD   United Kingdom
SILVER   Germany
BRONZE   Netherlands

WOMEN

Women's Single Sculls
GOLD   Kimberley Brennan, Australia
SILVER   Gevvie Stone, United States
BRONZE   Duan Jingli, China

Women's Double Sculls
GOLD   Magdalena Fularczyk-Kozlowska and Natalia Madaj, Poland
SILVER   Katherine Grainger and Victoria Thornley, United Kingdom
BRONZE   Milda Valciukaite and Donata Vistartaite, Lithuania

Women's Lightweight Double Sculls
GOLD   Maaike Head and Ilse Paulis, Netherlands
SILVER   Lindsay Jennerich and Patricia Obee, Canada
BRONZE   Huang Wenyi and Pan Feihong, China

Women's Quadruple Sculls
GOLD   Germany
SILVER   Netherlands
BRONZE   Poland

Women's Pair
GOLD   Helen Glover and Heather Stanning, United Kingdom
SILVER   Genevieve Behrent and Rebecca Scown, New Zealand
BRONZE   Anne Andersen and Hedvig Rasmussen, Denmark

Women's Eight
GOLD   United States
SILVER   United Kingdom
BRONZE   Romania

RUGBY SEVENS

Men
GOLD	Fiji
SILVER	United Kingdom
BRONZE	South Africa

Women
GOLD	Australia
SILVER	New Zealand
BRONZE	Canada

SAILING

MEN

Men's RS:X
GOLD	Dorian van Rijsselberghe, Netherlands
SILVER	Nick Dempsey, United Kingdom
BRONZE	Pierre Le Coq, France

Men's Laser
GOLD	Tom Burton, Australia
SILVER	Tonci Stipanovic, Croatia
BRONZE	Sam Meech, New Zealand

Men's Finn
GOLD	Giles Scott, United Kingdom
SILVER	Vasilij Zbogar, Slovenia
BRONZE	Caleb Paine, United States

Men's 470
GOLD	Sime Fantela and Igor Marenic, Croatia
SILVER	Mathew Belcher and William Ryan, Australia
BRONZE	Pavlos Kagialis and Panagiotis Mantis, Greece

Men's 49er
GOLD	Peter Burling and Blair Tuke, New Zealand
SILVER	Iain Jensen and Nathan Outteridge, Australia
BRONZE	Erik Heil and Thomas Ploessel, Germany

WOMEN

Women's RS:X
GOLD	Charline Picon, France
SILVER	Chen Peina, China
BRONZE	Stefania Elfutina, Russia

Women's Laser Radial
GOLD	Marit Bouwmeester, Netherlands
SILVER	Annalise Murphy, Ireland
BRONZE	Anne-Marie Rindom, Denmark

New Zealand's Peter Burling, *left*, and Blair Tuke celebrate their victory in the men's 49er FX (2-person skiff) race in Rio de Janeiro on Aug. 18, 2016.

Women's 470
GOLD   Saskia Clark and Hannah Mills, United Kingdom
SILVER   Jo Aleh and Polly Powrie, New Zealand
BRONZE   Hélène Defrance and Camille Lecointre, France

Women's 49er
GOLD   Martine Grael and Kahena Kunze, Brazil
SILVER   Alex Maloney and Molly Meech, New Zealand
BRONZE   Jena Hansen and Katja Salskov-Iversen, Denmark

MIXED
Nacra 17
GOLD   Santiago Lange and Cecilia Carranza Saroli, Argentina
SILVER   Lisa Darmanin and Jason Waterhouse, Australia
BRONZE   Tanja Frank and Thomas Zajac, Austria

SHOOTING

Men's 10m Air Rifle
GOLD   Niccolò Campriani, Italy
SILVER   Serhiy Kulish, Ukraine
BRONZE   Vladimir Maslennikov, Russia

Men's 50m Rifle Prone
GOLD   Henri Junghaenel, Germany
SILVER   Kim Jong-hyun, South Korea
BRONZE   Kirill Grigoryan, Russia

Men's 50m Rifle 3 Positions
GOLD   Niccolò Campriani, Italy
SILVER   Sergey Kamenskiy, Russia
BRONZE   Alexis Raynaud, France

Men's 10m Air Pistol
GOLD   Hoang Xuan Vinh, Vietnam
SILVER   Felipe Almeida Wu, Brazil
BRONZE   Pang Wei, China

Men's 50m Pistol
GOLD   Jim Jongoh, South Korea
SILVER   Hoang Xuan Vinh, Vietnam
BRONZE   Kim Song Guk, North Korea

Men's 25m Rapid Fire Pistol
GOLD   Christian Reitz, Germany
SILVER   Jean Quiquampoix, France
BRONZE   Li Yuehong, China

Men's Trap
GOLD   Josip Glasnovic, Croatia
SILVER   Giovanni Pellielo, Italy
BRONZE   Edward Ling, United Kingdom

Men's Double Trap
GOLD   Fehaid Aldeehani, Independent
        Olympic Athletes
SILVER   Marco Innocenti, Italy
BRONZE   Steven Scott, United Kingdom

Men's Skeet
GOLD   Gabriele Rossetti, Italy
SILVER   Marcus Svensson, Sweden
BRONZE   Abdullah Al-Rashidi, Independent
        Olympic Athletes

Women's 10m Air Rifle
GOLD   Virginia Thrasher,
        United States
SILVER   Du Li, China
BRONZE   Yi Siling, China

Women's 50m Rifle 3 Positions
GOLD   Barbara Engleder,
        Germany
SILVER   Zhang Binbin, China
BRONZE   Du Li, China

Women's 10m Air Pistol
GOLD   Zhang Mengxue,
        China
SILVER   Vitalina Batsarashkina,
        Russia
BRONZE   Anna Korakaki,
        Greece

Women's 25m Pistol
GOLD   Anna Korakaki,
        Greece
SILVER   Monika Karsch,
        Germany
BRONZE   Heidi Diethelm Gerber,
        Switzerland

Women's Trap
GOLD   Catherine Skinner,
        Australia
SILVER   Natalie Rooney,
        New Zealand
BRONZE   Corey Cogdell,
        United States

Women's Skeet
GOLD   Diana Bacosi,
        Italy
SILVER   Chiara Cainero,
        Italy
BRONZE   Kim Rhode,
        United States

SOCCER

Men
GOLD   Brazil
SILVER   Germany
BRONZE   Nigeria

Women
GOLD   Germany
SILVER   Sweden
BRONZE   Canada

SWIMMING

MEN

Men's 50m Freestyle
GOLD	Anthony Ervin, United States	21.40
SILVER	Florent Manaudou, France	
BRONZE	Nathan Adrian, United States	

Men's 100m Freestyle
GOLD	Kyle Chalmers, Australia	47.58
SILVER	Pieter Timmers, Belgium	
BRONZE	Nathan Adrian, United States	

Men's 200m Freestyle
GOLD	Sun Yang, China	1:44.65
SILVER	Chad le Clos, South Africa	
BRONZE	Conor Dwyer, United States	

Men's 400m Freestyle
GOLD	Mack Horton, Australia	3:41.55
SILVER	Sun Yang, China	
BRONZE	Gabriele Detti, Italy	

Men's 1,500m Freestyle
GOLD	Gregorio Paltrinieri, Italy	14:34.57
SILVER	Connor Jaeger, United States	
BRONZE	Gabriele Detti, Italy	

Men's 100m Butterfly
GOLD	Joseph Schooling, Singapore	50.39†
SILVER	Lászió Cseh, Hungary, Chad le Clos, South Africa, and Michael Phelps, United States	

Men's 200m Butterfly
GOLD	Michael Phelps, United States	1:53.36
SILVER	Masato Sakai, Japan	
BRONZE	Tamás Kenderesi, Hungary	

Men's 100m Breaststroke
GOLD	Adam Peaty, United Kingdom	57.13*
SILVER	Cameron van der Burgh, South Africa	
BRONZE	Cody Miller, United States	

Men's 200m Breaststroke
GOLD	Dmitriy Balandin, Kazakhstan	2:07.46
SILVER	Josh Prenot, United States	
BRONZE	Anton Chupkov, Russia	

Men's 100m Backstroke
GOLD	Ryan Murphy, United States	51.97†
SILVER	Xu Jiayu, China	
BRONZE	David Plummer, United States	

Men's 200m Backstroke
GOLD	Ryan Murphy, United States	1:53.62
SILVER	Mitchell Larkin, Australia	
BRONZE	Evgeny Rylov, Russia	

Men's 200m Individual Medley
GOLD	Michael Phelps, United States	1:54.66
SILVER	Kosuke Hagino, Japan	
BRONZE	Wang Shun, China	

Men's 400m Individual Medley
GOLD	Kosuke Hagino, Japan	4:06.05
SILVER	Chase Kalisz, United States	
BRONZE	Daiya Seto, Japan	

Men's 4x100m Freestyle Relay
GOLD	United States	3:09.92
SILVER	France	
BRONZE	Australia	

Men's 4x200m Freestyle Relay
GOLD	United States	7:00.66
SILVER	United Kingdom	
BRONZE	Japan	

Men's 4x100m Medley Relay
GOLD	United States	3:27.95†
SILVER	United Kingdom	
BRONZE	Australia	

Men's Open Water 10km Marathon
GOLD	Ferry Weertman, Netherlands	1:52:59.8
SILVER	Spiros Gianniotis, Greece	
BRONZE	Marc-Antoine Olivier, France	

WOMEN

Women's 50m Freestyle
GOLD	Pernille Blume, Denmark	24.07
SILVER	Simone Manuel, United States	
BRONZE	Aliaksandra Herasimenia, Belarus	

Women's 100m Freestyle
GOLD	Simone Manuel, United States, and Penny Oleksiak, Canada	52.70†
BRONZE	Sarah Sjöström, Sweden	

Women's 200m Freestyle
GOLD	Katie Ledecky, United States	1:53.73
SILVER	Sarah Sjöström, Sweden	
BRONZE	Emma McKeon, Australia	

Women's 400m Freestyle
GOLD	Katie Ledecky, United States	3:56.46*
SILVER	Jazmin Carlin, United Kingdom	
BRONZE	Leah Smith, United States	

Women's 800m Freestyle
GOLD	Katie Ledecky, United States	8:04.79*
SILVER	Jazmin Carlin, United Kingdom	
BRONZE	Boglárka Kapás, Hungary	

Women's 100m Butterfly
GOLD	Sarah Sjöström, Sweden	55.48*
SILVER	Penny Oleksiak, Canada	
BRONZE	Dana Vollmer, United States	

* World record
† Olympic record

U.S. swimmer Katie Ledecky swims ahead of the pack in the women's 800-meter freestyle final at Olympic Aquatics Stadium in Rio de Janeiro on Aug. 12, 2016. Ledecky won gold in the race and set a new world record.

SWIMMING, continued

Women's 200m Butterfly
GOLD	Mireia Belmonte Garcia, Spain	2:04.85
SILVER	Madeline Groves, Australia	
BRONZE	Natsumi Hoshi, Japan	

Women's 100m Breaststroke
GOLD	Lilly King, United States	1:04.93†
SILVER	Yulia Efimova, Russia	
BRONZE	Katie Meili, United States	

Women's 200m Breaststroke
GOLD	Rie Kaneto, Japan	2:20.30
SILVER	Yulia Efimova, Russia	
BRONZE	Shi Jinglin, China	

Women's 100m Backstroke
GOLD	Katinka Hosszú, Hungary	58.45
SILVER	Kathleen Baker, United States	
BRONZE	Kylie Masse, Canada, and Fu Yuanhui, China	

Women's 200m Backstroke
GOLD	Madeline DiRado, United States	2:05.99
SILVER	Katinka Hosszú, Hungary	
BRONZE	Hilary Caldwell, Canada	

Women's 200m Individual Medley
GOLD	Katinka Hosszú, Hungary	2:06.58†
SILVER	Siobhan-Marie O'Connor, United Kingdom	
BRONZE	Madeline DiRado, United States	

Women's 400m Individual Medley
GOLD	Katinka Hosszú, Hungary	4:26.36*
SILVER	Madeline Dirado, United States	
BRONZE	Mireia Belmonte Garcia, Spain	

Women's 4x100m Freestyle Relay
GOLD	Australia	3:30.65*
SILVER	United States	
BRONZE	Canada	

Women's 4x200m Freestyle Relay
GOLD	United States	7:43.03
SILVER	Australia	
BRONZE	Canada	

Women's 4x100m Medley Relay
GOLD	United States	3:53.13
SILVER	Australia	
BRONZE	Denmark	

Women's Open Water 10km Marathon
GOLD	Sharon van Rouwendaal, Netherlands	1:56:32.1
SILVER	Rachele Bruni, Italy	
BRONZE	Poliana Okimoto, Brazil	

SYNCHRONIZED SWIMMING

Teams
GOLD	Russia
SILVER	China
BRONZE	Japan

Duets
GOLD	Natalia Ishchenko and Svetlana Romashina, Russia
SILVER	Huang Xuechen and Sun Wenyan, China
BRONZE	Yukiko Inui and Risako Mitsui, Japan

TABLE TENNIS

Men's Singles
GOLD	Ma Long, China
SILVER	Zhang Jike, China
BRONZE	Jun Mizutani, Japan

Women's Singles
GOLD	Ding Ning, China
SILVER	Li Xiaoxia, China
BRONZE	Kim Song I, North Korea

Men's Team
GOLD	China
SILVER	Japan
BRONZE	Germany

Women's Team
GOLD	China
SILVER	Germany
BRONZE	Japan

* World Record
† Olympic Record

A CLOSER
LOOK

TEAM HANDBALL

Men

GOLD	Denmark
SILVER	France
BRONZE	Germany

Women

GOLD	Russia
SILVER	France
BRONZE	Norway

TENNIS

Men's Singles

GOLD	Andy Murray, United Kingdom
SILVER	Juan Martín del Potro, Argentina
BRONZE	Kei Nishikori, Japan

Men's Doubles

GOLD	Marc López and Rafael Nadal, Spain
SILVER	Florin Mergea and Horia Tecau, Romania
BRONZE	Steve Johnson and Jack Sock, United States

Women's Singles

GOLD	Mónica Puig, Puerto Rico
SILVER	Angelique Kerber, Germany
BRONZE	Petra Kvitová, Czech Republic

Women's Doubles

GOLD	Ekaterina Makarova and Elena Vesnina, Russia
SILVER	Timea Bacsinszky and Martina Hingis, Switzerland
BRONZE	Lucie Safárová and Barbora Strycová, Czech Republic

Mixed Doubles

GOLD	Bethanie Mattek-Sands and Jack Sock, United States
SILVER	Rajeev Ram and Venus Williams, United States
BRONZE	Lucie Hradecká and Radek Stepánek, Czech Republic

TAE KWON DO

Men's under 58 kg (128 lb)

GOLD	Zhao Shuai, China
SILVER	Tawin Hanprab, Thailand
BRONZE	Tae-hun Kim, South Korea, and Luisito Pie, Dominican Republic

Men's under 68 kg (150 lb)

GOLD	Ahmad Abughaush, Jordan
SILVER	Alexey Denisenko, Russia
BRONZE	Joel González Bonilla, Spain, and Lee Dae-hoon, South Korea

Men's under 80 kg (176 lb)

GOLD	Cheick Sallah Cissé, Côte d'Ivoire
SILVER	Lutalo Muhammad, United Kingdom
BRONZE	Milad Beigi, Azerbaijan, and Oussama Oueslati, Tunisia

Men's over 80 kg (176 lb)

GOLD	Radik Isaev, Azerbaijan
SILVER	Abdoulrazak Issoufou Alfaga, Niger
BRONZE	Dong-min Cha, South Korea, and Maicon Siqueira, Brazil

Women's under 49 kg (108 lb)

GOLD	Kim So-hui, South Korea
SILVER	Tijana Bogdanovic, Serbia
BRONZE	Patimat Abakarova, Azerbaijan, and Panipak Wongpattanakit, Thailand

Women's under 57 kg (126 lb)

GOLD	Jade Jones, United Kingdom
SILVER	Eva Calvo Gómez, Spain
BRONZE	Kimia Alizadeh Zenoorin, Iran, and Hedaya Wahba, Egypt

Women's under 67 kg (148 lb)

GOLD	Oh Hye-ri, South Korea
SILVER	Haby Niare, France
BRONZE	Ruth Gbagbi, Côte d'Ivoire, and Nur Tatar, Turkey

Women's over 67 kg (148 lb)

GOLD	Zheng Shuyin, China
SILVER	María Espinoza, Mexico
BRONZE	Jackie Galloway, United States, and Bianca Walkden, United Kingdom

TRACK AND FIELD

MEN

Men's 100m
GOLD	Usain Bolt, Jamaica	9.81
SILVER	Justin Gatlin, United States	
BRONZE	Andre De Grasse, Canada	

Men's 200m
GOLD	Usain Bolt, Jamaica	19.78
SILVER	Andre De Grasse, Canada	
BRONZE	Christophe Lemaitre, France	

Men's 400m
GOLD	Wayde van Niekerk, South Africa	43.03*
SILVER	Kirani James, Grenada	
BRONZE	LaShawn Merritt, United States	

Men's 800m
GOLD	David Rudisha, Kenya	1:42.15
SILVER	Taoufik Makhloufi, Algeria	
BRONZE	Clayton Murphy, United States	

Men's 1,500m
GOLD	Matthew Centrowitz, Jr., United States	3:50.00
SILVER	Taoufik Makhloufi, Algeria	
BRONZE	Nick Willis, New Zealand	

Men's 5,000m
GOLD	Mohamed Farah, United Kingdom	13:03.30
SILVER	Paul Kipkemoi Chelimo, United States	
BRONZE	Hagos Gebrhiwet, Ethiopia	

Men's 10,000m
GOLD	Mohamed Farah, United Kingdom	27:05.17
SILVER	Paul Kipngetich Tanui, Kenya	
BRONZE	Tamirat Tola, Ethiopia	

Men's Marathon
GOLD	Eliud Kipchoge, Kenya	2:08.44
SILVER	Feyisa Lilesa, Ethiopia	
BRONZE	Galen Rupp, United States	

Men's 3,000m Steeplechase
GOLD	Conseslus Kipruto, Kenya	8:03.28†
SILVER	Evan Jager, United States	
BRONZE	Mahiedine Mekhissi, France	

Men's 4x100m Relay
GOLD	Jamaica	37.27
SILVER	Japan	
BRONZE	Canada	

Men's 4x400m Relay
GOLD	United States	2:57.30
SILVER	Jamaica	
BRONZE	Bahamas	

Men's 110m Hurdles
GOLD	Omar McLeod, Jamaica	13.05
SILVER	Orlando Ortega, Spain	
BRONZE	Dmitri Bascou, France	

Men's 400m Hurdles
GOLD	Kerron Clement, United States	47.73
SILVER	Boniface Mucheru Tumuti, Kenya	
BRONZE	Yasmani Copello, Turkey	

Men's Shot Put
GOLD	Ryan Crouser, United States	22.52 m (73.88 ft)†
SILVER	Joe Kovacs, United States	
BRONZE	Tomas Walsh, New Zealand	

Men's Discus
GOLD	Christoph Harting, Germany	68.37 m (224.31 ft)
SILVER	Piotr Malachowski, Poland	
BRONZE	Daniel Jasinski, Germany	

Men's Hammer
GOLD	Dilshod Nazarov, Tajikistan	78.68 m (258.14 ft)
SILVER	Ivan Tsikhan, Belarus	
BRONZE	Wojciech Nowicki, Poland	

Men's Javelin
GOLD	Thomas Röhler, Germany	90.30 m (296.26 ft)
SILVER	Julius Yego, Kenya	
BRONZE	Keshorn Walcott, Trinidad and Tobago	

Men's High Jump
GOLD	Derek Drouin, Canada	2.38 m (7.81 ft.)
SILVER	Mutasz Essa Barshim, Qatar	
BRONZE	Bohdan Bondarenko, Ukraine	

Men's Pole Vault
GOLD	Thiago Braz da Silva, Brazil	6.03 m (19.78 ft)†
SILVER	Renaud Lavillenie, France	
BRONZE	Sam Kendricks, United States	

Men's Long Jump
GOLD	Jeff Henderson, United States	8.38 m (27.49 ft)
SILVER	Luvo Manyonga, South Africa	
BRONZE	Greg Rutherford, United Kingdom	

Men's Triple Jump
GOLD	Christian Taylor, United States	17.86 m (58.60 ft)
SILVER	Will Claye, United States	
BRONZE	Dong Bin, China	

Men's 20km Walk
GOLD	Wang Zhen, China	1:19:14
SILVER	Cai Zelin, China	
BRONZE	Dane Bird-Smith, Australia	

Men's 50km Walk
GOLD	Matej Tóth, Slovakia	3:40:58
SILVER	Jared Tallent, Australia	
BRONZE	Hirooki Arai, Japan	

Men's Decathlon
GOLD	Ashton Eaton, United States	8,893 points†
SILVER	Kévin Mayer, France	
BRONZE	Damian Warner, Canada	

WOMEN

Women's 100m
GOLD	Elaine Thompson, Jamaica	10.71
SILVER	Tori Bowie, United States	
BRONZE	Shelly-Ann Fraser-Pryce, Jamaica	

Women's 200m
GOLD	Elaine Thompson, Jamaica	21.78
SILVER	Dafne Schippers, Netherlands	
BRONZE	Tori Bowie, United States	

* World record
† Olympic record

A CLOSER LOOK

Jamaican sprinter Usain Bolt grins at his lead in the men's 100-meter semifinals at Olympic Stadium in Rio de Janeiro on Aug. 14, 2016. Bolt won his third consecutive Olympic gold in the event.

TRACK AND FIELD, continued

Women's 400m

GOLD	Shaunae Miller, Bahamas	49.44
SILVER	Allyson Felix, United States	
BRONZE	Shericka Jackson, Jamaica	

Women's 800m

GOLD	Caster Semenya, South Africa	1:55.28
SILVER	Francine Niyonsaba, Burundi	
BRONZE	Margaret Wambui, Kenya	

Women's 1,500m

GOLD	Faith Chepngetich Kipyegon, Kenya	4:08.92
SILVER	Genzebe Dibaba, Ethiopia	
BRONZE	Jennifer Simpson, United States	

Women's 5,000m
GOLD   Vivian Cheruiyot, Kenya   14:26.17†
SILVER   Hellen Onsando Obiri, Kenya
BRONZE Almaz Ayana, Ethiopia

Women's 10,000m
GOLD   Almaz Ayana, Ethiopia   29:17.45*
SILVER   Vivian Cheruiyot, Kenya
BRONZE Tirunesh Dibaba, Ethiopia

Women's Marathon
GOLD   Jemima Jelagat Sumgong, Kenya   2:24:04
SILVER   Eunice Jepkirui Kirwa, Bahrain
BRONZE Mare Dibaba, Ethiopia

Women's 3,000m Steeplechase
GOLD   Ruth Jebet, Bahrain   8:59.75
SILVER   Hyvin Jepkemoi, Kenya
BRONZE Emma Coburn, United States

Women's 4x100m Relay
GOLD   United States   41.01
SILVER   Jamaica
BRONZE United Kingdom

Women's 4x400m Relay
GOLD   United States   3:19.06
SILVER   Jamaica
BRONZE United Kingdom

Women's 100m Hurdles
GOLD   Brianna Rollins, United States   12.48
SILVER   Nia Ali, United States
BRONZE Kristi Castlin, United States

Women's 400m Hurdles
GOLD   Dalilah Muhammad, United States   53.13
SILVER   Sara Petersen, Denmark
BRONZE Ashley Spencer, United States

Women's Shot Put
GOLD   Michelle Carter, United States   20.63 m (67.68 ft)
SILVER   Valerie Adams, New Zealand
BRONZE Anita Márton, Hungary

Women's Discus
GOLD   Sandra Perkovic, Croatia   69.21 m (227.06 ft)
SILVER   Mélina Robert-Michon, France
BRONZE Denia Caballero, Cuba

Women's Hammer
GOLD   Anita Wlodarczyk, Poland   82.29 m (269.98 ft)*
SILVER   Zhang Wenxiu, China
BRONZE Sophie Hitchon, United Kingdom

Women's Javelin
GOLD   Sara Kolak, Croatia   66.18 m (217.12 ft)
SILVER   Sunette Viljoen, Russia
BRONZE Barbora Spotáková, Czech Republic

Women's High Jump
GOLD   Ruth Beitia, Spain   1.97 m (6.46 ft)
SILVER   Mirela Demireva, Bulgaria
BRONZE Blanka Vlasic, Croatia

Women's Pole Vault
GOLD   Ekateríni Stefanídi, Greece   4.85 m (15.91 ft)
SILVER   Sandi Morris, United States
BRONZE Eliza McCartney, New Zealand

Women's Long Jump
GOLD   Tianna Bartoletta, United States   7.17 m (23.52 ft)
SILVER   Brittney Reese, United States
BRONZE Ivana Spanovic, Serbia

Women's Triple Jump
GOLD   Caterine Ibargüen, Colombia   15.17 m (49.77 ft)
SILVER   Yulimar Rojas, Venezuela
BRONZE Olga Rypakova, Kazakhstan

Women's 20km Walk
GOLD   Liu Hong, China   1:28:35
SILVER   María Guadalupe González, Mexico
BRONZE Lü Xiuzhi, China

Women's Heptathlon
GOLD   Nafissatou Thiam, Belgium   6,810 pts
SILVER   Jessica Ennis-Hill, United Kingdom
BRONZE Brianne Theisen-Eaton, Canada

* World Record
† Olympic Record

A CLOSER
LOOK

TRIATHLON

Men

GOLD	Alistair Brownlee, United Kingdom
SILVER	Jonathan Brownlee, United Kingdom
BRONZE	Henri Schoeman, South Africa

Women

GOLD	Gwen Jorgensen, United States
SILVER	Nicola Spirig, Switzerland
BRONZE	Vicky Holland, United Kingdom

VOLLEYBALL

Men

GOLD	Brazil
SILVER	Italy
BRONZE	United States

Women

GOLD	China
SILVER	Serbia
BRONZE	United States

WATER POLO

Men

GOLD	Serbia
SILVER	Croatia
BRONZE	Italy

Women

GOLD	United States
SILVER	Italy
BRONZE	Russia

WEIGHTLIFTING

Men's 56 kg (123 lb)

GOLD	Long Qingquan, China	307 kg (677 lb) *
SILVER	Om Yun-chol, North Korea	
BRONZE	Sinphet Kruaithong, Thailand	

Men's 62 kg (136 lb)

GOLD	Óscar Figueroa, Colombia	318 kg (701 lb)
SILVER	Eko Yuli Irawan, Indonesia	
BRONZE	Farkhad Kharki, Kazakhstan	

Men's 69 kg (152 lb)

GOLD	Shi Zhiyong, China	352 kg (776 lb)
SILVER	Daniyar Ismayilov, China	
BRONZE	Luis Javier Mosquera, Colombia	

Men's 77 kg (169 lb)

GOLD	Nijat Rahimov, Kazakhstan	379 kg (836 lb)
SILVER	Lü Xiaojun, China	
BRONZE	Mohamed Mahmoud, Egypt	

Men's 85 kg (187 lb)

GOLD	Kianoush Rostami, Iran	396 kg (873 lb)*
SILVER	Tian Tao, China	
BRONZE	Gabriel Sîncraian, Romania	

Men's 94 kg (207 lb)

GOLD	Sohrab Moradi, Iran	403 kg (888 lb)
SILVER	Vadzim Straltsou, Belarus	
BRONZE	Aurimas Didzbalis, Lithuania	

Men's 105 kg (231 lb)

GOLD	Ruslan Nurudinov, Uzbekistan	431 kg (950 lb)†
SILVER	Simon Martirosyan, Armenia	
BRONZE	Alexandr Zaichikov, Kazakhstan	

Men's over 105 kg (over 231 lb)

GOLD	Lasha Talakhadze, Georgia	473 kg (1,043 lb)*
SILVER	Gor Minasyan, Armenia	
BRONZE	Irakli Turmanidze, Georgia	

Women's 48 kg (106 lb)

GOLD	Sopita Tanasan, Thailand	200 kg (441 lb)
SILVER	Sri Wahyuni Agustiani, Indonesia	
BRONZE	Hiromi Miyake, Japan	

Women's 53 kg (117 lb)

GOLD	Hsu Shu-Ching, Taiwan	212 kg (467 lb)
SILVER	Hidilyn Diaz, Philippines	
BRONZE	Yoon Jin-hee, South Korea	

Women's 58 kg (128 lb)

GOLD	Sukanya Srisurat, Thailand	240 kg (529 lb)
SILVER	Pimsiri Sirikaew, Thailand	
BRONZE	Kuo Hsing-chun, Taiwan	

WEIGHTLIFTING, continued

Women's 63 kg (139 lb)
GOLD   Deng Wei, China   262 kg (578 lb) *
SILVER   Choe Hyo Sim, North Korea
BRONZE   Karina Goricheva, Kazakhstan

Women's 69 kg (152 lb)
GOLD   Xiang Yanmei, China   261 kg (575 lb)
SILVER   Zhazira Zhapparkul, Kazakhstan
BRONZE   Sara Ahmed, Egypt

Women's 75 kg (165 lb)
GOLD   Rim Jong-sim, North Korea   274 kg (604 lb)
SILVER   Darya Naumava, Belarus
BRONZE   Lidia Valentín Pérez, Spain

Women's over 75 kg (over 165 lb)
GOLD   Meng Suping, China   307 kg (677 lb)
SILVER   Kim Kuk-hyang, North Korea
BRONZE   Sarah Robles, United States

WRESTLING

Men's Greco-Roman 59 kg (130 lb)
GOLD   Ismael Borrero Molina, Cuba
SILVER   Shinobu Ota, Japan
BRONZE   Stig André Berge, Norway, and Elmurat Tasmuradov, Uzbekistan

Men's Greco-Roman 66 kg (145 lb)
GOLD   Davor Stefanek, Serbia
SILVER   Migran Arutyunyan, Armenia
BRONZE   Shmagi Bolkvadze, Georgia, and Rasul Chunayev, Azerbaijan

Men's Greco-Roman 75 kg (165 lb)
GOLD   Roman Vlasov, Russia
SILVER   Mark Overgaard Madsen, Denmark
BRONZE   Saeid Abdevali, Iran, and Kim Hyeon-woo, South Korea

Men's Greco-Roman 85 kg (187 lb)
GOLD   Davit Chakvetadze, Russia
SILVER   Zhan Beleniuk, Ukraine
BRONZE   Javid Hamzatau, Belarus, and Denis Kudla, Germany

Men's Greco-Roman 98 kg (216 lb)
GOLD   Artur Aleksanyan, Armenia
SILVER   Yasmany Daniel Lugo Cabrera, Cuba
BRONZE   Cenk Ildem, Turkey, and Ghasem Rezaei, Iran

Men's Greco-Roman 130 kg (287 lb)
GOLD   Mijaín López, Cuba
SILVER   Riza Kayaalp, Turkey
BRONZE   Sergey Semenov, Russia, and Sabah Shariati, Azerbaijan

Men's Freestyle 57 kg (126 lb)
GOLD   Vladimer Khinchegashvili, Georgia
SILVER   Rei Higuchi, Japan
BRONZE   Haji Aliyev, Azerbaijan, and Hassan Rahimi, Iran

Men's Freestyle 65 kg (143 lb)
GOLD   Soslan Ramonov, Russia
SILVER   Toghrul Asgarov, Azerbaijan
BRONZE   Frank Chamizo, Italy, and Ikhtiyor Navruzov, Uzbekistan

Men's Freestyle 74 kg (163 lb)
GOLD   Hassan Yazdani, Iran
SILVER   Aniuar Gedeuv, Russia
BRONZE   Soner Demirtas, Turkey, and Jabrayil Hasnov, Azerbaijan

Men's Freestyle 86 kg (190 lb)
GOLD   Abdulrashid Sadulaev, Russia
SILVER   Selim Yasar, Turkey
BRONZE   J'den Cox, United States, and Sharif Sharifov, Azerbaijan

Men's Freestyle 97 kg (214 lb)
GOLD   Kyle Snyder, United States
SILVER   Khetag Gazyumov, Azerbaijan
BRONZE   Magomed Ibragimov, Uzbekistan, and Albert Saritov, Romania

Men's Freestyle 125 kg (276 lb)
GOLD   Taha Akgül, Turkey
SILVER   Komeil Ghasemi, Iran
BRONZE   Geno Petriashvili, Georgia, and Ibrahim Saidau, Belarus

Women's Freestyle 48 kg (106 lb)
GOLD   Eri Tosaka, Japan
SILVER   Mariya Stadnik, Azerbaijan
BRONZE   Sun Yanan, China, and Elitsa Yankova, Bulgaria

Women's Freestyle 53 kg (117 lb)
GOLD   Helen Maroulis, United States
SILVER   Saori Yoshida, Japan
BRONZE   Sofia Mattsson, Sweden, and Natalya Sinishin, Azerbaijan

Women's Freestyle 58 kg (128 lb)
GOLD   Kaori Icho, Japan
SILVER   Valeriia Koblova, Russia
BRONZE   Marwa Amri, Tunisia, and Sakshi Malik, India

Women's Freestyle 63 kg (139 lb)
GOLD   Risako Kawai, Japan
SILVER   Maryia Mamashuk, Belarus
BRONZE   Yekaterina Larionova, Kazakhstan, and Monika Michalik, Poland

Women's Freestyle 69 kg (152 lb)
GOLD   Sara Dosho, Japan
SILVER   Natalia Vorobieva, Russia
BRONZE   Jenny Fransson, Sweden, and Elmira Syzdykova, Kazakhstan

Women's Freestyle 75 kg (165 lb)
GOLD   Erica Wiebe, Canada
SILVER   Guzel Manyurova, Kazakhstan
BRONZE   Ekaterina Bukina, Russia, and Zhang Fengliu, China

* World record
† Olympic record

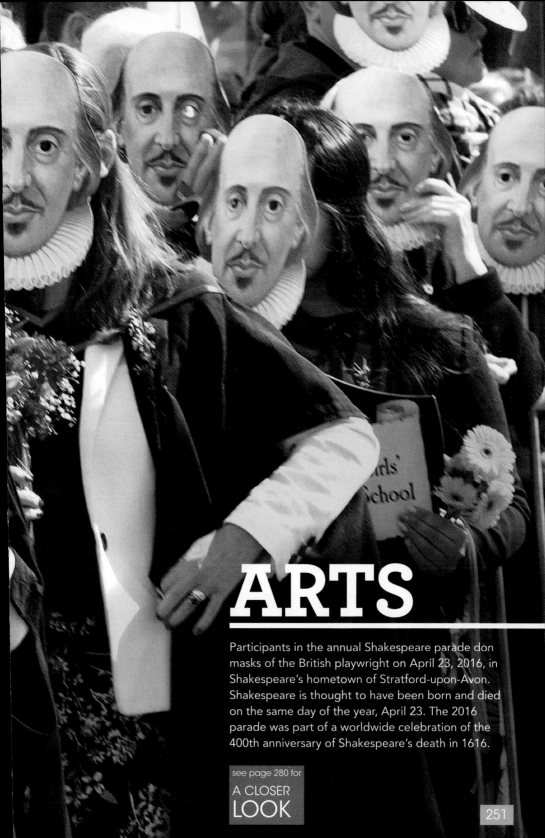

ARTS

Participants in the annual Shakespeare parade don masks of the British playwright on April 23, 2016, in Shakespeare's hometown of Stratford-upon-Avon. Shakespeare is thought to have been born and died on the same day of the year, April 23. The 2016 parade was part of a worldwide celebration of the 400th anniversary of Shakespeare's death in 1616.

see page 280 for
A CLOSER LOOK

THE NATIONAL MUSEUM OF AFRICAN AMERICAN HISTORY AND CULTURE

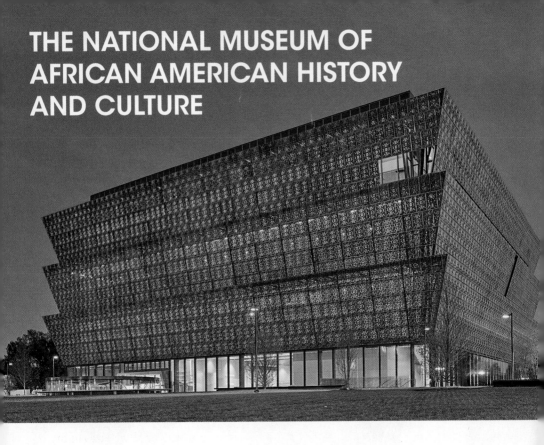

The National Museum of African American History and Culture stands on the National Mall in Washington, D.C.

On Sept. 24, 2016, the National Museum of African American History and Culture (NMAAHC) opened to the public in Washington, D.C. Prominently sited on the National Mall, the museum details the history of slavery, the period of Reconstruction, the Harlem Renaissance, segregation, and civil rights. It also highlights African Americans' achievements in the arts, entertainment, military, politics, sports, and other aspects of the wider culture. The NMAAHC is a bureau of the Smithsonian Institution.

President Barack Obama, together with his family, helped dedicate the museum. "This national museum helps to tell a richer and fuller story of who we are," he said. "Hopefully, this museum can help us to talk to each other. And more importantly, listen to each other. And most importantly, see each other. Black and white and Latino and Native American and Asian American—see how our stories are bound together." In 2009, Obama made history as the first African American president of the United States. His dedication speech came amid racial tensions stirred by September police shootings of black men in Charlotte,

North Carolina, and Tulsa, Oklahoma.

Former President George W. Bush, who authorized construction of the museum in 2003, joined President Obama at the NMAAHC dedication. "A great nation," he said, "does not hide its history. It faces its flaws and it corrects them."

Cultural material collected by the museum includes works of art, historical artifacts, photographs, moving images, archival documents, electronic data, audio recordings, books, and manuscripts. The museum's notable collections include the Harriet Tubman Collection, featuring dozens of artifacts that belonged to the Underground Railroad leader; the Ernest C. Withers Photography Collection; and the Black Fashion Museum Collection.

The $540-million museum was designed by Ghanaian-British architect David Adjaye, who was inspired by Yoruban art from West Africa. The building achieved LEED Gold certification, the second highest rating for environmental sustainability. Among the museum's "green" qualities are solar hot water panels on the roof and a geothermal ground water system.

The NMAAHC's three-tier bronzed aluminum skin contrasts starkly with the white marble of the nearby Washington Monument.

Harriet Tubman's shawl and hymnal are among the highlights of the NMAAHC collections. Tubman, a former slave who escaped to freedom, helped others do so as well through the Underground Railroad in the 1800's.

ZAHA HADID 1950-2016

Iraqi-born British architect Zaha Hadid died on March 31, 2016. Hadid contracted bronchitis shortly before suffering a fatal heart attack in Miami, Florida. She was 65.

In 2004, Hadid became the first woman to win the Pritzker Architecture Prize, the most prestigious international award in architecture. Hadid gained recognition for her visionary designs that reflected major art movements of the 1900's, especially the Russian movement called *Suprematism*. Hadid's designs show the Suprematist influence in their fragmented geometric forms that define the surrounding space in highly imaginative ways.

Many of Hadid's projects were so daring they were never built. Some projects exist only as paintings and drawings, which themselves have been praised as distinctive works of art. However, many Hadid designs were built, including the Vitra fire station (1993) in Weil am Rhein, Germany; the Lois and Richard Rosenthal Center for Contemporary Art (2003) in Cincinnati; the Phaeno Science Center (2005) in Wolfsburg, Germany; the "Spittelau viaduct" housing project (2005) in Vienna, Austria; an opera house (2010) in Guangzhou, China; the Eli and Edythe Broad Art Museum (2012) at Michigan State University in East Lansing, Michigan; and the Heydar Aliyev cultural center (2012) in Baku, Azerbaijan. Hadid also designed the Aquatics Center for the 2012 Olympic Games in London and the stadium for the 2020 Olympics in Tokyo. In addition, she designed exhibitions and interiors, such as the "Mind Zone" interior for the Millennium Dome in London in 1999.

Hadid was born on Oct. 31, 1950, in Baghdad, Iraq. She studied at the Architectural Association in London. Hadid opened her first architecture firm in London in 1979.

NOBEL PRIZE IN LITERATURE

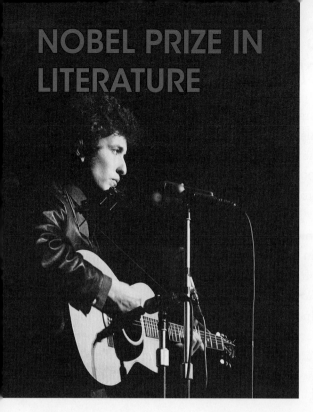

U.S. folk singer Bob Dylan, seen here on tour in England in May 1965, became the first songwriter to win the Nobel Prize in literature in 2016.

On Oct. 13, 2016, the Swedish Academy in Stockholm, Sweden, awarded the 2016 Nobel Prize in literature to the U.S. composer, singer, and musician Bob Dylan "for having created new poetic expressions within the great American song tradition." Dylan, the first songwriter to win the award, has been one of the most influential songwriters of the past 50 years. His early songs, aimed at what many people considered the wrongs of society, were often performed simply with acoustic guitar and harmonica. Such songs as "Blowin' in the Wind" and "The Times They Are A-Changin'" became anthems that helped galvanize the civil rights movement and captured the spirit of young American protesters who opposed the country's involvement in the Vietnam War.

In the late 1960's and early 1970's, Dylan produced such lasting hits as "Like a Rolling Stone," "Mr. Tambourine Man," "Subterranean Homesick Blues," "Rainy Day Women #12 & 35," "Just Like a Woman," "Lay Lady Lay," "Knockin' on Heaven's Door," and "Tangled Up in Blue."

Dylan was born Robert Zimmerman in Duluth, Minnesota, on May 24, 1941. Throughout his long and ongoing career, he has won numerous Grammy Awards and was inducted into the Rock and Roll Hall of Fame in 1988. He won an Academy Award for his song "Things Have Changed" from the 2000 motion picture *Wonder Boys*. Dylan received a Pulitzer Prize in 2008 for "his profound impact on popular music and American culture, marked by lyrical compositions of extraordinary poetic power." He also received the Presidential Medal of Freedom, one of the nation's highest civilian honors, in 2012.

FAIRY TALES FAR OLDER THAN ONCE THOUGHT

In January 2016, folklore scholars analyzing the language of popular fairy tales found that some of the stories originated more than 6,000 years ago. Sara Graca da Silva from the New University of Lisbon, Portugal, and anthropologist Jamshid Tehrani of Durham University in the United Kingdom published the findings January 20 in the journal *Royal Society Open Science*. The findings indicate that some fairy tales, such as "Rumpelstiltskin" and "Jack and the Beanstalk," are older than the myths of ancient Egypt, Greece, and Rome, and predate most of the world's religions.

Between 1807 and 1814, German brothers Jakob and Wilhelm Grimm compiled a collection of European fairy tales. The most popular tales include "Hansel and Gretel," "Little Red Riding Hood," "Sleeping Beauty," and "Rapunzel." By 1857, *Grimm's Fairy Tales* included a total of 210 stories. The Grimms collected many of the stories from printed sources, but also from tales passed down by families over generations. Most scholars believe that such tales likely originated not long before they were first written down. This would make the oldest fairy tales only a few centuries old. However, the Grimms believed many of the stories were much more ancient. They thought the basic themes of the tales were rooted in a common European culture that existed thousands of years earlier.

Graca da Silva and Tehrani conducted a linguistic analysis of 275 different fairy tales. They found that some stories originated in earlier tales. From this group, they identified 75 basic stories. They then analyzed the linguistic elements of these tales, creating a *phylogenetic tree*—a kind of "family tree" indicating the age and relationship of each story—back to their earliest origins.

They estimated that many of the tales were more than 1,000 years old. "Jack and the Beanstalk" may first have been told 5,000 years ago in a language that is no longer spoken. Another tale called "The Smith and the Devil" appears to be the most ancient. This story can be traced back some 6,000 years to the Bronze Age. The scholars found that these fairy tales date back to the birth of the Indo-European language family. Many languages spoken in India, western Asia, and Europe originated from Indo-European, including English, German, Latin, Greek, Russian, Farsi, Hindi, and Urdu.

HARPER LEE 1926-2016

American author Harper Lee died on Feb. 19, 2016, at age 89. Lee became one of the most beloved writers in American literature through the success of a single novel, *To Kill a Mockingbird*. The novel was published in 1960 and won the Pulitzer Prize for fiction in 1961. It was adapted into a popular motion picture in 1962.

The plot of *To Kill a Mockingbird* centers on Atticus Finch, a compassionate small-town white lawyer in Alabama during the mid-1930's who defends a young black man falsely accused of raping a white woman. The lawyer's six-year-old daughter, nicknamed Scout, tells the story. The appeal of the novel lies in the author's ability to weave together the vivid eccentric characters of a Southern town, the observations of a sensitive child, and a plea for social justice.

During the mid-1950's, Lee wrote a novel that took place 20 years after the events of *To Kill a Mockingbird*. The book centered on Finch's daughter, now a 26-year-old woman, returning to the small Alabama town where she was raised. The unpublished manuscript was forgotten until Lee's lawyer rediscovered it in 2014. The book was published in 2015 as *Go Set a Watchman*. The sequel became a best seller but also created controversy. The book portrayed Atticus Finch as a racist with bigoted attitudes rather than the humane and tolerant figure of the first novel.

Nelle Harper Lee was born on April 28, 1926, in Monroeville, Alabama. She grew up in the state and attended the University of Alabama. After leaving school without a degree, Lee split her time between New York City and Monroeville. In New York City, Lee often spent time with a childhood friend, author Truman Capote, who had spent part of his youth in Monroeville.

UMBERTO ECO 1932-2016

Italian philosopher, novelist, and literary critic Umberto Eco died on Feb. 19, 2016. Eco, a highly respected scholar, was best known for his writings in the field of semiotics, the study of how cultures communicate through signs and symbols. Unexpectedly, however, Eco became internationally famous in the literary world with a best-seller—his first novel, *The Name of the Rose* (*Il nome della rosa*). The murder mystery is set in a monastery in northern Italy in 1327. An English monk named William of Baskerville and his assistant, Adso (who narrates the story as an old man), are brought to the monastery to investigate the unexplained killing of a young monk found at the bottom of a well. The novel deals with the nature of truth as seen from the viewpoints of theology, philosophy, history, and scholarship. A film was made of the book in 1986, starring Sean Connery as William and Christian Slater as his assistant. Eco's later novels include *Foucault's Pendulum* (1988), *The Island of the Day Before* (1994), *Baudolino* (2002), *The Mysterious Flame of Queen Loana* (2004), *The Prague Cemetery* (2011), and *Numero Uno* (2015). His books on semiotics include *A Theory of Semiotics* (1976) and *Semiotics and the Philosophy of Language* (1984). Eco also wrote about aesthetics, beauty, ugliness, and language.

Eco was born on Jan. 5, 1932, in Alessandria, Italy. He studied philosophy at Turin University and worked for Italian state television (1954-1959) before becoming a lecturer at Turin (1961-1964). He spent periods teaching at the universities of Milan and Florence, and from 1971 to 2007 he was professor of semiotics at Bologna.

ELIE WIESEL 1928-2016

On July 2, 2016, Romanian-American author Elie Wiesel died at age 87. Wiesel dedicated his life to describing the horrors he witnessed during the Holocaust and to helping victims of oppression and racism. The Holocaust was the systematic, state-sponsored murder of Jews and others by the Nazis during World War II (1939-1945). Wiesel wrote dozens of books and won the 1986 Nobel Peace Prize.

Eliezer Wiesel was born on Sept. 30, 1928, in Sighet, Romania. In 1944, he was sent with his family and the town's other Jews to a camp at Auschwitz (now Oświęcim), Poland, near Krakow. He was later sent to a camp at Buchenwald, Germany, near Weimar. Wiesel's parents and a sister died at these camps. After Buchenwald was liberated in 1945, Wiesel settled in France. He later studied philosophy at the University of Paris, became a journalist, and moved to the United States. In 1976, Wiesel became a professor of humanities at Boston University. President Jimmy Carter appointed him chairman of the President's Commission on the Holocaust in 1979. In 1980, Wiesel was named head of the United States Holocaust Memorial Council.

Wiesel's humanitarian efforts earned him the 1986 Nobel Peace Prize. The Nobel citation reads in part: "Wiesel is a messenger to mankind. His message is one of peace, atonement, and human dignity. His belief that the forces fighting evil in the world can be victorious is a hard-won belief."

Wiesel's books include *Night* (1958, revised edition 2006), *Dawn* (1960), *The Accident* (1961), *The Jews of Silence* (1966), *A Beggar in Jerusalem* (1968), *The Testament* (1980), *Wise Men and Their Tales* (2003), and *A Mad Desire to Dance* (2009).

THE 88TH ACADEMY AWARDS

On Feb. 28, 2016, the 88th Academy Awards were presented at the Dolby Theatre in Hollywood, California. The Academy of Motion Picture Arts and Sciences supervises the awards, which are presented annually for outstanding achievements in filmmaking.

Spotlight won best picture of the year. The film tells the true story of how the *Boston Globe* newspaper uncovered a child molestation scandal and cover-up within the local Roman Catholic archdiocese. Alejandro Iñárritu won the best director Oscar for *The Revenant,* the gritty story of a frontiersman in the 1820's who fights for survival after being mauled by a bear and left for dead by members of his own hunting party. Iñárritu also won best director in 2015 for *Birdman.* Leonardo DiCaprio's performance in *The Revenant* earned him this year's Academy Award for best actor—his first Oscar win after five previous nominations. Brie Larson received best actress for her performance as a woman who is abducted and raped and then gives birth to a boy in *Room.* Mark Rylance won best supporting actor for his portrayal of a man who is captured for spying on the United States during the Cold War in *Bridge of Spies.* The Academy Award for best supporting actress went to Alicia Vikander for her performance as the wife of a transgender pioneer in *The Danish Girl. Mad Max: Fury Road* won awards for costume design, film editing, makeup and hairstyling, production design, sound editing, and sound mixing.

A number of prominent African American Hollywood stars boycotted the Oscars to protest the Academy's lack of diversity. For the second year in a row,

Leonardo DiCaprio's character fights against man and nature in the Oscar-winning film *The Revenant.*

The following winners of the 2015 Academy Awards were announced in February 2016:

Best Picture	*Spotlight*
Best Actor	Leonardo DiCaprio, *The Revenant*
Best Actress	Brie Larson, *Room*
Best Supporting Actor	Mark Rylance, *Bridge of Spies*
Best Supporting Actress	Alicia Vikander, *The Danish Girl*
Best Director	Alejandro G. Iñárritu, *The Revenant*
Best Original Screenplay	Josh Singer and Tom McCarthy, *Spotlight*
Best Adapted Screenplay	Charles Randolph and Adam McKay, *The Big Short*
Best Animated Feature	*Inside Out*
Best Cinematography	Emmanuel Lubezki, *The Revenant*
Best Film Editing	Margaret Sixel, *Mad Max: Fury Road*
Best Original Score	Ennio Morricone, *The Hateful Eight*
Best Original Song	"Writing's on the Wall" from *Spectre*
Best Foreign-Language Film	*Son of Saul* (Hungary)
Best Production Design	Colin Gibson and Lisa Thompson, *Mad Max: Fury Road*
Best Costume Design	Jenny Beavan, *Mad Max: Fury Road*
Best Sound Mixing	Chris Jenkins, Gregg Rudloff, and Ben Osmo, *Mad Max: Fury Road*
Best Sound Editing	Mark Mangini and David White, *Mad Max: Fury Road*
Best Makeup and Hairstyling	Lesley Vanderwalt, Elka Wardega, and Damian Martin, *Mad Max: Fury Road*
Best Visual Effects	Andrew Whitehurst, Paul Norris, Mark Ardington, and Sara Bennett, *Ex Machina*
Best Animated Short Film	*Bear Story*
Best Live-Action Short Film	*Stutterer*
Best Feature Documentary	*Amy*
Best Short Subject Documentary	*A Girl in the River: The Price of Forgiveness*

The characters of this year's best picture winner, *Spotlight,* discuss how they will investigate and expose a child molestation scandal within the Roman Catholic Church.

Oscar nominees in the top four acting categories included only white actors and actresses. The Twitter hashtag #OscarSoWhite, which began last year, saw a resurgence among users of the social networking website. Among the most outspoken Hollywood celebrities calling for a boycott were director Spike Lee and actress Jada Pinkett Smith, both of whom skipped the Oscars ceremony. Lee's film *Chi-Raq* failed to garner any nominations, while Pinkett Smith's husband, Will Smith, was also left out despite his strong performance in the biopic *Concussion.* Other notable omissions were British actor Idris Elba, who was projected to secure a best supporting actor nomination for his performance as an African warlord in *Beasts of No Nation;* Michael B. Jordan, who portrayed a boxer in the *Rocky* sequel *Creed;* and the cast of the biopic *Straight Outta Compton,* about the influential rap group N.W.A.

Many protesters called for the evening's host, African American comedian and actor Chris Rock, to join the boycott. Instead, Rock made the Academy's lack of diversity the target of his opening monologue and the butt of many jokes.

ALAN RICKMAN 1946-2016

British actor Alan Rickman died on Jan. 14, 2016, at age 69. Rickman was an admired actor of the British stage and on British television, but he gained international notice as a sardonic terrorist in the American action movie *Die Hard* (1988). It was Rickman's first movie.

For younger movie fans, Rickman is best known as the menacing Severus Snape in evolving roles in the eight movie versions of the "Harry Potter" books.

Although Rickman had great success playing villains in *Die Hard* and in *Robin Hood: Prince of Thieves* (1991), he won acclaim for a broad range of roles. He played a cellist in the supernatural romance *Truly, Madly, Deeply* (1991). In 1995, he played the decent and modest Colonel Brandon in the movie adaptation of the Jane Austen novel *Sense and Sensibility*, and co-starred in the romantic comedy *Love Actually* (2003). On television, Rickman won a Golden Globe award for best actor in the 1997 historical drama *Rasputin*.

Rickman was one of the most admired stage actors of his time. He appeared in classic plays by William Shakespeare, Henrik Ibsen, and Noël Coward as well as in modern plays. His stage breakthrough came in London in 1986 as a cynical aristocrat—Vicomte de Valmont—in the British play *Les Liaisons Dangereuses* (Dangerous Liaisons). Rickman repeated the role on Broadway in 1987.

Alan Sidney Patrick Rickman was born in London on Jan. 14, 1946. He opened a successful graphics design business with friends and ran it for several years, but his love of the theater led him to seek an audition with the famous Royal Academy of Dramatic Art. At the relatively late age of 26, Rickman received an Academy scholarship, launching his professional acting career.

GENE WILDER 1933-2016

American comic actor Gene Wilder, whose wild dark blond curls and blue eyes accompanied an uncanny wit and neurotic sensitivity, died on Aug. 29, 2016. Wilder starred in such legendary comedy films as *Blazing Saddles*, *The Producers*, and *Young Frankenstein*, but he is best remembered for his eccentric lead role in *Willy Wonka & the Chocolate Factory*. Wilder worked closely with Hollywood icon Mel Brooks and fellow comic actor Richard Pryor. Wilder's rule for comedy—don't try to make it funny; try to make it real—is summed up in his often-quoted statement, "I'm an actor, not a clown." He was 83.

Wilder was born Jerome Silberman on June 11, 1933, in Milwaukee, Wisconsin. He began acting as a teenager and—after graduating from the University of Iowa and a hitch in the U.S. Army—was later accepted into New York City's famous Actors Studio. Adopting the name Gene Wilder, he acted in numerous theater productions before appearing in his first film, *Bonnie and Clyde*, in 1967. The following year, he was nominated for Best Supporting Actor for his role as Leo Bloom in Mel Brooks's *The Producers*. In 1971, Wilder took his turn as Willy Wonka, and three years later he starred in the Mel Brooks comedy hits *Blazing Saddles* and *Young Frankenstein*, the latter of which Wilder co-wrote with Brooks. Over the next few years, Wilder acted in several films, including the comedy hits *Silver Streak* and *Stir Crazy* with Richard Pryor.

Wilder appeared in numerous other films in the 1980's, but never achieved the success of his early career. As a writer, Wilder collaborated on numerous film and television scripts and produced a short story collection, three novels, and a 2005 memoir. Wilder married four times. His third wife was "Saturday Night Live" actress Gilda Radner, who died of ovarian cancer a few years after their marriage in 1984.

SUMMER'S HITS

The 2016 summer movie season saw some surprises, but most of them were negative. Movies with high expectations—such as *Ghostbusters, Independence Day: Resurgence, The Legend of Tarzan, Suicide Squad*, and *Warcraft*—all flopped with audiences, critics, or both (albeit with mostly rich ticket sales). Solid formulas paid off for other films, however, as the kid-targeted and parent-approved computer animations *Finding Dory* and *The Secret Life of Pets* raked in the dollars along with the "thumbs up," as did the action films *Jason Bourne* and *Star Trek Beyond*.

▲ *Finding Dory*, a sequel to the 2003 hit *Finding Nemo*, was a hit in its own right, topping the summer box office charts in 2016.

Louis C.K. gives voice to ▶ Max the Jack Russell terrier in the 2016 summer smash, *The Secret Life of Pets*.

Matt Damon returned as *Jason Bourne* in 2016, the fifth film in the successful Bourne franchise and the first starring Damon since 2007.

MERLE HAGGARD 1937-2016

American country music legend Merle Haggard died on April 6, 2016. Haggard recorded about 40 number-one songs, many of them dealing with working-class and rebellious themes. He composed hundreds of songs, many of them country music standards. His compositions blended influences of folk music, jazz, and the blues. A member of the Country Music Hall of Fame since 1994 and a Kennedy Center Honoree in 2010, Haggard died of pneumonia after years of poor health. He was 79. In the weeks after his death, a number of country artists paid tribute to Haggard and his legacy, including Toby Keith, Scotty McCreery, and George Strait.

Merle Ronald Haggard was born on April 6, 1937, in Bakersfield, California. His parents were migrant workers from Oklahoma. Haggard quit school in the eighth grade and spent much of his youth as a drifter. He served several stints in reformatories and prisons. In 1960, Haggard started singing in Bakersfield nightclubs. He made his first recording in 1962 and his first successful record, "Sing a Sad Song," in 1963. Some of Haggard's songs reflect his troubled early life, notably "Branded Man" and "Sing Me Back Home" (both 1967).

Haggard formed his own band, the Strangers, in 1965. In 1966, Haggard recorded his first number-one hit, "I'm a Lonesome Fugitive." His best-known song is probably "Okie from Muskogee" (1969). His other hits include "Mama Tried" (1968), "Hungry Eyes" (1969), "The Fightin' Side of Me" (1970), "If We Make It Through December" (1973), "It's All in the Movies" (1975), "I'm Always on a Mountain When I Fall" (1978), "Bar Room Buddies" (a duet with Clint Eastwood, 1980), "Big City" (1981), and "Reasons to Quit" (a duet with Willie Nelson, 1983).

DAVID BOWIE 1947-2016

The music world was shocked and saddened to learn of the death on Jan. 10, 2016, of British musician, composer, and actor David Bowie, one of the most creative figures in rock history. According to a statement on his official Facebook page, Bowie died "surrounded by his family after a courageous 18-month battle with cancer." Bowie turned 69 on January 8, the day his 26th studio album, *Blackstar*, was released.

Although Bowie had kept news of his illness secret until the announcement of his death, *Blackstar* was described as a "parting gift" to his fans, according to Bowie's longtime producer and collaborator Tony Visconti. Writing on his Facebook page, Visconti said: "[Bowie] always did what he wanted to do. And he wanted to do it his way and he wanted to do it the best way. His death was no different from his life—a work of art. He made *Blackstar* for us, his parting gift."

In his haunting last music video for one of the album's songs, "Lazarus," Bowie sings eerily from his apparent death bed, "Look up here, I'm in heaven/I've got scars that can't be seen." The song also appears in the off-Broadway musical *Lazarus* by Bowie and Enda Wash that premiered on Dec. 7, 2015. The musical was inspired by the 1963 science-fiction novel, *The Man Who Fell to Earth,* by Walter Tevis. The book centers on the character of Thomas Jerome Newton, an alien from outer space, famously portrayed by Bowie in the 1976 motion-picture adaptation.

Bowie was born in London in 1947. His real name was David Robert Jones. He first attracted attention with his hit recording "Space Oddity" (1969). His reputation grew with his album *The Rise and Fall of Ziggy Stardust and the Spiders from Mars* (1972). Bowie soon became famous for his bizarre, gender-bending costumes in concerts and for his experimentation with many musical styles and themes. His hit songs include "Fame" (1975), "Heroes" (1977), "Let's Dance" (1983), "Modern Love" (1983), "Without You" (1984), and "Day-In Day-Out" (1987). Bowie was inducted into the Rock and Roll Hall of Fame in 1996.

Bowie acted in a number of films after *The Man Who Fell to Earth*, including *The Hunger* (1983), *Merry Christmas Mr. Lawrence* (1983), *The Last Temptation of Christ* (1988), *Basquiat* (1995), and *August* (2008). Bowie also performed on Broadway in the drama *The Elephant Man* (1980). Bowie's son, Duncan Jones, is a motion-picture director.

PRINCE 1958-2016

Pop music icon Prince died suddenly on April 21, 2016. The singer, musician, and songwriter was found unresponsive by Carver County sheriff's deputies in his Paisley Park studio and residence in Chanhassen, Minnesota. A private gathering was held at Paisley Park on April 23 to mourn the musician. Autopsy results later showed that Prince died of an accidental overdose of the opioid fentanyl. He was 57.

Tributes to Prince from fans and celebrities poured out over social media the weekend after his death. United States President Barack Obama, a noted fan, released a statement, calling Prince "one of the most gifted and prolific musicians of our time." At a press conference on April 22, the president said that he and his staff listened to Prince's music ahead of a meeting with British Prime Minister David Cameron. Prince performed at the White House along with Stevie

Wonder at a private concert in 2015.

An electrifying and versatile performer, Prince's music reflected many styles, including rhythm and blues, pop, soul, jazz, funk, and hip-hop. He played guitar, keyboards, and drums. Prince became a rock music superstar in the 1980's with the hits "Controversy" (1981); "1999" (1982); "Little Red Corvette" and "Delirious" (both 1983); "When Doves Cry," "Let's Go Crazy," and "Purple Rain" (all 1984); "Raspberry Beret" and "Pop Life" (both 1985); "Kiss" (1986); and "Sign o' the Times" and "U Got the Look" (both 1987). Prince's fame spread with his starring role in the motion picture *Purple Rain* (1984), for which he won the 1984 Academy Award for best original score. He also composed the soundtracks for several other films, including *Batman* (1989) with its hit song, "Batdance."

Prince also aroused controversy. He was criticized for the strong sexual nature of his public performances and his song lyrics. In 1993, out of protest against his record label over artistic independence, he changed his name to an unpronounceable symbol and then to "The Artist Formerly Known as Prince." He changed his name back to Prince in 2000.

Prince was born on June 7, 1958, in Minneapolis, Minnesota. His full name was Prince Rogers Nelson. His first album, *For You,* was released in 1978. Prince played all the instruments on the record himself. He went on to record hundreds of compositions, including many songs that became hits for other performers, including the Bangles, Sheila E., Sheena Easton, Tom Jones, Chaka Khan, and Sinead O'Connor. Prince also produced a number of groups, including the Time and Vanity 6 (whose lead singer, Denise Matthews, died earlier in 2016).

Prince continued to record and perform live throughout the 1990's and early 2000's. His later hits included "The Most Beautiful Girl in the World" (1995), "Call My Name" (2004), and "Cinnamon Girl" (2004). He made a highly praised appearance during the halftime show of the 2007 Super Bowl before an estimated television audience of 140 million people. Prince was inducted into the Rock and Roll Hall of Fame in 2004.

Fentanyl, the drug that killed Prince, is a synthetic opioid painkiller. It is similar to such opioids as codeine, hydrocodone, and oxycodone, but fentanyl is much stronger and more addictive. According to the Centers for Disease Control and Prevention (CDC), fentanyl is 50 to 100 times more potent than the opiates heroin and morphine.

GRAMMY AWARD WINNERS IN 2016

Record of the Year	"Uptown Funk," Mark Ronson, featuring Bruno Mars
Album of the Year	*1989*, Taylor Swift
Song of the Year	"Thinking Out Loud," Ed Sheeran and Amy Wadge, songwriters (Ed Sheeran)
New Artist	Meghan Trainor
Pop Solo Performance	"Thinking Out Loud," Ed Sheeran
Pop Duo/Group Performance	"Uptown Funk," Mark Ronson, featuring Bruno Mars
Traditional Pop Vocal Album	*The Silver Lining: The Songs of Jerome Kern*, Tony Bennett and Bill Charlap
Pop Vocal Album	*1989*, Taylor Swift
Dance Recording	"Where Are Ü Now," Skrillex and Diplo with Justin Bieber
Dance/Electronic Album	*Skrillex and Diplo Present Jack Ü*, Skrillex and Diplo
Rock Performance	"Don't Wanna Fight," Alabama Shakes
Metal Performance	"Cirice," Ghost
Rock Song	"Don't Wanna Fight," Alabama Shakes, songwriters (Alabama Shakes)
Rock Album	*Drones*, Muse
Alternative Music Album	*Sound & Color*, Alabama Shakes
Rhythm-and-Blues Performance	"Earned It (Fifty Shades of Grey)," the Weeknd
Traditional Rhythm-and-Blues Performance	"Little Ghetto Boy," Lalah Hathaway
Rhythm-and-Blues Song	"Really Love," D'Angelo, Gina Figueroa, and Kendra Foster, songwriters (D'Angelo and the Vanguard)
Urban Contemporary Album	*Beauty Behind the Madness*, the Weeknd
Rhythm-and-Blues Album	*Black Messiah*, D'Angelo and the Vanguard
Rap Performance	"Alright," Kendrick Lamar
Rap/Sung Collaboration	"These Walls," Kendrick Lamar, featuring Bilal, Anna Wise, and Thundercat
Rap Song	"Alright," Kendrick Duckworth, Kawan Prather, Mark Anthony Spears, and Pharrell Williams, songwriters (Kendrick Lamar)
Rap Album	*To Pimp a Butterfly*, Kendrick Lamar
Country Solo Performance	"Traveller," Chris Stapleton
Country Duo/Group Performance	"Girl Crush," Little Big Town
Country Song	"Girl Song," Hillary Lindsey, Lori McKenna, and Liz Rose, songwriters (Little Big Town)
Country Album	*Traveller*, Chris Stapleton
New Age Album	*Grace*, Paul Avgerinos
Improvised Jazz Solo	"Cherokee," Christian McBride, soloist
Jazz Vocal Album	*For One to Love*, Cécile McLorin Salvant
Jazz Instrumental Album	*Past Present*, John Scofield
Large Jazz Ensemble Album	*The Thompson Fields*, Maria Schneider Orchestra
Latin Jazz Album	*Made in Brazil*, Eliane Elias
Gospel Performance/Song	"Wanna Be Happy?," Kirk Franklin, songwriter (Kirk Franklin)

Contemporary Christian Music Performance/Song	"Holy Spirit," Francesca Battistelli, songwriter (Francesca Battistelli)
Gospel Album	*Covered: Alive in Asia* [Live], Israel & New Breed
Contemporary Christian Music Album	*This Is Not a Test*, Tobymac
Latin Pop Album	*A Quien Quiera Escuchar* [Deluxe Edition], Ricky Martin
Latin Rock, Urban, or Alternative Album	*Hasta la Raíz*, Natalia Lafourcade and *Dale*, Pitbull (tie)
Regional Mexican Album (including Tejano)	*Realidades* [Deluxe Edition], Los Tigres del Norte
Tropical Latin Album	*Son de Panamá*, Rubén Blades with Roberto Delgado and Orchestra
Americana Album	*Something More Than Free*, Jason Isbell
Bluegrass Album	*The Muscle Shoals Recordings*, the SteelDrivers
Blues Album	*Born to Play Guitar*, Buddy Guy
Folk Album	*Béla Fleck and Abigail Washburn*, Béla Fleck and Abigail Washburn
Regional Roots Music Album	*Go Go Juice*, Jon Cleary
Reggae Album	*Strictly Roots*, Morgan Heritage
World Music Album	*Sings*, Angelique Kidjo
Children's Album	*Home*, Tim Kubart
Musical Theater Album	*Hamilton*
Score Soundtrack for Visual Media	*Birdman*, Antonio Sanchez
Song Written for Visual Media	"Glory" (from *Selma*), Lonnie Lynn, Che Smith, and John Stephens, songwriters (Common and John Legend)
Instrumental Composition	"The Afro Latin Jazz Suite," Arturo O'Farrill, composer (Arturo O'Farrill and the Afro Latin Jazz Orchestra, featuring Rudresh Mahanthappa)
Instrumental or A Cappella Arrangement	"Dance of the Sugar Plum Fairy," Ben Bram, Mitch Grassi, Scott Hoying, Avi Kaplan, Kirstin Maldonado, and Kevin Olusola, arrangers (Pentatonix)
Arrangement, Instruments, and Vocals	"Sue (Or in a Season of Crime)," Maria Schneider, arranger (David Bowie)
Music Video	"Bad Blood," Taylor Swift, featuring Kendrick Lamar
Orchestral Performance	*Shostakovich: Under Stalin's Shadow—Symphony No. 10*, Andris Nelsons, conductor (Boston Symphony Orchestra)
Opera Recording	*Ravel: L'Enfant et les Sortilèges; Shéhérazade*, Seiji Ozawa, conductor (Saito Kinen Orchestra; SKF Matsumoto Chorus and SKF Matsumoto Children's Chorus)
Choral Performance	*Rachmaninoff: All-Night Vigil*, Charles Bruffy, conductor (Paul Davidson, Frank Fleschner, Toby Vaughn Kidd, Bryan Pinkall, Julia Scozzafava, Bryan Taylor, and Joseph Warner; Kansas City Chorale and Phoenix Chorale)
Chamber Music/ Small Ensemble Performance	*Filament*, Eighth Blackbird
Classical Instrumental Solo	*Dutilleux: Violin Concerto, L'Arbre des Songes*, Augustin Hadelich, soloist
Classical Solo Vocal Album	*Joyce & Tony—Live from Wigmore Hall*, Joyce DiDonato, soloist
Contemporary Classical Composition	*Paulus: Prayers and Remembrances*, Stephen Paulus, composer

THE 2016 PULITZER PRIZE WINNERS

The Reuters news photography staff shared the Pulitzer Prize for a collection of photos recording the migrant crisis in Europe and the Middle East in 2015. This Reuters photo shows a Syrian refugee and his daughter walking in the rain near Greece's border with Macedonia.

The annual Pulitzer Prizes for journalism, literature, drama, and music are awarded at Columbia University in New York City.

JOURNALISM

Public Service	Associated Press
Breaking News Reporting	Los Angeles Times Staff
Investigative Reporting	Leonora LaPeter Anton and Anthony Cormier of the Tampa Bay Times and Michael Braga of the Sarasota Herald-Tribune
Explanatory Reporting	T. Christian Miller of ProPublica and Ken Armstrong of The Marshall Project
Local Reporting	Michael LaForgia, Cara Fitzpatrick, and Lisa Gartner of the Tampa Bay Times
National Reporting	The Washington Post Staff
International Reporting	Alissa J. Rubin of The New York Times
Feature Writing	Kathryn Schulz of The New Yorker
Commentary	Farah Stockman of The Boston Globe
Criticism	Emily Nussbaum of The New Yorker
Editorial Writing	John Hackworth and Brian Gleason of Sun Newspapers, Charlotte Harbor, FL
Editorial Cartooning	Jack Ohman of The Sacramento Bee
Breaking News Photography	Mauricio Lima, Sergey Ponomarev, Tyler Hicks, and Daniel Etter of The New York Times and Photography Staff of Reuters
Feature Photography	Jessica Rinaldi of The Boston Globe

LETTERS, DRAMA, AND MUSIC

Fiction	*The Sympathizer* by Viet Thanh Nguyen (Grove Press)
Drama	*Hamilton* by Lin-Manuel Miranda
History	*Custer's Trials: A Life on the Frontier of a New America* by T. J. Stiles (Alfred A. Knopf)
Biography	*Barbarian Days: A Surfing Life* by William Finnegan (Penguin Press)
Poetry	*Ozone Journal* by Peter Balakian (University of Chicago Press)
Nonfiction	*Black Flags: The Rise of ISIS* by Joby Warrick (Doubleday)
Music	*In for a Penny, In for a Pound* by Henry Threadgill (Pi Recordings)

A FINAL IDOL

On April 7, 2016, the singing competition television show "American Idol" crowned its final winner as it ended its 15-year run. Country crooner Trent Harmon became the show's final winner—much to the surprise of judges Harry Connick, Jr., Jennifer Lopez, and Keith Urban.

But "the people had spoken," a theme emphasized in a special opening segment featuring United States President Barack Obama. Obama congratulated the show on its long run as he urged Americans to vote: "For over a decade, this show has motivated millions of young Americans to vote.... We should do the same in our lives as citizens of this country we love.... Not all of us can sing like Kelly Clarkson [the show's first winner] but all our voices matter. This show reached historic heights not only because Americans watched it, but because you participated in its success."

"American Idol," which had aired on the Fox network since 2002, discovered new singing talent through a series of auditions and televised performances. While the judges commented on each contestant's performance, the show's viewers determined which contestants would advance to the next round of the competition. Viewers voted by calling a special telephone number or by text messaging after each show. The results were announced during the following night's broadcast. After several weeks of performances and voting, the competition was eventually narrowed down to two finalists. The winner received a recording contract and the title of "American Idol."

The final show featured special segments and appearances by such former contestants as Clarkson, Jennifer Hudson, and Carrie Underwood. Original judges Simon Cowell, Randy Jackson, and Paula Abdul also appeared. Over the years, the show's judges included comedian and TV personality Ellen DeGeneres, rock musician Steven Tyler, singer Mariah Carey, and rap artist Nicki Minaj. The show's notable contestants included Clay Aiken, Fantasia Barrino, David Cook, Chris Daughtry, Taylor Hicks, Adam Lambert, Jordin Sparks, and Ruben Studdard.

Ratings for "American Idol," which once attracted some of the biggest audiences in television history, had been down in recent years. A decade ago, "Idol" drew up to 40 million viewers. The final show drew nearly 13 million viewers, the best ratings for an "Idol" finale since 2013.

"American Idol" creator Simon Fuller claimed a reboot of the show was in the works. Ryan Seacrest, the show's host since season one, hinted at the show's return with his sign-off: "Goodnight America, for now."

2016 EMMY AWARDS

On Sept. 18, 2016, the Emmy Awards were presented at the Microsoft Theater in Los Angeles. The awards recognized excellence in programming and individual achievement for the 2015-2016 television season. Comedian Jimmy Kimmel hosted the awards' live telecast for the second time.

Including the Emmy Creative Arts Awards presented earlier in September, HBO's epic medieval fantasy series, "Game of Thrones," won a record 12 awards for a fictional series for the second consecutive year, including best drama, best directing, and best writing for a drama series. The series, which began airing in 2011, has won a record 38 total Emmy Awards.

FX's crime anthology, *The People v. O. J. Simpson: American Crime Story,* won best limited series and best writing for a limited series. HBO's political satire "Veep" won best comedy series, and the show's star, Julia Louis-Dreyfus, won best actress for the fifth straight year. Jeffrey Tambor repeated as best actor in a comedy for Amazon's "Transparent." Rami Malek won best lead actor in a drama for the USA Network thriller, "Mr. Robot." Tatiana Maslany won best lead actress in a drama for the BBC America series "Orphan Black." Maggie Smith won her third Emmy for her role in the British television series "Downton Abbey." HBO's "Last Week Tonight with John Oliver" won best variety talk series and Comedy Central's "Key & Peele" won best variety sketch series.

In contrast to the lack of diversity among nominees at the Academy Awards earlier in 2016, 25 percent of this year's Emmy nominations went to people of color.

Kit Harington stars as Jon Snow in the sixth season of the medieval fantasy television series, "Game of Thrones." The show won a record 12 Emmy Awards for the second consecutive year in 2016.

PRIMETIME EMMY AWARD WINNERS IN 2016

COMEDY

Best Series	"Veep"
Lead Actress	Julia Louis-Dreyfus, "Veep"
Lead Actor	Jeffrey Tambor, "Transparent"
Supporting Actress	Kate McKinnon, "Saturday Night Live"
Supporting Actor	Louie Anderson, "Baskets"

DRAMA

Best Series	"Game of Thrones"
Lead Actress	Tatiana Maslany, "Orphan Black"
Lead Actor	Rami Malek, "Mr. Robot"
Supporting Actress	Maggie Smith, "Downton Abbey"
Supporting Actor	Ben Mendelsohn, "Bloodline"

OTHER AWARDS

Limited Series	The People v. O. J. Simpson: American Crime Story
Television Movie	Sherlock: The Abominable Bride
Reality/Competition Series	"The Voice"
Variety Sketch Series	"Key & Peele"
Variety Talk Series	"Last Week Tonight with John Oliver"
Lead Actress in a Limited Series or Movie	Sarah Paulson, The People v. O. J. Simpson: American Crime Story
Lead Actor in a Limited Series or Movie	Courtney B. Vance, The People v. O. J. Simpson: American Crime Story
Supporting Actress in a Limited Series or Movie	Regina King, American Crime
Supporting Actor in a Limited Series or Movie	Sterling K. Brown, The People v. O. J. Simpson: American Crime Story

STAR TREK TURNS 50

On Sept. 8, 1966, the science-fiction television program "Star Trek" first aired in the United States and Canada. The show's ratings were never strong, and the series lasted just three seasons. But reruns in the 1970's gained the show legions of ardent fans (called *Trekkies*), giving birth to an entire "Star Trek" culture. The show birthed spin-off TV shows with much longer runs than the original "Star Trek" series, and the strong "Star Trek" movie franchise, begun in 1979, continued in 2016 with *Star Trek Beyond*. Numerous events and and conventions—too many to list here—marked the show's 50th anniversary in cities around the world.

"Star Trek" was created by Gene Roddenberry. It followed the adventures of the starship USS *Enterprise* (NCC-1701) as it explored outer space—"the final frontier." The ship's

The original "Star Trek" crew gather on the bridge of the starship Enterprise. *The popular television show first aired 50 years ago on Sept. 8, 1966.*

crew—led by Captain James T. Kirk (William Shatner) and his first officer, Mr. Spock (Leonard Nimoy)—endeared themselves to audiences of all ages and walks of life.

"Star Trek" has had a significant impact on arts and culture—even on the English language. No explanation is needed when someone asks to be "beamed up" or to travel at "warp speed." "Star Trek" listings in the *Oxford English Dictionary* include weaponry—*phaser* and *photon torpedo*—and the humanoid alien races *Klingon* and *Vulcan*. Most people probably know Spock's catch phrase, "Live long and prosper," as well as the *Enterprise* crew's mission "to boldly go where no man has gone before."

MORLEY SAFER 1931-2016

On May 19, 2016, longtime CBS correspondent Morley Safer died at age 84. Safer, whose broadcast journalism career began in the 1950's, had been a contributor and host for the popular television news magazine "60 Minutes" since 1970. The witty and debonair Safer retired from the show the week before his death from pneumonia in New York City.

Morley Safer was born Nov. 8, 1931, in Toronto, Ontario, Canada, where his father ran an upholstery shop. After attending the University of Western Ontario (now Western University), he worked at Ontario newspapers and for the Reuters news agency in London, England. In 1955, he began reporting for the Canadian Broadcasting Corporation. In 1964, he joined the CBS London bureau. CBS (Columbia Broadcasting System) is one of the largest broadcasting networks in the United States.

Safer's long CBS career included a wide variety of stories. He covered conflict in Algeria, Cyprus, Czechoslovakia, Israel, Nigeria, Northern Ireland, and, most famously, in Vietnam. A 1965 broadcast on American troops at Cam Ne earned him widespread renown as well as sharp rebukes from the U.S. military and government. Safer profiled people from all walks of life, including centenarians, criminals, homeless people, opera stars, world leaders, writers, and the unemployed. He did features on bureaucracy, crime, heart attack treatments, insomnia, strip mining, Swiss bank accounts, unsafe building practices, the benefits of red wine, and the questionable quality of modern art. Safer won every major award given for broadcast journalism, including 12 Emmys, 3 Peabodys for public service, and the George Polk Award for career achievement.

THEATER 2016

Hamilton, the smash Broadway musical hit of 2015, continued as the dominant stage event of 2016. Remaining the toughest ticket in recent Broadway history, the hip-hop retelling of the founding of the United States has become a cultural event that transcends the boundaries of theater. The *Hamilton* saga expanded in 2016 with new productions in Chicago and on the West Coast, with a London production slated for 2017.

As expected, *Hamilton* won the 2016 Tony Award for best musical (plus 10 other Tony awards), along with the 2016 Pulitzer Prize for drama, a rare honor for a musical. Lin-Manuel Miranda, both star and author-composer of *Hamilton,* was the toast of the American theater scene.

With no new hit shows during the 2015-2016 season (straight plays continued to flounder), Broadway relied on the luster of long-running musicals in 2016. The year's biggest "new" production was the restaging of *Cats,* which closed in New York City in 2000 after an 18-year run and has returned, to the delight of the tourist trade. The same can be said for *Les Misérables,* a Broadway staple from 1987 to 2003 that came back for a well-received encore run. Other veteran shows that thrived at the 2016 box office included *The Book of Mormon, Chicago, The Lion King,* and *Wicked.*

Lin-Manuel Miranda, *right,* performs in a scene from *Hamilton* at the Tony Awards at New York City's Beacon Theatre on June 12, 2016.

TONY AWARD WINNERS IN 2016

Best Play	*The Humans*
Best Musical	*Hamilton*
Best Play Revival	*A View from the Bridge*
Best Musical Revival	*The Color Purple*
Leading Actor in a Play	Frank Langella, *The Father*
Leading Actress in a Play	Jessica Lange, *Long Day's Journey Into Night*
Leading Actor in a Musical	Leslie Odom, Jr., *Hamilton*
Leading Actress in a Musical	Cynthia Erivo, *The Color Purple*
Featured Actor in a Play	Reed Birney, *The Humans*
Featured Actress in a Play	Jayne Houdyshell, *The Humans*
Featured Actor in a Musical	Daveed Diggs, *Hamilton*
Featured Actress in a Musical	Renée Elise Goldsberry, *Hamilton*
Direction of a Play	Ivo van Hove, *A View from the Bridge*
Direction of a Musical	Thomas Kail, *Hamilton*
Book of a Musical	Lin-Manuel Miranda, *Hamilton*
Original Musical Score	Lin-Manuel Miranda, *Hamilton*
Choreography	Andy Blankenbuehler, *Hamilton*
Orchestrations	Alex Lacamoire, *Hamilton*
Scenic Design of a Play	David Zinn, *The Humans*
Scenic Design of a Musical	David Rockwell, *She Loves Me*
Costume Design of a Play	Clint Ramos, *Eclipsed*
Costume Design of a Musical	Paul Tazewell, *Hamilton*
Lighting Design of a Play	Natasha Katz, *Long Day's Journey into Night*
Lighting Design of a Musical	Howell Binkley, *Hamilton*
Regional Theater	Paper Mill Playhouse, Millburn, NJ
Isabelle Stevenson Award	Brian Stokes Mitchell
Excellence in the Theater	Seth Gelblum, Joan Lader, and Sally Ann Parsons
Lifetime Achievement in the Theater	Sheldon Harnick and Marshall W. Mason
Special Tony Award	National Endowment for the Arts and Miles Wilkin

An image of William Shakespeare illuminates London's
famous Guildhall prior to events on April 23, 2016,
marking the 400th anniversary of the playwright's death.

THE PLAY'S THE THING

BY DAVID BEVINGTON

April 23, 2016, marked 400 years since the death of English playwright William Shakespeare in 1616. To commemorate the day, Professor David Bevington, a Shakespearean scholar at the University of Chicago, considered how productions of Shakespeare's plays have changed over four centuries.

The 400th anniversary of the death of William Shakespeare seems a good time to reflect on how his wonderful plays have fared on stage over the centuries. In Shakespeare's own day, his productions were highly professional and very successful. From 1594 to 1603, Shakespeare belonged to an acting company known as the Lord Chamberlain's Men, so named because technically and legally, they were "servants" of the lord chamberlain, an influential member of Queen Elizabeth I's government. In practice, their status as his "men" gave the company the license they needed to perform publicly, at first at a building called The Theatre just north of London's city walls.

Plays in London were subject to strict laws because attending them was thought to lead to the spread of plague as well as immorality. Outside of London's city limits, actors were not subject to London's regulations and to Puritan mistrust of dramatic activity. The company also acted at The Curtain, a new building of a similar type near The Theater. When the actors encountered difficulty with their landlord in 1599, they moved to a location on the south side of the River Thames, across from the city of London. In this new open-air theater, the Globe, they performed *As You Like It, Hamlet, Henry V,* and the great plays that followed in Shakespeare's writing career, including *Othello, King Lear, Macbeth, Antony and Cleopatra,*

Britain's Queen Elizabeth II and the Duke of Edinburgh (first balcony, upper right) attend the opening of the reconstructed Globe Theatre in London, on June 12, 1997. The reconstruction was built 200 yards (183 meters) from the site of the original Globe Theatre.

and *The Tempest*. Toward the end of this period, the company also performed indoors in the Blackfriars Theater, close to Saint Paul's Cathedral.

The Globe playhouse was a polygonal structure enclosing an arena of some 70 feet (21 meters) in diameter, with galleries for seated audiences on most sides and a platform stage that measured approximately 43 feet (13 meters) across and 27 feet (8 meters) deep. To the rear were two doors leading into the actors' *attiring space* (dressing rooms) backstage. Probably between these doors was a "discovery space" that was useful for scenes of concealment and eavesdropping. Over this back wall was a gallery where actors could appear "above" and where spectators sometimes sat as well. Surrounding the stage on three sides was "the yard," where spectators could stand and watch the play

without having to pay for seats. The audience was of mixed social status, from the well-to-do to apprentices and workmen who might stand in the yard. Over the stage was a small roof sheltering the actors from the weather. The building was otherwise open to the sky. Performances in the afternoons depended on natural light for illumination. Lighting effects were impractical. The actors could mime nighttime, as in the opening of *Hamlet,* by their gestures and apprehensive whispers. Audiences were thus able to see and hear everything.

Scenery was essentially nonexistent, though chairs and other furniture might sparingly be brought on stage as needed. The acting environment was accordingly swift and flexible. Actors quickly came on stage in a new scene as the performers of the previous scene exited. Well-designed costumes enabled playgoers to understand a scene's location by what the actors wore and what they said. The audience was invited to join with the actors to create an illusion through costuming, gesture, and a willingness to picture in their minds what they were asked to imagine: a field of battle, a sea voyage, a room in a courtly palace, a family home, a forest. "Piece out our imperfections with your thoughts," says the Chorus of *Henry V.* "Think, when we talk of horses, that you see them / Printing their proud hoofs i'th' receiving earth." Shakespeare was thus able to rely on his spectators' imaginations to enact the marvelous stories he chose to dramatize. As Duke Theseus explains in Act 5 of *A Midsummer Night's Dream,* theatrical imagination "bodies forth / The forms of things unknown." The dramatist turns his ideas and dreams into shapes, giving "to airy nothing / A local habitation and a name." Shakespeare was and is a dramatist of the imagination. He was materially assisted in this artistic enterprise by his theater, one that provided the actors an open and flexible stage where they could enact any location and bridge any gap of time.

After Shakespeare's death in 1616, many of his plays continued in repertory down to the time of the closing of the theaters by a Puritan Parliament in 1642. During the years of the English Civil War, fragments of plays were occasionally secretly performed, but otherwise England was officially without dramatic entertainment

In early April 2016, this rare and valuable *First Folio*—a 1623 collection of 36 Shakespeare plays—was found at Mount Stuart, an aristocratic home on the Isle of Bute off Scotland's west coast.

from 1642 until the Restoration of the monarchy in 1660.

King Charles II, son of the executed Charles I, returned to England from France in 1660 with an intent to turn back the clock to days of indulgent pleasure. Two theaters were licensed for performance, one (the Duke of York's Men) under the management of William Davenant and the other (the King's Company) entrusted to Thomas Killigrew, soon at a new theater building in Drury Lane. Shakespeare's plays were popular and often performed in these years, though generally in adapted form. *Romeo and Juliet* sometimes alternated between a tragical version with the deaths of the *protagonists* (leading characters) and on other days, a tragicomic version in which the lovers managed to survive. Thomas Otway, in his play *Caius Marius* (1679), adapted the play to a neoclassical tale of star-crossed lovers set in ancient Rome. William Davenant's *The Law Against Lovers* (1662) combined *Much Ado About Nothing* with *Measure for Measure* by making Beatrice of the first play a ward of Lord Angelo in the second, and Benedick his brother. *Twelfth Night* was transformed into an adaptation by Charles Burnaby called *Love Betrayed, or the Agreeable Disappointment* (1703), centering on

Malvolio, in which all the characters were renamed and only 58 lines of Shakespeare's text were retained. Perhaps most famously, Nahum Tate's *History of King Lear* (1681) introduced a happy ending in which Cordelia was reunited with her royal father and with Edgar, her partner in the play's love story. Presumably Tate did this in response to the insistence of popular audiences, for whom the death of Cordelia in Shakespeare's version violated the age's ideas of what was right and proper. The Tate version held the stage until well past the year 1800.

Only in the Restoration period did women first appear in English theater. Before then, boys played the parts of such characters as Juliet and Lady Macbeth. The theater was considered unsuitably sinful for female players, but the court of King Charles II changed all that. Nell Gwynn, one of the first actresses to appear on stage, was a mistress of the king himself. Leading members of the court had their stage mistresses as well. From that time onward, women were increasingly a center of interest for new, middle-class audiences who were fascinated by the tragic death of Desdemona in *Othello,* the mad scenes of Ophelia in *Hamlet,* and the sleepwalking of Lady Macbeth. Operatic versions by Giuseppe Verdi added to the glamour and excitement. Such actresses as Peg Woffington, Susannah Cibber, Helen Faucit, Sarah Siddons, Charlotte Cushman, Lily Langtry, Ada Rehan, Ellen Terry, and Sarah Bernhardt were justly famous.

The years from 1800 to 1899 featured large and expensive productions of Shakespeare's plays staged in theater buildings increasingly designed to hold thousands of spectators. Productions by David Garrick, Edmund Kean, John Philip Kemble, William Charles Macready, and Henry Irving, among others, featured elaborate sets built to look as natural as possible for showing the Battle of Agincourt in *Henry V,* the Roman Forum in *Julius Caesar,* or the court of Henry VIII in the history play named for him. Gothic windows, battlements, moonlit scenes at night, and the like were manufactured with new technologies and especially with artificial lighting. Herbert Beerbohm Tree's *Twelfth Night* in 1901 featured a terrace for Countess Olivia's house with real grass, fountains, pathways, and staircases in the style of an Italian garden. Tree's production of *A Midsummer Night's Dream* provided live rabbits scurrying across the stage.

A notable feature of productions of Shakespeare from 1900 until today is that they have turned their back, by and large, on the massive sets and scenery of previous centuries, returning in effect to the open and flexible stage of Shakespeare's own day. William Poel pioneered experiments for his Elizabethan Stage Society in the early twentieth century. Barry Jackson staged a quick-paced *Twelfth Night* on an apron stage at the Birmingham Repertory Theatre in 1913. Glen Byam Shaw's set for *Romeo and Juliet* at Stratford-upon-Avon in 1947 consisted of a partly abstract and geometrical arrangement of concentric circles. Peter Brook's concept for a *Midsummer Night's Dream* in 1970 found disillusionment in a play traditionally peopled by cute little fairies with gossamer wings. Brook chose for his set a white box, with the actors as circus performers sometimes on swings and Bottom the Weaver as a circus clown with large shoes. Visible in such productions was a response to a twentieth-century world of political revolution, world war, and existential philosophical despair. Laurence Olivier's *Hamlet,* on stage and on screen (1948), explored Sigmund Freud's psychoanalytic interpretation of Hamlet as suffering an Oedipal crisis. Grigori Kozintsev's *Hamlet* (1964) resonated to disturbing visions of Soviet concentration camps under Joseph Stalin. The same play proved to be a powerful vehicle for dissident playwrights in Egypt protesting authoritarian rule under Gamal Abed Nasser. Cheek by Jowl's production of *As You Like It* in 1991 employed an all-male cast as a means of exploring themes of gender, identity, and power on a stage that was essentially devoid of realistic scenery. Akira Kurosawa's films *Throne of Blood* (1957) and *Ran* (1965) offer devastating interpretations of *Macbeth* and *King Lear* as seen from the perspective of Japanese warlord history. Productions of *Othello* have witnessed a sea change in racial casting. The role of Othello, once the property of white actors in blackface, such as Macready and Kean, shifted to enactments by such black actors as

Ira Aldridge and Paul Robeson. It has shifted again in the modern world, where casting is either racially neutral or more pointedly tries out every possible variation in the performances of Othello and Iago.

This experimentation, even if sometimes overdone, has given to Shakespearean theater the freshness and immediacy that it justly deserves and needs. The result is what we see today: a thriving theatrical enterprise of imagination that gives continual new insight to an amazing body of work by a fruitful combination of irreverence and lasting admiration.

Sir Laurence Olivier directed and starred in the 1948 British film adaptation of Shakespeare's *Hamlet*. Olivier played Prince Hamlet and Eileen Herlie (in the background) played his mother, Queen Gertrude.

THOMAS EAKINS, AMERICAN REALIST

June 25, 2016, marked the 100th anniversary of the death of the great American Realist painter Thomas Eakins (1844-1916). At a time when many American painters were under the spell of new modern movements in Europe, Eakins believed that progress in American art should be home-grown. He spent most of his career in Philadelphia, Pennsylvania, and he painted the subjects he knew best—sports, outdoor recreation, domestic life, and the people of Philadelphia.

Eakins rejected the symbolism and sentimentality favored by many American artists of the later 1800's. Using

The Champion Single Sculls (Max Schmitt in a Single Scull) (1871), oil on canvas by Thomas Eakins

Eakins was born in Philadelphia on July 25, 1844. He began art training in the early 1860's at the Pennsylvania Academy of Fine Arts and studied anatomy at Jefferson Medical College. After studying in Europe, Eakins returned to Philadelphia and taught at the Pennsylvania Academy of Fine Arts from 1876 to 1886. During these years, he became a leader of the Realist painters in the United States.

In 1875, Eakins completed *The Clinic of Dr. Gross*. One of the great paintings in American art, the work portrays the famous surgeon Samuel David Gross in an operating theater, performing an operation surrounded by students. The painting was rejected as part of the art gallery in the Centennial Exhibition world's fair of 1876 because its bold naturalism was considered too graphic. Eakins's painting on a similar subject, *The Clinic of Dr. Agnew* (1889), won acclaim at the 1893 World's Columbian Exposition in Chicago.

Eakins painted several famous pictures of sporting life, notably *Max Schmitt in a Single Scull* (1871), with its subtle effects of light and atmosphere, as well as several scenes of boxing and wrestling in the 1890's. His later portraits include character studies of unsmiling men and women isolated against dark backgrounds. Aside from painting, Eakins made a number of sculptures for public monuments and experimented with various forms of photography.

bold brushstrokes and thick layers of paint, Eakins filled his paintings with emotional truth as well as visual reality. While his style was honest and objective, it was also warm and compassionate. These qualities appear in his famous 1887 portrait of American poet Walt Whitman.

ECONOMICS, LAW, AND GOVERNMENT

People attend a rally during primary voting in Brooklyn, New York, on June 7, 2016. The United States presidential primary season and election campaign were filled with drama in 2016, right up to election day on November 8.

see page 306 for
A CLOSER
LOOK

PROMISING PUERTO RICO

On June 30, 2016, U.S. President Barack Obama signed into law the Puerto Rico Oversight, Management, and Economic Stability Act to address the worsening debt crisis in Puerto Rico, a U.S. possession with commonwealth status. The law, also known as PROMESA, provides an oversight board to temporarily manage Puerto Rico's finances and restructure its accumulated debt of about $70 billion. PROMESA (*promise* in Spanish) also places a stay on lawsuits by creditors in the event of Puerto Rico's failure to make debt payments. The act became law just one day before Puerto Rico was due to make an approximately $2-billion debt payment that included general obligation bonds, the repayment of which is guaranteed by Puerto Rico's constitution.

Puerto Rico has been in an economic recession since the first decade of the 2000's. The commonwealth acquired much of its debt by issuing municipal bonds to cover budget shortfalls. The bonds are exempt from taxation, making them especially attractive to American investors. The 2006 expiration of certain corporate tax incentives in Puerto Rico further damaged the island's economy, as it resulted in both businesses and workers moving elsewhere. Since 2000, more than 300,000 people have emigrated, and three-fourths of those have left since 2010.

In April 2016, Puerto Rico's Governor Alejandro García Padilla declared a financial state of emergency and placed a moratorium on debt payments. In early May, the government defaulted on a debt payment of nearly $400 million. It also defaulted on much of the $2-billion payment due July 1. Padilla's administration said that such defaults were necessary to ensure that the government had enough money to provide essential services to Puerto Ricans.

Puerto Rico's commonwealth status complicates its financial situation. U.S. bankruptcy law permits financially distressed municipalities and public agencies, including utilities, in the 50 U.S. states to file for bankruptcy and restructure their debt. Because Puerto is not a state, it is not eligible for such restructuring. In 2014, Puerto Rico passed the Recovery Act, a law allowing its public utilities to file for bankruptcy and reorganize their substantial debt, but the U.S. Supreme Court struck down the law on June 13, 2016.

PROMESA also provides for a temporary freeze on bond repayments, the enforcement of balanced budgets, a mandate for the continued funding of pensions, and a possible decrease in the minimum wage.

PANAMA PAPERS
HEAT UP ICELAND

On April 6, 2016, Iceland's Prime Minister Sigmundur Davíð Gunnlaugsson resigned from office. Gunnlaugsson had enjoyed fair popularity since taking office in 2013, but his downfall came quickly and loudly. On April 3, Gunnlaugsson and his wife were among the international figures named in the controversial *Panama Papers*. The papers consist of millions of confidential documents detailing secret offshore bank accounts used by wealthy world leaders, celebrities, and others for various purposes, including money laundering and to avoid paying taxes in their home countries. The papers—leaked from the Panama-based international law firm Mossack Fonseca—raised widespread questions of corruption or at least of unseemly legal deception.

The Panama Papers revealed transactions between the Gunnlaugssons, offshore companies, and the Icelandic banks that were at the heart of that nation's financial collapse in 2008. While the nation plunged into economic chaos, the Gunnlaugssons profited handsomely—and secretively. Gunnlaugsson denied any legal wrongdoing, but the people of Iceland, who paid a hefty price for their nation's financial recovery, were not interested in the legality of his actions. Large protests and demonstrations erupted immediately, calling for Gunnlaugsson's resignation. After failing to rally support, Gunnlaugsson stepped down.

Other world notables mentioned in the documents include top leaders (or their friends and relatives) from Argentina, Brazil, China, Chile, India, Malaysia, Mexico, Pakistan, Peru, Qatar, Romania, Russia, Saudi Arabia, South Africa, Spain, Syria, Ukraine, the United Arab Emirates, and the United Kingdom. Others named in the papers include world soccer's already-troubled governing body, FIFA, as well as many of the sport's star players. Many others have been named too, and the investigation is just gaining traction.

Offshore companies often provide financial and legal advantages for investors. Among the benefits are privacy, little or no taxation, and no deposit regulation—meaning no alarms are raised if you suddenly deposit, say, $1 million. If you put $1 million in your local bank, the Internal Revenue Service would soon be in contact with a list of questions beginning with *where did you get it?*

VENEZUELA'S DIRE STRAITS

On May 13, 2016, Venezuelan President Nicolás Maduro decreed a 60-day state of economic emergency that increased presidential, military, and police powers in his country. It was the second time in 2016 that Maduro, who leads the United Socialist Party of Venezuela, had issued such a decree. The first, issued in mid-January, gave the Socialist president greater executive control over Venezuela's companies and currency. The country's opposition-dominated National Assembly rejected both decrees. But the Supreme Tribunal of Justice, stacked with appointees of the previous legislature, overruled the new Assembly. Maduro said the latest emergency measure was meant "to tend to our country and, more importantly, to prepare to denounce, neutralize, and overcome the external and foreign aggressions against our country." The president accused his political opposition and foreign powers, particularly the United States, with economic and political sabotage.

In February 2016, Venezuela's central bank reported that the country's gross domestic product (GDP) had shrunk by 5.7 percent and inflation had reached 180.9 percent in 2015. In April 2016, the International Monetary Fund (IMF) estimated that the GDP would decrease by a further 8 percent for the year and inflation would increase by another 481 percent. By early 2016, Venezuela could not afford much-needed imports. As the year progressed, ordinary Venezuelans suffered from severe shortages of staple foods, domestic products, and basic medicines. In addition, skyrocketing inflation reduced the worth of their salaries. Health workers lacked medicines and supplies, and broken medical equipment could not be replaced. Shortages of water and electric power (caused by a drought) also had a large impact. To save power, the government declared a two-day work week for civil servants and began a program of energy rationing. In many cases, hospitals lacked electricity to operate life-saving machines and even water to clean medical facilities. The education system deteriorated as students and teachers abandoned classes to stand in line for groceries and other scarce commodities.

Analysts and critics of Maduro attributed Venezuela's dire economic situation to a number of factors. Like his predecessor, President Hugo Chávez, Maduro has relied upon revenue from oil to support the national economy. A sharp fall in the global price of oil in the early 2000's ravaged the economy. From mid-2014 to early 2016, the price of crude oil plummeted from more than $100 per barrel to less than $30. Like Chávez, Maduro has poured oil revenue into social-benefit programs and neglected investing in the development of domestic industries, leaving Venezuela dependent upon imports. The government has favored making payments on its large foreign debt over buying more of the imports that Venezuelans so desperately need. In addition, currency controls in place since 2003 have contributed to extreme inflation and strong growth of the black market.

Critics and observers also have blamed Venezuela's crisis on the widespread nationalization of economic sectors and the government's failure to save and invest in such services as education and health care. To make matters worse, the government has refused help from such international lending organizations as the IMF.

Venezuela's economic crisis coincided with a political struggle between Maduro and the National

On May 25, 2016, a Venezuelan woman's sign reads in Spanish, "Venezuela is hungry," during a protest outside court offices in Caracas, the capital. Opposition members held a demonstration demanding a recall referendum to shorten Nicolás Maduro's troubled presidency.

Assembly. In December 2015, the Democratic Unity Roundtable opposition coalition, led by Henrique Capriles, won a majority of Assembly seats. It was the first time in more than 15 years that the Socialists lost control of the legislature. However, Maduro and the Supreme Tribunal repeatedly blocked the Assembly's attempts to pass new legislation, and Maduro said it was only a matter of time before the Assembly would cease to exist. Opposition members in the Assembly vowed to remove Maduro from office by legal means.

In April 2016, Venezuela's Supreme Tribunal blocked an attempt by the legislature to shorten Maduro's term, from six to four years, by constitutional amendment. Maduro's term is set to end in 2019. In May 2016, opposition leaders submitted a petition with nearly 2 million signatures, far more than needed, to begin proceedings for a recall referendum on Maduro's presidency. However, electoral authorities took measures to stall such proceedings. A recall vote held by Jan. 10, 2017, would result in a new presidential election. A vote held after that date still could end Maduro's term. Instead of an election, however, Socialist Vice President Aristóbulo Istúriz would ascend to the presidency.

Amidst this economic and political climate, public demonstrations, looting, riots, and street violence became common throughout the country. Hungry and desperate Venezuelans scavenged for food in trash bins, broke into shops, attacked food-transport trucks, and vandalized Socialist Party headquarters. In July 2016, tens of thousands of people took advantage of brief border openings to buy food and other supplies in neighboring Colombia.

Opinion polls indicate that most people want Maduro out of office, but with or without Maduro, the country will face a long, difficult road to remedy its economic and political problems.

THE U.S. ECONOMY

The United States economy—still the largest in the world at about 20 percent of the total global output—continued its slow and steady growth in 2016. Exports outpaced imports, businesses and individuals increased their investments, and consumer spending grew as the gross domestic product (GDP) expanded by 1.4 percent in the year's second quarter, and by a healthy 2 percent in the third quarter (ideal GDP growth is 2 to 3 percent). These modest numbers sound small but they represent large increases when the size of the GDP—more than $18 trillion—is considered. The United States still has the world's sixth highest per capita GDP (more than $53,000), surpassed only by small countries such as Norway and Singapore. The healthy but uneven U.S. economy relied on its highly developed and technologically advanced services sector, which accounted for about 80 percent of its output. Services-oriented industries, such as finance, healthcare, retail, and technology, enjoyed solid growth in 2016. Manufacturing represented about 15 percent of the U.S. economy and agriculture made up 2 percent. That 2 percent is deceiving, however, as the United States remained the largest agricultural exporting country in the world in 2016.

Oil prices remained low, about $50 per barrel, throughout the year. This is good for the individual but it drags down overall economic numbers. The continued decrease in the nation's oil reliance hurt oil-reliant Texas, the second most populous state. Payroll increases there lagged behind the national average throughout the year, and the state's economy leveled out in 2016 after steady growth over the previous five years. Texas unemployment was above the national average, forcing many energy sector employees to find work in other areas or other industries. Texas represents about 9 percent of the nation's total economic output.

The number of Americans filing for unemployment benefits reached a 43-year low in October 2016, and the U.S. Bureau of Labor Statistics put the unemployment rate at 5 percent. The rate—which reached its low point of 4.7 percent in May—represented unemployment's continued downward trend since it peaked at 9.9 percent early in 2010 following the Great Recession of 2008. Job growth in 2016 averaged 178,000 per month, a decrease from the 229,000 jobs per month added in 2015, a year in which household incomes increased by 5.2 percent after seven years of stagnant and declining earnings. Federal Reserve officials noted that improvements in current immigration laws—specifically those dealing with the immigration of skilled workers—could boost the employment rate as well as the overall economy, refuting the theory that skilled immigrants take jobs away from natural-born Americans. Simply put, the economy suffers from a lack of suitably trained or experienced workers.

To reduce the chances of inflation, Federal Reserve policy makers planned an interest rate hike for the end of 2016. And the Fed expects a 2-percent GDP increase in 2017. Officials were holding their breath during the turmoil of the 2016 presidential election, however. A number of economic reports listed dysfunction in the U.S. political system as the single biggest threat to economic progress.

THE U.S. ECONOMY

SELECT U.S. ECONOMIC INDICATORS

Gross domestic product

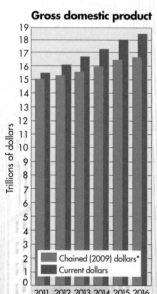

Trillions of dollars

- Chained (2009) dollars*
- Current dollars

2011 2012 2013 2014 2015 2016

*Chained dollars show the amount adjusted for inflation.

Unemployment rate

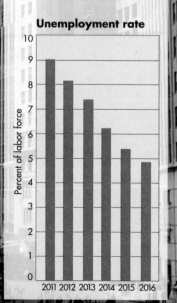

Percent of labor force

2011 2012 2013 2014 2015 2016

STOCK MARKET LEVELS IN 2016

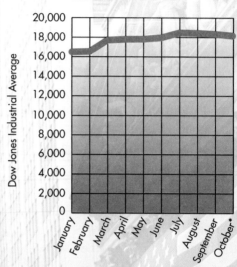

Dow Jones Industrial Average

January February March April May June July August September October*

Closing month averages for 2016
*October figure is as of the 15th

CHANGES IN THE UNITED STATES LABOR FORCE

	2015	2016
Civilian labor force	157,126,000	159,049,000
Total employment	148,839,000	151,241,000
Unemployment	8,287,000	7,808,000
Unemployment rate	5.3%	4.9%

Median usual weekly earnings of full-time employed wage and salary workers age 25 years or older by highest educational attainment

	2015	2016
Less than a high school diploma	$499	$499
High school diploma	$678	$690
Some college or an associate's degree	$757	$767
Bachelor's degree	$1,130	$1,155
Advanced degree	$1,377	$1,425

*Employment data are averages for all of 2015; the figures for 2016 are averages for the first 9 months of the year. Earnings numbers are the second-quarter figures for each year and exclude the value of benefits.

Source: World Book estimates based on data from the U.S. Bureau of Labor Statistics.

THE CANADIAN ECONOMY

FEDERAL SPENDING IN CANADA
ESTIMATED BUDGET FOR FISCAL 2016-2017*

Department or agency	Millions of dollars†
Agriculture and agri-food	2,273
Canadian heritage	3,204
Environment and climate change	2,107
Families, children, and social development; employment, workforce development, and labour	63,675
Finance	90,028
Fisheries and oceans	2,241
Foreign affairs; international trade	5,526
Governor general	23
Health	6,123
Immigration, refugees, and citizenship	1,765
Indigenous and northern affairs	7,525
Infrastructure and communities	4,437
Innovation, science, and economic development	6,503
International development and La Francophonie	149
Justice and attorney general	1,605
National defence	19,237
National revenue	4,086
Natural resources	2,787
Parliament	810
Privy Council	177
Public safety and emergency preparedness	8,527
Public services and procurement	4,526
Status of women	32
Transport	2,472
Treasury board	6,659
Veterans affairs	3,639
Total	**250,136**

*April 1, 2016, to March 31, 2017.
†Rounded in Canadian dollars; $1 = U.S. $0.76 as of Sept. 30, 2016.
Source: Treasury Board of Canada.

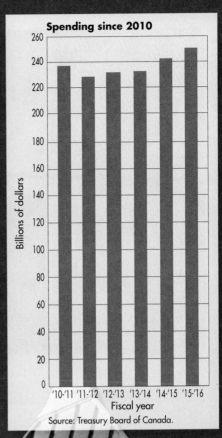

Spending since 2010

Billions of dollars / Fiscal year: '10-'11, '11-'12, '12-'13, '13-'14, '14-'15, '15-'16

Source: Treasury Board of Canada.

ANTONIN SCALIA 1936-2016

On Feb. 13, 2016, U.S. Supreme Court Justice Antonin Scalia died at age 79. At the time of his death, he was the longest-serving justice on the court. President Ronald Reagan appointed him to the post in 1986.

Antonin Scalia was born in Trenton, New Jersey, in 1936, to Italian immigrant parents. His family moved to the New York City borough of Queens when Scalia was a small child. Scalia attended Xavier High School, a Jesuit military academy in Manhattan.

Scalia studied at Georgetown University in Washington, D.C., before graduating from Harvard Law School in Cambridge, Mas-

sachusetts. He practiced law before becoming a law professor at the University of Virginia and then at the University of Chicago. President Reagan made Scalia a judge for the United States Court of Appeals for the District of Columbia Circuit in 1982. In 1986, Scalia was the first Italian American to be appointed a justice to the Supreme Court.

Scalia was a very conservative member of the court. He argued there was no constitutional right to abortion. He opposed gay rights, favored the death penalty, and opposed gun control measures. Scalia followed an "originalist" view when deciding cases. For originalists, the U.S. Constitution is fixed in the time it was created by the Founding Fathers. If no mention is made of an issue in the Constitution, originalists believe the issue is to be decided by the legislatures of the individual states and not by the Supreme Court.

Scalia's death left the Supreme Court evenly split between four liberal and four conservative justices. Republican legislators blocked the nominee to the court put forth by President Barack Obama, hoping that, if a Republican won the presidential election, a conservative justice could be appointed in 2017.

"FREEDOM SUMMER" MURDER CASE CLOSED

On June 20, 2016, after an investigation that continued for more than half a century, U.S. federal and Mississippi state authorities officially closed the books on one of the most heinous, racially motivated criminal cases in the history of the country's civil rights movement. Known as the "Freedom Summer" murder case or the "Mississippi Burning" murder case, it was notable as the first successful federal prosecution of a civil rights case in Mississippi. Outrage over the case helped gain passage of the Voting Rights Act of 1965.

In June 1964, Andrew Goodman and Michael Schwerner, two white civil rights volunteers from New York City, and James Chaney, a black volunteer from Meridian, Mississippi, were working together in Meridian as part of the "Freedom Summer" campaign to help African Americans register to vote. The campaign was organized primarily by the Student Nonviolent Coordinating Committee (SNCC), a civil rights organization. At that time, many Southern States used various methods to deprive blacks of their voting rights. On June 21, the three men were on their way to investigate the burning of an African American church in Neshoba County when they were taken into custody for speeding by a deputy sheriff. After the men were released from county jail in Philadelphia, Mississippi, a Ku Klux Klan mob forced their car off the road and shot the men to death. Initially classified as a missing persons case, the men's disappearance sparked national outrage and an investigation by the Federal Bureau of Investigation (FBI). The FBI found the bodies of the three men 44 days later, buried in an earthen dam.

In 1967, 18 men were tried on federal civil rights charges in the case (7 were convicted), but none were tried for murder. The plot leader, Edgar Ray Killen, a Baptist minister, avoided a trial due to a hung jury. Killen was finally convicted in a 2005 trial based on evidence unveiled in 2000. He was convicted of manslaughter and sentenced to 60 years in prison, where he remains today at age 91.

In 2010, federal authorities reopened the investigation in search of evidence that could convict the remaining suspects. However, that investigation ended after a key witness refused to sign a statement that would have implicated a suspect, according to Mississippi Attorney General Jim Hood. The case closure decision meant that no other suspects would be prosecuted.

FAREWELL TO THE CHIEF

U.S. President Barack Obama marked the eighth and final year of his administration in 2016. Looking back over the Democrat's two terms, his accomplishments are many. Obama began his first term with a surprise Nobel Peace Prize, illustrating the global expectations placed on the new president, particularly in light of the economic and foreign relations failures of his predecessor, George W. Bush. Right away, the Hawaii-born Obama risked becoming a one-term first-African-American-president by insisting Congress put health insurance reform—a political hot potato—atop its priority list. The Patient Protection and Affordable Care Act brought health coverage to millions of previously uninsured citizens, but it also stoked the ire of Congressional Republicans—a running theme throughout his presidency.

Obama, who inherited an economic recession, presided over a U.S. economy which grew slowly but steadily during his time in office, while unemployment numbers dropped dramatically. Obama's administration refused to defend a federal law banning same-sex marriage and later celebrated a Supreme Court decision allowing same-sex marriage throughout the country. Obama signed a law ending the ban on openly homosexual soldiers in the military, and his Department of Defense later lifted the ban on women combat soldiers. The president encouraged the use of clean energy, directing automakers to improve fuel economy and proposing rules to cut greenhouse gas emissions from electric power plants. He also expanded existing national parks and created new national monuments. Obama Supreme Court nominees Sonia Sotomayor and Elena Kagan were both confirmed, but, in 2016, Senate Republicans refused to act on the nomination of Merrick Garland (to replace the late Antonin Scalia), leaving the court a justice short. Obama's administration restored diplomatic ties with Cuba and significantly thawed relations with Iran. Under his command, U.S. troops killed terrorist leader Osama bin Laden and left Iraq at the end of 2011. In 2015, however, U.S. troops returned to Iraq to confront Islamic State terrorists.

Congressional Republicans scuttled many other presidential nominees and voted down or filibustered hundreds of bills, including such important parts of the president's agenda as gun control, immigration reform, political finance reform, unemployment benefit expansion, and closing the detention center at Guantanamo Bay. Nonpartisan critics objected to the government's surveillance programs and the military's use of drones.

NANCY REAGAN 1921-2016

On March 6, 2016, former U.S. First Lady Nancy Davis Reagan died at age 94 in Los Angeles. From 1981 to 1989, Reagan shared the White House with her husband, President Ronald Reagan (1911-2004).

Mrs. Reagan was born Anne Frances Robbins in 1921. Nicknamed Nancy, she grew up in New York City and Chicago. Her mother's second husband, Loyal Davis, adopted Nancy, and her last name changed from Robbins to Davis.

Nancy Davis graduated from Smith College in 1943, where she majored in drama. She became an actress in Hollywood, where she appeared in such films as *East Side, West Side* (1949), *Night into Morn-*ing (1951), *Donovan's Brain* (1953), and *Hellcats of the Navy* (1957).

Nancy Davis met actor Ronald Reagan in 1951, and they married the following year. They had two children, Patricia Ann, in 1952; and Ronald Prescott, in 1958. Ronald Reagan became active in conservative politics in the 1950's. He served as the Republican governor of California before being elected president in 1980. As first lady, Nancy Reagan was a force behind the scenes in the White House. Her husband listened to her and most often followed her advice—from firing staff members she felt to be incompetent to apologizing on national television for his role in the Iran-contra scandal of the 1980's. Mrs. Reagan spoke out against the use of illegal drugs, especially by young people. The slogan of the effort, "Just Say No," became nationally known. After Ronald Reagan's presidency ended in 1989, the Reagans moved to their ranch near Santa Barbara, California.

Ronald Reagan later suffered from Alzheimer's disease, and Mrs. Reagan became known as a supporter of research on embryonic stem cells to find a treatment or cure for the disease.

UNITED KINGDOM VOTES FOR
BREXIT

On June 23, 2016, British voters shocked the world—and many in their own nation—by choosing to leave the European Union (EU). The contentious referendum, nicknamed "Brexit" (*British exit*), passed by a narrow margin, 51.9 to 48.1 percent, sending shock waves throughout the UK as well as the rest of the world. Most world business and political leaders had backed and expected a "remain" victory, and opinion polls too had predicted a narrow "remain"

majority. Global economic markets and currencies dropped sharply upon the news, and British Prime Minister David Cameron, a strong "remain" backer, resigned shortly thereafter. His replacement, fellow Conservative Theresa May, also did not support Brexit, but she placed Brexit backers in key positions among her Cabinet.

The UK government is not bound by the "leave" vote, but politicians will no doubt respect its result. The process to leave the EU could take years,

On June 24, 2016, a taxi driver waves the Union Jack in Westminster, London, after British voters narrowly chose to leave the European Union in the historic "Brexit" referendum.

but the UK's place in the partnership was immediately jeopardized. The UK will be excluded from votes on long-lasting matters and other topics of importance (such as its own Brexit). The European Parliament held an emergency session the week after the Brexit vote, urging British leaders to speed the departure.

The consequences of the "leave" vote—beyond removing the UK from the EU—are widespread, long term, and somewhat uncertain. Aside from the changeover in government, the economy has slumped, and the pound has lost value since the vote. A significant political ramification could be the dissolution of the United Kingdom itself, as Northern Ireland and Scotland, which both voted against the Brexit, will be forced out of the EU against their will. Scotland will likely revisit an independence referendum that was voted down two years ago, while Northern Ireland will weigh the possibility of uniting with the Republic of Ireland. The vote also weakens the EU and gives hope and strength to budding exit movements in other European countries. The Brexit vote also created panic and uncertainty among the hundreds of thousands of British citizens living and working in other parts of Europe.

To drum up support from right-wing political parties (which had long called for an EU exit) in 2013, Prime Minister Cameron promised a future "in/out" EU referendum. The move helped Conservatives win parliamentary elections in 2015, but many party members then went against Cameron, who did not support a so-called Brexit. A "remain" victory—which at first seemed a near certainty—then fell into doubt. Right-wing groups and many others joined the "leave" camp. They based their support for an EU withdrawal on hopes of cutting off immigration, extricating the nation from the EU's perceived heavy-handed bureaucracy, and "taking back control" of the UK's place in the world. They also blamed Europe—the perceived gateway for migrants and refugees from elsewhere in the world—for such domestic problems as unemployment, stagnant wage growth, and high home prices. "Remain" voters supported the generally more favorable diplomatic, economic, logistical, political, and social conditions of EU membership.

The UK has been an unusual EU member since the partnership began in 1993. The UK does not use the euro currency; it is not part of the Schengen zone of passport-free travel; and, although the UK is the third largest contributor to the EU budget, it adds the least among the members as a percentage of its gross national income.

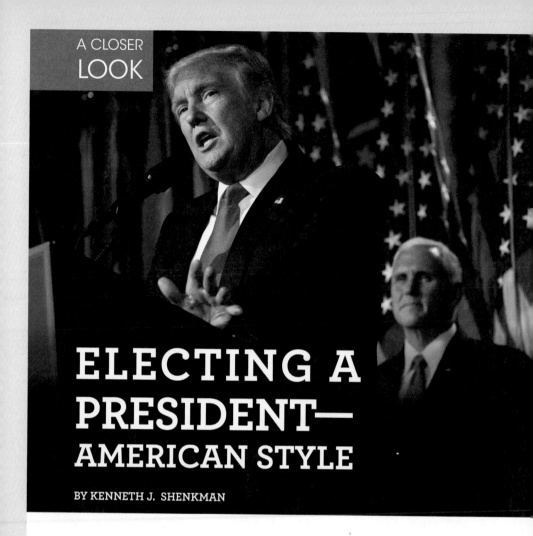

ELECTING A PRESIDENT— AMERICAN STYLE

BY KENNETH J. SHENKMAN

In a shocking result on Nov. 8, 2016, voters in the United States elected Republican businessman Donald Trump to be the nation's next president. Trump upended Democrat Hillary Rodham Clinton, who had been widely expected to win the election.

President-elect Donald Trump speaks during an election night rally in New York City on Nov. 8, 2016. Trump pulled off a surprise victory over Democratic candidate Hillary Rodham Clinton.

Polls had given Clinton a 90-percent chance of winning the presidency, but Trump claimed narrow victories in most of the so-called *swing states* (states that do not vote predictably Democratic or Republican) en route to a slim electoral victory. With 270 electoral votes needed to win, Trump claimed 279 (as of November 9).

Trump's surprise win came at the end of a long and heated campaign that left much of the United States deeply divided politically.

As voting results came in on November 8, Trump's path to reaching the 270 electoral vote threshold widened after he captured the closely contested swing states of Florida, North Carolina, and Ohio. The real estate developer and reality television personality proved popular in such regularly "blue" (Democratic) states as Pennsylvania and Wisconsin, increasing turnout in conservative suburbs and rural areas.

In a small consolation to Clinton, she appeared to win the popular vote after running up large margins in the West Coast states. It was the first time since 2000 that a candidate won the Electoral College while losing the national popular vote. In that election, Republican George W. Bush edged out Democrat Al Gore, who had won the popular vote, after a U.S. Supreme Court ruling ended weeks of contested recounts in Florida.

Clinton had been seeking to succeed popular outgoing President Barack Obama and largely continue his policies. Healthy economic indicators, three strong debate performances, and polls showing a small-but-steady lead appeared to make Clinton poised to become the nation's first woman president. She had garnered the endorsements of the editorial boards of countless newspapers, and numerous current and former Republican officeholders supported her over an opponent they called dangerous for what they labeled his ill-considered pronouncements on foreign policy.

The surfacing, late in the campaign, of a 2005 recording of Trump seemingly promoting aggressive sexual behavior toward women also seemed to have discredited his candidacy. But conventional wisdom did not sway Trump voters. Pollsters hinted that potential voters, aware of the labeling of the Republican as racist and sexist, understated their support of the populist businessman. Political observers failed to gauge the thirst of the electorate to change business-as-usual in Washington, D.C.

In Trump, many saw a champion who would challenge the status quo. His statements about curbing Muslim immigration spoke to some voters' fears about terrorist threats. Trump's lambasting of international trade deals gave supporters hope of overcoming the challenges of a global economy that had "left American workers behind." Furthermore, right-wing news sources popularized the notion that Clinton was an untrustworthy and corrupt—even evil—opportunist who heeded no

Republican presidential candidates (left to right) Ohio Governor John Kasich, former Florida Governor Jeb Bush, Texas Senator Ted Cruz, businessman Donald Trump, Florida Senator Marco Rubio, and Dr. Ben Carson debate in Greenville, South Carolina, on Feb. 13, 2016.

limits in her pursuit of political power and personal enrichment. During his speech accepting the Republican nomination in July, Trump said, "I alone can fix" the nation's apparent dysfunction. In his victory speech late on election night, he struck a conciliatory tone:

"Now it's time for America to bind the wounds of division; [we] have to get together. To all Republicans and Democrats and independents across this nation, I say it is time for us to come together as one united people.

"It's time. I pledge to every citizen of our land that I will be president for all Americans, and this is so important to me. For those who have chosen not to support me in the past, of which there were a few people ... I'm reaching out to you for your guidance and your help so that we can work together and unify our great country."

A divisive, surprising campaign. The 2016 presidential campaign started early in the spring of 2015, when a handful of Democratic candidates—notably Clinton, Vermont Senator Bernie Sanders, former Virginia Senator James Webb, and

former Rhode Island Governor Lincoln Chafee—declared their intention
to seek the party's nod. Sanders proved to be Clinton's strongest rival.
Their contest became a battle between the establishment and progressive wings of the Democratic Party. Sanders, representing the progressive wing, focused on issues surrounding economic inequality. He and
his message proved popular with the Democratic electorate, and the
front-running Clinton found herself in a bruising primary fight.

Clinton and Sanders competed in 57 nominating contests in U.S.
states and territories. Sanders and his supporters criticized Clinton for
her ties to Wall Street banks, her changing positions on trade agree-
ments, and what they called her questionable judgment in handling
international crises as secretary of state. Clinton countered that she had
spent decades fighting for fair pay for women and had led a crusade
for universal health care in the 1990's. Sanders won 23 contests, and
Clinton carried 34. In July 2016, Sanders acknowledged his campaign's
defeat and endorsed Clinton for president.

More than a dozen contenders sought the Republican nomination.
Political observers predicted that Wisconsin Governor Scott Walker
would duke it out with former Florida Governor Jeb Bush for the right
to face Clinton—the long-assumed Democratic nominee—in the general
election. Other well-known candidates included moderate Florida Senator Marco Rubio and ultra-conservative Senator Ted Cruz of Texas.

Dr. Ben Carson and Ohio Governor John Kasich were also lasting contenders.

After Donald Trump announced the start of his presidential campaign in June 2015, however, he shot to the top of the Republican list. Huge crowds and ratings-loving television executives thrilled to Trump's combination of stardom—he had hosted the reality television series "The Apprentice"—and blunt talk linking immigration to crime. Trump panned trade deals for hollowing out American industries and sending jobs to Mexico and overseas. He promised to build a huge wall on the U.S.-Mexico border to curb illegal immigration—and make Mexico pay for it. Opinion polls showed that Trump's campaign, with its slogan "Make America Great Again," appealed strongly to working-class voters, particularly white males.

Despite Trump's early lead in the Republican polls, some prognosticators doubted his earnest desire to become president, and few believed he could go the distance. Often speaking in a carnival-like atmosphere, he belittled his main rivals with such labels as "Little" Marco Rubio, "Lyin'" Ted Cruz, and "Low-energy" Jeb Bush. Scott Walker dropped out early in the campaign, and Bush—despite his presidential pedigree as the son of George H. W. Bush and brother of George W. Bush—failed to distinguish himself among the crowded Republican field. Trump outlasted his rivals and emerged victorious from the primary contests.

The Republicans opened their party's July convention in Cleveland, Ohio, with a stern message of law and order, delivered in the wake of shootings that targeted police officers in Texas and Louisiana; social unrest surrounding the killings of African Americans by police; and a horrific terror attack in Nice, France.

Political observers noted that the party's gathering lacked the star power of prior conventions. Prominent Republicans refusing to attend the convention included members of the Bush family and former Republican nominees Mitt Romney and John McCain. Ohio Governor John Kasich, calling for a dignified and respectful campaign, pointedly refused to endorse the Republican nominee. Trump ended the convention by naming Indiana Governor Mike Pence as his vice-presidential running mate.

One week later, the Democratic Convention featured plenty of star power. First Lady Michelle Obama delivered a ringing endorsement of Clinton, and former President Bill Clinton touted his wife's lifelong drive to be a "change maker" for children and families. Barack Obama strongly backed Clinton as the right choice to continue his fights for better health care, a cleaner environment, and a fair economic system. Clinton accepted the nomination with an inspiring speech detailing her plans as president and noting the significance of being the first female major party nominee. Clinton named Tim Kaine, a genial U.S. senator and former Virginia governor, as her running mate. Their campaign slogan was "Stronger Together."

In the general election race, Trump's campaign suffered from the candidate's lack of discipline. His near-daily stream of provocative and often offensive comments distracted the media from pressing both candidates about policy matters. Many Americans shuddered as he engaged in a war of words with the

Vermont Senator Bernie Sanders speaks during a campaign rally in Santa Fe, New Mexico, on May 20, 2016. Sanders, a Democrat, ran a popular presidential campaign, finishing a close second to eventual nominee Hillary Clinton.

Pakistani-American parents of a U.S. marine who had been killed in combat. Trump also faced criticism for not releasing his tax returns, a tradition candidates had followed since the 1970's. As early as August, many Trump supporters feared that their candidate would lose by huge margins. In September, however, Trump began to narrow the gap in the polls. He focused on Clinton's unauthorized use of a private e-mail server while she served as secretary of state, asking her to produce "33,000 missing e-mails." Many poll respondents said that they doubted Clinton's honesty and appreciated Trump's promises to shake up Washington.

Democratic presidential candidate Hillary Clinton speaks during her debate with Republican Donald Trump on Oct. 9, 2016, at Washington University in St. Louis, Missouri. It was the second of the three debates between the political opponents.

During the fall of 2016, the two candidates participated in three debates. Clinton's strong debate performances, together with media reports detailing graphic statements Trump had made about women, propelled her to a wide polling lead in October. Trump rallied again in the race's closing weeks, however, to produce a historic result.

CHANGING LEADERS IN 2016

The list below, in alphabetical order by country, shows notable leadership events and elections that resulted in a new head of state or government. The entries are current as of the end of October 2016.

Armenia. *September 8* Civil unrest and economic woes force the resignation of Prime Minister Hovik Abrahamyan. *September 13* Energy executive and former Yerevan mayor Karen Karapetyan becomes the southwestern Asian nation's new prime minister.

Austria. *May 9* Chancellor Werner Faymann resigns after far-right advances in national elections. *May 17* Railway executive and businessman Christian Kern is named the nation's new chancellor. *May 22* A presidential election is held, but the results are annulled because of improperly handled postal ballots.

Benin. *March 20* Businessman Patrice Talon is elected the next president of the small West African nation.

Brazil. *May 13* Vice President Michel Temer assumes presidential powers and duties during the impeachment trial of President Dilma Rousseff. *August 31* Brazil's senate impeaches Rousseff, formally dismissing her from

President Michel Temer, Brazil

office. Michel Temer is sworn in as the nation's new president.

Central African Republic. *February 19* Voters elected former Prime Minister Faustin-Archange Touadéra as the nation's next president.

Chad. *February 12* Albert Pahimi Padacké is appointed the new prime minister of the north-central African nation.

Comoros. *April 10* Azali Assoumani is elected president of the small Indian Ocean island nation.

Congo, Republic of the. *April 23* President Denis Sassou Nguesso

President Htin Kyaw (L), Myanmar

names former opposition leader Clément Mouamba as prime minister.

Croatia. *October 19* Parliament names Croatian Democratic Union leader Andrej Plenković as the nation's new prime minister.

Estonia. *October 3* Parliament elects European Union accountant Kersti Kaljulaid to become the Baltic nation's first woman president.

Gabon. *August 28* President Ali Bongo Ondimba claims victory over his main challenger, former Foreign Minister Jean Ping, in the small West African nation's presidential election. *September 27* Despite unrest in the capital, Libreville, and allegations of electoral fraud, Ali Bongo is sworn in

for a second 7-year term.

Guatemala. *January 14* Former comic actor Jimmy Morales is sworn in as the small Central American nation's new president.

Haiti. *February 7* Political dysfunction forces the resignation of President Michel Martelly. *February 14* Senator Jocelerme Privert takes over as acting president until a popular election can be held.

Iceland. *April 6* In the wake of revelations in the Panama Papers scandal, Prime Minister Sigmundur Davíð Gunnlaugsson resigns from office and is replaced by Agriculture Minister Sigurður Ingi Jóhannsson. *June 25* Voters elect independent historian Guðni Jóhannesson to become the island nation's next president.

Jordan. *May 29* King Abdullah II names Hani Al-Mulki as the nation's new prime minister.

Kiribati. *March 9* Voters elect Taneti Maamau as the next president of the Central Pacific island nation.

Kosovo. *February 26* Members of parliament elect former Prime Minister Hashim Thaçi as the southeastern European nation's new president.

Lebanon. *October 31* Parliament elects former army chief Michel Aoun as the nation's new president, ending more than two years of vacancy in the post. Saad Hariri is then named prime minister.

Macedonia. *January 18* Emil Dimitriev becomes prime minister on an interim basis following the resignation of Nikola Gruevski.

Marshall Islands. *January 28* Hilda Heine becomes the first woman president of the North Pacific Ocean island country. Heine took over for President Casten Nemra, who briefly held office earlier in the month.

Monaco. *February 1* Serge Telle replaces Michel Roger as minister of state in the small French Riviera country.

Montenegro. *October 26* Prime Minister Milo Djukanovic steps down and is replaced by Deputy Prime Minister Duško Markovic.

Myanmar. *March 15* Htin Kyaw, a longtime ally of democracy activist and Nobel laureate Aung San

President Rodrigo Duterte, Philippines

Suu Kyi, is elected as the Southeast Asian nation's new president. *March 30* Kyaw becomes Myanmar's first civilian leader since 1962.

Nepal. *July 24* Prime Minister Khadga Prasad Oli resigns after the defection of allies from his coalition government. *August 3* Former Communist rebel leader Pushpa Kamal Dahal becomes prime minister for the second time.

Peru. *June 5* Voters elect former Prime Minister Pedro Pablo Kuczynski to be the South American nation's next president.

Philippines. *May 9* Filipino voters elect populist Davao City Mayor Rodrigo Duterte to be the next

President Tsai Ing-wen, Taiwan

president of the Pacific Islands nation. *June 30* Duterte takes office.

Portugal. *January 24* Former law professor and member of European Parliament Marcelo Rebelo de Sousa is elected as the European nation's new president.

São Tomé and Príncipe. *July 17* Voters elect former Prime Minister Evaristo Carvalho as the Atlantic two-island nation's new president.

Seychelles. *October 16* President James Alix Michel resigns and is replaced by Vice President Danny Faure.

Switzerland. *January 1* Johann

Schneider-Ammann is sworn in as the European nation's new president.

Syria. *June 23* Imad Khamis is named the Middle Eastern nation's new prime minister.

Taiwan. *January 16* Voters elect Democratic Progressive Party candidate Tsai Ing-wen to become that nation's first female president.

Thailand. *October 13* Military chief and Privy Council President Prem Tinsulanonda is named regent pro tempore until the succession of Crown Prince Maha Vajiralongkorn to replace King Bhumibol Adulyadej, who died earlier that day.

Prime Minister Theresa May, United Kingdom

United Kingdom. *July 13* Conservative Home Secretary Theresa May becomes the nation's second-ever woman prime minister.

Uzbekistan. *September 2* President Islam Karimov dies after suffering a stroke days earlier. *September 8* Parliament appoints Prime Minister Shavkat Mirziyoyev as interim president until elections can be held.

Vanuatu. *February 11* The parliament of the southwest Pacific Island nation elects Charlot Salwai as the nation's new prime minister.

Tunisia. *July 30* Lawmakers dismiss Prime Minister Habib Essid from office during a no-confidence ballot in parliament. *August 3* Agricultural science specialist Youssef Chahed is named the north African nation's new prime minister.

Turkey. *May 23* Cabinet Minister Binali Yıldırım is named the nation's new prime minister, replacing Ahmet Davutoğlu, who resigned.

Ukraine. *April 14* Parliament appoints Volodymyr Groysman as the nation's new prime minister, replacing Arseny Yatseniuk, who resigned.

Vietnam. *April 2* Parliament elects government security minister Tran Dai Quang as the southeast Asian nation's new president. *April 7* Deputy Prime Minister Nguyen Xuân Phúc is named the country's new prime minister.

Yemen. *April 4* Ahmed Obeid bin Daghr is named the Arabian Peninsula nation's new prime minister.

Zambia. *August 11* Voters elect President Edgar Lungu to a full 5-year term in office. Lungu took over in early 2015 after the death of President Michael Sata.

THE AUSTRALIAN GOVERNMENT

THE CABINET OF AUSTRALIA*

Malcolm Turnbull	prime minister
Barnaby Joyce	deputy prime minister; minister for agriculture and water resources
Nigel Scullion	minister for indigenous affairs
Michaelia Cash	minister for women; minister for employment
Julie Bishop	minister for foreign affairs
Steven Ciobo	minister for trade, tourism, and investment
George Brandis	attorney-general
Scott Morrison	treasurer
Kelly O'Dwyer	minister for revenue and financial services
Mathias Cormann	minister for finance
Fiona Nash	minister for regional development; minister for local government and territories; minister for regional communications
Darren Chester	minister for infrastructure and transport
Marise Payne	minister for defence
Christopher Pyne	minister for defence industry
Peter Dutton	minister for immigration and border protection
Greg Hunt	minister for industry, innovation, and science
Matt Canavan	minister for resources and Northern Australia
Sussan Ley	minister for health and aged care; minister for sport
Mitch Fifield	minister for communication; minister for the arts
Christian Porter	minister for social services
Simon Birmingham	minister for education and training
Josh Frydenberg	minister for the environment and energy

*As of Sept. 1, 2016.

MEMBERS OF THE AUSTRALIAN SENATE

The Senate of the 45th Parliament first met on Aug. 30, 2016. On that date, the Senate consisted of the following members: 26 Australian Labor Party, 24 Liberal Party of Australia, 9 Australian Greens, 5 National Party of Australia, 4 Pauline Hanson's One Nation party, 3 Nick Xenophon Team, 1 County Liberal Party, 1 Derryn Hinch's Justice Party, 1 Family First Party, 1 Jacqui Lambie Network, and 1 Liberal Democratic Party. This table shows each legislator and party affiliation.

Australian Capital Territory
Katy Gallagher, A.L.P.
Zed Seselja, L.P.

New South Wales
Brian Burston, P.H.O.N.
Doug Cameron, A.L.P.
Sam Dastyari, A.L.P.
Concetta Fierravanti-Wells, L.P.
David Leyonhjelm, L.D.P.
Jenny McAllister, A.L.P.
Fiona Nash, N.P.
Deborah O'Neill, A.L.P.
Marise Payne, L.P.
Lee Rhiannon, A.G.
Arthur Sinodinos, L.P.
John Williams, N.P.

Northern Territory
Malarndirri McCarthy, A.L.P.
Nigel Scullion, C.L.P.

Queensland
George Brandis, L.P.
Matthew Canavan, N.P.
Anthony Chisholm, A.L.P.
Pauline Hanson, P.H.O.N.
Chris Ketter, A.L.P.
Ian Macdonald, L.P.
James McGrath, L.P.
Claire Moore, A.L.P.

Barry O'Sullivan, N.P.
Malcolm Roberts, P.H.O.N.
Larissa Waters, A.G.
Murray Watt, A.L.P.

South Australia
Cory Bernardi, L.P.
Simon Birmingham, L.P.
Bob Day, F.F.P.
Don Farrell, A.L.P.
David Fawcett, L.P.
Alex Gallacher, A.L.P.
Stirling Griff, N.X.T.
Sarah Hanson-Young, A.G.
Skye Kakoschke-Moore, N.X.T.
Anne Ruston, L.P.
Penny Wong, A.L.P.
Nick Xenophon, N.X.T.

Tasmania
Eric Abetz, L.P.
Catryna Bilyk, A.L.P.
Carol Brown, A.L.P.
David Bushby, L.P.
Jonathon Duniam, L.P.
Jacqui Lambie, J.L.N.
Nick McKim, A.G.
Stephen Parry, L.P.
Helen Polley, A.L.P.
Lisa Singh, A.L.P.

Anne Urquhart, A.L.P.
Peter Whish-Wilson, A.G.

Victoria
Kim Carr, A.L.P.
Jacinta Collins, A.L.P.
Stephen Conroy, A.L.P.
Richard Di Natale, A.G.
Mitch Fifield, L.P.
Derryn Hinch, D.H.J.P
Jane Hume, L.P.
Gavin Marshall, A.L.P.
Bridget McKenzie, N.P.
James Paterson, L.P.
Janet Rice, A.G.
Scott Ryan, L.P.

Western Australia
Chris Back, L.P.
Michaelia Cash, L.P.
Mathias Cormann, L.P.
Rodney Culleton, P.H.O.N.
Patrick Dodson, A.L.P.
Sue Lines, A.L.P.
Scott Ludlam, A.G.
Louise Pratt, A.L.P.
Linda Reynolds, L.P.
Rachel Siewert, A.G.
Dean Smith, L.P.
Glenn Sterle, A.L.P.

CHIEF MINISTERS OF AUSTRALIAN MAINLAND TERRITORIES

Australian Capital Territory	Andrew Barr	Northern Territory	Michael Gunner

PREMIERS OF AUSTRALIAN STATES

State	Premier
New South Wales	Mike Baird
Queensland	Annastacia Palaszczuk
South Australia	Jay Weatherill
Tasmania	Will Hodgman
Victoria	Daniel Andrews
Western Australia	Colin Barnett

MEMBERS OF THE AUSTRALIAN HOUSE OF REPRESENTATIVES

The House of Representatives of the 45th Parliament first met on Aug. 30, 2016. On that date, the House of Representatives consisted of the following members: 69 Australian Labor Party, 60 Liberal Party of Australia, 16 National Party of Australia, 2 Independents, 1 Australian Greens, 1 Katter's Australian Party, and 1 Nick Xenophon Team. This table shows each legislator and party affiliation. An asterisk (*) denotes those who served in the 44th Parliament.

Australian Capital Territory
Gai Brodtmann, A.L.P.*
Andrew Leigh, A.L.P.*

New South Wales
Tony Abbott, L.P.*
Anthony Albanese, A.L.P.*
John Alexander, L.P.*
Sharon Bird, A.L.P.*
Chris Bowen, A.L.P.*
Tony Burke, A.L.P.*
Linda Burney, A.L.P.
Jason Clare, A.L.P.*
Sharon Claydon, A.L.P.*
David Coleman, L.P.*
Pat Conroy, A.L.P.*
Mark Coulton, N.P.*
Justine Elliot, A.L.P.*
Jason Falinski, L.P.
Joel Fitzgibbon, A.L.P.*
Paul Fletcher, L.P.*
Mike Freelander, A.L.P.
Andrew Gee, N.P.

David Gillespie, N.P.*
Luke Hartsuyker, N.P.*
Alex Hawke, L.P.*
Chris Hayes, A.L.P.*
Kevin Hogan, N.P.*
Emma Husar, A.L.P.
Ed Husic, A.L.P.*
Stephen Jones, A.L.P.*
Barnaby Joyce, N.P.*
Craig Kelly, L.P.*
Mike Kelly, A.L.P.
Craig Laundy, L.P.*
Julian Leeser, L.P.
Sussan Ley, L.P.*
Emma McBride, A.L.P.
Michael McCormack, N.P.*
Scott Morrison, L.P.*
Julie Owens, A.L.P.*
Tanya Plibersek, A.L.P.*
Michelle Rowland, A.L.P.*
Anne Stanley, A.L.P.
Ann Sudmalis, L.P.*
Meryl Swanson, A.L.P.

Angus Taylor L.P.*
Susan Templeman, A.L.P.
Matt Thistlethwaite, A.L.P.*
Malcolm Turnbull, L.P.*
Lucy Wicks, L.P.*
Trent Zimmerman, L.P.*

Northern Territory
Luke Gosling, A.L.P.
Warren Snowdon, A.L.P.*

Queensland
Karen Andrews, L.P.*
Scott Buchholz, L.P.*
Terri Butler, A.L.P.*
Jim Chalmers, A.L.P.*
George Christensen, N.P.*
Steven Ciobo, L.P.*
Milton Dick, A.L.P.
Peter Dutton, L.P.*
Warren Entsch, L.P.*
Trevor Evans, L.P.
Luke Howarth, L.P.*

Bob Katter, K.A.P.*
Susan Lamb, A.L.P.
Andrew Laming, L.P.*
Michelle Landry, N.P.*
David Littleproud, N.P.
John McVeigh, L.P.
Shayne Neumann, A.L.P.*
Llew O'Brien, N.P.
Ted O'Brien, L.P.
Ken O'Dowd, N.P.*
Cathy O'Toole, A.L.P.
Graham Perrett, A.L.P.*
Keith Pitt, N.P.*
Jane Prentice, L.P.*
Stuart Robert, L.P.*
Wayne Swan, A.L.P.*
Bert van Manen, L.P.*
Ross Vasta, L.P.*
Andrew Wallace, L.P.

South Australia
Mark Butler, A.L.P.*
Nick Champion, A.L.P.*
Kate Ellis, A.L.P.*
Nicolle Flint, L.P.
Steve Georganas, A.L.P.
Tony Pasin, L.P.*
Christopher Pyne, L.P.*
Rowan Ramsey, L.P.*
Amanda Rishworth, A.L.P.*
Rebekha Sharkie, N.X.T.
Tony Zappia, A.L.P.*

Tasmania
Julie Collins, A.L.P.*
Ross Hart, A.L.P.
Justine Keay, A.L.P.
Brian Mitchell, A.L.P.
Andrew Wilkie, Ind.*

Victoria
Kevin Andrews, L.P.*
Adam Bandt, A.G.*
Julia Banks, L.P.
Andrew Broad, N.P.*
Russell Broadbent, L.P.*
Anthony Byrne, A.L.P.*
Darren Chester, N.P.*
Lisa Chesters, A.L.P.*
Chris Crewther, L.P.
Michael Danby, A.L.P.*
Mark Dreyfus, A.L.P.*
Damian Drum, N.P.
David Feeney, A.L.P.*
Josh Frydenberg, L.P.*
Andrew Giles, A.L.P.*
Sarah Henderson, L.P.*
Julian Hill, A.L.P.
Greg Hunt, L.P.*
Peter Khalil, A.L.P.
Catherine King, A.L.P.*
Jenny Macklin, A.L.P.*
Richard Marles, A.L.P.*
Cathy McGowan, Ind.*
Rob Mitchell, A.L.P.*

Brendan O'Connor, A.L.P.*
Kelly O'Dwyer, L.P.*
Clare O'Neil, A.L.P.*
Joanne Ryan, A.L.P.*
Bill Shorten, A.L.P.*
Tony Smith, L.P.*
Michael Sukkar, L.P.*
Dan Tehan, L.P.*
Alan Tudge, L.P.*
Maria Vamvakinou, A.L.P.*
Tim Watts, A.L.P.*
Timothy Wilson, L.P.
Jason Wood, L.P.*

Western Australia
Anne Aly, A.L.P.
Julie Bishop, L.P.*
Ian Goodenough, L.P.*
Tim Hammond, A.L.P.
Andrew Hastie, L.P.*
Steve Irons, L.P.*
Michael Keenan, L.P.*
Matt Keogh, A.L.P.
Madeleine King, A.L.P.
Nola Marino, L.P.*
Ben Morton, L.P.
Christian Porter, L.P.*
Melissa Price, L.P.*
Josh Wilson, A.L.P.
Rick Wilson, L.P.*
Ken Wyatt, L.P.*

THE CANADIAN GOVERNMENT

MEMBERS OF THE CANADIAN SENATE

The Senate of the 42nd Parliament convened on Dec. 3, 2015. On Sept. 1, 2016, the House of Commons consisted of the following members: 41 Conservative Party of Canada, 23 Independents, 21 Liberal Party of Canada, and 20 vacancies. This table shows each legislator and party affiliation.

Alberta
Douglas Black, Ind.
Elaine McCoy, Ind.
Grant Mitchell, Ind.
Scott Tannas, C.P.C.
Claudette Tardif, L.P.C.
Betty E. Unger, C.P.C.

British Columbia
Larry W. Campbell, Ind.
Mobina S.B. Jaffer, L.P.C.
Yonah Martin, C.P.C.
Richard Neufeld, C.P.C.
Nancy Greene Raine, C.P.C.
1 vacancy

Manitoba
Raymond Gagné, Ind.
Janis G. Johnson, C.P.C.
Donald Neil Plett, C.P.C.
Murray Sinclair, Ind.
2 vacancies

New Brunswick
Joseph A. Day, L.P.C.
Sandra Lovelace Nicholas, L.P.C.
Paul E. McIntyre, C.P.C.
Percy Mockler, C.P.C.
Rose-May Poirier, C.P.C.
Pierrette Ringuette, Ind.
Carolyn Stewart Olsen, C.P.C.
John D. Wallace, Ind.
2 vacancies

Newfoundland and Labrador
George Baker, L.P.C.
Norman E. Doyle, C.P.C.
George J. Furey, Ind.
Fabian Manning, C.P.C.

Elizabeth Marshall, C.P.C.
David M. Wells, C.P.C.

Northwest Territories
Nick G. Sibbeston, Ind.

Nova Scotia
Jane Cordy, L.P.C.
James S. Cowan, L.P.C.
Stephen Greene, C.P.C.
Michael L. MacDonald, C.P.C.
Thomas Johnson McInnis, C.P.C.
Terry M. Mercer, L.P.C.
Wilfred P. Moore, L.P.C.
Kelvin Kenneth Ogilvie, C.P.C.
2 vacancies

Nunavut
Dennis Glen Patterson, C.P.C.

Ontario
Salma Ataullahjan, C.P.C.
Lynn Beyak, C.P.C.
Anne C. Cools, Ind.
Nicole Eaton, C.P.C.
Art Eggleton, L.P.C.
Tobias C. Enverga, Jr., C.P.C.
Linda Frum, C.P.C.
Peter Harder, Ind.
Colin Kenny, L.P.C.
Frances Lankin, Ind.
Don Meredith, Ind.
Jim Munson, L.P.C.
Thanh Hai Ngo, C.P.C.
Victor Oh, C.P.C.
Ratina Omidvar, Ind.
Bob Runciman, C.P.C.
Nancy Ruth, C.P.C.
Vernon White, C.P.C.
6 vacancies

Prince Edward Island
Percy E. Downe, L.P.C.
Michael Duffy, Ind.
Elizabeth Hubley, L.P.C.
1 vacancy

Quebec
Diane Bellemare, Ind.
Pierre-Hugues Boisvenu, Ind.
Patrick Brazeau, Ind.
Claude Carignan, C.P.C.
Jean-Guy Dagenais, C.P.C.
Dennis Dawson, L.P.C.
Jacques Demers, Ind.
Joan Fraser, L.P.C.
Leo Housakos, C.P.C.
Serge Joyal, L.P.C.
Ghislain Maltais, C.P.C.
Paul J. Massicotte, L.P.C.
Chantal Petitclerc, Ind.
André Pratte, Ind.
Judith Seidman, C.P.C.
Larry Smith, C.P.C.
Josée Verner, C.P.C.
Charlie Watt, L.P.C.
6 vacancies

Saskatchewan
Raynell Andreychuk, C.P.C.
Denise Batters, C.P.C.
Lillian Eva Dyck, L.P.C.
Pana Merchant, L.P.C.
David Tkachuk, C.P.C.
Pamela Wallin, Ind.

Yukon
Daniel Lang, C.P.C.

THE MINISTRY OF CANADA*

Justin Trudeau	prime minister
Ralph Goodale	minister of public safety and emergency preparedness
Lawrence MacAulay	minister of agriculture and agri-food
Stéphane Dion	minister of foreign affairs
John McCallum	minister of immigration, refugees, and citizenship
Carolyn Bennett	minister of indigenous and northern affairs
Scott Brison	president of the Treasury Board
Dominic LeBlanc	minister of fisheries, oceans, and the Canadian Coast Guard
Navdeep Bains	minister of innovation, science, and economic development
Bill Morneau	minister of finance
Jody Wilson-Raybould	minister of justice; attorney general of Canada
Judy Foote	minister for public services and procurement
Chrystia Freeland	minister of international trade
Jane Philpott	minister of health
Jean-Yves Duclos	minister of families, children, and social development
Marc Garneau	minister of transport
Marie-Claude Bibeau	minister of international development and la Francophonie
Jim Carr	minister of natural resources
Mélanie Joly	minister of Canadian heritage
Diane Lebouthillier	minister of national revenue
Kent Hehr	minister of veterans affairs, associate minister of national defence
Catherine McKenna	minister of environment and climate change
Harjit Singh Sajjan	minister of national defence
MaryAnn Mihychuk	minister of employment, workforce development, and labour
Amarjeet Sohi	minister of infrastructure and communities
Maryam Monsef	minister of democratic institutions
Carla Qualtrough	minister of sport and persons with disabilities
Kirsty Duncan	minister of science
Patricia Hajdu	minister of status of women
Bardish Chagger	minister of small business and tourism; leader of the government in the House of Commons

*As of Sept. 1, 2016.

LOCAL GOVERNMENT HEADS

Premiers of Canadian provinces

Alberta	Rachel Notley
British Columbia	Christy Clark
Manitoba	Brian Pallister
New Brunswick	Brian Gallant
Newfoundland and Labrador	Dwight Ball
Nova Scotia	Stephen McNeil
Ontario	Kathleen Wynne
Prince Edward Island	Wade MacLauchlan
Quebec	Philippe Couillard
Saskatchewan	Brad Wall

Premiers of Canadian territories

Northwest Territories	Bob McLeod
Nunavut	Peter Taptuna
Yukon	Darrell Pasloski

SUPREME COURT OF CANADA

Chief Justice

Beverley McLachlin

Puisne Justices

Rosalie Silberman Abella

Michael J. Moldaver

Andromache Karakatsanis

Richard Wagner

Clément Gascon

Suzanne Côté

Russell Brown

Malcolm Rowe

MEMBERS OF THE CANADIAN HOUSE OF COMMONS

The House of Commons of the 42nd Parliament convened on Dec. 3, 2015. On Sept. 1, 2016, the House of Commons consisted of the following members: 182 Liberal Party, 97 Conservative Party of Canada, 44 New Democratic Party, 10 Bloc Québécois, 1 Green Party, 1 Independent, and 3 vacancies. This table shows each legislator and party affiliation. An asterisk (*) denotes those who served in the 41st Parliament.

Alberta
Ziad Aboultaif, C.P.C.
Rona Ambrose, C.P.C.*
John Barlow, C.P.C.*
Randy Boissonnault, Lib.
Blaine Calkins, C.P.C.*
Michael Cooper, C.P.C.
Kerry Diotte, C.P.C.
Earl Dreeshen, C.P.C.*
Linda Francis Duncan, N.D.P.*
Jim Eglinski, C.P.C.*
Garnett Genuis, C.P.C.
Rachael Harder, C.P.C.
Kent Hehr, Lib.
Matt Jeneroux, C.P.C.
Darshan Singh Kang, Lib.
Pat Kelly, C.P.C.
Jason Kenney, C.P.C.*
Tom Kmiec, C.P.C.
Mike Lake, C.P.C.*
Ron Liepert, C.P.C.
Kelly McCauley, C.P.C.
Deepak Obhrai, C.P.C.*
Michelle Rempel, C.P.C.*
Blake Richards, C.P.C.*
Martin Shields, C.P.C.
Amarjeet Sohi, Lib.
Kevin Sorenson, C.P.C.*
Shannon Stubbs, C.P.C.
Arnold Viersen, C.P.C.
Chris Warkentin, C.P.C.*
Len Webber, C.P.C.
David Yurdiga, C.P.C.
2 vacancies

British Columbia
Dan Albas, C.P.C.*
John Aldag, Lib.
Mel Arnold, C.P.C.
Terry Beech, Lib.
Rachel Blaney, N.D.P.
Richard Cannings, N.D.P.
Nathan Cullen, N.D.P.*
Don Davies, N.D.P.*
Sukh Dhaliwal, Lib.
Todd Doherty, C.P.C.
Fin Donnelly, N.D.P.*
Edward Fast, C.P.C.*
Hedy Fry, Lib.*
Stephen Fuhr, Lib.
Randall Garrison, N.D.P.*
Pam Goldsmith-Jones, Lib.
Ken Hardie, Lib.
Gord Johns, N.D.P.
Peter Julian, N.D.P.*
Jenny Wai Ching Kwan, N.D.P.
Alistair MacGregor, N.D.P.

Sheila Malcolmson, N.D.P.
Elizabeth May, Green*
Ron McKinnon, Lib.
Cathy McLeod, C.P.C.*
Joyce Murray, Lib.*
Joe Peschisolido, Lib.
Carla Qualtrough, Lib.
Murray Rankin, N.D.P.*
Dan Ruimy, Lib.
Harjit Singh Sajjan, Lib.
Randeep Sarai, Lib.
Jati Sidhu, Lib.
Wayne Stetski, N.D.P.
Kennedy Stewart, N.D.P.*
Mark Strahl, C.P.C.*
Mark Warawa, C.P.C.*
Dianne Lynn Watts, C.P.C.
Jonathan Wilkinson, Lib.
Jody Wilson-Raybould, Lib.
Alice Wong, C.P.C.*
Bob Zimmer, C.P.C.*

Manitoba
Niki Ashton, N.D.P.*
Candice Bergen, C.P.C.*
James Bezan, C.P.C.*
Daniel Blaikie, N.D.P.
James Gordon Carr, Lib.
Terry Duguid, Lib.
Doug Eyolfson, Lib.
Ted Falk, C.P.C.*
Kevin Lamoureux, Lib.*
Larry Maguire, C.P.C.*
MaryAnn Mihychuk, Lib.
Robert-Falcon Ouellette, Lib.
Robert Sopuck, C.P.C.*
Dan Vandal, Lib.

New Brunswick
René Arseneault, Lib.
Serge Cormier, Lib.
Matt DeCourcey, Lib.
Pat Finnigan, Lib.
TJ Harvey, Lib.
Dominic LeBlanc, Lib.*
Alaina Lockhart, Lib.
Wayne Long, Lib.
Karen Ludwig, Lib.
Ginette Petitpas Taylor, Lib.

Newfoundland and Labrador
Judy Foote, Lib.*
Gudie Hutchings, Lib.
Yvonne Jones, Lib.*
Ken McDonald, Lib.
Seamus O'Regan, Lib.
Scott Simms, Lib.*
Nick Whalen, Lib.

Northwest Territories
Michael McLeod, Lib.

Nova Scotia
Scott Brison, Lib.*
William D. (Bill) Casey, Lib.
Rodger Cuzner, Lib.*
Mark Eyking, Lib.*
Andy Fillmore, Lib.
Darren Fisher, Lib.
Colin Fraser, Lib.
Sean Fraser, Lib.
Bernadette Jordan, Lib.
Geoff Regan, Lib.*
Darrell Samson, Lib.

Nunavut
Hunter Tootoo, Ind.

Ontario
Harold Albrecht, C.P.C.*
Omar Alghabra, Lib.
Leona Alleslev, Lib.
Dean Allison, C.P.C.*
Gary Anandasangaree, Lib.
Charlie Angus, N.D.P.*
Chandra Arya, Lib.
Vance Badawey, Lib.
Navdeep Singh Bains, Lib.
Carolyn Bennett, Lib.*
Chris Bittle, Lib.
Bill Blair, Lib.
Mike Bossio, Lib.
John Brassard, C.P.C.
Bob Bratina, Lib.
Gordon Brown, C.P.C.*
Celina Caesar-Chavannes, Lib.
Colin Carrie, C.P.C.*
Bardish Chagger, Lib.
Arnold Chan, Lib.*
Shaun Chen, Lib.
Michael D. Chong, C.P.C.*
David Christopherson, N.D.P.*
Tony Clement, C.P.C.*
Julie Dabrusin, Lib.
Pam Damoff, Lib.
Francis Drouin, Lib.
Kirsty Duncan, Lib.*
Scott Duvall, N.D.P.
Julie Dzerowicz, Lib.
Ali Ehsassi, Lib.
Neil Ellis, Lib.
Nathaniel Erskine-Smith, Lib.
Diane Finley, C.P.C.*
Peter Fonseca, Lib.
Peter Fragiskatos, Lib.
Chrystia Freeland, Lib.*
Cheryl Gallant, C.P.C.*

Mark Gerretsen, Lib.
Marilyn Gladu, C.P.C.
Karina Gould, Lib.
Raj Grewal, Lib.
Patricia Hajdu, Lib.
Cheryl Hardcastle, N.D.P.
Mark Holland, Lib.
Carol Hughes, N.D.P.*
Ahmed Hussen, Lib.
Majid Jowhari, Lib.
Peter Kent, C.P.C.*
Iqra Khalid, Lib.
Kamal Khera, Lib.
Guy Lauzon, C.P.C.*
Paul Lefebvre, Lib.
K. Kellie Leitch, C.P.C.*
Andrew Leslie, Lib.
Michael Levitt, Lib.
Ben Lobb, C.P.C.*
Lloyd Longfield, Lib.
Dave MacKenzie, C.P.C.*
James Maloney, Lib.
Brian Masse, N.D.P.*
Irene Mathyssen, N.D.P.*
Bryan May, Lib.
John McCallum, Lib.*
Phil McColeman, C.P.C.*
Karen McCrimmon, Lib.
David McGuinty, Lib.*
John McKay, Lib.*
Catherine Mary McKenna, Lib.
Marco Mendicino, Lib.
Larry Miller, C.P.C.*
Maryam Monsef, Lib.
William Francis Morneau, Lib.
John Nater, C.P.C.
Robert Daniel Nault, Lib.
Rob Nicholson, C.P.C.*
Alex Nuttall, C.P.C.
Jennifer O'Connell, Lib.
Robert Oliphant, Lib.
John Oliver, Lib.
Erin O'Toole, C.P.C.*
Kyle Peterson, Lib.
Jane Philpott, Lib.
Pierre Poilievre, C.P.C.*
Lisa Raitt, C.P.C.*
Tracey Ramsey, N.D.P.
Yasmin Ratansi, Lib.
Scott Reid, C.P.C.*
Anthony Rota, Lib.
Kim Rudd, Lib.
Don Rusnak, Lib.
Ruby Sahota, Lib.
Raj Saini, Lib.
Ramesh Sangha, Lib.
Bob Saroya, C.P.C.
Jamie Schmale, C.P.C.
Deb Schulte, Lib.
Marc Serré, Lib.
Judy Sgro, Lib.*
Terry Sheehan, Lib.
Bev Shipley, C.P.C.*

Sonia Sidhu, Lib.
Gagan Sikand, Lib.
Francesco Sorbara, Lib.
Sven Spengemann, Lib.
Bruce Stanton, C.P.C.*
David Sweet, C.P.C.*
Marwan Tabbara, Lib.
Geng Tan, Lib.
Filomena Tassi, Lib.
David Allan Tilson, C.P.C.*
Dave Van Kesteren, C.P.C.*
Peter Van Loan, C.P.C.*
Anita Vandenbeld, Lib.
Adam Vaughan, Lib.*
Karen Louise Vecchio, C.P.C.
Arif Virani, Lib.
Borys Wrzesnewskyj, Lib.
Kate Young, Lib.
Salma Zahid, Lib.
1 vacancy

Prince Edward Island
Sean Casey, Lib.*
Arnold Wayne Easter, Lib.*
Lawrence MacAulay, Lib.*
Robert Morrissey, Lib.

Quebec
William Amos, Lib.
Robert Aubin, N.D.P.*
Ramez Ayoub, Lib.
Xavier Barsalou-Duval, B.Q.
Frank Baylis, Lib.
Mario Beaulieu, B.Q.
Maxime Bernier, C.P.C.*
Luc Berthold, C.P.C.
Marie-Claude Bibeau, Lib.
Steven Blaney, C.P.C.*
Sylvie Boucher, C.P.C.
Michel Boudrias, B.Q.
Alexandre Boulerice, N.D.P.*
Marjolaine Boutin-Sweet, N.D.P.*
Pierre Breton, Lib.
Ruth Ellen Brosseau, N.D.P.*
Guy Caron, N.D.P.*
François-Philippe Champagne, Lib.
François Choquette, N.D.P.*
Alupa Clarke, C.P.C.
Gérard Deltell, C.P.C.
Anju Dhillon, Lib.
Nicola Di Iorio, Lib.
Stéphane Dion, Lib.*
Matthew Dubé, N.D.P.*
Emmanuel Dubourg, Lib.*
Jean-Yves Duclos, Lib.
Pierre-Luc Dusseault, N.D.P.*
Fayçal El-Khoury, Lib.
Greg Fergus, Lib.
Rhéal Fortin, B.Q.
Marc Garneau, Lib.*
Bernard Généreux, C.P.C.
Marilène Gill, B.Q.
Joël Godin, C.P.C.
Jacques Gourde, C.P.C.*

David Graham, Lib.
Anthony Housefather, Lib.
Angelo Iacono, Lib.
Mélanie Joly, Lib.
David Lametti, Lib.
Linda Lapointe, Lib.
Stéphane Lauzon, Lib.
Hélène Laverdière, N.D.P.*
Denis Lebel, C.P.C.*
Diane Lebouthillier, Lib.
Denis Lemieux, Lib.
Joël Lightbound, Lib.
Steven MacKinnon, Lib.
Simon Marcil, B.Q.
Rémi Massé, Lib.
Alexandra Mendès, Lib.
Marc Miller, Lib.
Christine Moore, N.D.P.
Thomas J. Mulcair, N.D.P.*
Pierre Nantel, N.D.P.*
Eva Nassif, Lib.
Denis Paradis, Lib.
Pierre Paul-Hus, C.P.C.
Monique Pauzé, B.Q.
Michel Picard, Lib.
Louis Plamondon, B.Q.*
Jean-Claude Poissant, Lib.
Anne Minh-Thu Quach, N.D.P.*
Alain Rayes, C.P.C.
Jean Rioux, Lib.
Yves Robillard, Lib.
Pablo Rodriquez, Lib.
Sherry Romanado, Lib.
Romeo Saganash, N.D.P.*
Brigitte Sansoucy, N.D.P.
Francis Scarpaleggia, Lib.*
Peter Schiefke, Lib.
Brenda Shanahan, Lib.
Gabriel Ste-Marie, B.Q.
Luc Thériault, B.Q.
Justin Trudeau, Lib.*
Karine Trudel, N.D.P.

Saskatchewan
David Anderson, C.P.C.*
Sheri Benson, N.D.P.
Kelly Block, C.P.C.*
Ralph Goodale, Lib.*
Randy Hoback, C.P.C.*
Georgina Jolibois, N.D.P.
Robert Gordon Kitchen, C.P.C.
Tom Lukiwski, C.P.C.*
Gerry Ritz, C.P.C.*
Andrew Scheer, C.P.C.*
Brad Trost, C.P.C.*
Cathay Wagantall, C.P.C.
Kevin Waugh, C.P.C.
Erin Weir, N.D.P.

Yukon
Larry Bagnell, Lib.

THE GOVERNMENT OF THE UNITED KINGDOM

THE CABINET OF THE UNITED KINGDOM*

Theresa May	prime minister; first lord of the treasury; minister for the civil service
Philip Hammond	chancellor of the exchequer
Amber Rudd	home secretary
Boris Johnson	secretary of state for foreign and commonwealth affairs
Michael Fallon	secretary of state for defence
Elizabeth Truss	lord chancellor; secretary of state for justice
Justine Greening	secretary of state for education
David Davis	secretary of state for exiting the European Union
Liam Fox	secretary of state for international trade; president of the Board of Trade
Greg Clark	secretary of state for business, energy, and industrial strategy
Jeremy Hunt	secretary of state for health
Damian Green	secretary of state for work and pensions
Chris Grayling	secretary of state for transport
Sajid Javid	secretary of state for communities and local government
David Lidington	lord president of the council; leader of the House of Commons
Baroness Evans of Bowes Park	leader of the House of Lords; lord privy seal
David Mundell	secretary of state for Scotland
Alun Cairns	secretary of state for Wales
James Brokenshire	secretary of state for Northern Ireland
Andrea Leadsom	secretary of state for environment, food, and rural affairs
Priti Patel	secretary of state for international development
Karen Bradley	secretary of state for culture, media, and sport
Patrick McLoughlin	chancellor of the duchy of Lancaster

*As of Sept. 1, 2016.

HOUSE OF COMMONS

Queen Elizabeth II opened the 2016-2017 session of Parliament on May 18, 2016. As of Sept. 13, 2016, the House of Commons consisted of the following:

329	Conservative Party
230	Labour Party
54	Scottish National Party
8	Democratic Unionist Party
8	Liberal Democrats
4	Independent
4	Sinn Fein
3	Plaid Cymru
3	Social Democratic and Labour Party
2	Ulster Unionist Party
1	Green Party
1	UK Independence Party
2	Vacant

THE GOVERNMENT OF THE UNITED STATES

SELECTED HEADS OF THE UNITED STATES EXECUTIVE BRANCH*

President	Barack Obama
Vice President	Joe Biden
Secretary of Agriculture	Thomas J. Vilsack
Secretary of Commerce	Penny Pritzker
Secretary of Defense	Ashton Carter
Secretary of Education	John King
Secretary of Energy	Ernest Moniz
Secretary of Health and Human Services	Sylvia M. Burwell
Secretary of Homeland Security	Jeh Johnson
Secretary of Housing and Urban Development	Julián Castro
Secretary of the Interior	Sally Jewell
Attorney General	Loretta E. Lynch
Secretary of Labor	Thomas E. Perez
Secretary of State	John Kerry
Secretary of Transportation	Anthony Foxx
Secretary of the Treasury	Jack Lew
Secretary of Veterans Affairs	Robert McDonald

*As of Oct. 14, 2016.

SUPREME COURT
OF THE UNITED STATES

Chief Justice of the
United States

John G. Roberts, Jr.

Associate Justices

Anthony M. Kennedy

Clarence Thomas

Ruth Bader Ginsburg

Stephen G. Breyer

Samuel A. Alito, Jr.

Sonia Sotomayor

Elena Kagan

MEMBERS OF THE UNITED STATES SENATE

The Senate of the 115th Congress will convene on Jan. 3, 2017. The Senate will consist of 51 Republicans, 48 Democrats, and 1 undecided at press time. The names are color coded according to party affiliation: Republican—red and Democrat—blue. The first date in each listing shows when the senator's term began. The second date shows when the senator's term expires.

STATE	TERM	STATE	TERM	STATE	TERM
Alabama		**Kentucky**		**North Dakota**	
Richard C. Shelby	1987-2023	Mitch McConnell	1985-2021	John Hoeven	2011-2023
Jeff Sessions	1997-2021	Rand Paul	2011-2023	Heidi Heitkamp	2013-2019
Alaska		**Louisiana**		**Ohio**	
Lisa Murkowski	2002-2023	Bill Cassidy	2015-2021	Sherrod Brown	2007-2019
Dan Sullivan	2015-2021	Undecided		Rob Portman	2011-2023
Arizona		**Maine**		**Oklahoma**	
John McCain III	1987-2023	Susan M. Collins	1997-2021	James M. Inhofe	1994-2021
Jeff Flake	2013-2019	Angus King	2013-2019	James Lankford	2015-2023
Arkansas		**Maryland**		**Oregon**	
John Boozman	2011-2023	Benjamin L. Cardin	2007-2023	Ron Wyden	1996-2023
Tom Cotton	2015-2021	Chris Van Hollen	2017-2023	Jeff Merkley	2009-2021
California		**Massachusetts**		**Pennsylvania**	
Dianne Feinstein	1992-2019	Elizabeth Warren	2013-2019	Bob Casey, Jr.	2007-2019
Kamala Harris	2017-2023	Ed Markey	2013-2021	Pat Toomey	2011-2023
Colorado		**Michigan**		**Rhode Island**	
Michael F. Bennet	2009-2023	Debbie Stabenow	2001-2019	Jack Reed	1997-2021
Cory Gardner	2015-2021	Gary Peters	2015-2021	Sheldon Whitehouse	2007-2019
Connecticut		**Minnesota**		**South Carolina**	
Richard Blumenthal	2011-2023	Amy Klobuchar	2007-2019	Lindsey Graham	2003-2021
Chris Murphy	2013-2019	Al Franken	2009-2021	Tim Scott	2013-2023
Delaware		**Mississippi**		**South Dakota**	
Thomas Carper	2001-2019	Thad Cochran	1978-2021	John Thune	2005-2023
Christopher Coons	2011-2021	Roger Wicker	2007-2019	Mike Rounds	2015-2021
Florida		**Missouri**		**Tennessee**	
Bill Nelson	2001-2019	Claire C. McCaskill	2007-2019	Lamar Alexander	2003-2021
Marco Rubio	2011-2023	Roy Blunt	2011-2023	Bob Corker	2007-2019
Georgia		**Montana**		**Texas**	
Johnny Isakson	2005-2023	Jon Tester	2007-2019	John Cornyn	2003-2021
David Perdue	2015-2021	Steve Daines	2015-2021	Ted Cruz	2013-2019
Hawaii		**Nebraska**		**Utah**	
Brian Schatz	2012-2023	Deb Fischer	2013-2019	Orrin G. Hatch	1977-2019
Mazie Hirono	2013-2019	Ben Sasse	2015-2021	Mike Lee	2011-2023
Idaho		**Nevada**		**Vermont**	
Mike Crapo	1999-2023	Dean Heller	2011-2019	Patrick J. Leahy	1975-2023
Jim Risch	2009-2021	Catherine Cortez Masto	2017-2023	Bernie Sanders	2007-2019
Illinois		**New Hampshire**		**Virginia**	
Richard J. Durbin	1997-2021	Jeanne Shaheen	2009-2021	Mark Warner	2009-2021
Tammy Duckworth	2017-2023	Maggie Hassan	2017-2023	Tim Kaine	2013-2019
Indiana		**New Jersey**		**Washington**	
Joe Donnelly	2013-2019	Robert Menendez	2006-2019	Patty Murray	1993-2023
Todd Young	2017-2023	Cory Booker	2013-2021	Maria Cantwell	2001-2019
Iowa		**New Mexico**		**West Virginia**	
Charles E. Grassley	1981-2023	Tom Udall	2009-2021	Joe Manchin III	2010-2019
Joni Ernst	2015-2021	Martin Heinrich	2013-2019	Shelley Moore Capito	2015-2021
Kansas		**New York**		**Wisconsin**	
Pat Roberts	1997-2021	Charles E. Schumer	1999-2023	Ron Johnson	2011-2023
Jerry Moran	2011-2023	Kirsten E. Gillibrand	2009-2019	Tammy Baldwin	2013-2019
		North Carolina		**Wyoming**	
		Richard Burr	2005-2023	Mike Enzi	1997-2021
		Thom Tillis	2015-2021	John Barrasso	2007-2019

CONGRESSIONAL OFFICIALS

President of the Senate pro tempore	Orrin G. Hatch	Speaker of the House	Paul Ryan
Senate Majority Leader	Mitch McConnell	House Majority Leader	Kevin McCarthy
Senate Minority Leader	Harry M. Reid	House Democratic Leader	Nancy Pelosi

MEMBERS OF THE UNITED STATES HOUSE OF REPRESENTATIVES

The House of Representatives of the 115th Congress will convene on Jan. 3, 2017. The House of Representatives will consist of 238 Republicans, 193 Democrats, and 4 not decided at press time (not including representatives from American Samoa, the District of Columbia, Guam, the Northern Mariana Islands, Puerto Rico, and the Virgin Islands). This table shows congressional district, legislator, and party affiliation. The names are color coded according to party affiliation: Republican—red and Democrat—blue. Asterisk (*) denotes those who served in the 114th Congress; dagger (†) denotes "at large."

Alabama
1. Bradley Byrne*
2. Martha Roby*
3. Mike Rogers*
4. Robert Aderholt*
5. Mo Brooks*
6. Gary Palmer*
7. Terri Sewell*

Alaska
†Donald E. Young*

Arizona
1. Tom O'Halleran*
2. Martha McSally*
3. Raul Grijalva*
4. Paul Gosar*
5. Andy Biggs*
6. David Schweikert*
7. Ruben Gallego*
8. Trent Franks*
9. Kyrsten Sinema*

Arkansas
1. Rick Crawford*
2. French Hill*
3. Steve Womack*
4. Bruce Westerman

California
1. Doug La Malfa*
2. Jared Huffman*
3. John Garamendi*
4. Tom McClintock*
5. Mike Thompson*
6. Doris Matsui*
7. Undecided
8. Paul Cook*
9. Jerry McNerney*
10. Jeff Denham*
11. Mark DeSaulnier*
12. Nancy Pelosi*
13. Barbara Lee*
14. Jackie Speier*
15. Eric Swalwell*
16. Jim Costa*
17. Ro Khanna
18. Anna Eshoo*
19. Zoe Lofgren*

20. Jimmy Panetta
21. David Valadao*
22. Devin Nunes*
23. Kevin McCarthy*
24. Salud Carbajal
25. Steve Knight*
26. Julia Brownley*
27. Judy Chu*
28. Adam Schiff*
29. Tony Cárdenas*
30. Brad Sherman*
31. Pete Aguilar*
32. Grace Napolitano*
33. Ted Lieu*
34. Xavier Becerra*
35. Norma Torres*
36. Raul Ruiz*
37. Karen Bass*
38. Linda Sánchez*
39. Ed Royce*
40. Lucille Roybal-Allard*
41. Mark Takano*
42. Ken Calvert*
43. Maxine Waters*
44. Nanette Barragán*
45. Mimi Walters*
46. Lou Correa*
47. Alan Lowenthal*
48. Dana Rohrabacher*
49. Undecided
50. Duncan Hunter*
51. Juan Vargas*
52. Scott Peters*
53. Susan Davis*

Colorado
1. Diana DeGette*
2. Jared Polis*
3. Scott Tipton*
4. Ken Buck*
5. Doug Lamborn*
6. Mike Coffman*
7. Ed Perlmutter*

Connecticut
1. John Larson*
2. Joe Courtney*

3. Rosa DeLauro*
4. Jim Himes*
5. Elizabeth Esty*

Delaware
†Lisa Blunt Rochester

Florida
1. Matt Gaetz
2. Neal Dunn
3. Ted Yoho*
4. John Rutherford
5. Al Lawson
6. Ron DeSantis*
7. Stephanie Murphy
8. Bill Posey*
9. Darren Soto
10. Val Demings
11. Daniel Webster*
12. Gus Bilirakis*
13. Charlie Crist
14. Kathy Castor*
15. Dennis Ross*
16. Vern Buchanan*
17. Tom Rooney*
18. Brian Mast
19. Francis Rooney
20. Alcee Hastings*
21. Ted Deutch*
22. Lois Frankel*
23. Debbie Wasserman Schultz*
24. Frederica Wilson*
25. Mario Diaz-Balart*
26. Carlos Curbelo*
27. Ileana Ros-Lehtinen*

Georgia
1. Buddy Carter*
2. Sanford Bishop, Jr.*
3. Drew Ferguson
4. Hank Johnson, Jr.*
5. John Lewis*
6. Tom Price*
7. Rob Woodall*
8. Austin Scott*
9. Doug Collins*
10. Jody Hice*
11. Barry Loudermilk*

12. Rich Allen*
13. David Scott*
14. Tom Graves*

Hawaii
1. Colleen Hanabusa*
2. Tulsi Gabbard*

Idaho
1. Raul Labrador*
2. Mike Simpson*

Illinois
1. Bobby Rush*
2. Robin Kelly*
3. Daniel Lipinski*
4. Luis Gutierrez*
5. Mike Quigley*
6. Peter J. Roskam*
7. Danny Davis*
8. Raja Krishnamoorthi
9. Jan Schakowsky*
10. Brad Schneider
11. Bill Foster*
12. Mike Bost*
13. Rodney Davis*
14. Randy Hultgren*
15. John Shimkus*
16. Adam Kinzinger*
17. Cheri Bustos*
18. Darin LaHood*

Indiana
1. Peter Visclosky*
2. Jackie Walorski*
3. Jim Banks
4. Todd Rokita*
5. Susan Brooks*
6. Luke Messer*
7. André Carson*
8. Larry Bucshon*
9. Trey Hollingsworth

Iowa
1. Rod Blum*
2. David Loebsack*
3. David Young*
4. Steve King*

Kansas
1. Roger Marshall
2. Lynn Jenkins*
3. Kevin Yoder*
4. Mike Pompeo*

Kentucky
1. James Comer*
2. Brett Guthrie*
3. John Yarmuth*
4. Thomas Massie*
5. Harold (Hal) Rogers*
6. Andy Barr*

Louisiana
1. Steve Scalise*
2. Cedric Richmond*
3. Undecided
4. Undecided

5. Ralph Abraham*
6. Garret Graves*

Maine
1. Chellie Pingree*
2. Bruce Poliquin*

Maryland
1. Andy Harris*
2. Dutch Ruppersberger*
3. John Sarbanes*
4. Anthony Brown
5. Steny Hoyer*
6. John Delaney*
7. Elijah Cummings*
8. Jamie Raskin

Massachusetts
1. Richard Neal*
2. James McGovern*
3. Niki Tsongas*
4. Joe Kennedy*
5. Katherine Clark*
6. Seth Moulton*
7. Michael Capuano*
8. Stephen Lynch*
9. Bill Keating*

Michigan
1. Jack Bergman
2. Bill Huizenga*
3. Justin Amash*
4. John Moolenaar*
5. Daniel Kildee*
6. Fred Upton*
7. Tim Walberg*
8. Mike Bishop*
9. Sander Levin*
10. Paul Mitchell
11. Dave Trott*
12. Debbie Dingell*
13. John Conyers, Jr.*
14. Brenda Lawrence*

Minnesota
1. Timothy Walz*
2. Jason Lewis
3. Erik Paulsen*
4. Betty McCollum*
5. Keith Ellison*
6. Tom Emmer*
7. Collin Peterson*
8. Rick Nolan*

Mississippi
1. Trent Kelly*
2. Bennie Thompson*
3. Gregg Harper*
4. Steven Palazzo*

Missouri
1. William Lacy Clay, Jr.*
2. Ann Wagner*
3. Blaine Luetkemeyer*
4. Vicky Hartzler*
5. Emanuel Cleaver II*
6. Samuel Graves*

7. Billy Long*
8. Jason Smith*

Montana
†Ryan Zinke*

Nebraska
1. Jeff Fortenberry*
2. Undecided - Don Bacon
3. Adrian Smith*

Nevada
1. Dina Titus*
2. Mark Amodei*
3. Jacky Rosen
4. Ruben Kihuen

New Hampshire
1. Carol Shea-Porter*
2. Ann McLane Kuster*

New Jersey
1. Donald Norcross*
2. Frank LoBiondo*
3. Tom MacArthur*
4. Christopher Smith*
5. Joshua Gottheimer*
6. Frank Pallone, Jr.*
7. Leonard Lance*
8. Albio Sires*
9. William Pascrell, Jr.*
10. Donald Payne, Jr.*
11. Rodney Frelinghuysen*
12. Bonnie Watson Coleman*

New Mexico
1. Michelle Lujan Grisham*
2. Steve Pearce*
3. Ben Lujan*

New York
1. Lee Zeldin*
2. Peter King*
3. Thomas Suozzi
4. Kathleen Rice*
5. Gregory Meeks*
6. Grace Meng*
7. Nydia Velázquez*
8. Hakeem Jeffries*
9. Yvette Clarke*
10. Jerrold Nadler*
11. Daniel Donovan*
12. Carolyn Maloney*
13. Adriano Espaillat
14. Joseph Crowley*
15. José Serrano*
16. Eliot Engel*
17. Nita Lowey*
18. Sean Patrick Maloney*
19. John Faso
20. Paul Tonko*
21. Elise Stefanik*
22. Claudia Tenney
23. Thomas Reed*
24. John Katko*
25. Louise Slaughter*
26. Brian Higgins*
27. Chris Collins*

North Carolina
1. G. K. Butterfield*
2. George Holding*
3. Walter Jones, Jr.*
4. David Price*
5. Virginia Foxx*
6. Mark Walker*
7. David Rouzer*
8. Richard Hudson*
9. Robert Pittenger*
10. Patrick McHenry*
11. Mark Meadows*
12. Alma Adams
13. Ted Budd

North Dakota
†Kevin Cramer*

Ohio
1. Steve Chabot*
2. Brad Wenstrup*
3. Joyce Beatty*
4. Jim Jordan*
5. Robert Latta*
6. Bill Johnson*
7. Bob Gibbs*
8. Warren Davidson*
9. Marcy Kaptur*
10. Michael Turner*
11. Marcia Fudge*
12. Pat Tiberi*
13. Timothy Ryan*
14. David Joyce*
15. Steve Stivers*
16. Jim Renacci*

Oklahoma
1. Jim Bridenstine*
2. Markwayne Mullin*
3. Frank Lucas*
4. Tom Cole*
5. Steve Russell*

Oregon
1. Suzanne Bonamici*
2. Greg Walden*
3. Earl Blumenauer*
4. Peter DeFazio*
5. Kurt Schrader*

Pennsylvania
1. Robert Brady*
2. Dwight Evans
3. Mike Kelly*
4. Scott Perry*
5. Glenn Thompson*
6. Ryan Costello*
7. Patrick Meehan*
8. Michael Fitzpatrick*
9. Bill Shuster*
10. Thomas Marino*
11. Lou Barletta*
12. Keith Rothfus*
13. Brendan Boyle
14. Michael Doyle*
15. Charles Dent*
16. Lloyd Smucker

17. Matt Cartwright*
18. Tim Murphy*

Rhode Island
1. David Cicilline*
2. James Langevin*

South Carolina
1. Mark Sanford*
2. Joe Wilson*
3. Jeff Duncan*
4. Trey Gowdy*
5. Mick Mulvaney*
6. James Clyburn*
7. Tom Rice*

South Dakota
†Kristi Noem*

Tennessee
1. David Phil Roe*
2. John J. Duncan, Jr.*
3. Chuck Fleischmann*
4. Scott DesJarlais*
5. Jim Cooper*
6. Diane Black*
7. Marsha Blackburn*
8. David Kustoff
9. Steve Cohen*

Texas
1. Louie Gohmert*
2. Ted Poe*
3. Sam Johnson*
4. John Ratcliffe*
5. Jeb Hensarling*
6. Joe Barton*
7. John Culberson*
8. Kevin Brady*
9. Al Green*
10. Michael McCaul*
11. Mike Conaway*
12. Kay Granger*
13. Mac Thornberry*
14. Randy Weber*
15. Vicente Gonzalez
16. Beto O'Rourke*
17. Bill Flores*
18. Sheila Jackson Lee*
19. Jodey Arrington
20. Joaquin Castro*
21. Lamar Smith*
22. Pete Olson*
23. Will Hurd*
24. Kenny Marchant*
25. Roger Williams*
26. Michael Burgess*
27. Blake Farenthold*
28. Henry Cuellar*
29. Gene Green*
30. Eddie Bernice Johnson*
31. John Carter*
32. Pete Sessions*
33. Marc Veasey*
34. Filemon Vela*
35. Lloyd Doggett*
36. Brian Babin*

Utah
1. Rob Bishop*
2. Chris Stewart*
3. Jason Chaffetz*
4. Mia Love*

Vermont
†Peter Welch*

Virginia
1. Robert Wittman*
2. Scott Taylor
3. Robert Scott*
4. Donald McEachin
5. Tom Garrett
6. Robert Goodlatte*
7. Dave Brat*
8. Donald Beyer*
9. Morgan Griffith*
10. Barbara Comstock*
11. Gerry Connolly*

Washington
1. Suzan DelBene*
2. Rick Larsen*
3. Jaime Herrera Beutler*
4. Dan Newhouse*
5. Cathy McMorris Rodgers*
6. Derek Kilmer*
7. Pramila Jayapal
8. Dave Reichert*
9. Adam Smith*
10. Dennis Heck*

West Virginia
1. David McKinley*
2. Alex Mooney*
3. Evan Jenkins*

Wisconsin
1. Paul Ryan*
2. Mark Pocan*
3. Ron Kind*
4. Gwen Moore*
5. James Sensenbrenner, Jr.*
6. Glenn Grothman*
7. Sean Duffy*
8. Mike Gallagher

Wyoming
† Liz Cheney

NONVOTING REPRESENTATIVES
American Samoa
Aumua Amata*
District of Columbia
Eleanor Holmes Norton*
Guam
Madeleine Bordallo*
Northern Mariana Islands
Gregorio "Kilili" Camacho Sablan*
Puerto Rico
Jenniffer González
Virgin Islands
Stacey Plaskett*

SELECTED STATISTICS ON STATE GOVERNMENTS

State	Resident population*	Governor†	Legislators‡ Senate	Legislators‡ House	State tax revenue§	Tax revenue per capita§
Alabama	4,858,979	Robert Bentley (R)	35	105	$ 9,755,000,000	$ 2,010
Alaska	738,432	Bill Walker (I)	20	40	864,000,000	1,170
Arizona	6,828,065	Doug Ducey (R)	30	60	14,082,000,000	2,060
Arkansas	2,978,204	Asa Hutchinson (R)	35	100	9,190,000,000	3,090
California	39,144,818	Jerry Brown (D)	40	80	151,173,000,000	3,860
Colorado	5,456,574	John Hickenlooper (D)	35	65	12,811,000,000	2,350
Connecticut	3,590,886	Dan Malloy (D)	36	151	16,232,000,000	4,520
Delaware	945,934	John Carney (D)	21	41	3,514,000,000	3,710
Florida	20,271,272	Rick Scott (R)	40	120	37,218,000,000	1,840
Georgia	10,214,860	Nathan Deal (R)	56	180	19,724,000,000	1,930
Hawaii	1,431,603	David Ige (D)	25	51	6,486,000,000	4,530
Idaho	1,654,930	C. L. "Butch" Otter (R)	35	70	3,975,000,000	2,400
Illinois	12,859,995	Bruce Rauner (R)	59	118	39,283,000,000	3,050
Indiana	6,619,680	Eric Holcomb (R)	50	100	17,400,000,000	2,630
Iowa	3,123,899	Terry Branstad (R)	50	100	9,189,000,000	2,940
Kansas	2,911,641	Sam Brownback (R)	40	125	7,884,000,000	2,710
Kentucky	4,425,092	Matt Bevin (R)	38	100	11,598,000,000	2,620
Louisiana	4,670,724	Jon Bel Edwards (D)	39	105	9,719,000,000	2,080
Maine	1,329,328	Paul LePage (R)	35	151	4,064,000,000	3,060
Maryland	6,006,401	Larry Hogan (R)	47	141	19,850,000,000	3,300
Massachusetts	6,794,422	Charlie Baker (R)	40	160	27,012,000,000	3,980
Michigan	9,922,576	Rick Snyder (R)	38	110	26,957,000,000	2,720
Minnesota	5,489,594	Mark Dayton (D)	67	134	24,439,000,000	4,450
Mississippi	2,992,333	Phil Bryant (R)	52	122	7,907,000,000	2,640
Missouri	6,083,672	Eric Greitens (R)	34	163	11,956,000,000	1,970
Montana	1,032,949	Steve Bullock (D)	50	100	2,843,000,000	2,750
Nebraska	1,896,190	Pete Ricketts (R)	49 (unicameral)		5,087,000,000	2,680
Nevada	2,890,845	Brian Sandoval (R)	21	42	7,533,000,000	2,610
New Hampshire	1,330,608	Chris Sununu (R)	24	400	2,488,000,000	1,870
New Jersey	8,958,013	Chris Christie (R)	40	80	31,568,000,000	3,520
New Mexico	2,085,109	Susana Martinez (R)	42	70	6,009,000,000	2,880
New York	19,795,791	Andrew Cuomo (D)	63	150	78,243,000,000	3,950
North Carolina	10,042,802	Undecided	50	120	25,062,000,000	2,500
North Dakota	756,927	Doug Burgum (R)	47	94	5,740,000,000	7,580
Ohio	11,613,423	John Kasich (R)	33	99	28,297,000,000	2,440
Oklahoma	3,911,338	Mary Fallin (R)	48	101	9,407,000,000	2,410
Oregon	4,028,977	Kate Brown (D)	30	60	10,575,000,000	2,620
Pennsylvania	12,802,503	Tom Wolf (D)	50	203	36,110,000,000	2,820
Rhode Island	1,056,298	Gina Raimondo (D)	38	75	3,197,000,000	3,030
South Carolina	4,896,146	Nikki Haley (R)	46	124	9,633,000,000	1,970
South Dakota	858,469	Dennis Daugaard (R)	35	70	1,674,000,000	1,950
Tennessee	6,600,299	Bill Haslam (R)	33	99	12,698,000,000	1,920
Texas	27,469,114	Greg Abbott (R)	31	150	55,086,000,000	2,010
Utah	2,995,919	Gary Herbert (R)	29	75	6,703,000,000	2,240
Vermont	626,042	Phil Scott (R)	30	150	3,043,000,000	4,860
Virginia	8,382,993	Terry McAuliffe (D)	40	100	20,537,000,000	2,450
Washington	7,170,351	Jay Inslee (D)	49	98	20,644,000,000	2,880
West Virginia	1,844,128	Jim Justice (D)	34	100	5,566,000,000	3,020
Wisconsin	5,771,337	Scott Walker (R)	33	99	17,019,000,000	2,950
Wyoming	586,107	Matthew Mead (R)	30	60	2,356,000,000	4,020

*July 1, 2015, estimates. Source: U.S. Census Bureau.
†As of January 2017. Source: National Governors Association.
‡Source: National Conference of State Legislatures.
§2015 figures. Source: U.S. Census Bureau.

COUNTRY GOVERNMENT AND ECONOMY

This table lists the chiefs of state and heads of government, major currencies, and gross domestic product and per capita gross domestic product for each of the independent countries of the world.
*GDP figures are in U.S. dollars and are for 2015 or latest available year.
†Claimed by China.

Country	Government	Monetary unit	GDP* (in millions)	GDP* per capita
Afghanistan	President Ashraf Ghani	afghani	19,202	586
Albania	President Bujar Nishani Prime Minister Edi Rama	lek	11,500	3,785
Algeria	President Abdelaziz Bouteflika Prime Minister Abdelmalek Sellal	dinar	169,559	4,224
Andorra	French Coprince, François Hollande; Spanish Coprince, Joan Enric Vives Sicilia, Bishop of Urgel Executive Council President Antoni Martí Petit	euro	3,249	40,111
Angola	President Jose Eduardo dos Santos	kwanza	102,811	4,370
Antigua and Barbuda	Queen Elizabeth II, represented by Governor General Rodney Williams Prime Minister Gaston Browne	East Caribbean dollar	1,292	13,892
Argentina	President Mauricio Macri	peso	566,839	13,049
Armenia	President Serzh Sargsyan Prime Minister Karen Karapetian	dram	10,566	3,465
Australia	Queen Elizabeth II, represented by Governor General Peter Cosgrove Prime Minister Malcolm Turnbull	Australian dollar	1,281,713	52,806
Austria	Acting Presidents Doris Bures, Norbert Hofer, and Karlheinz Kopf Chancellor Christian Kern	euro	374,090	43,774
Azerbaijan	President Ilham Aliyev Prime Minister Artur Rasizade	manat	53,548	5,503

Bahamas	Queen Elizabeth II, represented by
	    Governor General Dame Marguerite
	    Pindling
	Prime Minister Perry Christie
		dollar	8,795	22,550

Bahrain	King Sheikh Hamad bin Isa Al Khalifa Prime Minister Khalifa bin Salman Al Khalifa	dinar	31,316	22,385
Bangladesh	President Abdul Hamid Prime Minister Sheikh Hasina Wajed	taka	200,397	1,241
Barbados	Queen Elizabeth II, represented by Acting Governor General Elliot Belgrave Prime Minister Freundel Stuart	dollar	4,432	15,334
Belarus	President Aleksandr Lukashenko Prime Minister Andrei Kobyakov	ruble	54,609	5,790
Belgium	King Philippe Prime Minister Charles Michel	euro	454,363	40,673
Belize	Queen Elizabeth II, represented by Governor General Sir Colville Young, Sr. Prime Minister Dean Barrow	dollar	1,763	4,952

Country	Government	Monetary unit	GDP* (in millions)	GDP* per capita
Benin	President Patrice Talon	CFA franc	8,474	780
Bhutan	King Jigme Khesar Namgyel Wangchuck Prime Minister Tshering Tobgay	ngultrum	2,088	2,694
Bolivia	President Evo Morales	boliviano	33,204	2,963
Bosnia-Herzegovina	Members of the Presidency Bakir Izetbegovic (Chairman), Dragan Covic, and Mladen Ivanic Chairman of the Council of Ministers Denis Zvizdic	marka	15,895	4,169
Botswana	President Ian Khama	pula	13,626	6,373
Brazil	President Michael Temer	real	1,773,657	8,630
Brunei	Sultan and Prime Minister Haji Hassanal Bolkiah	dollar	13,639	31,354
Bulgaria	President Rosen Plevneliev Prime Minister Boiko Borisov	lev	48,955	6,934
Burkina Faso	President Roch Marc Christian Kaboré Prime Minister Paul Kaba Thieba	CFA franc	11,054	586
Burundi	President Pierre Nkurunziza	franc	2,983	267
Cambodia	King Norodom Sihamoni Prime Minister Hun Sen	riel	18,103	1,164
Cameroon	President Paul Biya Prime Minister Philemon Yang	CFA franc	28,838	1,203
Canada	Queen Elizabeth II, represented by Governor General David Johnston Prime Minister Justin Trudeau	Canadian dollar	1,551,462	42,830
Cape Verde	President Jorge Carlos Fonseca Prime Minister Ulisses Correia e Silva	escudo	1,613	3,077
Central African Republic	President Faustin-Archange Touadéra Prime Minister Simplice Sarandji	CFA franc	1,554	311
Chad	President Idriss Déby Prime Minister Albert Pahimi Padacké	CFA franc	10,892	778
Chile	President Michelle Bachelet	peso	240,219	13,344
China	President Xi Jinping Premier Li Keqiang	yuan (also called renminbi)	10,924,637	7,886
Colombia	President Juan Manuel Santos	peso	292,662	5,974
Comoros	President Azali Assoumani	franc	607	769
Congo, Democratic Republic of the	President Joseph Kabila Prime Minister Augustin Matata Ponyo Mapon	franc	37,056	493
Congo, Republic of the	President Denis Sassou Nguesso	CFA franc	8,716	1,817
Costa Rica	President Luis Guillermo Solís	colón	52,003	10,634

Country	Government	Monetary unit	GDP* (in millions)	GDP* per capita
Côte d'Ivoire	President Alassane Ouattara	CFA franc	31,463	1,397
Croatia	President Kolinda Grabar-Kitarovic Prime Minister Andrej Plenkovic	kuna	48,791	11,475
Cuba	President of the Council of State and President of the Council of Ministers Raúl Castro	peso	77,150	6,874
Cyprus	President Nicos Anastasiades	euro	19,325	16,405
Czech Republic	President Miloš Zeman Prime Minister Bohuslav Sobotka	koruna	181,835	17,231
Denmark	Queen Margrethe II Prime Minister Lars Løkke Rasmussen	krone	295,058	52,020
Djibouti	President Ismail Omar Guelleh Prime Minister Abdoulkader Kamil Mohamed	franc	1,658	1,794
Dominica	President Charles Savarin Prime Minister Roosevelt Skerrit	East Caribbean dollar	518	6,993
Dominican Republic	President Danilo Medina	peso	67,298	6,301
East Timor	President Taur Matan Ruak Prime Minister Rui Maria de Araújo	U.S. dollar	2,016	1,582
Ecuador	President Rafael Correa	U.S. dollar	99,850	6,114
Egypt	President Abdel Fattah el-Sisi Prime Minister Sherif Ismail	pound	330,772	3,743
El Salvador	President Salvador Sánchez Cerén	colón, U.S. dollar	25,808	3,991
Equatorial Guinea	President Teodoro Obiang Nguema Mbasogo Prime Minister Francisco Pascual Obama Asue	franc	9,401	11,436
Eritrea	President Issaias Afewerki	nakfa	4,666	682
Estonia	President Kersti Kaljulaid Prime Minister Taavi Roivas	euro	22,698	17,353
Ethiopia	President Mulatu Teshome Wirtu Prime Minister Hailemariam Desalegn	birr	61,583	607
Fiji	President Jioji Konrote Prime Minister Frank Bainimarama	dollar	4,584	5,093
Finland	President Sauli Niinistö Prime Minister Juha Sipilä	euro	229,741	41,718
France	President François Hollande Prime Minister Manuel Valls	euro	2,421,621	37,163
Gabon	President Ali Ben Bongo Prime Minister Daniel Ona Ondo	CFA franc	14,345	8,100
Gambia	President Yahya A. J. J. Jammeh	dalasi	872	429
Georgia	President Giorgi Margvelashvili Prime Minister Giorgi Kvirikashvili	lari	13,986	3,120

Country	Government	Monetary unit	GDP* (in millions)	GDP* per capita
Germany	President Joachim Gauck Chancellor Angela Merkel	euro	3,356,693	41,583
Ghana	President John Dramani Mahama	cedi	36,952	1,339
Greece	President Prokopis Pavlopoulos Prime Minister Alexis Tsipras	euro	195,266	17,558
Grenada	Queen Elizabeth II, represented by Governor General Cécile La Grenade Prime Minister Keith Mitchell	East Caribbean dollar	966	8,944
Guatemala	President Jimmy Morales	quetzal	63,853	3,833
Guinea	President Alpha Condé Prime Minister Mamady Youla	franc	6,698	549
Guinea-Bissau	President José Mário Vaz Prime Minister Baciro Djá	CFA franc	1,057	593
Guyana	President David Granger Prime Minister Moses Nagamootoo	dollar	3,165	4,170
Haiti	Provisional President Jocelerme Privert Prime Minister Enex Jean-Charles	gourde	8,748	810
Honduras	President Juan Orlando Hernández	lempira	20,224	2,363
Hungary	President János Áder Prime Minister Viktor Orbán	forint	120,662	12,198
Iceland	President Guðni Jóhannesson Prime Minister Sigurður Ingi Jóhannsson	krona	16,658	49,577
India	President Pranab Mukherjee Prime Minister Narendra Modi	rupee	2,082,125	1,602
Indonesia	President Joko Widodo	rupiah	860,444	3,328
Iran	Supreme Leader Ayatollah Ali Khamenei President Hassan Rouhani	rial	406,469	5,095
Iraq	President Fouad Massoum Prime Minister Haider al-Abadi	dinar	169,034	4,649
Ireland	President Michael D. Higgins Prime Minister Enda Kenny	euro	238,026	50,493
Israel	President Reuven Rivlin Prime Minister Benjamin Netanyahu	shekel	296,074	36,507
Italy	President Sergio Mattarella Prime Minister Matteo Renzi	euro	1,815,260	29,577
Jamaica	Queen Elizabeth II, represented by Governor General Patrick Allen Prime Minister Portia Simpson Miller	dollar	13,965	4,938
Japan	Emperor Akihito Prime Minister Shinzo Abe	yen	4,123,258	32,544
Jordan	King Abdullah II Prime Minister Hani Mulki	dinar	37,569	5,391

Country	Government	Monetary unit	GDP* (in millions)	GDP* per capita
Kazakhstan	President Nursultan A. Nazarbayev Prime Minister Bakytzhan Sagintayev	tenge	178,787	10,092
Kenya	President Uhuru Kenyatta	shilling	62,402	1,370
Kiribati	President Taneti Maamau	Australian dollar	154	1,435
Korea, North	First Chairman of the National Defense Commission Kim Jong-un Premier Pak Pong-ju	won	28,563	1,143
Korea, South	President Park Geun-hye Prime Minister Hwang Kyo-ahn	won	1,377,371	27,182
Kosovo	President Hashim Thaçi Prime Minister Isa Mustafa	euro	6,371	3,419
Kuwait	Emir Sabah al-Ahmad al-Jabir al-Sabah Prime Minister Jaber al-Mubarak al-Hamad al-Sabah	dinar	116,747	32,942
Kyrgyzstan	President Almazbek Atambayev Prime Minister Sooronbay Jeenbekov	som	6,611	1,145
Laos	President Bounnhang Vorachith Prime Minister Thongloun Sisoulith	kip	12,415	1,763
Latvia	President Raimonds Vejonis Prime Minister Maris Kucinskis	euro	27,042	13,420
Lebanon	President Michel Aoun Prime Minister Saad Hariri	pound	49,136	10,675
Lesotho	King Letsie III Prime Minister Pakalitha Mosisili	loti	2,107	1,005
Liberia	President Ellen Johnson-Sirleaf	dollar	2,044	441
Libya	President of the House of Representatives Aguila Saleh Issa Prime Minister Abdullah al-Thinni	dinar	33,727	5,170
Liechtenstein	Prince Hans-Adam II Prime Minister Adrian Hasler	Swiss franc	5,487	144,395
Lithuania	President Dalia Grybauskaite Prime Minister Algirdas Butkevicius	euro	41,256	13,863
Luxembourg	Grand Duke Henri Prime Minister Xavier Bettel	euro	57,609	101,782
Macedonia	President Gjorge Ivanov Interim Prime Minister Emil Dimitriev	denar	10,004	4,739
Madagascar	President Hery Rajaonarimampianina Prime Minister Solonandrasana Olivier Mahafaly	ariary	9,859	396
Malawi	President Peter Mutharika	kwacha	6,491	365
Malaysia	Sultan Abdul Halim Mu'adzam Shah Prime Minister Najib Razak	ringgit	296,219	9,563

Country	Government	Monetary unit	GDP* (in millions)	GDP* per capita
Maldives	President Abdulla Yameen	rufiyaa	3,137	8,593
Mali	President Ibrahim Boubacar Keïta Prime Minister Modibo Keïta	CFA franc	13,083	775
Malta	President Marie-Louise Coleiro Preca Prime Minister Joseph Muscat	euro	9,702	22,775
Marshall Islands	President Hilda Heine	U.S. dollar	185	3,304
Mauritania	President Mohamed Ould Abdel Aziz Prime Minister Yahya Ould Hademine	ouguiya	5,097	1,285
Mauritius	President Ameenah Gurib-Fakim Prime Minister Anerood Jugnauth	rupee	11,560	8,824
Mexico	President Enrique Peña Nieto	peso	1,144,333	9,332
Micronesia, Federated States of	President Peter M. Christian	U.S. dollar	318	3,000
Moldova	President Nicolae Timofti Prime Minister Pavel Filip	leu	6,483	1,864
Monaco	Prince Albert II Minister of State Serge Telle	euro	6,063	155,462
Mongolia	President Tsakhiagiin Elbegdorj Prime Minister Jargaltulga Erdenebat	tugrik	11,747	3,958
Montenegro	President Filip Vujanovic Prime Minister Duško Markovic	euro	4,016	6,457
Morocco	King Mohammed VI Prime Minister Abdelilah Benkirane	dirham	101,751	2,956
Mozambique	President Filipe Nyusi	metical	14,827	563
Myanmar	President Htin Kyaw	kyat	65,925	1,207
Namibia	President Hage Geingob	dollar	12,189	5,006
Nauru	President Baron Waqa	Australian dollar	151	15,100
Nepal	President Bidhya Devi Bhandari Prime Minister Pushpa Kamal Dahal	rupee	21,119	737
Netherlands	King Willem-Alexander Prime Minister Mark Rutte	euro	745,483	44,059
New Zealand	Queen Elizabeth II, represented by Governor General Dame Patsy Reddy Prime Minister John Key	dollar	173,001	37,724
Nicaragua	President Daniel Ortega	gold cordoba	12,458	1,978
Niger	President Mahamadou Issoufou Prime Minister Brigi Rafini	CFA franc	7,147	372
Nigeria	President Muhammadu Buhari	naira	485,637	2,604

Country	Government	Monetary unit	GDP* (in millions)	GDP* per capita
Norway	King Harald V Prime Minister Erna Solberg	krone	388,899	74,745
Oman	Sultan and Prime Minister Qaboos bin Said	rial	64,373	19,193
Pakistan	President Mamnoon Hussain Prime Minister Nawaz Sharif	rupee	269,971	1,377
Palau	President Tommy Remengesau, Jr.	U.S. dollar	287	13,667
Panama	President Juan Carlos Varela	balboa	52,132	12,975
Papua New Guinea	Queen Elizabeth II, represented by Governor General Sir Michael Ogio Prime Minister Peter O'Neill	kina	16,510	2,117
Paraguay	President Horacio Cartes	guarani	27,850	3,951
Peru	President Pedro Pablo Kuczynski	new sol	192,113	6,124
Philippines	President Rodrigo Duterte	peso	291,965	2,820
Poland	President Andrzej Duda Prime Minister Beata Szydlo	zloty	474,838	12,421
Portugal	President Marcelo Rebelo de Sousa Prime Minister António Costa	euro	199,004	19,698
Qatar	Emir Tamim bin Hamad al-Thani Prime Minister Abdullah bin Nasser bin Khalifa al-Thani	riyal	176,152	79,027
Romania	President Klaus Iohannis Prime Minister Dacian Ciolos	leu	177,635	8,388
Russia	President Vladimir Putin Prime Minister Dmitry Medvedev	ruble	1,325,375	9,263
Rwanda	President Paul Kagame Prime Minister Anastase Murekezi	franc	8,182	641

Saint Kitts and Nevis	Queen Elizabeth II, represented by
	    Governor General Samuel
	    Weymouth Tapley Seaton
	Prime Minister Timothy Harris
		East Caribbean dollar	909	16,232

Saint Lucia	Queen Elizabeth II, represented by Governor General Pearlette Louisy Prime Minister Allen Chastanet	East Caribbean dollar	1,426	7,708

Saint Vincent and the Grenadines	Queen Elizabeth II, represented by
	    Governor General Sir Frederick
	    Nathaniel Ballantyne
	Prime Minister Ralph E. Gonsalves
		East Caribbean dollar	754	6,917

Samoa	Head of State Tuiatua Tupua Tamasese Efi Prime Minister Tuila'epa Sailele Malielegaoi	tala	800	4,121

San Marino	Captain-Regent Gian Nicola Berti and
	    Captain-Regent Massimo Andrea Ugolini
	Secretary of State for Foreign and Political
	    Affairs Pasquale Valentini
		euro	1,566	47,455

Country	Government	Monetary unit	GDP* (in millions)	GDP* per capita
São Tomé and Príncipe	President Evaristo Carvalho Prime Minister Patrice Trovoada	dobra	328	1,605
Saudi Arabia	King and Prime Minister Salman	riyal	649,611	21,327
Senegal	President Macky Sall Prime Minister Mohamed Dionne	CFA franc	13,723	932
Serbia	President Tomislav Nikolic Prime Minister Aleksandar Vucic	dinar	36,513	5,157
Seychelles	President James Michel	rupee	1,407	14,651
Sierra Leone	President Ernest Bai Koroma	leone	4,321	670
Singapore	President Tony Tan Prime Minister Lee Hsien Loong	dollar	292,737	51,655
Slovakia	President Andrej Kiska Prime Minister Robert Fico	euro	86,606	15,847
Slovenia	President Borut Pahor Prime Minister Miro Cerar	euro	42,758	20,576
Solomon Islands	Queen Elizabeth II, represented by Governor General Frank Kabui Prime Minister Manasseh Sogavare	dollar	1,152	1,849
Somalia	President Hassan Sheik Mohamud Prime Minister Omar Abdirashid Ali Sharmarke	shilling	5,877	529
South Africa	President Jacob Zuma	rand	312,878	5,792
South Sudan	President Salva Kiir Mayardit	pound	9,015	709
Spain	King Felipe VI Acting Prime Minister Mariano Rajoy	euro	1,199,386	25,224
Sri Lanka	President Maithripala Sirisena	rupee	82,206	3,917
Sudan	President Umar Hassan Ahmad al-Bashir	pound	83,840	2,074
Suriname	President Desi Bouterse	dollar	5,035	9,056
Swaziland	King Mswati III Prime Minister Barnabas Sibusiso Dlamini	lilangeni	4,044	3,020
Sweden	King Carl XVI Gustaf Prime Minister Stefan Löfven	krona	492,618	49,987
Switzerland	President Johann Schneider-Ammann	franc	664,671	80,042
Syria	President Bashar al-Assad Prime Minister Imad Khamis	pound	22,165	958
Taiwan[†]	President Tsai Ing-wen Premier (President of the Executive Yuan) Lin Chuan	dollar	523,581	22,269
Tajikistan	President Emomali Rahmon Prime Minister Kokhir Rasulzoda	somoni	7,835	913
Tanzania	President John Magufuli	shilling	44,900	834

Country	Government	Monetary unit	GDP* (in millions)	GDP* per capita
Thailand	Vacant‡ General Prayuth Chan-ocha	baht	395,285	5,800
Togo	President Faure Gnassingbé Prime Minister Komi Sélom Klassou	CFA franc	4,084	555
Tonga	King Topou VI Prime Minister `Akilisi Pohiva	pa'anga	424	4,000
Trinidad and Tobago	President Anthony Carmona Prime Minister Keith Rowley	dollar	26,180	19,364
Tunisia	President Beji Caid Essebsi Prime Minister Habib Essid	dinar	43,298	3,822
Turkey	President Recep Tayyip Erdogan Prime Minister Binali Yildirim	new lira	725,932	9,193
Turkmenistan	President Gurbanguly Berdimuhammedov	manat	36,507	6,708
Tuvalu	Queen Elizabeth II, represented by Governor General Sir Iakoba Italeli Prime Minister Enele Sopoaga	Australian dollar	36	3,227
Uganda	President Yoweri Museveni	shilling	25,555	651
Ukraine	President Petro Poroshenko Prime Minister Volodymyr Groysman	hryvnia	90,570	2,026
United Arab Emirates	President Khalifa bin Zayed al-Nahyan Prime Minister Mohammad bin Rashid al-Maktum	dirham	357,888	36,223
United Kingdom	Queen Elizabeth II Prime Minister Theresa May	pound	2,849,050	44,310
United States	President Barack Obama	U.S. dollar	17,946,998	55,414
Uruguay	President Tabaré Vázquez	peso	53,619	15,578
Uzbekistan	Acting President and Prime Minister Shavkat Mirziyoyev	som	66,208	2,185
Vanuatu	President Baldwin Lonsdale Prime Minister Charlot Salwai	vatu	790	2,801
Vatican City	Pope Francis Secretary of State Archbishop Pietro Parolin		n/a	n/a
Venezuela	President Nicolás Maduro	bolívar fuerte	305,455	9,819
Vietnam	Communist Party Secretary-General Nguyen Phú Trong President Tran Dai Quang Prime Minister Nguyen Xuan Phuc	dong	192,527	2,081
Yemen	President Abd-Rabbu Mansour Hadi Prime Minister Ahmed Obaid bin Daghr	rial	36,404	1,335
Zambia	President Edgar Lungu	new kwacha	21,546	1,370
Zimbabwe	President Robert Gabriel Mugabe	U.S. dollar	14,081	916

‡King Bhumibol Adulyadej died on Oct. 13, 2016. Crown Prince Maha Vajiralongkorn, his son and successor, announced that he would delay his coronation for at least a year while he mourned his father.

SCIENCE AND TECHNOLOGY

NASA astronaut Scott Kelly took this dazzling photo of the aurora borealis above the Pacific Northwest of the United States and Canada on Jan. 20, 2016, during his 340-day stay aboard the International Space Station. Kelly returned to Earth on March 1, 2016.

see page 362 for

A CLOSER
LOOK

A CAVE OF **ART** AND **GOD**

On July 19, 2016, a team of British and Puerto Rican researchers published an article in the journal *Antiquity* detailing drawings on the walls and ceilings of a cave on the Puerto Rican island of Mona (*Isla Mona* in Spanish). Cave drawings are not especially rare on islands in the Caribbean, but the rich imagery of this cave, called *Cave 18*, proved to be something special. Many of the inscriptions were made by native Taíno people, and some date back nearly 1,000 years. Most of the inscriptions, however, date from the 1500's, during the early years of the Spanish conquest of the region. And many of the inscriptions were made by Spanish colonists, side-by-side with Taíno drawings. Most of the inscriptions depict a variety of religious and spiritual symbols, with space given to both Taíno and Spanish beliefs. The researchers claim the inscriptions are evidence of mutual religious exchange and tolerance, a rare occurrence at a time when the Spanish sought to convert native peoples to Christianity, often through force.

Cave 18's inscriptions include crosses, Christian phrases written in Latin and Spanish, names of Christian saints, and *Christograms* (abbreviations of the name of Christ). There are also many Taíno symbols, including complex figures with human and animal features, human faces, wavy lines, and different styles of crosses. The Spanish inscriptions were made with a metal dagger or other sharp object. They are easily distinguished from Taíno etchings made with fingers in the soft limestone.

The mix of religious symbols suggests that the Taíno were able to communicate and explain their religious beliefs while receiving Spanish suggestions at the same time.

Mona Island lies some 41 miles (66 kilometers) west of Puerto Rico. The Taíno people lived there and in other areas of the Caribbean. They were the first Native Americans encountered by Christopher Columbus after he arrived in the region in 1492. Christian Spanish missionaries soon established themselves among the Taíno, and native spiritual beliefs were largely repressed. Cave 18, however, shows not all Spanish colonists treated religion with so heavy a hand. Unfortunately for the Taíno, the Spanish arrival proved their undoing. By 1600, most had been killed or had died of diseases brought by the Spanish and against which the Taíno had no natural immunity.

Today, remnants of Taíno beliefs survive in the practices of *espiritismo*, a form of traditional religious healing in Puerto Rico.

SUNNY *SOLAR IMPULSE 2*

On July 26, 2016, the solar-powered airplane *Solar Impulse 2* landed in Abu Dhabi in the United Arab Emirates, completing the first-ever zero-fuel flight around Earth. Swiss pilot Bertrand Piccard flew the final leg from Cairo, Egypt, to Abu Dhabi, a grueling 48 ½-hour journey buffeted by hot desert air-driven turbulence. Speaking from the runway tarmac, a tired Piccard commented: "I hope people will understand that it is not just a first in the history of aviation, but also a first in the history of energy... These [clean] technologies now can make the world much better and we have to use them, not only for the environment, but also because they are profitable and create jobs." Piccard has made aviation news before. In 1999, he completed the world's first nonstop balloon flight around the world.

Piccard thanked the large Solar Impulse ground team as well as fellow Swiss pilot André Borschberg, who was the first to greet Piccard out of the cockpit. Piccard and Borschberg took turns at the controls during the long legs of the round-the-world flight. The cockpit of *Solar Impulse 2* is large enough for just one person at a time. The circumnavigation, which began in March 2015, was completed in 17 legs

covering some 26,000 miles (42,000 kilometers) and more than 500 flight hours. Along the way, *Solar Impulse 2* set numerous solar-powered flight records, but it also set the general aviation record for longest solo flight—a brutal 4-day, 21-hour, and 51-minute journey made by Borschberg from Japan to Hawaii.

Solar Impulse 2 was built in Switzerland and first flew in 2014. The aircraft flies at an average speed of 44 miles (70 kilometers) per hour. Lithium batteries charged by more than 17,000 solar cells power the plane's four propeller engines. The cells are located in the aircraft's 236-foot- (72-meter-) wide wings. The carbon fiber plane weighs about as much as a car, some 5,000 pounds (2.3 metric tons). The small cockpit snugly fits the pilot and reclining chair (which includes a toilet feature), along with flight instruments, computers, food, water, and other supplies. There is no automatic pilot, but a rudimentary electronic co-pilot keeps the plane steady enough for catnaps. Flashing lights in the pilot's goggles and other alarms wake the aviator if the plane suddenly changes course.

The first *Solar Impulse,* a smaller aircraft meant to test the technology, flew safely from 2010 to 2013.

THE AIR FORCE'S NEW *LIGHTNING*

On Aug. 2, 2016, the United States Air Force declared its new F-35 Lightning II fighter planes ready for combat. The F-35 is a "fifth generation" fighter, combining advanced stealth technology with heavy firepower, long range, high speed, and remarkable agility. Variants of the F-35 will be the core fighters throughout the Air Force, Navy, and Marine Corps. Such allied nations as Australia, Italy, and the United Kingdom will also fly F-35 squadrons.

The Lockheed Martin Corporation designed the F-35 Lightning II. Development began in 2001, and the first production F-35 flew in 2006. Variants were tested over the next several years. The program took longer than expected, and it cost more, too (the average price tag is $178 million per aircraft). The first F-35 military training squadrons were activated in 2013.

F-35 variants include fighters modified for use on aircraft carriers and aircraft with short take-off / vertical landing (STOVL) capability. STOVL variants have special propulsion systems and swiveling engines that allow the plane to fly straight up and down and stop and turn in midair. Over the next several years, the Lightning II will replace older fighters such as the F-16 Falcon, F/A-18 Hornet, A-10 Warthog, and AV-8 Harrier. Lockheed's first "Lightning," the P-38, was one of the most famous fighters of World War II.

A Lockheed Martin F-35 Lightning II lands at Hill Air Force Base, Utah, on Sept. 2, 2015.

NhMcTsOg: PERIODIC TABLE COMPLETES 7TH ROW

The year 2016 heralded the addition of four new chemical elements to the periodic table. The new elements are numbers 113, 115, 117, and 118 on the table. The International Union of Pure and Applied Chemistry (IUPAC) recognized the new elements on Dec. 30, 2015. Teams of scientists from America, Japan, and Russia discovered the new elements, and—with IUPAC approval—suggested the following names in June 2016: Nihonium (Nh) for element 113; Moscovium (Mc) for element 115; Tennessine (Ts) for element 117; and Oganesson (Og) for element 118.

The periodic table is one of the most useful tools in science. It organizes the chemical elements into rows and columns that show how the elements are related and what properties they share. For example, elements in the left and center of the table are metallic. Elements in the far right column are noble gases. The new elements—NhMcTsOg together—complete the table's seventh row.

Each chemical element is a kind of atom. The core of an atom, called a nucleus, contains even smaller particles called protons. An atom's proton count determines its number on the periodic table. The lightest element, hydrogen, has just one proton,

so it is the first chemical element on the table. Helium—element #2—has two protons. Carbon has six protons, oxygen has eight, and iron has 26. The more protons an element has, the heavier it is.

Extremely heavy elements are unstable, tending to fall apart like towers of loose blocks. Elements 113, 115, 117, and 118 are so heavy and unstable that they do not even exist in nature. Scientists created them in the lab by smashing together the nuclei of lighter atoms. They then observed the resulting new atoms—easier said than done, since the heavy atoms disintegrate into lighter atoms and particles in just a fraction of a second.

IUPAC guidelines allow newly discovered elements to be named after a mythological concept or character (including an astronomical object); a mineral or similar substance; a place or geographical region; a property of the element; or a scientist. Elements 113, 115, and 117 all honor the labs and origins of the participating researchers. Nihonium (Nh) is named for *Nihon,* a word for *Japan* in Japanese. Moscovium (Mc) and Tennessine (Ts) are named for Moscow and Tennessee. Number 118, Oganesson (Og), is named for Russian heavy metal expert Yuri Oganessian.

ANCIENT WINGS IN AMBER

In late June 2016, *paleontologists* (scientists who study fossils) announced an amazing discovery. Researchers led by Lida Xing at the China University of Geosciences in Beijing had discovered two bird wings preserved in amber. They published their findings in the journal *Nature Communications*.

Amber is a hard, yellowish-brown fossilized resin. It comes chiefly from the resins of pine trees that grew millions of years ago. These resins were gummy materials mixed with oils in the trees. When the oils *oxidized* (combined with oxygen), hard resins were left. These pine trees were then buried underground or underwater, and the resins slowly changed into lumps of amber. These lumps often contain insects trapped as the resins flowed from the trees. But finding larger animals such as small vertebrates (animals with backbones) is incredibly rare. In the 1993 science fiction film *Jurassic Park*, dinosaur DNA (*deoxyribonucleic acid*) is discovered in the blood of an ancient mosquito fossilized in amber.

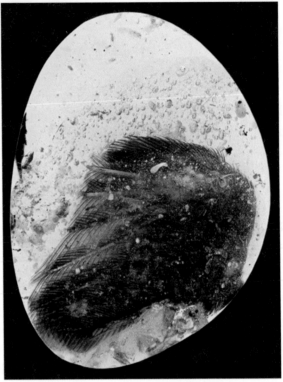

Amber preserved this 100-million-year-old wing tip featuring bones, feathers, and soft tissue.

Movie scientists then used the DNA to recreate dinosaurs—an improbable, yet intriguing, plot line.

The wing fossil subjects of the June 2016 report were formed about 100 million years ago, in the Cretaceous Period, in what is now Myanmar (also called Burma). Two birds apparently became stuck in the sticky resin of a tree and died. The amber preserved the three-dimensional structure of the birds' wings, as well as the wings' feathers, skin, and bones—even the color patterns!

Xing and his team think the wings came from a group of birds called enantiornithines, which means *opposite birds* in Greek. These birds had claws and teeth, and they went extinct along with the nonflying dinosaurs about 65 million years ago. The fossils showed that the wings were from young birds and that the birds hatched as miniature adults, ready to fly. This is different from modern birds, which must develop for weeks or months before they can leave the nest.

The structure of the wings and the arrangement of feathers are similar to modern bird wings. Birds evolved about 150 million years ago from meat-eating dinosaurs, so they must have quickly developed modern-looking wings, before *enantiornithines* and the ancestors of modern birds developed independently.

Unlike science fiction, these fossils won't resurrect the extinct *enantiornithines*, even if they do contain DNA. The technology to create entire animals from bits of ancient DNA does not yet—and might never—exist. The fossils do, however, offer paleontologists a treasure trove of information that will help us better understand early birds and their world.

REALLY **BIG** FEET

Eons ago, a monstrous beast stalked an ancient South American floodplain. One of its enormous footprints in the soft clay was covered with layers of silt and preserved for some 70 million years. In July 2016 the track was discovered, revealing that huge predatory dinosaurs lived in South America up until the extinction of the group about 65 million years ago.

Dinosaurs are a group of prehistoric reptiles that ruled Earth for about 160 million years. Most of these animals died millions of years ago, but their direct descendants—birds—continue to flourish today. Dinosaurs have fascinated people ever since they were first described in the early 1800's as having strange appearances and huge sizes. Scientists now know that not all dinosaurs were large. Many, such as the microraptor and compsognathus, were, in fact, quite small.

The South American footprint, however, belonged to something gigantic with *really big feet*. It was found about 45 miles (60 kilometers) outside of Sucre, the official capital city of Bolivia, by a local tour guide. At some 45 inches (115 centimeters) wide, it is the largest *car-*

nivorous (meat-eating) dinosaur footprint ever discovered. The previous record was nothing to sneeze at either: a 40-inch- (110-centimeter-) wide track from New Mexico, a state in the southwestern United States.

The animal that made the South American print probably belonged to a group of dinosaurs called *abelisaurids*, large meat-eaters with short skulls and tiny arms that lived in South America, Africa, and India. Based on the enormous size of the footprint, scientists think the dinosaur could have been up to 40 feet (12 meters) long.

The discovery of this footprint helps paleontologists fill in the history of large meat-eating dinosaurs in South America. *Giganotosaurus*, one of the largest meat-eating dinosaurs known, stalked the continent some 95 million years ago. But *Giganotosaurus* probably died out after 5 million years or so, and paleontologists had not found fossil evidence of any large carnivores taking its place. The print was dated at 70 million years old, showing that abelisaurids took over after the demise of *Giganotosaurus*.

On July 21, 2016, paleontologist Sebastian Apesteguia measures a record-setting dinosaur footprint made by a meat-eating predator some 70 million years ago. The giant track was found at Maragua Crater near Sucre, Bolivia, a site already known for other, smaller dinosaur tracks.

EINSTEIN WAS RIGHT

On Feb. 11, 2016, scientists from the Laser Interferometer Gravitational-Wave Observatory (LIGO) announced a monumental discovery: they had detected *gravitational waves*. These tiny ripples in the fabric of space-time were predicted exactly 100 years ago by Albert Einstein's general theory of relativity, but even Einstein himself doubted that they could ever be found. Their detection ushers in a new age in astrophysics.

Gravitational waves are a type of radiation that carries gravitational force. According to the general theory of relativity, time and space are not absolutely separate. The theory refers to them instead as a single entity, space-time. Gravitational waves can be thought of as moving ripples in space-time. The ripples stretch and shrink space-time, changing the distance between objects without causing them to move.

Scientists have long suspected that violent cosmic events create powerful gravitational waves. The waves, however, grow weaker as they travel outward from their source. Waves are so weak by the time they reach Earth that they are extremely difficult to detect.

After several rounds of upgrades since their initial construction in 2002, the LIGO detectors, located in Richland, Washington, and Livingston, Louisiana, picked up the signal of gravitational waves in September 2015. Two black holes collided over 1.5 billion years ago, producing ripples in space-time that finally reached Earth. Both observatories, which are shaped like giant L's, detected minute changes in the length of each arm of the "L." After all other possibilities, such as earthquakes, were ruled out, the only possible explanation for such a change in distance was the passing of gravitational waves through Earth.

This detection is not the end of scientists' interest in gravitational waves, but rather the beginning of a new type of astronomy. Now that we know gravitational waves exist, LIGO and other observatories will continue to look for them. They will help astronomers learn more about black holes, ultra-dense stars called *neutron stars*, and even about the origins of the universe itself.

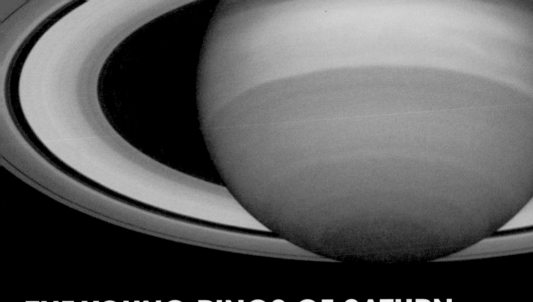

THE YOUNG RINGS OF SATURN

Imagine what Saturn would be like without its rings. Though large, it would be quite unremarkable as a planet compared to Jupiter, a planet with greater size, colorful cloud bands, and swirling storms. Aside from Saturn's large moon Titan, there would be little about the planet to excite astronomers and the telescoping public. This ringless state, however, may have been Saturn's plight in the relatively recent past, according to Matija Cuk from the Search for Extraterrestrial Intelligence (SETI) Institute and Luke Dones and David Nesvorny from the Southwest Research Institute of San Antonio, Texas. The trio published an article on March 24, 2016, in *The Astrophysical Journal* suggesting that Saturn's rings and some of its moons are only about 100 million

A 2016 study speculated that Saturn's famous rings are much younger than the planet itself.

years old—quite young by planetary standards.

Scientists had assumed that Saturn's rings and *satellites* (moons) formed about 4.6 billion years ago along with the planet itself and the rest of the solar system. In 2012, however, a team of French scientists suggested that *tidal forces* (forces created by the uneven pull of gravity on large objects) should have pushed Saturn's rings and inner moons farther from the planet. Thus, the researchers thought the rings might not be as old as the rest of the Saturn system.

Cuk, Dones, and Nesvorny helped support this idea. Occasionally, moons of large planets drift into orbital *reso-*

nances, when moons orbit in regular, but different orbits. For example, if one moon orbits a planet two times for every three orbits another moon makes, those moons are in orbital resonance. When this happens, the interaction of gravity between the moons—even if they are small—can fling them into longer, more eccentric, orbits. The three scientists found that the orbits of three satellites of Saturn—Dione, Rhea, and Tethys—had not changed much due to the effects of orbital resonance. They suggested the moons were formed—along with Saturn's rings—close to where they orbit today about 100 million years ago.

While 100 million years seems like quite a long time indeed, it is the blink of an eye in astronomical terms. Most of the solar system hasn't changed much in 4 billion years. The scientists speculate that around 100 million years ago, changes in the orbits of two or more earlier moons caused them to collide. Dione, Rhea, and Tethys would have formed from portions of this debris. Some of the debris would have also rained down on the rest of the Saturn system, peppering older moons with fresh craters. The rest of the debris remained locked in orbit around Saturn as the gorgeous rings we see today.

JUNO JOINS JUPITER

On July 4, 2016, the National Aeronautics and Space Administration (NASA) celebrated Independence Day with fireworks of the deep-space variety as its probe Juno fired its engine for 35 minutes to enter into orbit around Jupiter. After a five-year voyage from Earth, Juno had finally reached its destination.

Jupiter is the largest planet in our solar system. It has a *mass* (amount of matter) that is greater than the masses of all the other planets in the solar system added together. Astronomers call Jupiter a gas giant because the planet consists mostly of hydrogen and helium, and it has no solid surface. Jupiter is named for the king of the gods in Roman mythology. Juno was Jupiter's wife and queen of the gods.

Since July, Juno has been studying Jupiter from an elongated polar orbit. The probe reaches 4,900 miles (7,200 kilometers) from Jupiter at the farthest point in its orbit, and dives to within 2,600 miles (4,200 kilometers) of the Jovian clouds, flying over the planet's north and south poles. Mission scientists planned this orbit to keep

Juno out of Jupiter's radiation belts as much as possible. Any spacecraft entering these belts would be bombarded by huge doses of radiation, which is just as dangerous to electronics as it is to living things.

Scientists shielded Juno's most important electronics in a thick titanium case. But no spacecraft can stand exposure to such highly charged particles for long. NASA scientists do not expect the craft to survive much longer than its 20-month mission.

Scientists hope Juno will discover if Jupiter has a rocky core and why the planet has such a high concentration of elements heavier than hydrogen and helium. Juno will also study Jupiter's famous Great Red Spot, a storm that has been churning in the planet's atmosphere for centuries.

Launched from Earth in 2011, the Juno spacecraft arrived at Jupiter on July 4, 2016, to study the giant planet from an elliptical polar orbit.

THE FALCON HAS LANDED

On April 8, 2016, the Space Exploration Technologies Corporation (commonly called *SpaceX*) landed the *first stage* of a Falcon 9 rocket on a *drone ship* (crewless barge) in the Atlantic Ocean. The first stage is the fuel-and-engine part of a rocket. Typically, when the first stage runs out of propellant, it drops away and burns up in the atmosphere. The single-use aspect of first stage rockets has always been an expensive part of the rocket business. Falcon 9, however, can descend back to Earth, use its engines to slow itself, and land vertically—either on a runway or, in this case, on a ship at sea. The sea landing followed Falcon 9's first ground-based landing in December 2015.

The importance of landing at sea has to do with the amount of fuel a rocket can carry. The *trajectory* (curved path of flight) of a rocket's launch usually takes it over the ocean. Thus, it takes less fuel for a discarded first stage to land on a ship in the ocean than to reverse course and land back near the ground-based launch pad. Most Falcon 9's carry enough fuel for a sea landing, where the drone ship can move to "catch" the descending rocket.

Since the Falcon 9's first successful sea landing, SpaceX has landed three more rockets at sea and another on land. Another Falcon 9 crashed—experienced a "rapid unscheduled disassembly," or *RUD*—trying to land in June. If the company can make such landings routine, it will slash the cost of delivering cargo to space. Updating and refurbishing a relatively unscathed Falcon 9 costs much less than the $60 million needed to build a new one.

A Falcon 9 rocket slows to land on a drone ship in the Atlantic Ocean on April 8, 2016.

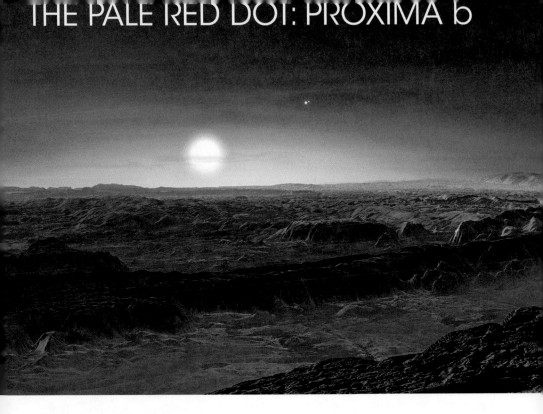

On Aug. 24, 2016, scientists from the European Southern Observatory (ESO) announced that they had discovered an *extrasolar* (beyond our solar system) planet, or *exoplanet,* that may harbor conditions favorable to life. This exoplanet, called *Proxima b*, orbits Proxima Centauri, the star closest to the sun. Astronomers have nicknamed Proxima b the "pale red dot," a play on Earth's appearance as a "pale blue dot" in a distant photo taken by the Voyager 1 space probe in 1990. Astronomers believe that Proxima Centauri, a red dwarf star, will cast its close-orbiting planet in a pale red glow. The search for a planet orbiting Proxima Centauri, which began in January 2016, was dubbed the "Pale Red Dot" campaign.

Proxima Centauri is part of a three-star system called Alpha Centauri. Two of the stars, Centauri A and Centauri B, are roughly the size of the sun and orbit each other. Proxima Centauri is a much smaller red dwarf star and orbits the larger pair of stars every million years or so.

The newly discovered exoplanet, Proxima b, is at least 1.3 times the size of Earth. Its size indicates that it is probably a rocky planet, like Earth and Mars. It orbits Proxima every 11 Earth days (Mercury, the closest planet

stars in the universe. They also burn slowly and steadily, for up to 10 trillion years. In contrast, the sun has a stable lifespan of only 10 billion years. As a result, if favorable conditions exist, life could have countless chances to form over countless eons. Astronomers still have a lot to learn about Proxima b and whether it can host life. It might lack an atmosphere or get bombarded by powerful X-ray blasts from Proxima. The James Webb Space Telescope (JWST), to be launched in 2018, should answer some of these questions. It will be able to determine the exoplanet's composition and whether it has an atmosphere. JWST will also gather more information on the planet's size and makeup. Future space telescopes may even be powerful enough to see the "pale red dot" directly. Most exoplanets are too far away to be explored by spacecraft from Earth. They orbit stars many *light-years* away. A light-year is the distance light travels in a year, or about 5.88 trillion miles (9.46 trillion kilometers). Nothing can travel faster than the speed of light. Proxima Centauri, however, is just 4.2 light-years away, tantalizingly close in astronomical terms. But the fastest

to the sun, completes a year every 88 Earth days). If Proxima Centauri were a star like our sun, the planet would be little more than a charred husk. But red dwarf stars are small and relatively cool. Consequently, it is possible that liquid water could exist on the exoplanet's surface. Scientists call this region around a star, where temperatures are suitable for liquid water, its *habitable zone*. Liquid water is a necessary building block for life as we know it. If red dwarf stars can harbor habitable worlds, then the odds that life exists elsewhere in the universe increase significantly. Red dwarfs make up about 70 percent of the spacecraft ever created have reached just tiny fractions of the speed of light. Using such technology, a traditional space probe would still take thousands of years to reach the system. A private initiative called Breakthrough Starshot, however, has proposed launching a tiny spacecraft to the system that would take as little as 20 years to get there. The probe would be only a gram or two (the equivalent of less than an ounce on Earth) and be propelled by large Earth-based lasers to 20 percent of the speed of light. There are many technical hurdles to be overcome, however, and the group does not anticipate launching a probe for at least another 20 years, but there is hope that the planet could be explored close-up before 2100. Soon, we may get to say hello to our closest potential neighbor. Will it say hi back?

WHERE NO MEERKAT HAS GONE BEFORE

On July 16, 2016, a South African meerkat made international news, but it wasn't one of the cute critters of the Kalahari Desert. This meerkat—or, rather, *MeerKAT*—is a radio telescope complex under construction near Carnarvon, South Africa. On July 16, images from the first 16 MeerKAT *reflectors* (dish antennas)—in operation for only a few hours and looking at only a tiny corner of the universe—revealed black holes some 200 million light-years away and hundreds of previously unknown galaxies. A radio telescope consists of a radio receiver with an antenna fixed on a wide, bowl-shaped reflector that records radio waves coming from stars and other objects in outer space. A radio receiver amplifies the signals and sends them to a computer. The computer then analyzes the radio spectrum of the wave source to produce an image.

The *KAT* in MeerKAT stands for *Karoo Array Telescope*, which refers to the complex's location in South Africa's remote Karoo semidesert region. MeerKAT, which will have 64 reflectors when completed in late 2017, is the first phase of Square Kilometer Array (SKA) South Africa that will eventually have 250 antennas. SKA South Africa will then pair with a SKA complex of 256 antennas being built in Western Australia. Together, they will explore and measure the universe at different radio frequencies. If the first few hours of the first 16 SKA reflectors—which glimpsed less than 1/100th of 1 percent of the celestial sphere—are any indication, imagine what 64, then 250, then 506 antennas scanning the entire sky might find!

SKA Phase 2—scheduled to be operating by the mid-2020's—will include thousands of radio telescope antennas throughout Africa and Australia. The SKA project has a number of key objectives, such as investigating the origins and structure of the universe and studying gravitational waves and *astrobiological* (the search for and study of life in the universe) possibilities. But the project's stated purpose, "Exploration of the Unknown," reflects the hope that SKA will discover things in the universe we cannot yet conceive.

In the large image below, a MeerKAT dish scans the night sky above the dry Karoo region of South Africa. In the smaller image, a portion of MeerKAT's first radio image shows more than 200 astronomical radio sources (white dots). Previous mapping of this area showed just five sources, marked here by the violet circles.

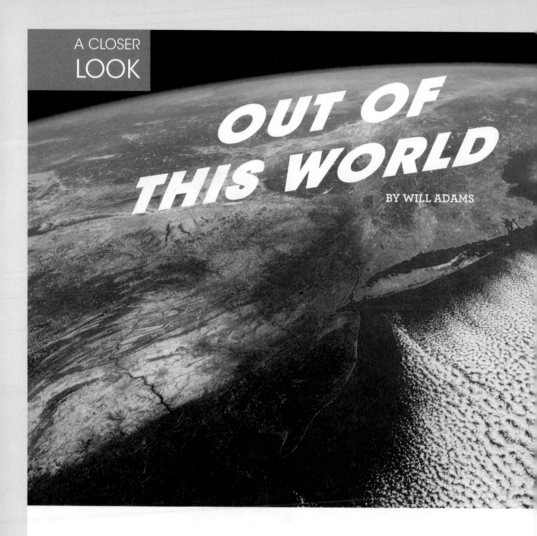

OUT OF THIS WORLD

BY WILL ADAMS

On March 1, 2016, United States National Aeronautics and Space Administration (NASA) astronaut Scott Kelly and Russian cosmonaut Mikhail Kornienko returned to Earth after a record 340 days aboard the International Space Station (ISS). The pair ended their long mission by landing in Kazakhstan in west-central Asia aboard a Soyuz TMA-18M spacecraft.

Scott Kelly was born in 1964 in New Jersey. A U.S. Navy aviator, Kelly was selected to be a NASA astronaut in 1996. In his first spaceflight in 1999, he served as pilot of the space shuttle Discovery. In 2007, Kelly commanded the shuttle Endeavor on a mission to the ISS. He later commanded the station from November 2010 to March 2011.

Above, Scott Kelly poses with the light blue waters of the Bahamas through a window of the ISS cupola, a special module that provides a 360-degree view of Earth. At left, a *polar vortex* (a severe winter storm) approaches the east coast of the United States on Valentine's Day 2016.

Kelly and Kornienko arrived at the ISS on March 27, 2015. They spent the better part of a year at the space station, performing scientific experiments and maintenance as other ISS crew came and went. Kelly and his crewmates grew lettuce and other plants on the space station, but the primary objective was to study the effects of long-duration space travel on the human body. Over the 340 days, tests compared Kelly's physical and mental well-being with that of his identical twin brother, retired NASA astronaut Mark Kelly, who was tested on Earth over the same period. Since identical twins have practically identical genomes, any differences between the Kelly brothers were almost certainly caused by Scott's extended stay at the ISS.

NASA astronauts Scott Kelly (left) and Terry Virts (right) work on a Carbon Dioxide Removal Assembly (CDRA) inside the ISS in May 2015. The CDRA removes carbon dioxide from the cabin air, allowing for an environmentally safe crew cabin.

On Aug. 9, 2015, the 135th day of Kelly's 340-day mission aboard the ISS, the astronaut took this star-spangled photograph of the Milky Way below the glowing curve of Earth.

Scientists studied how living in space affected Kelly's heart, fluid distribution in his body, behavior and decision-making skills, and even his microbiome (the diverse community of microbes that live within and on plants and animals). Kornienko also underwent a battery of tests during the mission. These studies will help identify potential health problems faced by astronauts travelling to Mars or living in a lunar base.

After returning to Earth and normal gravity, Kelly experienced flu-like symptoms, joint and muscle pain, swollen legs, and sensitive skin. In the microgravity of low-Earth orbit, an astronaut's skin touches very little besides the astronaut's clothes: they rarely sit, lie down, or touch other objects.

Kelly took this image of air pollution building up against the Indian Himalayas on Jan. 12, 2016. Kelly tweeted hundreds of images of Earth during his 340 days in space.

Kelly often came up with creative ways to pass the time. Here, he celebrates his 300th day in space—Jan. 21, 2016—by playing ping pong with a water droplet.

On Jan. 16, 2016, Kelly shared photographs of a blooming zinnia flower in the plant growth system aboard the ISS. Kelly wrote, "Yes, there are other life forms in space!" This flowering crop experiment began on Nov. 16, 2015, with the activation of the "Veggie" system and its rooting "pillows" containing zinnia seeds. The challenging process of growing the zinnias allowed scientists back on Earth to study how plants grow in microgravity. It also provided astronauts with space-gardening experience. Zinnias were also grown for comparison at NASA's Kennedy Space Center in Florida.

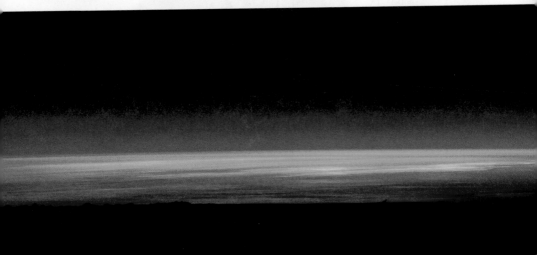

Kelly shared sunrise photographs with social media followers during his time aboard the ISS. This last one, taken on March 1, 2016, was captioned, "Rise and shine! My last sunrise from space then I gotta go!"

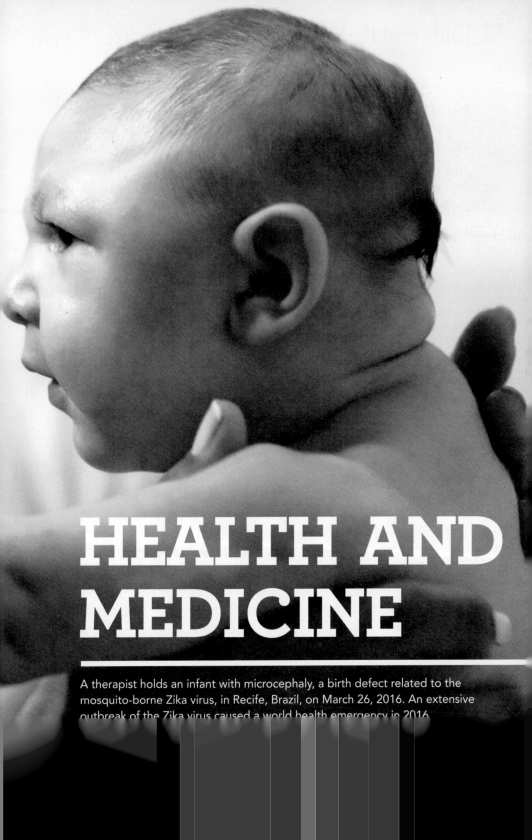

HEALTH AND MEDICINE

A therapist holds an infant with microcephaly, a birth defect related to the mosquito-borne Zika virus, in Recife, Brazil, on March 26, 2016. An extensive outbreak of the Zika virus caused a world health emergency in 2016.

SHINING LIGHT ON SCHIZOPHRENIA

On Jan. 27, 2016, scientists at Harvard University Medical School and Boston Children's Hospital in Massachusetts published a study on the cause of schizophrenia, one of the most common and devastating forms of mental illness. The study identified certain genes associated with the development of schizophrenia, providing crucial new information on the molecular foundation of the illness. The scientists hope the study will aid in the development of new and effective treatments for schizophrenia over the coming decades.

Schizophrenia affects about 1 percent of the world's population. It is characterized by unpredictable mental disturbances. People with the disease sometimes withdraw from reality and think in illogical, confused patterns. Many people with schizophrenia develop delusions or hear "voices" that others cannot hear. They often suffer disturbances in mood and behavior. Some patients seem to feel no emotions, but others may display inappropriate emotions, such as laughing at sad situations. Some patients withdraw from their family and friends and talk mainly to themselves or to their "voices."

Physicians do not know the exact cause of schizophrenia. A genetic component to the development of the disease has long been suspected because schizophrenia often runs in families. But no clear genetic cause has been discovered, and environmental factors—including stress or a traumatic emotional experience—are known to influence the development of schizophrenia.

Medical imaging studies show that schizophrenics have less neural tissue in their brains than healthy individuals. Studying both humans and mice, the researchers identified a particular gene, called *compliment component 4* (C4), that deletes connections between neurons (nerve cells) in the brain. As people grow from infants to adults, millions of neuron connections are established and deleted in the developing brain, in a normal process that scientists call "synaptic pruning." (A synapse is the place between nerve cells at which nerve impulses are passed.) Using genome databases, the C4 genes in 28,800 people with schizophrenia were compared to those in 36,000 people without the disease. The scientists identified a variation of the C4 gene that seems to be responsible for an abnormally high amount of synaptic pruning in adolescents, resulting in the loss of too many neurons and neural connections, leading to schizophrenia.

REAL-LIFE X-MEN

Could people with rare powers resulting from genetic mutations be living among us? On April 11, 2016, a genetic study of almost 600,000 people was published in the journal *Nature Biotechnology*. In the study, scientists identified 13 individuals believed to possess mutations that protect them from certain deadly inherited diseases. Sage Bionetworks, a biomedical research organization in Seattle, Washington, conducted the study. Sage researchers discovered a handful of people who, despite carrying mutations of hereditary diseases that should have either killed them or made them very ill, showed no signs of the diseases.

The researchers analyzed DNA from 589,306 people, focusing on 874 genes known to contain mutations that cause a variety of hereditary diseases. They compared this *genome* data with the health record of each person. (A genome is the entire set of chemical instructions that controls heredity in a species.) The researchers found 13 individuals whose genes normally caused hereditary diseases. These diseases included cystic fibrosis (CF), an incurable condition in which abnormally thick mucus affects the lungs and other organs. CF often causes premature death. Other individuals in the study should have suffered more rare hereditary conditions, including Smith-Lemli-Opitz syndrome, a severe and deadly developmental disorder; familial dysautonomia, a neurological disease that usually kills in early childhood; and epidermolysis bullosa, a condition which causes the skin to break out in painful blisters at the slightest touch. Yet, the health records of the 13 individuals showed no signs of such diseases.

The researchers suspect that the 13 patients possessed other mutations to counter the effects of the usually deadly or debilitating mutations. The protective mutations are reminiscent of the character "Wolverine" in the popular *X-Men* series of comic books and action films. Wolverine and other X-Men are superheroes who have gained their powers from genetic mutations. The super power of the character Wolverine, for example, is the ability to immediately heal from any wound, injury, or illness.

Understanding the mutations that protect these 13 individuals from hereditary diseases would be extremely useful in helping researchers better treat or even prevent such deadly conditions. Unfortunately, Sage Bionetworks cannot work with the 13 "mutants." Rules attached to the genetic study forbid researchers from identifying or contacting the participants.

SEASON OF ZIKA

BY NICK KILZER

*The rapid spread of an obscure mosquito-borne virus
caused a public health emergency following a wave of related
heartbreaking birth defects. The virus, known as Zika, also
cast a shadow on the 2016 Summer Olympic Games in Brazil.*

In January 2016, health officials at the United States Centers
for Disease Control and Prevention (CDC) issued a travel
alert for people, especially pregnant women or women of

child-bearing age, to avoid travel to Puerto Rico and several countries in Central and South America over fears of severe birth defects associated with the mosquito-borne Zika virus. The travel alert was issued following a rash of reports in late 2015 of birth defects in Brazil, where at least 1,500 babies were born with *microcephaly,* an uncommon condition in which a baby is born with a smaller-than-normal sized head and often with severely impaired brain development. This was an alarming increase compared to the 147 cases of microcephaly recorded in Brazil in all 2014.

Brazilian officials believed that the increase in the birth defect was somehow related to a recent outbreak of Zika virus in the country, but they could not explain how. Several of the babies with this condition and their mothers tested positive for exposure to the Zika virus, strongly indicating a link between the virus and the birth defect.

The CDC warning turned out to be the tip of the iceberg. On Feb. 1, 2016, the World Health Organization (WHO) declared Zika virus a *Public Health Emergency of International Concern.* WHO reserves such emergency declarations only for extraordinary events that are "serious, unusual, or unexpected." WHO officials found that Zika was spreading rapidly through numerous countries and territories in Central and South America and the Caribbean. Until then, the virus had never appeared in that part of the world.

A girl peeks through a window behind a Zika virus warning banner in Tegucigalpa, Honduras, on Feb 6, 2016. The small Central American country has reported over 20,000 Zika cases and about 100 related cases of Guillain-Barré syndrome.

By April, scientists had established that the Zika virus was directly responsible for the microcephaly birth defects. Evidence also emerged that infection with Zika virus was linked to a dramatic rise in *Guillain-Barré syndrome.* This condition causes progressive muscle weakness by damaging the peripheral nervous system.

By April 2016, the Zika virus had been detected in more than 50 countries worldwide. U.S. health officials scrambled to prepare for the inevitable spread of the virus to the United States.

Origins. Zika virus is named after the Zika Forest, near Lake Victoria in Uganda, where scientists first discovered it in monkeys in 1947. Scientists classify the Zika virus in the *flavivirus* family. This family of viruses is a subgroup of a larger group called *arboviruses*. The flavivirus family includes several viruses that cause disease in people. Such flaviviruses include yellow fever, dengue fever, and West Nile virus. In 1952, scientists found that the Zika virus also infects people. Over the next 60 years, outbreaks of Zika were reported in tropical Africa, Southeast Asia, and the Pacific Islands. However, none of these outbreaks was associated with birth defects.

Symptoms of Zika virus disease include fever, rash, joint pain, and conjunctivitis (eye inflammation). For adults and children, the illness is usually mild, with symptoms lasting from several days to a week. Severe Zika virus infections, requiring hospitalization or causing death, are rare.

Zika virus is spread to people through the bite of a mosquito, *Aedes aegypti,* which is common throughout the world's tropical regions. The disease may infect people who live or work in forested areas and are bitten by infected mosquitoes. Infected people may then carry the virus to urban areas, where it is transmitted to other people through mosquito bites. In the United States, *Aedes aegypti* mosquitoes occur naturally in Florida and the Gulf Coast. However, they are found as far north as New York during the hot and humid summer months.

In 2016, medical researchers also discovered that the Zika virus may be sexually transmitted between people. Doctors have detected Zika virus in semen, urine, and saliva from infected patients. Pregnant women have the most to fear because of the immediate risk to their unborn babies.

The Zika Zone

This map shows the origins of the Zika virus in Africa and its spread through the years to other parts of the world. Red zones mark the most recent outbreaks and areas of Zika-related microcephaly that hit hard in Central, South, and North America. More than 400,000 Zika virus cases have been reported throughout the Americas.

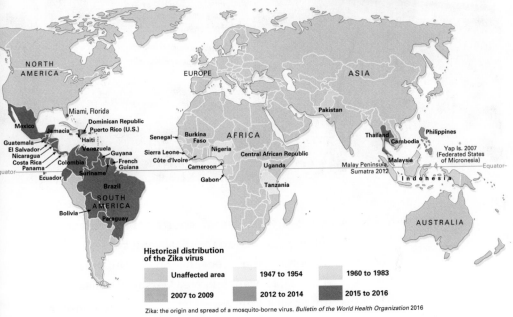

Zika: the origin and spread of a mosquito-borne virus. *Bulletin of the World Health Organization* 2016

Because the virus can be sexually transmitted, and scientists aren't sure how long it stays in an individual's system, all adults who plan on having children should do their best to avoid infection.

On January 15, the CDC reported that a mother and her infant born with microcephaly in the United States had both tested positive for a prior Zika infection. The mother had been in Brazil during her pregnancy. It was the first U.S. case of a birth defect linked to the virus. By May, Puerto Rico had over 900 confirmed cases of Zika virus infection, including over 100 in pregnant

On May 9, 2016, a Zika adivsory warns against mosquito bites at Hartsfield-Jackson Atlanta International Airport in Georgia.

women, with several reports of birth defects. By the end of June 2016, several babies with Zika-related microcephaly had been born in Florida, Hawaii, and New Jersey. All these infections were *travel-associated* cases, where the mothers contracted Zika while in other countries. In late July, the first *local* cases (transmitted directly by mosquitoes) were reported in southern Florida, and they soon appeared in other parts of the state as well. More than 10,000 Zika cases have now been reported in the United States and its territories, with the vast majority occurring in American Samoa, Puerto Rico, and the U.S. Virgin Islands.

Health officials expressed concerns that the virus will eventually appear and become established in other areas of the United States, much like the West Nile virus (another mosquito-borne viral disease) did in the 1990's. President

Barack Obama called on Congress to approve nearly 2 billion dollars to fund efforts to combat Zika in the United States. The administration had already reprogrammed nearly $600 million that had been set aside to help prevent the spread of Africa's 2014 outbreak of Ebola virus. Medical experts worried that precious time had been wasted as Congress argued over Zika funds while the virus spread in Puerto Rico and the Caribbean and alarming reports of birth defects surfaced in the mainland United States.

Olympic concerns. The Zika virus outbreak could not have come at a worse time for Brazil, which hosted the 2016 Summer Olympic Games in Rio de Janeiro in August and the Paralympic Games in September. Brazilian officials expressed concerns over the possibility of visitors staying away from Rio de Janeiro out of fear of contracting Zika. The city took precautions to ensure that tourists and Olympics athletes did not feel threatened, with crews on hand to eliminate any stagnant water that could serve as breeding grounds for mosquitoes.

In May, a group of more than 100 doctors and professors signed a letter to WHO, saying the Summer Games should be postponed or moved in light of the Zika threat. The letter stated that the medical consequences of the Zika virus were too great to run the risk of spreading the infection at the games. Health officials worried that travelers would also spread Zika to sexual partners back home, or to native mosquitoes that would transmit the virus locally. Many travelers to the Rio Olympics would be returning to their native countries just as mosquito populations were peaking.

By June, at least seven Olympic competitors, including top-ranked golfers Rory McIlroy of Ireland and Australia's Jason Day, announced they would not attend the games because of fears over the Zika virus. Citing concern for his pregnant wife, cyclist Tejay van Garderen was the first U.S. athlete to drop out of the games. Several other athletes expressed uncertainty about attending the games.

Yet some public health officials supported Brazil's decision to go on with the Olympic Games. Infectious disease experts pointed out that the games were to be held in one city during the region's cooler winter months. The mosquito population primarily spreading the virus reaches its lowest numbers during the Brazilian cool season, which includes August and September when the Olympics and Paralympics were held.

The U.S. Olympic Committee created an advisory panel to answer Olympians' questions and published recommendations to help keep U.S. team members and staff from becoming infected with Zika. Still, some athletes chose not to attend the games out of an abundance of caution.

WHO officials said that athletes and spectators, except for pregnant women, should not hesitate to attend so long as they take precautions against Zika infection. There is currently no vaccine to prevent or medicine to treat Zika. Pregnant women who must travel to a Zika-affected area should talk to their healthcare provider first and strictly follow steps to avoid mosquito bites.

People can limit the risk of Zika infection through basic mosquito-control measures. For example, people in affected areas should limit skin exposure by wearing long sleeves and pants, and wear mosquito repellent during the day, when the mosquitoes that transmit Zika virus are known to bite.

As it turned out, no reports of Zika infections came out of the Olympic Games. After the games, however, outbreaks in areas previously untouched by Zika illustrated the traveling threat of the virus.

Vaccine hopes. In June, scientists from the Walter Reed Army Institute of Research, the Beth Israel Deaconess Medical Center, and Harvard Medical School tested two potential Zika vaccines in mice with good results. The experimental vaccines protected all mice that were immunized against the virus, while the mice not given the vaccine caught Zika upon exposure.

However, additional testing is needed to determine if these vaccines are equally safe and effective in humans, and whether they will provide lasting protection from the Zika virus. That will take months or longer. Experts from the U.S. National Institutes of Health began clinical trials of a Zika vaccine in August. Depending on the results, larger trials could begin later in 2017. But experts caution that a safe and effective vaccine for widespread use to protect those at most risk—such as pregnant women—could still be years away.

Vaccine or not, scientists think that the Zika outbreak could possibly burn itself out in a few years, based on the fact that people develop immunity to the virus after an initial infection.

A Miami-Dade County mosquito-control worker sprays around a home in Miami on Aug. 1, 2016. The CDC warned that pregnant women should avoid a Zika-stricken part of Miami, and that pregnant women who live there should take steps to prevent mosquito bites and the sexual spread of the virus.

LIVING WORLD

In the spring of 2016, lemon damselfish swim over bleached coral colonies of the Great Barrier Reef along the northeast coast of Australia. A 2016 study revealed that the Great Barrier Reef, the world's largest coral reef system, is suffering from potentially fatal bleaching.

see page 390 for

A CLOSER
LOOK

TULLY MONSTER

In March 2016, scientists from Yale University solved the mystery surrounding a 300-million-year-old "monster." In 1955, a fossil hunter named Francis Tully found a strange creature preserved in the Mazon Creek region of the Midwestern state of Illinois. Tully turned the fossil over to scientists at Chicago's Field Museum. The scientists named the creature *Tullymonstrum gregarium* in Tully's honor, but they could never identify the creature. This year, however, a team of scientists led by Victoria E. McCoy think they uncovered the true identity of the *Tully Monster*. Their findings were published in the journal *Nature* in March 2016.

The Mazon Creek area has numerous well-preserved fossils from the Carboniferous Period of some 300 million years ago (which predates the dinosaurs). The Tully Monster fossil looked somewhat like a leaf. The animal had a long, oval-shaped body with triangular tail fins. Its eyes rested on a skinny rod or bar. On top of all that, it had a long, wormlike snout ending in tiny, toothed jaws. From snout to tail, the whole creature grew little more than a foot (30 centimeters) long. Over the years, the "monster" was linked to squid, clams, snails, slugs, and different kinds of worms, but nothing quite fit the Tully Monster mold. The Yale scientists, however, noticed that the thin, light band running along the length of the Tully Monster, previously thought to be a digestive tract, was in fact a *notochord*, a flexible cord along the backs of many early vertebrates. That related the Tully Monster to fish, and the structure of the gills and teeth showed that it was an ancestor of modern lampreys.

A reconstruction of the Tully Monster as it would have looked 300 million years ago, swimming in Carboniferous waters. Notice the jointed snout, the multiple rows of teeth, and the eye bar on the animal's back.

THE LAST ELEPHANT SHOW

On May 1, 2016, Asian elephants appeared for the last time in the Ringling Bros. and Barnum & Bailey Circus. The circus, which had planned to retire the elephants by 2018, moved the date forward to accommodate requests from animal rights groups and some circus fans that felt the elephant act had outlived its era. The final elephant show was performed in Providence, Rhode Island. The 13 final elephants then moved to Florida—like so many other retirees—where they joined the rest of the circus herd at Ringling's Center for Elephant Conservation.

After 145 years of featuring the animals in its "Greatest Show on Earth," the circus now focuses its efforts on elephant conservation programs in North America and Sri

Elephants perform in the Ringling Bros. and Barnum & Bailey Circus in 2016.

Lanka. There are only about 40,000 to 50,000 of this endangered species remaining in the wild.

Ringling's retired elephants will now be a part of cancer research. Cancer is much more common in humans than elephants, even though elephants have many more cells in their bodies. Scientist believe this is the result of an abundance of specific cancer-suppressing genes in elephants. These genes help repair cells that have been exposed to cancer-causing substances.

The Ringling Bros. and Barnum & Bailey Circus no longer has elephants, but other animals—including tigers, lions, horses, dogs, and camels—still remain part of the show.

U.S. NATIONAL MAMMAL: THE BISON

On May 9, 2016, the National Bison Legacy Act made the American bison, or "buffalo," the first official national mammal of the United States. Once hunted to near extinction, conservation efforts and legal protection helped bison populations recover. Today, the animal endures and now takes its place beside the bald eagle, the national bird since 1782, as a beautiful American symbol. Despite its common name, the bison is not a true buffalo, but rather a type of wild ox.

Great herds of bison once roamed the vast, dry grasslands of North America. Indians depended upon bison meat for food and hides for clothing. In 1850, about 20 million bison thundered over the Great Plains. In the late 1800's, white American hunters slaughtered millions of bison, depriving Indians of their main source of food and almost wiping out the bison.

Today, some 500,000 bison live in the wild and in commercial and conservation herds in Canada and the United States. Yellowstone National Park, which lies in Wyoming, Idaho, and Montana, is the only place in the United States where bison populations never disappeared. It is also home to the nation's largest herd.

The American bison, commonly called the "buffalo," became the first official national mammal of the United States in 2016.

BELOVED GORILLA HARAMBE KILLED

Animal lovers were shocked on May 28, 2016, when workers at the Cincinnati Zoo in Ohio shot and killed a beloved western lowland gorilla. The incident began when a young boy slipped through a small opening and fell into the gorilla enclosure. The splashing of the boy in the enclosure's moat attracted the attention of the 17-year-old silverback Harambe. Silverbacks are mature, dominant male gorillas, known for the gray fur on their back and shoulders. The western lowland gorilla is an endangered animal.

The crowd looked on helplessly as the over-400-pound (180-kilogram) gorilla roughly handled the boy, dragging him around the enclosure and even knocking him into a wall. After removing the crowd and evacuating Harambe's penmates, zookeepers made the difficult decision to shoot the animal. They feared that subduing Harambe with a tranquilizer dart might take too long, exposing the child to further danger.

Many animal lovers were outraged by the incident and by the zoo's decision to kill the gorilla. Some noted that in video of the incident, Harambe appeared to be protecting the child. But several *primatologists* (scientists who study apes, monkeys, and other similar animals) observed that although male gorillas are not inherently aggressive, the gorilla's strength and its agitated state could have presented a mortal danger to the child. The child was treated for injuries and released.

An incident at the Cincinnati Zoo resulted in the death of Harambe, *pictured below*, in 2016.

AUSTRALIAN PEACOCK SPIDERS

The new species *maratus bubo* is named for the owlish pattern of the male spiders' colors. Several species of owl belong to the genus *Bubo*.

Scientists documented seven new species of peacock spider in 2016. Peacock spiders, found only in Australia, are less than a ¼ of an inch (6 millimeters) long. Males from these species are brightly colored and perform elaborate rolling and shaking dances and displays to win over potential mates. Peacock spiders are jumping spiders. Instead of spinning webs, they hunt by sneaking up and pouncing on their prey. These spiders have short legs, but they can jump more than 40 times the length of their bodies. Thick, colored hairs cover their bodies, especially on their first pair of legs. Male jumping spiders are among the most colorful of all spiders. Juvenile spiders and females lack the male's bright colors.

Jurgen Otto, a German-born Australian scientist, discovered and named these new peacock spiders—along with spider experts David Knowles and David Hill. The newly named species increase the number of peacock spider species to 16, with several more yet to be positively identified. The new species are all named after characteristics of their appearance.

THAILAND'S TROUBLING TIGER TEMPLE

In late May and early June 2016, Thai wildlife officials closed the famed Wat Pha Luang Ta Bua temple (commonly known as the "Tiger Temple"), west of Bangkok, the capital. Officials seized 137 tigers from the temple and relocated the animals to temporary facilities. Upon inspection of the temple and its grounds, officials found skins, goods made with tiger parts, and dozens of dead tiger cubs. The temple began caring for tigers in 1999. Visitors paid to feed and pet the animals and snap pictures with them.

The temple became a popular tourist destination, but animal rights activists accused the temple of mistreatment, claiming drugs were used to keep the tigers docile.

Investigators believe the temple bred the tigers in order to illegally sell their skin, meat, bones, and claws for use in traditional Chinese medicines and amulets believed to have magical powers. Tigers are endangered animals. WWF, formerly the World Wildlife Fund, estimates that fewer than 4,000 tigers remain in the wild. The temple denied any wrongdoing.

A sedated tiger is removed from the so-called Tiger Temple in Thailand's Kanchanaburi province on June 3, 2016.

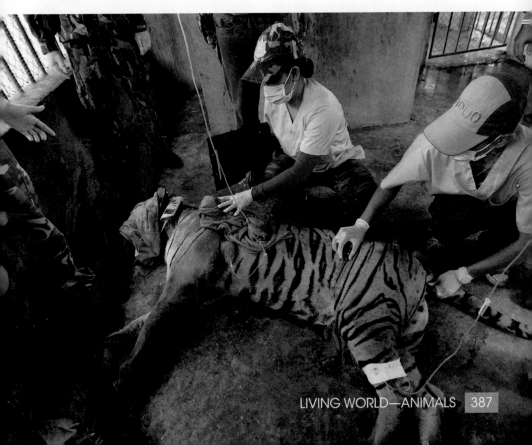

CLIMATE CHANGE
MAMMAL VICTIM ONE

On June 7, 2016, Australian authorities confirmed the extinction of a small rodent called the Bramble Cay melomys. The animal was native only to Bramble Cay, a small northern Australian island in the Torres Strait. The main reason for the rodent's extinction was the elimination of its habitat on the small, sandy reef island. Climate change has caused rising tides and sea levels, wiping out much of Bramble Cay's leafy plants—the rodent's main food source. Some rodents likely drowned, and the rest simply starved. The Bramble Cay melomys, then, became the first mammal casualty of *anthropogenic* (human-caused) climate change. In 1999, the death of the last golden toad in Central America marked the first documented species extinction driven by climate change.

The Bramble Cay melomys (*Melomys rubicola*)—seen here in 2002—has vanished from Earth. Scientists blame the small rodent's extinction on climate change.

Bramble Cay is a reef island of about 12 acres (5 hectares) at the northern end of the Great Barrier Reef near Papua New Guinea. At most, the island reaches 10 feet (3 meters) above sea level. The Bramble Cay melomys was first seen there in the 1800's. The small animal had a round brownish body, long whiskers, and a lumpy tail. In 1978, researchers counted several hundred of the rodents on Bramble Cay, noting that they were distinct from other types of Australian melomys. Since then, however, the island's population of the melomys—also called the *mosaic-tailed rat*—had dwindled along with its disappearing habitat. It was last seen in 2009.

YE OLDE GREENLAND SHARK

In August 2016, biologists identified the Greenland shark (*Somniosus microcephalus*) as one of the longest-living animals on Earth. These sharks, native to the frigid, deep waters of the Arctic and North Atlantic oceans, have a life span that may well exceed *400 years*. No other *vertebrate* (animal with a backbone) is known to live such a long life.

The remote habitat and shy nature of Greenland sharks means they are poorly studied, and few aspects of their lives are well understood. They are among the largest sharks, typically reaching more than 18 feet (5.5 meters) in length. They are nearly blind and swim slowly through the cold and murky northern waters. Greenland sharks grow slowly, less than half an inch (1 centimeter) per year—a trait that suggests an animal with a long life span.

Scientists with the Greenland Institute for Natural Resources used radiocarbon dating of tissue from the eye lenses to determine the age of 28 Greenland sharks caught during a study of commercial fishing. Scientists know that among these sharks, the lens of the eye grows by slowly adding layers of transparent tissue over the animal's lifetime. The innermost layers are formed before the shark is born. The smallest sharks in the study, around 7 feet (2 .2 meters) in length, showed a distinct spike in the ratio of radiocarbon, also known as Carbon 14, in the lens tissue that scientists know came from nuclear bomb testing done in the 1950's and 1960's. That spike indicated these sharks, which were not yet mature enough to reproduce, were at least 50 to 60 years old. The largest shark in the study, over 16 feet (5 meters) long, was determined to be at least 392 years old and possibly as old as 512 years!

Many people think that most vertebrates have life spans similar to our own, which rarely exceeds 100 years. The oldest known verified age of a human was just over 122 years, but some animals live much longer. Tortoises routinely live more than 100 years, and Bowhead whales are thought to survive around 200 years. But these new findings show without question that the Greenland shark is the oldest vertebrate animal in the world.

The flesh of Greenland sharks is poisonous, and they are not caught commercially or for sport fishing. However, some Greenland sharks are caught accidentally by commercial fishing vessels. Researchers think that Greenland sharks reproduce slowly and only after they grow to more than 7 feet (2.2 meters) length and have reached about 120 years of age. With such a slow rate of growth and reproduction, scientists worry that this life-span champion may be at risk of extinction.

CORAL IN CRISIS: RECORD BLEACHING OF THE GREAT BARRIER REEF

BY JEFF DE LA ROSA

"The hard corals were dead and covered in algae... The soft corals were still dying and the flesh of the animals was decomposing and dripping off the reef...." This is how diver Richard Vevers described a recent visit to the northern stretches of Australia's Great Barrier Reef, long considered one of the seven wonders of the natural world. In 2016, the reef's northern third, one of its more remote areas and thus, until recently, one of its most pristine, was ground zero for the worst coral bleaching event ever recorded in the region. Scientists estimate that the bleaching, triggered by unusually warm water temperatures, resulted in the death of

Empty waters surround the bleached corals of Australia's Lizard Island National Park, just off the coast of Queensland.

as much as half of the coral in many areas. Worse still, the bleaching event's cause was linked to *global warming*, signaling that such events may become more common in the coming years. Global warming is an observed increase in Earth's average surface temperature. Strong evidence links this increase to human activities, particularly the burning of such fossil fuels as coal, oil, and natural gas. Burning fossil fuels releases large amounts of carbon dioxide (CO_2) gas into the atmosphere. Carbon dioxide is a *greenhouse gas* that helps trap heat from the sun close to Earth's surface.

The Great Barrier Reef is made up of more than 3,000 individual reefs extending some 1,400 miles (2,300 kilometers) along the northeast coast of Australia. Together, they make up the world's largest reef system. Each reef has been built up over millions of years by animals called corals. An individual coral, called a *polyp*, constructs a skeleton by taking calcium from seawater and then depositing *calcium carbonate,* also known as limestone, around its body. Many corals grow in huge colonies, with new polyps attaching to one another or to the skeletons of dead corals, over time building up the limestone structure of the reef.

Coral reefs are hotbeds of *biodiversity,* variety among living things. The Great Barrier Reef is home to more than a thousand fish species, including over 100 unique species of sharks and rays. A variety of seabirds and sea mammals also depend on the reef system for food and shelter. Coral reefs have been compared to lovely sea gardens because of the many colorful sea animals that live among the corals. Thousands of divers and other tourists visit the Great Barrier Reef each year, contributing billions of dollars to the Australian economy.

Most reef-building corals cannot survive without single-celled algae called *zooxanthellae,* which live in the polyp's own tissue. The tiny algae provide up to 90 percent of the coral's food and also help the corals secrete their limestone skeletons. In addition, zooxanthellae provide much of living coral's often breathtaking color. For reasons not entirely understood, stressed corals—such as those exposed to unusually warm seawater—will often eject zooxanthellae from their bodies. Ejecting the colorful algae leaves the coral with a ghostly white appearance, giving the phenomenon its name: *bleaching.* If water temperatures recover soon, the coral may take up the algae again, helping to limit long-term damage. But if abnormally warm conditions persist, the coral can die. The decaying polyps serve as fertilizer for seaweed, which can overrun the remaining reef structure, contributing to the collapse of the entire ecosystem.

Reports of widespread bleaching were once relatively rare. Since the the early 1980's, however, reports of bleaching at the Great Barrier Reef have become all too common. The first reports occurred in conjunction with the El Niño of 1982-1983. El Niño is a periodic weather pattern that can bring warm weather and spread warm surface waters throughout much of the Pacific Ocean. Particularly strong El Niños occur about

At right, a few fish remain around bleached coral of the Great Barrier Reef in March 2016. *Far right,* fish abandon the same coral, now dun and lifeless, just two months later.

WHAT CAUSES BLEACHING?

HOT WATER
Water temperature being higher than the average summer maximum—just 1.8 °F (1 °C) higher for four weeks—can trigger bleaching.

SUNSHINE
Excessive sunlight adds to the impact of rising ocean temperatures and is made worse by calm seas and low tides.

HEALTHY
The colors of healthy coral colonies come from tiny plant-like cells that live inside the clear body tissue of the animal. These plant-like cells convert sunlight into food for the coral.

BLEACHED
The plant-like cells are expelled by the coral during mass bleaching events. The coral's white skeleton is revealed through the coral's clear body tissue.

DEAD
Without enough plant cells to provide the coral wth food, the coral soon starves or becomes diseased. Soon afterwards, the tissues of the coral disappear and seaweed covers the exposed skeleton.

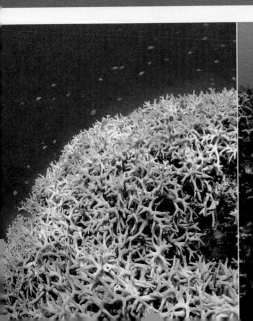

every two to seven years. Because they bring such great warmth, it is no surprise that extreme El Niño years have been linked to widespread bleaching. Bleaching in the El Niño year of 1997-1998 led the United States National Oceanographic and Atmospheric Administration (NOAA) to declare its first ever global bleaching event, with 50 percent of the individual reefs that make up the Great Barrier Reef being affected. Unusually warm temperatures produced another mass bleaching in the region in 2002, affecting 60 percent of the reefs.

The El Niño of 2015-2016 was the strongest on record, helping to make 2015 the hottest year yet recorded. The warming triggered the worst bleaching event yet observed at the Great Barrier Reef. The Australian Research Council (ARC) Center of Excellence for Coral Reef Studies announced that at least some bleaching had occurred in over *93 percent* of the reef. In the reef's northern third, the hardest hit area, a survey determined 81

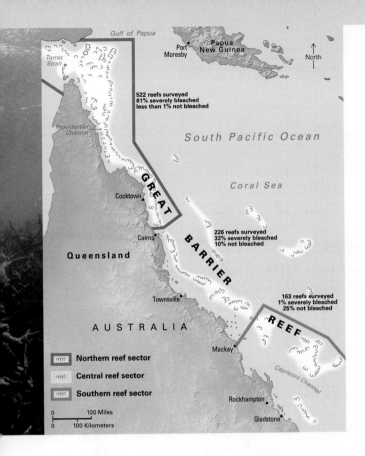

522 reefs surveyed
81% severely bleached
less than 1% not bleached

226 reefs surveyed
33% severely bleached
10% not bleached

163 reefs surveyed
1% severely bleached
25% not bleached

Gulf of Papua

Torres
Strait

Port
Moresby

Papua
New Guinea

North

Providential
Channel

South Pacific Ocean

Cooktown

Coral Sea

Cairns

Queensland

Townsville

AUSTRALIA

Mackay

Capricorn Channel

Rockhampton

Gladstone

GREAT

BARRIER

REEF

Northern reef sector

Central reef sector

Southern reef sector

0   100 Miles

0   100 Kilometers

This map shows how bleaching at the Great Barrier Reef gets worse as waters warm from south to north.

A researcher, *far left*, photographs dead corals in the hard-hit northern sector of the Great Barrier Reef in May 2016.

percent of the reefs to be severely bleached. Only 1 percent of the reefs in the southern third of the Great Barrier Reef were severely bleached. Yet even there, only 25 percent of the reefs remained completely unaffected. By the El Niño's end, about half the coral in the northern third of the reef was dead. Scientists expected that at some reefs, as few as 10 percent of corals would survive.

Severely bleached reefs can take several years or even decades to recover. But it is probably becoming less likely that damaged reefs will get the chance. Bleaching events have become more frequent as worldwide temperatures have risen due to global warming. Scientists estimate that the global average surface temperature has risen about 1.4 Fahrenheit degrees (0.76 Celsius degrees) since the late 1800's, with most of the warming occurring since the 1950's. Much of the excess heat has been absorbed by Earth's oceans, causing water temperatures to rise more quickly than those on land. Such rises may seem small, but at certain times of the year, a bleaching event can be triggered by a rise of just 1.8 Fahrenheit degrees (1 Celsius degree) lasting four weeks. So, while past episodes of bleaching have been triggered by seasonal weather events, global warming pushes average temperatures closer to the threshold that corals cannot withstand, making it more likely that bleaching will occur. "In a world without humans, it's not quite impossible that you'd get March sea surface temperatures as warm as [in 2016]," observed Andrew King, a climate scientist at the University of Melbourne, "but it's extremely unlikely." The Intergovernmental Panel on Climate Change (IPCC), a committee created to advise the United Nations on global warming and the climate change it can produce, has called coral bleaching the "most widespread and conspicuous impact of climate change."

Some action can be taken to help save the coral. The healthier a reef is to begin with, the more easily it may recover from bleaching. Thus, measures to reduce water pollution may help corals withstand and recover from bleaching. There is also some hope that heartier corals may survive and flourish. However, it is unlikely that corals will ultimately survive unless politicians can be moved to tackle the hard issue of climate change. Political leaders worldwide have been reluctant or unable to develop and agree to an effective plan to reduce the release of greenhouse gases and fight global warming. Tour operators at the Great Barrier Reef have also been traditionally reluctant to sound the alarm about coral bleaching, for fear of scaring away tourists. In addition, this year's worst damage occurred in the reef's least visited regions, making it easier for politicians to ignore.

Time may be running out for the Great Barrier Reef and for reefs worldwide. At the current pace of global warming, 2016's extreme highs will be considered average in the 2030's, resulting in progressively worse annual bleaching. The death of ocean reefs would take a terrible toll on marine life, and, consequently, on all life on Earth.

THE WEEKEND SNOWS OF JONAS

It was a mild winter in much of the United States this past year, but in late January 2016, the North Atlantic coast got a taste of what many other parts of the country were missing. From Friday, January 22, through Sunday, January 24, Winter Storm Jonas (see photo, p. 12) dumped more than 2 feet (61 centimeters) of snow in areas from Washington, D.C., to New York City. The storm, which blew in from the Atlantic Ocean, pushed heavy snows inland to parts of the South and the Ohio Valley as well. Snow totals peaked at 42 inches (107 centimeters) in the West Virginia panhandle, with parts of 14 states buried under 12 inches (30 centimeters) or more of snow.

Winter Storm Jonas was the largest snowstorm on record for several eastern locations, including Allentown and Harrisburg, Pennsylvania; New York City's Central Park; and both LaGuardia and JFK Airports. And if you live in Glengary, West Virginia; Philomont, Virginia; Redhouse, Maryland; Greencastle, Pennsylvania; or Morris Plains, New Jersey, you saw plenty of the white stuff—all more than 30 inches (76 centimeters)—during those cold late January days.

Jonas brought more than snow, too, as coastal flooding soaked parts of the Atlantic Coast. Record storm *surges* (sudden onrushes of tidal waves caused by strong winds) hit more than 4 feet (1.2 meters) above normal tides in Lewes, Delaware. Record flooding also hit several parts of New Jersey.

Some 75 million people were affected by the storm. Subways in Washington, D.C., closed for that snowy late January weekend, and tens of thousands of flights were canceled throughout the storm's area of impact.

CYCLONE WINSTON HITS FIJI

On Feb. 20, 2016, Tropical Cyclone Winston made landfall on the South Pacific island nation of Fiji. (Tropical cyclones are called hurricanes in many places.) Winston's winds averaged 185 miles (298 kilometers) per hour and peaked at 224 miles (360 kilometers) per hour. A Category 5 storm (the strongest storm level), Winston was the strongest tropical cyclone on record for the Southern Hemisphere. Winston made landfall along the north coast of Fiji's largest, most populous island, Viti Levu. The storm knocked out electric power, forced the closure of schools and government buildings, and flooded parts of Fiji's many islands. Winston thundered over other parts of the Coral Sea as well, lashing parts of Niue, Tonga, Vanuatu, and Queensland, Australia, with high winds and rain. The storm destroyed large parts of the region's banana, coconut, and vanilla crops. The storm also killed 44 people, left tens of thousands of others homeless, and caused some $1.4 billion in damage. Early warnings, mass evacuations, and other storm preparations prevented larger loss of life. Numerous nations sent aid to help Fiji and the rest of the region recover.

On Feb. 20, 2016, Tropical Cyclone Winston thrashed Fiji and other South Pacific islands. According to news and meteorological sources, it was the second-strongest landfalling cyclone in recorded history. The only storm to reach land with stronger winds was Super Typhoon Haiyan, which struck the Philippines in 2013.

BERTA CÁCERES   1971-2016

On March 3, 2016, noted human rights and environmental activist Berta Cáceres was gunned down in her home in La Esperanza, Honduras. For years, Cáceres had been trying to prevent construction of the Agua Zarca hydroelectric dam on the Río Gualcarque in western Honduras. Her efforts earned her the prestigious Goldman Environmental Prize for South and Central America in 2014. Unfortunately, her efforts also led to death threats and her eventual murder. Cáceres was 44 years old.

A member of the indigenous Honduran Lenca people, Cáceres co-founded the National Council of Popular and Indigenous Organizations of Honduras in 1993. For the past several years, the group was leading protests and a legal battle against construction of the Agua Zarca Dam. The hydroelectric project will cut off much of the Lenca's water supply from the Gualcarque—a river sacred to the Lenca people. Protests at the dam site, which occasionally led to violence, convinced Sinohydro, the Chinese company originally behind the dam project, to pull out of Honduras. A Honduran company took over the project and continued construction. Tensions rose and security forces repeatedly arrested environmental protesters.

Cáceres began receiving death threats in February 2016. Early on March 3, gunmen burst into her house and shot her to death. On March 14, a colleague of Cáceres, Nelson García, was also shot dead. Honduran officials said they had no suspects in the murders, but family members and fellow activists were quick to blame the government and the dam company.

Honduras is a small Central American country known for the production of bananas. A poor and politically unstable country, Honduras is also a very violent place with a poor human rights record.

HOTTEST YEAR (AGAIN)

Planet Earth just keeps getting hotter. May 2016 was the hottest month of May (breaking last year's record) since records began in 1880. This past July, in addition to being the hottest July in history, was the *hottest month ever recorded*. It was over 1.5 Fahrenheit degrees (0.8 Celsius degrees) warmer than the average temperature since 1900. A month later, August 2016 tied July's record heat.

The recent strong El Niño probably contributed to the record-shattering heat. It began in 2014 and ended in late spring of 2016. El Niños increase water temperatures, which then increase air temperatures around the planet. But Earth has continued to warm even in non-El Niño years. Since 2010, each year has been within the top 15 hottest years on record. 2015 ranked 1st, 2014 ranked 2nd, and 2013 ranked 4th. Of those years, only 2010 had a mild El Niño.

The surging temperatures of the past year serve as a stark reminder of the growing threat of climate change. As the Paris Agreement (a UN-brokered climate initiative) lumbers toward ratification, many countries are dragging their feet in enacting tougher restrictions on greenhouse gas emissions. But there is hope that greater public concern about climate change will compel world leaders to take the difficult steps necessary to reduce greenhouse gas emissions.

In the meantime, however, the situation remains mostly unchanged. People and ecosystems continue to feel the effects of climate change (such as the coral bleaching, flooding, severe storms, and wildfires mentioned elsewhere this book). Concentrations of carbon dioxide in the atmosphere reached the milestone number of 400 parts per million in March 2016 (scientists consider 350 parts per million to be the highest "safe" level of carbon dioxide in the atmosphere). Climate scientists are confident that the final months of 2016 will push the year's temperatures ahead of 2015, and we will have seen the hottest year on record—again.

INDEX

A

Abbott, Tony, 142
Abdeslam, Salah, 26
Abdullah II, 315
Abe, Shinzo, 43, 45, 56, 138
abelisaurids, 352
abortion, 11, 42, 52, 300
Abrahamyan, Hovik, 71-72, 313
Abu Dhabi, United Arab Emirates, 60, 347
Abu Sayyaf, 31, 69
Academy Awards, 21, 255, 260-262
Addis Ababa, Ethiopia, 70
Aden, Yemen, 28, 69
Adjaye, David, 253
Adonia (ship), 38
Aedes aegypti mosquito, 374
Affordable Care Act. *See* Patient Protection and Affordable Care Act
Afghanistan, 39-40, 54, 70
  tables, 158, 335
  terrorism, 140-141; January, 10; February, 14, 19, 21; March, 22; April, 31, 33, 34; May, 42-44; June, 49, 53; July, 59; August, 68; September, 70; October, 79-82, 84
Afghanistan War, 140
African Americans, 73, 106, 203, 257
  Academy Awards boycott, 260-262
  "Freedom Summer" case, 301
  national museum, 252-253
  police, relations with, 42, 55, 56, 58, 60, 64, 65, 74-75
  voting rights, 60
African helium field, 53, 154
African Union, 9-10, 47-48, 60
Afrikaans language, 107
agriculture, 297
Agua Zarca Dam, 399
AIDS, 130
Aikins, Luke, 61
Ailes, Roger, 58, 71
Air Force, U.S., 348
airplanes. *See* aviation
airship, 66-67
Alabama, U.S.A., 72-73, 77, 334
Alaska, U.S.A., 29, 334
Alaska Airlines, 30
Albania, 158, 335
Albee, Edward, 86, 87
Alberta, Canada, 38-39, 124
Aleppo, Syria, 36-37, 65, 75, 82, 150-151

Algeria, 29, 49, 158, 335
Ali, Muhammad, 48, 192-197
al-Jaf, Abdel, 155
All-Star Game
  baseball, 175
  basketball, 18, 184
Al-Mulki, Hani, 315
Alpha Centauri, 358
Alps, 46, 72
al-Qamishli, Syria, 60
al-Shabab, 9-10, 21, 46-48, 53, 57, 60, 67-69, 84
Altman, Adnan Abu, 155
Álvarez, Canelo, 39
Alzheimer's disease, 303
Amatrice, Italy, 114, 115
amber, 350-351
American Airlines, 43-44
"American Idol," 273
American League, 57, 83, 175
American Samoa, 376
American University of Afghanistan, 68
Andaman and Nicobar Islands, 59
Andorra, 158, 335
Angola, 158, 335
animals, 382-395
  oldest, 389
Ankara, Turkey, 18, 24
Anthony, Carmelo, 229
anthrax, 62
anthropology, 346
Antigua and Barbuda, 158, 335
Antony and Cleopatra (Shakespeare), 281
Anzac Day, 100
apartheid, 107
Apesteguia, Sebastián, 352
Apple Inc., 18, 69, 128
arboviruses, 374
archery, 228
architecture, 252-254
Arcidiacono, Ryan, 30, 186
Argentina, 30, 52
  independence, 96
  tables, 158, 335
Arizona, U.S.A., 27, 334
Arizona Wildcats, 53
Arkansas, U.S.A., 334
ARM (company), 58
Armenia, 30, 71-73, 313
  tables, 158, 335
Arrieta, Jake, 35
arts, 250-289
  See also specific arts and the Day by Day section of this volume
Aryan racial concept, 106

As You Like It (Shakespeare), 281, 286
Asadabad, Afghanistan, 21
Assad, Bashar al-, 150
Assam state, India, 62
Assange, Julian, 14
Associated Press, 34
Association of Muslim Scholars, 153
Assoumani, Azali, 313
Atatürk Airport, 52, 153
Atchison, Kansas, 84
Atlanta, Georgia, 76
Atlantic City, New Jersey, 72
Atlético Madrid, 44
atoms, 349
Auckland, New Zealand, 14
Aung San Suu Kyi, 26, 73, 315
Auriemma, Geno, 189
aurora borealis, 344-345
"Aurora Green" diamond, 45
Auschwitz, 259
Australia, 14, 78, 187, 360-361
  Anzac Day, 100
  election, 56, 142
  Long Tan, Battle of, 143
  rodent extinction, 388
  storms, 77, 398
  tables, 158, 318-321, 335
Australian Football League, 78
Australian Open, 11, 225
Australian Research Council (ARC), 394-395
Austria, 40, 43, 54, 313
  tables, 158, 335
automobile racing, 19, 44, 168, 198
automobiles
  airbag defects, 53, 72
  emissions tests, 34, 53
  traffic deaths, 55
aviation
  airlines, 30, 43-44; U.S.-Cuba flight, 69
  disasters, 19, 26, 42, 48, 59, 60, 77, 110
  new designs, 51, 60, 66-67, 347, 348
  See also helicopter crashes
axe, prehistoric, 40
Aylwin Azócar, Patricio, 86
Azerbaijan, 30, 158, 335

B

Babenco, Héctor, 86
babies, 44, 64
Bacha Khan University, 10
badminton, 228

ACKNOWLEDGMENTS

All maps, charts, and diagrams were prepared by staff unless otherwise noted.

6-7 © Mike Segar, Reuters
12 Scott Kelly, NASA
16-17 Bureau of Land Management
20 © Cal Sport Media/AP Photo
25 © Sipa/AP Photo
28-29 © Alexandre Meneghini, Reuters
32-33 © Athit Perawongmetha, Reuters
36-37 © Validated UGC/AP Photo
38-39 © Jonathan Hayward, AP Photo
45 © Kimimasa Mayama, AP Photo
46-47 © Christophe Ena, AP Photo
51 © Marcelo del Pozo, Reuters
56 © Jonathan Bachman, Reuters
61 © Sipa/AP Photo
63 © DPA/Zuma Press/Icon Sportswire/AP Photo
66-67 © TPG/ZUMA Press
71 © Viktor Drachev, Getty Images
74-75 © Adam Rhew, Charlotte Magazine/AFP/Getty Images
80-81 © Rebecca Blackwell, AP Photo
85 © Rex Features/AP Photo
87 © Truman Moore, The LIFE Images Collection/Getty Images
88 © H. Rumph Jr, AP Photo
91 © Touchstone Pictures/Alamy
91 © EPA/Alamy
92 © Tsafrir Abayov, AP Photo
92 © Kevork Djansezian, AP Photo
95 © Golden Richard, Alamy
96 © Shutterstock
97 United States Postal Service
98 Library of Congress
99 National Library of Ireland
100 © Shutterstock
101 © Gareth Fuller, Getty Images
102-103 © Shutterstock
103 National Park Service
104-105 WORLD BOOK photo
106 © Keystone Pictures USA/Alamy
107 © Foto24/Getty Images
108-109 © Han Yuqing Xinhua, eyevine/Redux Pictures
112 © Naoya Osato, Kyodo/AP Photo
113 © Luis Acosta, AFP/Getty Images
114-115 © Shutterstock
116-117 © Marcus Yam, Los Angeles Times/Getty Images
118-119 © Yu Congwen, Color China Photo/AP Photo
118-119 © Sanjeev Verma, Hindustan Times/Getty Images
119 © Steve Helber, AP Photo
120-121 © Erik McGregor, Pacific Press/LightRocket/Getty Images
123 © Pablo Martinez Monsivais, AP Photo
125 © Loren Elliott/The Tampa Bay Times/AP Photo
126-127 © Mel Evans, AP Photo
127 © Shutterstock
128 © Al Drago, CQ Roll Call/AP Photo
131 © Jacquelyn Martin, AP Photo
132-133 © Shutterstock

134-135 © Dario Lopez-Mills, AP Photo
137 © Sipa/AP Photo
139 © AP Photo
140-141 © Rahmat Gul, AP Photo
142 © Rick Rycroft, AP Photo
145 © John Stillwell, Getty Images
146-147 © Arnd Wiegmann, Reuters
148-149 © Claude Paris, AP Photo
150-151 © Bassam Khabieh, Reuters
153 © Emrah Gurel, AP Photo
154 © Shutterstock
156-167 © Shutterstock
168 © Fred Vuich, Sports Illustrated/Getty Images
170-171 © AP Photo
174 © Shutterstock
176 © Michael Reaves, The Denver Post/Getty Images
178 © Brian Rothmuller, Icon Sportswire/AP Photo
179 © AP Photo
182-183 © Marcio Jose Sanchez, AP Photo
185 © George Long, Sports Illustrated/Getty Images
188-189 © Zach Bolinger, Icon Sportswire/AP Photo
191 © Gerry Broome, AP Photo
192-193 © John Rooney, AP Photo
197 © David Guttenfelder, AP Photo
200-201 © Gregory Payan, AP Photo
204-209 © Shutterstock
210 © Rob Schumacher, USA TODAY Sports/Reuters
211 © PA Wire/AP Photo
214-215 © Samuel Stringer, Icon Sportswire/AP Photo
217 © AP Photo
218 © David J. Phillip, AP Photo
220-221 © Frank Augstein, AP Photo
223 © Leslie Plaza Johnson, Icon Sportswire/AP Photo
225 © Thomas Samson, Getty Images
226-227 © Dominic Ebenbichler, Reuters
229 © Mark Ralston, Reuters
230 © Rio 2016
234-235 © ZUMA Press/Alamy
236 © Ramil Sitdikov, Sputnik/AP Photo
238-239 © Bernat Armangue, AP Photo
242-243 © Stefan Wermuth, Reuters
246-247 © Kai Pfaffenbach, Reuters
250-251 © Lucy Ford, Alamy
252-253 © Alan Karchmer, National Museum of African American History and Culture
253 Smithsonian National Museum of African American History and Culture Collection, Gift of Charles L. Blockson
254 © Steve Forrest, The New York Times/Redux Pictures
255 © Trinity Mirror/Mirrorpix/Alamy
257 © AP Photo
258 Rob Bogaerts, National Archives of the Netherlands/Anefo (CC BY 4.0)
259 © Gary Cameron, Reuters
260-261 Twentieth Century Fox
262 Open Road Films
263-264 Warner Brothers

265 Pixar/Walt Disney Pictures
265 Universal Pictures
266 © Mark Humphrey, AP Photo
267 © AP Photo
268 © Andreas Terlaak, Hollandse Hoogte/Redux Pictures
270-271 © Shutterstock
272 © Yannis Behrakis, Reuters
274-275 HBO
276 NBC
277 © Hulton Archive/Getty Images
278-279 © Evan Agostini, Invision/AP Photo
280-281 © Rex Features/AP Photo
282-283 © AP Photo
284 © Russell Cheyne, Reuters
287 Two Cities Films
288-289 The Metropolitan Museum of Art, New York City
290-291 © Justin Sullivan, Getty Images
295 © Fernando Llano, AP Photo
298-299 © Shutterstock
300 Supreme Court of the United States
303 Library of Congress
304-305 © Stefan Rousseau, AP Photo
306 © AP Photo
308-309 © Jonathan Ernst, Reuters
311 © Eddie Moore, The Albuquerque Journal/AP Photo
312 © Saul Loeb, AP Photo
313 Licurgo Miranda (CC BY-SA 4.0)
314 © Ye Aung Thu, Reuters
315 Keith Bacongco (CC BY 2.0)
316 © Damir Sagolj, Reuters
316-317 © Stefan Wermuth, Reuters
318-327 © Shutterstock
328 Pete Souza, The White House
330-331 © Shutterstock
332-333 The White House Photo
334-343 © Shutterstock
344-345 Scott Kelly, NASA
348 Todd Cromar, U.S. Air Force
350 © Ryan C. McKellar, Royal Saskatchewan Museum
352 © Reuters/Alamy
354-356 NASA
357 SpaceX
358-359 ESO/M. Kornmesser
361 © SKA South Africa
362-367 NASA
368-369 © Paulo Whitaker, Reuters
372-373 © Jorge Cabrera, Reuters
375 © Dreamstime
376 © Mike Stewart, AP Photo
379 © Alan Diaz, AP Photo
380-381 © Gary Bell, SeaPics
382 © Sean McMahon, Yale University
383-384 © Shutterstock
385 © Cincinnati Zoo and Botanical Garden
386 © Jurgen Otto
387 © Chaiwat Subprasom, Reuters
388 Queensland Department of Environment and Heritage Protection
390-394 XL Catlin Seaview Survey
398 NASA
399 Goldman Environmental Prize
401 © Shutterstock